7001 Resumes-Plus Second Edition

The Job Search Tool to Get You That Job

Dr. Ferris E. Merhish

authorHOUSE

AuthorHouse™
1663 Liberty Drive
Bloomington, IN 47403
www.authorhouse.com
Phone: 1-800-839-8640

©2010 Dr. Ferris E. Merhish. All rights reserved.

No part of this book may be reproduced, stored in a retrieval system, or transmitted by any means without the written permission of the author.

First published by AuthorHouse 4/27/2010

ISBN: 978-1-4490-9220-7 (sc)

Library of Congress Control Number: 2010904738

Printed in the United States of America
Bloomington, Indiana

This book is printed on acid-free paper.

ABOUT THE AUTHOR

Dr. Ferris E. Merhish (Gene) is a college, adult education, and high school instructor with over seventeen years of teaching experience. Trained in Business Education he has been recognized as a Business Education Consultant for the State of California. Several years ago he operated one of the most advanced programs in the teaching of retail merchandising in the Western States. More recently he has been a Department Chair in a Southern California High School where he has also been teaching Computer Technology.

In addition, Dr. Merhish has over twenty-six years of business and marketing experience with such firms as Proctor and Gamble, Gardner-Denver, Harnischfeger Corporation, and has created and operated an entrepreneurial company. Dr. Merhish has more than fifteen years military experience with the Navy, Air Force Reserves, and National Guard. In California he has served as a Business and Marketing (Adjunct) instructor for Ivy University in Alhambra, Riverside Community College, Chaffey Community College in Rancho Cucamonga, and others. He has a good number of years teaching adult education for a number of school districts. He has also taught in consort with The China Training Center for Senior Civil Servants, Ministry of Personnel, and the People's Republic of China. Furthermore, Dr. Merhish works with small Businesses as a Marketing and Sales Consultant.

You will find that this will be Dr. Merhish's third book and a second addition of his first book 7,001 RÉSUMÉS. His second book JUMP START YOUR COMPUTER SKILL was written for Adults and High School Graduates entering the 'World of Work' for the first time. This book and his first were written as a general job search book which can be used by anyone but was designed for individuals that already have been in the labor force.

HOW TO USE THIS BOOK

Like the first book 7,**001 Résumés Plus**, The Job Search Workbook guides you step-by-step through the job search process. It is designed to help you develop and execute a job search as well as help you develop a career plan.

The best way to use this book is to start with the Introduction, which will give you the opportunity to get your bearings, and help you evaluate where you are in your current position. It will also give you an idea of how to understand the challenges facing 'you', the job searcher. Armed with this knowledge you can progress quickly through the book and start advancing your career by finding that next position.

In this book you will find employment references. Many of these resources are available at you local college and university libraries; some of the information will also be found at your city libraries. I will provide potential employers and organizations that you might want to consider for possible employment, but remember, these are only a small sample of the opportunities that await you out there in the world of work. You may however need to do additional research to find what you are looking for.

This is a job search 'workbook', I designed the book for you to write in as you come across answers and find '**key**' points that you want to remember and use. I hope you refer to the book as you advance your career. Some of the chapters include additional worksheets to log answers as you evaluate yourself. Samples have been provided to show you what employers are looking for so you can incorporate this information into your interview style. Remember the information is designed to help you evaluate what you have to offer a potential employer and assist you in presenting the information in a way that puts you in the best light.

In conclusion, I do give you a sampling of résumés, but there are <u>not</u> 7,001 in this book. The title is based on real job search experiences that I went through at one time or another and the title is more of a personal challenge to achieve what I need to do during my job search quest. So please, don't hold my feet to the fire when you only find a few samples. This book is more than just résumés.

DEDICATION

I am going to take a moment to dedicate this book to my Dad, and I am sorry to say, I did not know him very well. He was from the old country, the Middle-East, and sort of had that old style mentality or nature that set him apart from his family, or he was just the way he was. We did not have a lot of time together as father and son, but I am sure he did the best he could.

I look back and realize how hard he had to work to make a living; he was a quick order chief and a waiter. As a boy I can remember the way he could balance about a dozen plates and dishes on his arm as he rushed here and there bringing food to hungry customers. At times as I would visit him, I would see him filling orders from the hot kitchen. For a short time I worked with him, he was the cook and I was the dishwasher.

Maybe my dad wasn't the best dad one could have, but he was my dad and I have to thank him for bringing me into this world. I can remember having a taste of his beer on Friday night. He would get a quart of Slitz, sit at the kitchen table with his glass and relax. I used to ask him for a taste, and he would give me one. I can also remember going down to where he worked, Bolton & Hase in Des Moines, and ask him for a few bucks, he would always show me is wallet, which would be empty, but he would somehow get me an open faced hot beef sandwich to eat.

Looking back I wish we would have had more time together. I told my own son that I would like to be able to talk to him now. I would say sorry dad for 'trashing your car' which I did on more than one occasion in order to use it without his permission. I also want to say sorry dad that we could not have bought that duplex together as we planned; I really wanted us to have something together, and I wanted a grandpa for my kids!

I believe I lost him too soon, which now, looking back, I wish I had done more to be a better son. I know that this can't be done, so I am hoping I can be a better father to my son Kirk, daughter Debi, and my 16 grandchildren.

If there is one thing that I have learned it's that life can be very short and we all should make the best of what we have. One of the things that I have decided to do, if I can, is to help others through my self help books.

My works have come out of 26 years experience in industry and my training in Education, which I hope can help those who strive to better themselves through their use. Let me say this, you can achieve your goals, but not without a degree of self-sacrifice, motivation, and hard work. As they say 'there's no free lunch'. I have found this to be very true. You can get out of life what you want, but you and only you can make it happen.

Let me say this one more thing to my Dad, 'hey dad, this is my third book, what do you think'?

ACKNOWLEDGEMENTS

I would like to take a moment to acknowledge several people that helped me accomplish the task of writing this book. I have to say that it takes dedication, perseverance, teamwork, sacrifices, patience, and cooperation to do something like this. I would like to thank my wife Bobbie, who helped me get started with my writing and has been there through several re-writes, the marketing process, and has helped me with my various book signings. Also, she has been supportive while having spent hundreds of dollars getting the word out that we have a job search book on the market.

Bobbie has been very helpful, supportive, patient as well as understanding, and without her help there was a good chance I would have given up. We ran into a number of challenges that set us back, but with her support we were able to overcome.

I also want to thank my new re-writer and book editor Karen Rivello for her help in the proofreading and copyediting of this book. She came in after my other editor was called away on another project. I also want to thank Sean Hudson in his assistance in finalizing the editing of this book.

Also, I want to give credit to my new book illustrator, Tessa Mullins, for her work developing cartoons and illustrations for various chapters in this book. As you will find this is my third attempt to develop a Self-help book but a complete new experience for Tessa and I have to say, I enjoyed collaborating with her and look forward to working with her again.

I would like to thank my son-in-law Kirk Rhoade for putting up with me while I was going though the process of writing and developing this book. He was great at lending me his ear as I talked about the various phases of my undertaking. Also Branne, my daughter-in-law, who I am sure, got tired of me talking about advertising, marketing, and the other phases of business, but especially the big 'if'.

I also would like to take a moment to acknowledge my friend and one time Educational Supervisor Jerry Lambert for not only his ear over the years as I developed my second book Jump Start Your Career, but his interest and assistance in expanding the exposure of not only my books, but also his time and trouble in introducing me to other Educators who could influence their School Districts in establishing my books as Educational sources for their students. Thanks Jerry!

I would also like to recognize Mrs. Jacqueline Jacobs for her contribution to this book and for her enthusiasm in helping me develop a great interest in my work in providing Self-help training and Career Development.

Last but not least, I would like to thank a long-time Friend, Kathy J. Watson, for her support in helping me develop awareness of my books and providing Self-help training and Career Development. Thank you for your help and support everyone!

Published by Camelsealbooks – Inc.

C 2010

Manufactured and Printed in the United States of America

Copyrighted – Do Not Duplicate

IN MEMORY AND HONOR OF MY MOTHER

I know my mother loved to write short stories and I know she would have been pleased to have some of her work printed, but during her life time she was not able to do this. I am very good at judging other peoples work, my mother included, so I thought it might be nice to honor her by putting some of her work into print. By in large, none of her work has anything to do with the subject matter of my book, but now she can take a moment to look down from her little organ bench, take a little time away from one of her other pleasures, like singing and playing music, to enjoy having some of her work shared with others. Hey mom, how are you doing and here is a surprise for you. I know you will be pleased to have your work put to paper and be published. I can remember many of our good times together.

From your son,

Gene

Reminiscing-The Past, Anticipating- The Future

By: Eula Merhish

As the morning sun comes up, I start my day with the usual cup of coffee, only this Saturday is different. Today I am fifty -eight years old. Until just recently I have always thought young and enjoyed being with young people, but somehow the years are reaching out and surrounding me. I sit down and sigh and tell myself, 'Grandma, you are getting old.'

I think of my two grandchildren, a girl six and a boy that will soon be two. I wonder; what will their future be? What hardships will they have? Will my grandson grow up to go to war, or will he have a chance to have a happy and peaceful life.

My mind drifts back to my childhood. It was carefree, yet hard work was all I knew as a farm girl. I think of my parents, good honest people, always willing to lend a helping hand to a neighbor who needed help. My parents were strict and they believed in the old saying, 'spare the rod and spoil the child' (I think the rod was worn out because I sure wasn't spoiled). I was taught early in life to respect elderly people and to be quiet when they were talking, because children were to be seen and not heard in those days.

I don't remember learning to milk cows or driving a team of horses. I try to remember, but I must have started very young. As far back as I can remember, I was doing my share of the work as a daily job. In the summer there was the garden to plant and care for. Then we would have vegetables to can for winter food. The hay field in the hot sun, driving a team of horses or the job of stacker horse, the oats and wheat to be harvested, and to carry these heavy bundles and put them in shocks was no easy job. Then later the threshing machine would come, and the grain was threshed and put into bens for the winter. In the fall there was corn to be harvested; shucking corn would mean more sore hands and aching backs. There was all this work in the summer and fall so there would be food for us to eat, also the livestock could be fed in the cold winter months.

There wasn't such a thing as an allowance in those days. I had plenty of food, good clothes, and a warm home. I did my share of work and was happy. Once in a while there would be a sack of store bought candy hidden in the grocery box when we came home on Saturday from town; most of the time the candy was made from sorghum molasses. Sometimes dad would have a cane patch and we would strip the leaves from the stalk and then take the load of stalk to a mill. I remember the green juice coming from the stalks as they were crushed and then put into hot vats of oil which turned them into a beautiful amber syrup. On cold mornings this syrup was wonderful on my mother's hot biscuits.

During the cold winter evenings, when the snow was blowing and the winter wind was howling, there were many things to do. Mom, dad, and I would play games like dominoes, checkers, and rock. It seemed dad always won in the checkers game. Other evenings we would read books like Zane Gray Westerns, and Uncle Tom's Cabin. (I shall never forget how we cried when we read that sad book about Uncle Tom.). Then some evenings there was music when dad would play the fiddle and mom or I would play the organ. That was real old fashion music—from the waltz to the toe tapping of the old hoedown. When I got a little older I bought a guitar and soon learned to play. The neighbors would come over and bring their guitars, mandolins and fiddles, and we would roll up the rug to have a square dance. The refreshments were popcorn and apples, or gingerbread and coffee. I wonder if there are any homes like that today.

I think of my schooldays. The teacher was the boss and not the children. If I got punished at school, I was punished when I got home. My dad would say, 'I'm sending you to school to learn and to get the education I never had, and that is what I expect of you'.

Ah, yes, I have much to remember, the happy days, sad days, and days filled with fun, and still other days of hard work. I only wish there were more parents like mine today, hard-working and God-fearing. They taught me the good things in life, so many things to cherish and to be thankful for.

I remember when I was around eight years old we went to the county fair. We started early in the morning because we went in a buggy and the town was around twenty miles away. We took our lunch; some feed for the horses, and stayed all day. Everything was fine until we started home and it began to rain. My new crepe dress started to shrink and by the time we got home mom had to cut it with the scissors before I could get in off. I cried because my beautiful blue dress that mom hand made me was ruined.

I think of the new home my dad built when I was around fourteen years old. We had to sleep in the barn until it was built. That was quite an inconvenience and we were very happy when the house was finished. That same year dad bought me a riding horse. I was so happy because now I could go to town and see my friends whenever I wanted to. Five miles was quite a ways to walk.

I remember going to visit my married sister when there was another family there at the time. The men went outside to talk, but when they came in they showed us that they had taken the clippers and cut their hair as short as they could.

This made my mother very angry, so angry that she had her beautiful long black hair cut. I was so sad that I cried and I think my mom did too, but no one ever saw her do so. She never let it grow long again.

During these happy years there were sad things happening too. World war one was taking place in Germany and many wives and sweethearts were waiting and praying for news of their loved ones. I remember the joy when it was over as the older folks were talking. Now there would be peace. (I close my eyes and pray. Will there ever be peace?)

I remember the roaring twenties. Dresses were up to the knees. Also, there was the bath tub gin (as it was called). Home brew was made up in the hills, and the sheriff was always trying to find the stills. But no one would talk. He had quite a time trying to locate them.

I remember the gangsters that terrorized the county; robbing banks and trains. The bank in our little town where I went to school was robbed. For a quiet little community that was a frightening thing.

I remember when our home was never locked. If a neighbor needed something he came and borrowed it, even when we weren't home. When he was through he would bring it home. Who today would leave their home unlocked?

I remember that when anyone lived on the county welfare, he was considered shiftless and lazy. But today it seems to be the 'in' thing to do.

I remember the crystal radio with the earphones to listen on, and the old phonograph with the cylinder records and big horn for the music to come through. I think of the old kerosene lamp with the glass chimney to keep clean, the old curling iron I would put in the chimney to heat so I could curl my hair, and the high button shoes I used to wear with the buttonhook I kept on a nail so I wouldn't loose it; if I did loose it I couldn't fasten them. I also think of those old ribbed stockings I wore. What a difference from the ones I wear today!

I think of the depression, so many people loosing their homes, the banks going broke, old folks worried and wondering what would they do. So many people were out of work in the cities and the farmer had no market for their produce.

I remember the tragedy and heartache of the Lindbergh family when their baby son was kidnapped, and the long days of waiting. Then there was the death of their son. I remember years later hearing Lindbergh talk in Des Moines, Iowa, warning the people of World War Two. I don't think many people believed him.

In 1935, I left home to find work. I went to Knoxville, Iowa and found a job for three dollars a week. While I was there the C.C.C. (Civilian Conservation Corps) was formed for young boys so they could have jobs. With the W.P.A (Work Projects Administration) for the men, there was work on the roads and parks. For the women there were jobs in the factories, working on sewing machines so they could earn money for food. The welfare offices were formed. Surplus feed was given to the hungry who could not find work.

During this turmoil of the depression I went to Des Moines, Iowa. Soon afterwards, with no thought of the future or the problems it will bring, I got married. In 1939 my son was born, and oh so many headaches and worries were created. Work was so hard to find and wages were so low. My husband worked for fourteen dollars a week and I helped when I could, by making three dollars a week. Today, as I think back, that doesn't seem like very much money, but the food was so much cheaper then. For three or four dollars we had quite a nice sack of food.

Then World War Two was declared. Again young men were gong overseas to fight for the safety of America. A large ammunitions plant was built in Des Moines and with thousands of other mothers I went to work there. Soon came the rationing of sugar, coffee, cigarette, gas and tires. To get a pair of nylon hose meant standing in line for hours just to buy them.

The W. A. C. (Women Army Core) was stationed out at the Fort Moines Army post. Part of them had to stay in the hotels in the downtown areas. A navy base was at Ames, Iowa. The old town of Des Moines became a swinging town. There were clubs on all the corners while new ones were being built.

People were working and the long lines of welfare were gone. Everyone was making money and spending it like there was no tomorrow.

After the war life became routine. My son was growing up. He went into the Cup Scouts and then into the Boy Scouts. With the Mitigwa Dancing group of the scouts, he got to travel through Colorado, Wyoming, and into the Dakotas where he met different tribes of Indians. There they would have friendship dances. When I was working in a factory and my son was going to school, these were happy years; also, he was a batboy for a baseball team in the evenings. One night he got to play on the team. He was so happy when be came home.

During these years there was the Korean Conflict, causing more worry and more boys going overseas into the service again. Mothers and wives were once more saying good-bye to those they loved; but in two years it was over, and once more there was talk of peace. Yet, there doesn't seem to ever be peace.

As in a lot of families there was the problem of divorce. I will not say either of us was completely at fault. I think there were a lot of problems, and each of us was not willing to admit our share of them. I only know that it doesn't matter what age a child is when his parents get a divorce, it does leave a scar on the child. My son was fifteen years old and although I thought he was old enough to understand, he didn't. He wasn't really a bad boy, but he started running around at night. He was so unhappy. I was working, and I'm sure, as I think back now, I was neglectful in my role as a mother.

In 1957 my son decided he wanted to go into the Navy so, I signed the papers because he was just seventeen years old. He was sent to Chicago for his basic training, to Norman, Oklahoma and then to Memphis, Tennessee. When he got his first leave he came home and wanted me to go with him to California because he was to be stationed there at Moffett Field. So with my clothes and $120.00 we started for California in an old 1951 Studebaker. Until then, I have never been more than a hundred miles away from the town where I was born.

I think back to the day when we left Des Moines, Iowa, we were a young boy of seventeen and a mother of forty five starting out for an unknown place over a thousand miles away with nothing but hope in our hearts that we would make it. It took three days and two nights to get there. We slept in the car to save the money that we had and bought a loaf of bread, lunch meat, and a bottle of milk for our meals. We had a flat tire and had to buy a new one. We reached Mountain View, California, on May 30, 1958, with $20.00 and the hope that we could find a place to live. Late that night we found an apartment. The owner trusted us to come up with the rest of the rent. The next morning I went job hunting and my son went to the base. I found a job taking care of an elderly couple, and my son was shipped overseas. I worked for quite some time, cooking and keeping house for the elderly couple. Then one of their daughters decided to move in with them. Again I went looking for work. This time it was work in a cannery, packing pickles. The smell was bad, but I didn't mind the work. Though working on a conveyor belt does make a person a little dizzy.

During the time that my son was gone I had bought another car and learned how to drive. With my drivers license I met his ship when it came in at the Alameda Navy Base. I was very proud of myself.

I think 'how did I do it!' A green country girl, that has never driven a car and was brave enough to get on those freeways and drive with my knees knocking and my heart pounding; I must have had more courage than brains. I know there were times when God was helping me, because I don't think I could have done it alone.

On my son's second trip oversees I went to San Francisco to work. That is a beautiful town with so many things to see and places to go. But it was very lonely because I didn't know anyone. I soon went back to Mountain View where I had met a few people and was happy there.

After my son got out of the Navy we bought a home in Sunnyvale, California and he went to work in a large factory near our home. It wasn't long before he started to think of love and marriage because he met a very wonderful girl. I had been going with a sailor. So while my son was busy with his romance, I had fallen in love, too. I got married in March, and my son in July of 1962.

My sailor retired after twenty years of service and in 1968 we move to his home state of Oklahoma, so far away from my son and his family who still lived in California. I miss them so much. Here we are, almost 2,000 miles apart. I know they are well and happy and their days are filled with work.

I think of all the sad and lonely mothers and wives waiting each day to hear some word from their loved ones so far away in Viet Nam. As I sit here and think of the past, about the wars and the hardships, somehow the future seems so much worse.

Something has gone wrong with so many boys and girls. They seem to have lost respect for themselves and their country. God has been cast aside. The old saying 'a family that prays together stays together' is forgotten quite often. I know that when a home is broken or the mother has to work, the children are the ones that get the worst part; they are neglected, given an allowance, and told to get out of the way. How do I know? I, too, was guilty of this. I think back to the many times when I told my son to go out and play when I should have given him love and understanding.

Today it seems like so many young teenagers seek excitement with pep pills, alcohol, or marijuana to ruin their life. The adults have to take pills to wake up, pills to get through the day, and pills to make them sleep. To relax and have fun they drink beer or hard liquor and get in a car and speed on the freeway to kill or be killed while looking for thrills and excitement.

I tremble with fear when I hear of all the riots in the schools and on the streets, of all the beatings, robberies, and the deaths of so many young people. These are needless ways to try to solve problems. No problem was ever solved by force, which causes the loss of many lives. I wonder, what will the next twenty years bring?

This is the most educated country in the world.

TABLE OF CONTENTS

About The Author   v

How To Use This Book   vii

Dedication   ix

Acknowledgements   xi

In Memory And Honor Of My Mother   xiii

Introduction   **xxvii**

Chapter One   **Getting Started**   **1**
Your introduction to the real world of job search starts here. This workbook will assist you in developing ideas, theories, and concepts to help you obtain your next job.

Chapter Two   **Supply And Demand**   **13**
This chapter introduces you to the concepts of supply and demand and how it can influence your job opportunities.

Chapter Three   **Effectiveness Vs. Efficiency**   **37**
You will find in this chapter how effectiveness and efficiency interrelates

Chapter Four   **Specialty Approaches To Job Search**   **41**
To set yourself apart from the pack, and I going to assume there is a pack out there, you may have to do something unique. This chapter addresses some unique approaches.

Chapter Five   **Tracking**   **45**
What tracking is and how you use it.

Chapter Six   **Career Planning**   **49**
The concept of career planning and how to formulate possible career strategies. Here we take a trip exploring how you can relate to work in general, your likes and dislikes

Chapter Seven   **Your Assets**   **53**
Here are tips to explore relating to what you have to sell to that potential employer.

Chapter Eight   **Developing Your Interviewing Skills**   **59**
The heart of getting the job is the interview. The cover letter, and your interview will get you up to the plate, but you get the job with a 'knock em dead' job interview.

Chapter Nine   **Networking**   **83**
The in's and out's of how to 'Network' which will be one of the most important tools in getting your next job.

Chapter Ten   **The Champion**   **89**

What, when, where, why, and how to put a Champion to work for you may be the most important person to assist you in getting your next job.

Chapter Eleven   **The Cover Letter (Letter Of Application)**   **93**

The foundation of your job search is the cover letter. This section explores the how, why, and how to development of a 'can do' cover letter. This is the 'tool' that sells you and gets you in the door.

Chapter Twelve   **The Résumé**   **113**

Now it is time to get it down on paper and develop the tool that presents your skills, experiences, and background to continue to sell you and help you close the door in getting the job.

Chapter Thirteen   **The Follow-Up Letter**   **151**

Once you have had some type of contact with a potential employer, be it verbal or in person, it is your responsibility to continue to sell yourself by sending a follow-up letter. This is your way to continue to get your qualifications and interests in front of the interviewer.

Chapter Fourteen   **Sources For Jobs**   **163**

There are many sources you can search to discover where to look for a job. This chapter will explore some alternatives.

Chapter Fifteen   **Is There A Job Internet For You?**   **199**

Today we have been given a new media to put in our arsenal of job search tools; this is the Internet and job search web sites. This source will expose us to a new horizon of jobs anywhere in the country and more, but at the same time also opens us up to greater competitors for these job opportunities.

Chapter Sixteen   **Preparing Your Résumé For Posting**   **235**

After you have taken the time to develop your Résumé it is important that it has the right presentation as you display your work to the audience you are trying to reach.

Chapter Seventeen   **Self Employment**   **247**

As you deliberate the ongoing process of seeking employment with another firm, you might want to consider the advantages and disadvantages of working for yourself. This chapter reviews some of these issues.

Chapter Eighteen   **Temporary Employment**   **251**

While you are seeking your dream job you may want to consider temporary employment as a stop gap until the right job comes along. This may be possible or it may be necessary.

Chapter Nineteen   **The Small Business: It Could Be For You (The Ideal Job)**   **255**

You will explore the dream of having and operating your own business, and look at some of the benefits and issues associated with this dream.

Chapter Twenty — How Should You Dress? **269**

The way you dress and look is an integral part of the hiring package. If the employer likes what they see it can be a big plus. This chapter looks at how you should look, dress, and present yourself.

Chapter Twenty One — The Multiple Party Interview **273**

As you get involved in the job search you may be exposed to another type of interviewing technique called the Multiple Party interview. You will find that executives do not want to totally be responsible for hiring new candidates, so in the Multiple Party Interview others will share the risk.

Chapter Twenty-Two — The Cost For Job Search **279**

Doing the job search isn't cheap, this chapter reviews some of the cost associated with finding a job.

Chapter Twenty-Three — Tax Deduction Job Search **281**

Job search is a lot of work and can also be expensive. This chapter touches on a number of items that you can deduct while you are seeking that 'dream Job'.

Chapter Twenty-Four — The Beginning – Not The End! **283**

Finding a new career/position is not the end, it is only the beginning in the process of building your future. Use this book as a tool to sharpen your awareness of your skills and abilities then build yourself that 'drop dead' résumé to get your dream job.

Chapter Twenty-Five — Headhunters And Recruiters **289**

In this chapter I am going to discuss different types of headhunters and recruiters and the advantages and disadvantages in using them.

Chapter Twenty-Six — The Top 100 Companies In The United States **295**

In this chapter you will find the 100 Best companies to work for as rated by the employees that work for said companies.

Chapter Twenty-Seven — Negotiate To Increase Your Financial Package **309**

We will discover how to use common sense and soft selling to negotiate your personal package.

Chapter Twenty-Eight — Your Background Check **315**

Passing your interview does not mean you have the job. Your background may hold the 'key' in determining if you have made the grade in getting your dream job.

Sample Résumés **321**

Market Study Package: **438**

Use these pages to plan and lay-out your job search program

Chapter Twenty-Nine   Top 100 Companies In The County   **439**

In this chapter, we are going to explore the top companies in America that would be worthwhile in taking your time to apply.

Chapter Thirty   How Much Are You Really Worth?   **501**

As you go through the process of job search it is important that you have some idea of what the positions you apply for are worth, and what you are worth based upon your education and experience.

Chapter Thirty-One   Digital Résumés   **531**

Samples of Applications   535

Glossary of Terms   543

INTRODUCTION

The purpose of this book is to discuss and help you with the real trials and tribulations of your job search, but more importantly explore how you **'really'** get a job today in these uncertain times using my experience, ideas, observations, inventories, planning, and information gathered and tried from many sources over the years. This information comes from all over the country from many levels within various organizations. Our leaders in government tell us 'there are <u>no</u> employment problems' and 'there is a shortage of workers'. But when the rubber meets the road, you still have your work cut out for you to find the job of your choice. Use this book as a 'tool', a workbook to build the ammunition you need to win that job. This is one of the most important battles of your life.

Historically, an individual use to work for one company, or organization for their entire working career of about forth-five years and then retired. This is <u>no longer</u> true. Today, we are finding little loyalty by companies to workers, and companies should not expect to get much back, this is not to say there no firms out there that look out for their employees, there are, but I believe this to be the minority and not the majority. Because of World Competition today we find organization downsizing, rightsizing, re-organizing, and firing employees in large numbers when the markets change, be it national or foreign, to gain a few profit points. We can be downsized for any number of reasons. Employers expect to pick up 'new' qualified, or cheaper employees in the future with often little regard for the employee economic situation or the employee's family. This is often done in the name of saving money, re-organization, progress, or whatever the poplar 'buzz' word is at the time.

Companies justify this in the eternal drive for higher profits for shareholders, and not to mention higher and higher bonuses for the top executives. On the other hand, increasing manufacturing costs, world wide competition, and obsolescent companies are forced to downsize or even go out of business. As examples there were companies that manufactured buggy whips, and shoes in the United States. Today we have no buggies, and most shoes are manufactured out of the county. I am sure you can think of other products that are made offshore. The world is getting smaller and smaller and companies are cutting corners everywhere. And if you are reading and planning to use this book, you may be a victim of this process; and this process results in higher prices and the reduction of services. In many cases companies are cutting services in the name of increasing or protecting their profits, believing that they could be in jeopardy, be it fact or fiction.

Efficiency is the name of the game; today the more efficient you are the more money or 'bigger' you get. This usually comes at the expense of the employee or the customer (or both). The key question for most people is, how do you adjust to this cold, new world; a reality in which everyone is out to get whatever they can at the expense of others? This may be a bit cynical, but it often seems true. This is the real world we face each day now and will be far into the future. You must be wary these days. I know of a friend who was happily retired for nearly ten years. He and his wife thought they had it made! Until one day one of this five children's husband was 'downsized' and guess who was back in the job market; always keep your résumé up-to-date. You never know what will happen next.

The managers today are mainly interested in protecting their 'fat' pay-check, bonuses and benefits, and you can't really blame them. They do not care much about the 'new' worker who must learn to do their job themselves or be fired. Many managers often cannot train them because they do not know the job themselves, and may not understand the job. However do expect that the work is done and done correctly.

You may feel that your termination was unfair. This may or may not be true, never-the-less most people do not have the time, or money to support a lawsuit. It is very time consuming, and an up hill battle. Many companies have unlimited resources and attorneys on call to handle the lawsuit. Often companies win the lawsuit anyway, but if you won, would you really like to be hired back? You are losing time and now have no income, the best solution might be to 'suck it up' and move on. You could also be included in the unpublished 'Black list' which is available on the internet to any employer willing to pay for them, and the word can get around. The employer wants to know if you are going to make trouble for them. Once on a 'Black List' an employee may have a difficult time getting a job.

Remember that a company can lay a person off for any reason; or in some cases no seemingly good one. I am going to have to tell you that in one or two cases I was let go for no apparent reason. I remember being laid off from a job by the Vice President of Engineering; he had my paycheck ready and there was little to no discussion. He called me in to a conference room and said 'I am going to have to let you go'. I was working in an area outside my experience, but as I said to him I am learning more and more each day, he said 'one of these days we are going to have an argument or disagreement', and he was going to let me go before that day came. When I was hired, which was less than 90 days earlier, I had reminded them that I was in the wrong department and had not used the appropriate skills necessary for years. There was nothing I could do but move on. As you can see, an organization can and will make up a reason (other than the real one) if no other reason comes to mind no matter whose fault it might be.

Companies can be very clever at disguising the real reason why a worker is being shown the door.

Another firm recently downsized an older dark-skinned employee for apparently no reason and won a lawsuit brought by the employee who sued for discrimination. The company claimed he was 'downsized' because he was unable to do the work that was left. The reason was due to his skin color. Some time ago I was aware of a School Superintendent who suggested that he wanted to replace all of his administrators with a specific ethnic group; does this go on, you bet! This does not mean you do not have a chance or that you should give up. No, it means that you need to be aware of what really goes on in the 'real' world of job search.

Older workers are particularly vulnerable to the trends toward downsizing and staff reduction. Older workers who earn very good salaries with benefits are being replaced by several workers with no experience for 1/3 their salaries and less or no benefits. This apparently has been a national trend since we can see the high numbers of employees over 50 years old being laid off, both sexes, and various ethnic groups. We also see these workers being replaced by off shore workers in countries that will work for concededly less. These same groups that are being replaced are having extreme difficulties finding worthwhile employment to match their experience and Education levels. We not only see this in business and industry, but in our Education Community.

This type of thinking ignores the fact that not as much work gets done because there is no one left who really knows how to do the job. The seasoned, laid-off employee gets frantic phone calls at home from the 'new' hires to find out what is going on or how to do their job. As an example I recently semi-retired from teaching Computer Technology and I received a phone call from an 'almost' Business/Computer teacher. The reason I call her almost is she had told me that she had not gotten her credential yet. She was asking me how to get her information off my classroom computer since she doesn't remember her password and the LCD monitor was stolen. By enlarge, few individuals in the school could teach the class, or solve the problem. And the trend in this district is to hire 'cheap' inexperienced teachers. Sometimes seasoned certified individuals may be called by desperate school districts to substitute, but not for a full-time job.

The people in management who lay off seasoned employees are supposed to know what is going on but they often do not. Organizations discover (too late) what was to be a money-savings idea more often than not costs these firms and companies a great deal more than if they had kept their original employees. They would have continued to do the job and make money, or gotten the job done without delays and disruptions, (not to mention the added cost of hiring, firing and other related administrative cost).

What I am going to say here as I indicated above is employers may reduce staff for a myriad of reasons and you may be the casualty of this action. You may or may not have cause to file a lawsuit. This action on your part may have further employment problems in the future, so I would suggest that you consider your actions because it might be better for you to move along then to fight for your old job back. I will leave this up to you, but I assure you, I would not want to be someplace where I was not wanted.

The employee should always have a current résumé and a letter of introduction at all times. If you are in Education you will always need three current letters of recommendation when applying for a position. Remember it is always easier to get a job while you are working. Do not wait until you get a 'Pink Slip' or a 'lay-off notice' to start a job search. This is a big mistake. Any individual should always be looking out for the next opportunity or career growth situation. Remember, not only is there little to no 'loyalty' by many companies today, the world is in flex, what is popular today may be subject to obsessions tomorrow and companies may have to adjust their labor force accordingly. Some might suggest that it can be very foolish to be too loyal these days. I am not going to say that it is foolish, you may know your situation better than I, but I am going to suggest that you be careful. There are good employers, businesses, school districts, government positions, and organizations out there; however, they are many times over-shadowed by the bad ones. Good organizations are like the baled eagle, they are in short supply. A person can never tell about an organization until it is too late. You may be able to find information such as 'the best 100' in the country to work for. I believe I ran across this list in the 'APR' magazine some months ago. But you may not always have this luxury available to you.

As you go through your life you can expect on an average to get seven lay-off notices in a forty-five year career. The average person will change careers at least four times during a lifetime. I myself for example started out working as a Hydraulic technician after being discharge from the Navy (another job), to working in Sales and Marketing, to Teaching High School and College, and now an Author. I will also let it be known that I sold shoes, pumped gas, made blue prints, and worked in engineering. Every one of these jobs was a move not always up, but to earn a living. In every case the change of career, or employment meant to start a job that had not been done before. This may mean a major change in salary (sometimes down, sometimes up) or it could mean an increase in experience that can be used in the new field. Most people starting a career are not aware of these facts as it is 'never' taught in school. Rarely does anyone discuss this with the new employee or applicant. In the beginning your career can be very rocky. You may not get the job you really want the first time out the gate. But, how and what you do will reflect on your next job.

A key point here is that every individual should always be involved in career training to get into or go to new fields of their choice like computers and the internet if there appears to be upward possibilities in those areas. The career training will always aid in upward mobility. Eighty-five percent of new career changes require some type of additional schooling or vocational training. This takes hard work, sacrifice, and commitment! It is important that as an employee you should take advantage of employer-paid, or provided training opportunities, but you may have to pay for additional training if the employer does not provide this benefit. If the additional training does not benefit you where you are it will make you more valuable in the future. Employee training can be obtained nearly everywhere these days it is to your advantage to seek it out and take as much as you can.

You should move toward jobs that appear to be in demand. New jobs are created all the time. Old jobs fall by the wayside, and are also outsourced to other countries. For example, the fireman in the railroad industry, the gas station attendant, the blueprint checker in the aerospace industry, and customer service. These jobs were all once very important jobs that have been replaced by changes in the workplace. This is supply and demand at work, it is nothing personal. Jobs can (and do) come and go all the time, or are replaced because of cost or a new process.

The 'key' to your success is what you do with your time. Since we all have 365 days a year, we must manage the limited amount of time that we have. You are the only person who can control what you want to do with your time. It is your time while you are alive. It is like money in your pocket, you can spend it wisely or you can waste it. My advice is that you should invest it in the most important person you know and that is yourself and your future. Like the story of the ants and the grasshopper, the grasshopper watched and joked as the ants gathered food, then came that day the grasshopper was hungry and he had no stored food to fall back on, but the ants who used their time wisely had gathered food for that 'rainy day' and did not have to worry about being hungry. Are you the ant or the grasshopper? Using your time to train, go to school and improve your skills is the way to use your time wisely. Again, are you an ant or a grasshopper?

The highest-priced workers are those that do very little physical work, They are the ones who 'think', 'plan', 'manage', 'teach', 'control', and 'direct'. Thinking is one of the most highly prized and least understood functions in the economy. There are many common misunderstandings about those who think for a living, but in many cases receive a high salary.

The person who digs ditches for a living can get tired physically from this work, but the 'mind' of the worker however, will never get physically tired because the mind cannot get tired, though it may get bored. The mind is available for work at any time the person is awake. The mind can also offer solutions in dreams while we sleep.

The most important person to any economy is the 'mind' worker. The more you think, the better the worker you are. You solve problems, save time, overcome obstacles, find new ways to do things; and you make more money. This is a cycle that will repeat itself again and again. The highest paid workers are those who think the best. Non-thinking workers usually do not rise to great levels in any organization; they are quickly replaced by smarter thinking people.

It is important to work smarter not harder. This is better for you as well as your employer. The best work requires the least effort and the most creativity. It requires you to look at what you are doing and think of ways to improve things. This initiative will be rewarded by your employer. The most important worker in the organization is the employee who thinks and asks himself 'how can I be more profitable for my company'. Being more profitable for your employer is being more profitable for yourself. These workers are few and far between, but you know them. They are the rising stars, the ones that go the 'extra' mile.

Thirty years ago 20 percent of the workforce was represented by college grads, 70 percent by manual laborers, and 10 percent by technical people. Thirty years from now there will still be a need for 20 percent college graduates, 79 percent technical people, but less than one (1) percent for manual laborers. The growth area will be for people with at least some technical training. Manual labor will be almost entirely gone! The 'Key' to all of this is Education (especially technical Education). And a key component of this Education will, to one degree or another, having a background of computer process knowledge. This exposure will help to carry you though. You will find though in all business and industry, a necessary need for this computer exposure.

In America we must focus also on competition and employment from a global work force. We must be preparing ourselves for the excelling of the Information Age, an era dominated by this technology and knowledge, as well as the globalization of employment. Today almost half of the U.S. workers will be in industries related to information technology. Already, the leading job category in the U.S. labor statistics is computer and data processing. The fastest growing occupations require the most Education and are concentrated in the business-services and health-services industries, this is much different from the last century. Highly educated professions such as doctors, engineers, and lawyers represented such a small percentage of the job market.

Those talented professionals will have more opportunities to work from their homes relying on the internet, computer power and faster broadband speeds. With more people working from home there will be more opportunities for door-to-door sales again.

Some of the good news is that we will see a rising rate of the re-hiring of retirees to teach remedial math, reading programs, customer service, and also occupations. But at the same time they are going to have to be ready with new skills as well. We will see more women making inroads into managerial and executive ranks. Today, the number of women earning four-year college degrees has surged 44 percent since 1979, and now 56 percent of the estimated 1,140,000 college graduates reported by the Department of Education are women.

When thinking about a place to go for a career change, a booming area of opportunity that is now coming to the forefront, is financial and retirement planning, as the nearly 77 million baby boomers begin to hit 65 in 2011.

Ex-retail workers will flood the job market as competition from catalogs and online centers force many retailers to consolidate or close. These retail people will compete for jobs in marketing and sales, making those sectors fiercely competitive.

Employers will become increasingly isolated, relying on digital communication rather than face to face interaction with applicants. If social skills diminish, this could hinder collaboration and threaten productivity. So it is safe to say, that in order to stay competitive one needs to maintain not only social skills, but also continue to train and develop technical skills that will keep you competitive into the 21st century and beyond. Surely the 'key' to career success is

Education and training! It is up to you to protect your job the best you can by exploring any and all Educational opportunity within your company or on your own to protect yourself within the company that you are with or to help make yourself more valuable if you have to move on to another job or make a career change.

CHAPTER ONE

GETTING STARTED

Hopefully, by the time you have purchased this book or you are reading it, you should have an idea of your career goals. This book can be used by anyone, but it is designed for the individual, or individuals who already have been in the world of work. I have another book that is published that is designed especially for High School graduates and adults moving into the employment market who basically have not worked before. The name of that Book is **JUMP START YOUR CAREER**. Both tools are useful, if you follow the techniques it will help in finding employment. As we discussed earlier you may have to make a number of job changes in your life time. These changes may be for career advancement or to stay employed. Across the county, millions of Americans have been forced to change their jobs or vocation. Some by choice, but others were not as fortunate. As an example, over the last year or so nearly the whole population of New Orleans was displaced do to a major Hurricane. Almost overnight their jobs were taken away from them; a perfect reason for continued education and training, as well as honing job skills, on the part of the applicant.

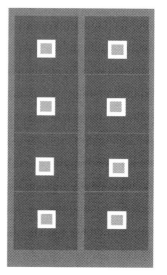

7001 Resumes-Plus Second Edition

You can look at the nation's employment record and see that last year over two million people were put out of work by 'downsizing', 'rightsizing', or 'pruning'. I suggest to you that this will continue to happen, just read the newspaper, or listen to the radio, or watch the news on TV. Over the last few months the Automobile industry has laid off large numbers of employees. So I want you to prepare, not just for that next job or career change, but to protect yourself in case of a negative turn of events.

I am sure this is not the first thing you wanted to hear, but I am going to tell you anyway to put you in the right prospective. You and I need to set some types of goals, a career map or as I call them, my A, B, and C plan. I am not going to recommend something I would not or have not done, in fact you may need a D, E, and F plan the way the economy is today. And some of you may have to add more letters of the alphabet. May I suggest that you have many goals to set, which should be short-term, intermediate, and long-term.

In many cases transition jobs are the wave of the future. Many of you are becoming 'underemployed' this is a term that rarely reaches the media (for good reason). Let me give you an example of a 'Transition' job. You might be an individual who was in industry, or a home maker who wants to go back into teaching, well the first and only thing you can find is a substituting position. Here is the job that you transition into to another career, but it also can be a position of underemployment. As a 'sub' you might receive $105.00 per day, maybe less, but if you would have gotten a full-time position you would have received $50,000 a year with benefits maybe more. I am sure you can think of examples in your industry, or your situation. Never the less, you are underemployed. You know who you are out there but our politicians refuse to touch or mention your group. Transitional jobs will continue forever, but we will see more of them at a faster and faster pace. By the way you are not a

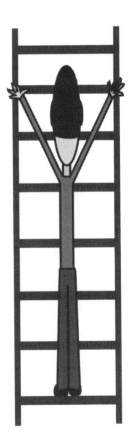

2

bad person if you have to take one of these jobs. The first responsibility is to take care of your basic needs.

I don't know if anyone has told you this before, or if you have ever thought of it, but the 'plan' concept is somewhat new to me. I didn't stumble on to it until a few years ago when I was in the 'Great Recession of 1989'. A lot of people were thrown out of work when 'peace' came. Real peace for the military and the aerospace workers meant a long time at the unemployment line.

This was the spoils of victors winning the cold war. That's right. Winning for many engineers, technicians, and high tech workers meant unemployment and underemployment. High-paying jobs were a thing of the past.

I can remember a long-time colleague of mine who was delighted to get a job at 50 percent of his previous income with a major aerospace company after months and months of job search. He had been with the first firm for over fifteen years, now in his 50s he has to seek out new employment. He was happy to get a job-any job.

What I am going to suggest to you on the positive side is that windows of opportunities open and close all the time, and as we gain maturity, experience, age, or get more education, we are more able to 'strike' as they avail themselves. This means of course we must have our eyes and ears open, as our plans or goals will change, and I assure you they will. Here's an example: when I first went to work as a kid my eyes were on this 'neat' navy blue 1950 Mercury. I am sure many of you can relate to my goal or dream. I have gone from wanting to work as a Hydraulic technician in the Aerospace industry to working as an Industrial Salesmen, and Manager in the same industry. We can adapt to these changes.

7001 Resumes-Plus Second Edition

As we all know the aerospace industry has changed and there has been a great deal of 'downsizing', but I was able to take what I leaned and transition to another opportunity, and a career advancement. Again some time later I moved into the Education field. I assure you some moves were to better my career, and others movers were to save my butt. The United States have lost many jobs to other countries which require that we are always on out toes. We want to be in control if you can and make changes and moves because we want to not because we have to. Understand the only thing we can count on is change, but as I suggest we want to try to be in control.

As I suggested earlier we must have a plan or a set of goals. For example, you may want to be a sales manager, teacher, architect, doctor, or engineer. Get a little book and write this down. Make a list of goals, or a list of how to accomplish your goals. Keep this list up to date. At first this may be hard to do because it is something 'new', though you will find that this is a positive habit. Like any habit it will take time to become accustomed to. If you like you could make this list out to be what you want. I call it a 'want list'. I have one today, I have it on my computer and I make a copy and carry it around with me all the time. When I complete a task or purchase an item from my list I drop it and add new items. Such as: purchase a 'hot tub', take a computer course, send out my résumé, ask for that raise, or get a new job. I do not care what you call this list, a 'Want list' or 'Goal list', what I am recommending here is that you start using a list. You can make it as detailed as you like, and carry it out as far as you want. You may want to start by setting times and dates. You should have short-term, intermediate, and long-term goals. Buy yourself a small 65 cent notebook and as your needs, ideas, and goals change, write them down. Carry this note book with you at all times and as ideas come to you make the modifications. As you achieve certain goals remove it from your book and add something new. Keep the list as current as you can and as I have suggested revise the list. You may want to have categories and keep each item in the right order.

This suggestion is not just for job search, but everything you want, or places you may want to go. This notebook will help you stay on 'task' and in the right direction you want to go. This simple process could even change your life. Finally, I am not asking you to do something that I am not doing and I find that it keeps me on the correct path.

EXAMPLE:

Income wanted (put a number here)

Position wanted (put a title here)

Part of the country you want to live in (put the place here)

Who you want to work for (You could even put a company name)

Vacation (put place here)

Education (Classes)

House

Hot Tub

Other needs

As you can see I am asking you to start to develop a new approach to job search, if you are using this skill than you are already ahead however, I am going to assume you are not so I am going to ask you to start thinking in short-term, intermediate, and long-term goals. I am going to suggest that you make this list long and refer to it on a daily and weekly basis. By doing this it will allow you to add, modify, and subtract items from it as you achieve them, as well as insert items that you want to accomplish. You will develop a sense of accomplishment as you find yourself making progress by doing this.

The new thing I am going to suggest to you is that you develop an attitude of persistence. You will have to understand that I have to make some assumptions. So if you are already persistent then we are on the right foot, but it not then we are moving into new territory. No matter what, never quit or give up. Now as

7001 Resumes-Plus Second Edition

you start your own job search program don't become discouraged if you don't get action right away when you are sending out your letters of application, and résumés. Another piece of information I would like to share would be right on target, you might get one job offer in ten job interviews. I would like to tell you some thing better, but this is the national average. Over the last year I have been seeing higher numbers than this. If you do better, then great, but this would an exception to the rule. Let me give you a couple of examples to think about on this subject. I am aware of a nurse who wanted to change jobs; she was faced with several reasons to move from her current place of employment. Besides upward mobility, there were some rumors of downsizing. She put together her résumé and cover letter then sent it out, and what do you know, she landed an interview right out of the gate. Why was this, well each one of us is different, are goals are different, the job market is different for every field. In this case there were extenuating circumstance, first her field was and is a 'hot' employment field and applicants are in high demand (with few applicants), and also in this case her reputation was known at the other company. But of course do not rule out timing. On the other hand, I am aware of a degreed applicant who was highly trained in his field; he sent out hundreds of applications and résumés and got very few answers let alone many interviews. In this case this applicant was facing a very competitive market with many other job seekers and few jobs. This does not mean though that you give up or not try.

You need to be aware that you're not the only one out there looking for employment, and that not only is there competition for various jobs, the job market varies with the economy and certain jobs more than others. You may see not only the jobs dropping off, but you may experience the quality of companies have dropped off also. This is another area which I would like to 'touch' base with you a bit. As a survivor and depending on your financial situation and goals, the duration of your job search can very greatly. I am going to remind you again, you must not give up and you must be consistent. How consistent you are will telegraph to the company you trying to work for. What makes advertising so successful is its consistency and this will work for you. Believe it, if you do what I suggest (don't give up, continually maintain your efforts), there will be a 'payoff'. Potential employers will call you for interviews. There will be times when you will get many calls from your efforts, and other times no calls at all. It will be feast or famine. Your job search will be somewhere in between. And as a group, employers, if they are not interested will not take the time to even to answer your letter of application. Don't get discouraged, just understand that this is just the way they are and it is not you. I am going to ask you to send out 80 to 100 letters of application, but not résumés, a week. Only send you résumé if it is asked for. I even developed a Newsletter designed around my qualifications, approaching it in a creative way of getting my skills across and get that interview. This is something 'new' in the job seeking tools that I have been experimenting with and will discuss later in another chapter. I will cover every phase of getting the right job.

Let's discuss getting a 'stop gap job'. You're going to have to search in phases. What do I mean by this? Well, since you know that many positions have been eliminated and a large number of people have been 'downsized', you are going to have to look outside your field. You may be forced to take a position for less money than you are used to making and a position of less authority. This is being 'under-employed', or a 'stop gap job'. It may be prudent to look at other industries for this and other employment opportunities. These are not bad moves; they keep money coming in and meat on the table. It may also bring new opportunities for you. I am sure you will be able to develop additional contacts for 'networking'. I will discuss this 'key' method of job search and finding that employment position you really want. Before moving on let me say this much about networking. The fact is, 'Networking' has been suggested, generates 64% to 74% of the jobs.

I want to talk next about recruitment advertising. It is suggested that they account for 10 to 14 percent of the hiring, and executive search and job agencies account for 9 to 14 percent of job placement. As you can see these numbers do not add up to 100%. These numbers change all the time and change for special circumstances. I would never suggest that you count any of these alternatives down and out. But keep in mind you're looking for employment, and of course knowing the statistics will help to keep you on track. I will try to point out ways you would need to travel to be successful in your job search. Networking is the 'key' method to finding that good job. You should be networking at all times. You should tell everyone you see what you want and what you are doing, also ask them for their help. You may be surprised to get help from an unlikely source like a neighbor who gives you a referral to a friend of his. One of my friends got a job referred by a gas station owner who knew a president of a company. You do not know who knows who knows who. Networking is now done cheaply and easily on the internet. The internet is a great way to keep phone bills low and keep in contact with people you know. The more people you know, the more likely it is for you to find someone who will put you in touch with the hiring manager or give you the ideas for your own business. Try to keep in contact with people as much as you can. Christmas cards are a good way to do this.

A shift must be made from the traditional sending out of your résumés which many people still do and I'm sure you may have to do. I have discovered the more effective way of getting a job/position is networking. The power of networking can not be over emphasized.

You may find that 'Networking' is challenging for you, as it is for me. Even with my years in Business, Education, Marketing, and Sales, I am still learning everyday. There will be times that you will have to force yourself to Network.

It may be hard for you to do, but remember this is your career and job we are talking about. You can network by making cold calls; you want to talk to anyone from the guy on the street to the gal in the club or in the grocery story. By the way, start going to various meetings. I am sure this may be challenging for you to do, it is for me. I want you to go to the Rotary Club, JC's, Lions Club, Chamber of Commerce's, Elks, Masons, your Church, or any other organization in your area to do your networking.

If you don't have referral names at this time, don't let that stop you. Go to the library and find at least two books that will identify businesses in your city, state, or country. Here in California we have the California Manufactures Directory and the California Business Directory, they are yellow and blue. You can find them at most city libraries and I have been told that they have them on their computer; go to the 'Reference Department'. There is also The Robert's Register. You will find similar directories in your state or city library. Talk to the Reference Librarian, he/she can help you identify these references books, which are updated yearly.

At one time I had the California Manufactures Directory on my computer and used it all the time. It will give you the city, product, and so forth. These business directories are very useful. If you are interested in buying this directory be prepared to put out more than $800.00. The library is a very cost effective resource.

You can identify the companies by there SIC code (this is the code that identifies what they do). Next select the company to be contacted. Say you identify one with 10 to 30 million gross sales per year as the firm size that you are interested in. If this is where you see yourself and feel that you could be of the most value, and has the greatest opportunities for **you**; then since you have the name of the company, the phone number, what they do, and the name of its president or CEO 'Viola', you can make the call, write that letter of application, Fax, or E-mail them.

No matter how you come up with a name, it is important that you develop a 'script'. This is especially true if you are calling. I am going suggest that it does not sound 'canned', but at the same time you do want it to sound professional and to the point. These people that you are calling are very busy and you will need to get the point across quickly and to hold their attention. You will also run up against what is known as the 'gatekeeper'. This is usually the secretary of the person you are trying to contact. Since most cases the person you want to talk to is the president of the company or a director of the firm, the 'gatekeeper' is the first one you will have to sell.

You may need to do this routine more than one time for you get it down. You may run into a company where the gatekeeper may not put you through to the people you first intended, however they may put you through to their own Human Resources Department. There is no

7001 Resumes-Plus Second Edition

question this is a hard way to network and it is hard to predict which way the job search well go, but remember, networking is 'critical' to your success in job search.

If possible remain on good terms with your former bosses. This may or may not be easy; however, they may have referrals in other areas of employment when you are 'downsized' out the door. Do not panic when you get 'downsized' it is not the end of the world. Try to leave on good terms with your old employer. Complete all of your projects and let your boss know how hard you've worked. There are good reasons for this. They may like you but cannot afford to keep you. Ask for a severance package. Some companies have severance packages, most do not.

Companies give severance packages to avoid bitterness and lawsuits especially for good employees who may be due things like bonuses. Always ask for letters of recommendation. This will make it harder for the employer to say you were downsized because you were a bad worker. You would have their word in writing as to what happened. Employers feel the need to justify why they let you go. Ask for an explanation as to why you were laid-off. This will help you to explain it to future employers. Be sure you tell the new employer what happened. Ask if the employers know of any openings in your company or any other companies or industries. Always go to the top of the company to get leads. You do not know who will help. Know your company policy regarding how to lay off workers. Find out if there is any possibility of recall by the company. Always get and read the personnel manual and be sure that the company follows manual guidelines. Many times the companies fail to follow the procedures required before you are laid off. You will never get any due process once you are gone.

You will be out of sight and out of the mind of the President and other key people within the organization. They will quickly forget everything about you while they try to figure out who will get stuck with your work. Someone will get stuck with it! The work does not go away.

You can ask for typing assistance on your résumé and letters of introduction. See if you can use the company phone, office, stationary, copier or desk to set up interviews with other firms. Also see if you can get time off with pay for interviewing. Finally, ask your employer if there is any other help they may want to give you like outplacement services. Outplacement service is going to an outside organization specializing in placement of workers who have been downsized.

Usually there is no cost to you. The cost is picked up by the employer. However in some situations, you may have to pay for your own outplacement work. Small firms will not have any benefits of this kind and you will more than likely be on your own. But before you leave the company that is letting you go ask about any other benefits or 401K funds you may be due. Find out when your last day at your current job will be. Large firms may give you some type of notice, small ones it may be immediate.

You will find that some companies will give you your last check and you will not be required to return to the work place. Ask about continuing your health benefits. There is a program called COBRA which is a good possibility if you need it.

You need to remember that you are the most important product you have. Market yourself well. You are a commodity that must compete to get that next job. For some people this is a 'new' concept for them to understand. Often non-marketing or sales types do not understand this, but the sooner you recognize this fact, the sooner you will understand the task you have at hand. I know that you may start thinking that you're a piece of meat, I do not think you need to go this far, but do not forget for a minute there are lots of applicants out there for nearly every job you are interested in. It has been estimated that each job will have from 20 to 300 applicants applying for it. This may sound hard to believe, but it is true, even in a good economy with low employment rates. I will give you some ideas how to get these down, but remember we will be competing, one way or another.

I am aware of a Regional Managers position which was advertised in a local Sunday Newspaper, the position was with the 'Staple' organization. As you may know they are a national retailing outlet. In conversation with the people conducting the interviews I discovered that they have eighty (80) applicants applying for the one position. This seems to be more the rule than the exceptions these days. This information is not to scare you but make you aware. And you may find in some cases the numbers can be much higher for better jobs. The better the job, the more people will apply. The better the job is publicized the more people will apply. Recently a group of positions was advertised in the local newspaper. There were 1,000 positions open of which 300 were reserved for women, however, it was reported that over 3,000 people applied for these jobs! Clearly there were three applicants for every position. Do not be disappointed if you fail to get a job in a situation like this. The jobs are there but you will have to keep trying. You will have to literally turn over every stone until you fin the job or position you really want. You will want to work smart not hard. Sometimes you can get a lucky break and walk into a great job. This is not true most of the time. You will have to look to find that ideal job. The job will rarely just find you

CHAPTER TWO

SUPPLY AND DEMAND

You should attempt to understand the basic laws of supply and demand. Supply and demand are 'key' things in any economy. The more supply of any given commodity, the less the demand there is for it. There is no demand at all for things when in infinite supply. Therefore, if you are highly skilled and there is a need for many persons with your skill you are in a positive position. But if there are many people with your skills the chance for future employment becomes difficult.

As we have discussed, you are a commodity. You <u>must</u> go out and sell your services to the highest bidder you can find. You are in constant competition with all the other people with your same level of skills or training, or maybe less.

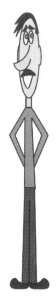

The market will give you a 'fair' price for your services. Most people feel that they are worth more than they are going to get. You are not alone if you feel this way.

7001 Resumes-Plus Second Edition

A recent newspaper article stated that the average college graduate expects to receive a salary of $38,000 per year. This is an optimistic view but is somewhat unrealistically high for many college graduates. As an example, the starting salaries of college graduates and full credentialed teachers have an average in California of $30,000 per year (in 1997). Furthermore it is projected that by 2005 almost half of the jobs in America will require that over 50% of the workers have training in technology. Therefore, if the applicant does not nave this training and background he/she will be in a position to <u>not</u> be hired at all. The fastest-growing occupations will require the most education and concentrate in the business-services and health-services industries. In some areas such as Law and Engineering you might find higher than the $38,000 per year. And since there is a high demand for qualified Nurses again you will find higher starting salaries than the average.

Many industries are going to a two-tiered wage system. This means older workers continue to get their higher salaries and benefits but new hired workers are brought in at much lower wages. This is more common in the blue collar fields. The new employees will receive about 1/3 the wages of the higher-paid, older employees for the same work. This trend is likely to continue as companies seek to drive cost down. Remember, companies are faced with World wide competition. The result is staying in business, less expensive products, and more sales and profit for the firm. It is also done to gain greater profits, efficiency, keeping up with the competition, and higher bonuses for the top people. In truth, I believe you will find that the lowering of wages is done for a combination of the above facts. The supposed shortage of skilled employees can be ignored by the company as long as there are persons applying to take these entry level openings.

Many companies believe that the older, higher-priced employees will train new, lesser-paid employees as long as they pay them and their benefits are not reduced. This strategy seems to be working especially in view of few labor strikes or work stoppages. The reason for this is 'downsizing'. There are very few labor unions to represent the workers; in fact, the percentage of workers represented by unions has dropped to an all-time low. The companies are not satisfied at leaving this situation alone. They offer the older employee a 'Golden Hand Shake' (retirement offer) once the new employees have been trained. The worker either takes the golden hand shake or does not. The company has eliminated the older employee if he/she accepts the golden handshake. The firm may lay off the employee the following year if he does not accept the retirement offer.

Either way, the company wins! Now the worker will be out of a job whether or not he takes the golden hand shake or not. The older worker might be offered his old position back within a year but at the new lower wage. Generally, the worker is better off taking the golden hand shake and looking for a new employment elsewhere. The older work will soon be looking for work with or without the golden hand shake.

The companies are justified in laying off older employees who refuse to take the golden hand shake for purely economic reasons; this has been upheld by some State Supreme Courts. The older worker has no recourse against the company once it has been refused. The firm may lay off the employee. Lastly, there may not be a golden hand shake at all. The cards are all stacked in the favor of the companies at this point.

It is true that in some work environments, there are genuine labor shortages. If you have these job skills, you will find a large demand for what you have to offer. And if this is the case, you are going to find more people attracted to your type of job which means greater competition, decreasing salaries, and the possibility of being 'downsized' when ripples occur in the economy.

Now you can increase your 'value' by getting extra training, more education, or obtaining additional work experience. You should always be looking for ways to improve your 'value'. There are areas with a limited supply of workers and hence a high salary. Great professional basketball players can demand and get a very good salary. On the other hand the trained 'fireman' for a train receives a low salary if any at all because there is a lower or no demand at all for this job.

In the age of the modern trains there is no job for a 'fireman'. The value for your skills is not determined by you but rather by the market. The market is not personal, but it is in control.

The market determines value by supply and demand, the greater the supply the less the demand, and vice versa. Every person has at least some value to market, if nothing else, as a consumer of products. The number of jobs created outside the farm sector far exceeds the forecast of 233,000 per year by private economists. So if you have the right experience there should be a slot for you out there, if not, you owe it to yourself to develop a salable skill that meets the needs of demand. Any material object has value to someone. '**One man's trash is another man's treasure**'. You need to develop talents into marketable skills that can be sold to the highest bidder.

You must first know what you have to sell. This Workbook is designed to help you inventory your skills and to help you make that import determination. Remember that supply and demand controls also most everything in the economy. Supply and demand apply to you and your organization. Supply and demand is everywhere. There were about 1.1 million new and good jobs created in the past year. So there is the demand, it is up to you to provide the supply!

You are going to need to find a '**niche**' where you can be happy, but at the same time make as much money as possible to meet your needs. There are trade-offs here and you must understand them. It has been discovered that all great business people have very diverse personalities and traits but they all spend a great deal of time at work. You must put in the hours if you are going to make it to the top. Most put in a lot of overtime for the company they work for. In the beginning, this overtime may not be compensated. At some point the organization naturally rewards this loyalty with promotion, responsibility, and a pay increase. This translates into spending less time with your family. You may or may not want to pay this price. You may find that your family may be more important to you. This is your call.

Most leaders in any organization put in at least 50 to 60 hours a week at work. I see my wife who is a manager not only put in extra hours on the weekend working at her office, but she also spends a lot of nights working on her computer. You may see a manager replacing a more capable person with one who is less capable who is willing to put in extra hours. If he starts to cut back on his hours, he can find this generally fatal to a career. However, in some cases, people can figure out how to use the time better to make even more money for the organization. These people can actually cut back on hours they work on the job but make more money for the firm. This is by far the best use of time and experience. And it is found to be good for them, but better for the company. It is a win win situation for all.

Everyone from the richest man in the world to the poorest man in the work force has at least one thing in common. They all have exactly 24 hours in a day, seven days in a week and 365 days in a year. No one has any more or any less time. The 'key' to success is what you do with the limited amount of time you have. You are the only person who can control what you do with your time. It is your time while you are alive. It is like money in your pocket. You may choose to spend it as you like. You should spend it wisely.

<u>Position Words</u>

To help you have a better understanding of your primary background and experience, I would like you to circle each word that most closely describes these areas:

Operation Management	Senior Management]
Sales	Computer Applications
Management	Sales Management
Manufacturing	Organizational Management
Management	Retail Management
Engineering	Program Management
Production Management	Educational Management

7001 Resumes-Plus Second Edition

Teacher

Training Management

Engineering

Marketing Management

Technical Applications

Any Other Area you May Have Experience:

Positions Words II

Note: Here is a second set of additional position words that may describe your overall accomplishments, duties, experiences, and background. Circle each word that correctly covers these areas:

Marketing	Import	Export
Financial	Projects	Media
MIS	Design	Promotions
Operations	Proposal	Project Management
Start-up	Financial Operation	Project
Training & Development	Organization	Account Retention
Administration	Reorganizing	Electronic
International Relations	Purchasing	Liaison
Business Development	Account Executive	Manufacturing
Information Systems	Productions Control	Administrative
Product Introduction	Customer Service	Programming
Government Requirement	Process Planning	Product Engineering
Computer Application	Sales	Sale Training
Franchise Operations	Negotiations	User Interface
Expansion Planning		

The Job Search Tool to Get You That Job

Position Statement

<u>Note:</u> Complete the following statement by checking all appropriate answers and filling in the requested information.

1. My experience and background can best be described as (choose all that apply)

Extensive   Management

Solid   Progressive

Well-rounded   Hands-on

Broad   In-depth

Technical   Comprehensive

<u>Any other experience you have:</u>

1. _____

2. _____

3. _____

4. _____

<u>The Environment under which Experience and Accomplishments Were Developed</u>

2. My experience, background, and accomplishments have been developed within or through the following types of environment (check all that apply):

Fast-paced	Highly competitive	Result oriented
Volatile	Technical	Marketing/sales
Operations	Creative	Engineering
Practical training	International	Diversified

19

7001 Resumes-Plus Second Edition

Financial	Education	Flexible
Ever-changing	High-stress	Management
Consulting	Service-oriented	Deadline sensitive
Successful	Top secret	Analytical
Sales intensive	Research	Profitable

<u>How I further Demonstrated my Background and Accomplishments</u>

3. My experience, background and accomplishments are further demonstrated through: (check all that apply and fill in the information when necessary):

A result oriented track record

Worldwide exposure

Exposure to complex situations

Continuous formal education

Rapid advancement

Progressive growth and accomplishments

Revenue enhancement

Problem solving challenges

Profitable accomplishments

Project development

Go the extra mile

Full responsibility for _____

Course work in _____

Direct interface with _____

Innovative design of _____

Production of _____

An education in _____

In-depth knowledge of _____

THE JOB SEARCH TOOL TO GET YOU THAT JOB

Job Functions

Note: It is hoped that you see where I am going here with this work. If you do not know or understand your background and what you are interested in you are going to have a hard time selling yourself to someone else.

1. Place a dash (-) in front of each function you have experience in (business or personal).

2. Place a plus (+) in front of each function for which you would like to be responsible in your next job.

3. Place a double plus (++) in front of the functions you want to be involved with on a hands on/day-to-day basis. Indicate a minimum of 3 but no more than five.

Accounting	Plant Management	Engineering
Administration	Pharmaceutical	Environmental
Advertising	Public relations	Executive
Agriculture	Personnel	Electronics
Artist	Planning	Field Service
Auditor	Pricing	Food service
Aviation	Product Engineering	Financial
Adjuster	Project Engineering	Banking
Psychology	Government	Health Recreation
Broker	Publishing	Graphics
Budget	Human Resources	Civil Engineering
Heath Care	Recruiting	Clergy
Research & Development	Industrial Engineer	Commercial Banking
Retailing	Communication	Insurance
Sales	Community Service	Security
Computer Programmer	International	Consultant

21

7001 Resumes-Plus Second Edition

Investment Counseling	Scientific Consultant Law	Surveyor
System Analyst	Contract Administrator	Copywriter
Labor Relations	Structural Engineering	Management
Costing	Software Systems	Marketing
Credit/collection	Manufacturing	Construction
Social Science	Ceramic	Technical
Mass Communications	Control	Material
Traffic & Shipping	Data Processing	Mechanical Eng.
Design & Drafting	Medical	Urban Development
Development engineering	Military	Metallurgy
Distribution	Merchandising	New Products
Editing	Natural resources	Operations
Energy	Other _____	Other _____

Additional areas in which you may have been involved _____

_____

_____

Additional areas in which you may have been involved: _____

_____

_____

_____

<u>In summary of this exercise</u>, you have now identified the areas in which you have experience, areas in which you would like to have more experience and responsibility, and three to five areas in which you would like to have hands on responsibility on a day to day basis. When writing your résumé use all of the words from these exercises that accurately describe your job functions.

QUESTIONS

Here is a list of questions and concerns which every employer would like to discover about every applicant. I can <u>not</u> tell you that you will be asked every one of these in a single interview, but I can state that you will be asked many of them. I am going to suggest that you prepare yourself by answering every question herein and review your answers many times so that when you are in an interview setting, you will be able to recall your response.

1. HONESTY

Rarely is an interviewer going to ask you, 'Are you honest', so somehow you are going to have to assure him that you are. You may provide letters which indicate you can be trusted and make a statement to that effect.

On the lines below, write a statement you feel comfortable with that would address this and assure the employer of your honesty.

_____

_____

_____

_____

2. RESPONSIBILITY

All employers want to know that you are the type of person who is going to be on the job every day and on time. He will also want to know that when given a job to do you will get it done, and done correctly.

On the lines below develop a statement that will indicate to the employer you are a responsible person.

_____

_____

3. CHARACTER

An employer is always seeking to discover character flaws or weaknesses. You will want to get across to them that you are not perfect but that you are constantly working on self-improvement.

_____

_____

_____

_____

4. PROBLEM SOLVER

An employer is always looking for employees that can solve problems, not create them. In doing this the employer may ask you perhaps the most difficult question of all to answer. The question, 'Why should we hire you'?

On the lines below write out a statement that you are comfortable with which indicates that you are in fact a problem solver, and why you are the correct person for the job.

_____

_____

_____

_____

5. FOLLOWS DIRECTIONS

Every employer is looking for people who can follow directions. Therefore, it is a good idea that you convey to the employer that you are a creative person, yet you believe that it is important to work within company procedures and regulations.

On the following lines write a statement that will indicate to the employer that you can follow directions and procedures.

_____

_____

_____

_____

6. PUTS COMPANY BUSINESS FIRST

Employers are always looking for employees who are interested in the growth and development of their business not just a pay check.

The applicant that projects a more positive image with regard to interest of the quality of the product, service, or the profit of the company, will stand a better chance of getting the position that he/she is interviewing for.

The self-centered individual who takes little interest in the growth of the company or wastes valuable time or resources would be the last kind of employee the company would want as an employee.

I believe what you are going to discover when doing this exercise is not only will you learn to respond to these various character questions, but also I believe that you will gain additional insights about yourself.

On the lines below, write a statement that you feel good about that would show the employer that you would indeed be an asset to their firm.

_____

_____

_____

_____

7001 Resumes-Plus Second Edition

7.   HEALTHY EMPLOYEE

With rising cost of health care, the employer has a great concern with health care issues and problems. There is a heavy cost to an employer when employees miss work frequently

If you are in good health, when asked simply state, "I am in great health and I will be at work everyday". You may want to stress attendance at your previous place of employment or your school attendance if it was good. (I remember getting a reward for perfect attendance from a major employer; this statement would send the message)

If you have letters, certificates, anything that relates your health, efficiency or punctuality, bring them.

You will want to point out that you have a strong sense of self-discipline and that any ailment you might have will not affect your work or attendance.

On the lines below, develop your own statement which you can use when asked about your health.

_____

_____

_____

_____

8.   ENTHUSIASM

An enthusiastic employee will be welcomed. The employer recognizes the values of a contented work environment. It is known that one negative employee can cause disputes, cliques, scandal, malice, jealousy and more.

The employer is looking for a person that can get along, one with charisma, and a good sense of humor. This type of person will get the job over someone who can not break into a smile.

You need to be warm, friendly, and relaxed, but above all be yourself. Smile and laugh at the interviewers jokes (be real).

Bear in mind, to get the job the interviewer must like you. The more he/she likes you, the less emphasis will be placed on your résumé and qualifications.

The interviewer will ask you questions about your personality. On the lines below write some short statements, one-liners that you can use in your interview as the opportunity comes up.

_____

_____

_____

_____

9. WHY DO YOU WANT TO WORK HERE?

We can't tell you how many times we have been asked, 'Why do you want to work here?' If you have done your research and goal setting, you will be in a position to answer this question in a positive manner.

An Important tip. You want to sound sincere and not 'canned'. You may want to suggest that you see the company as a place where you can make your mark, make a contribution and be successful. You can suggest here that you feel well qualified to be an asset to the firm.

On the lines below, write your own statement as to why you want to work for this company. (If you can not come up with anything positive it may be clear you really do not and you will want to put your effort toward a firm that you would).

_____

_____

_____

_____

10. CHANGE IN CAREER

This question you may find a bit challenging, but you can be assured that a potential employer is going to ask it of you if you are in fact making a career change. You may suggest that this was something you have been training for, for a long-time, or that you have, because of self-examination and research, decided to look at career options that could be better and more productive for your future.

Now take your time, but in your own words, develop a statement that best presents your reason for making a career change, if this is what you are doing. <u>Example</u>: I recently retired from teaching full-time at the High School level. For awhile I decided to go back into industry so I used a similar statement related to self-examination that would allow me to move back into the private sector and use my years of experience. Later, I decided to continue to write and publish though the statement was received at the time. I believe you will find that simply being in charge is respected on the part of the potential employer.

Now take your time, but in your own words, develop a statement that best presents your reason for making a career change. <u>If this is what you are doing</u>; remember you may use this statement in your cover letter as well as in your interview.

_____

_____

_____

_____

11. WHY WERE YOU OUT OF WORK FOR SUCH A LONG TIME?

If there is any question that I have some experience with, it is this one. I assure you that when you are in front of the interviewer, this question may be asked and it may be hard to answer. I believe that too often we take it on ourselves that it is shameful to be unemployed. It is not; in many cases today it is <u>not</u> your fault. I can recall not to long ago in the news it was announced that Ford Motor Company was going to lay-off 10,000 people. So it happens. Sometimes we get **'downsized'**. Nevertheless, it is up to you to come up with an answer that is acceptable in the eyes of the potential employer. **Be honest**. Any tale that you might weave can come back to harm you in the future. It may be painful, but as you know the Bible says, **'The Truth Will Set You Free'**. I believe this will be true when you discuss your work history.

Do not dwell on anything negative or place blame. You may discuss time in self-examination, not wanting to rush into another dead-end job. Of course you can also discuss time researching companies that you would have liked to have worked for.

Now on the lines below, write your own statement, Remember this will help you to sound honest and clear as to your position on this issue.

_____

_____

_____

_____

12. THE JOB HOPPER

The question of job-hopping may or may not come up in your interview, but I have seen it in the past. Over my 40 or more years working I have been employed by one of two companies that could not make payroll or have gone out of business. If you have had this experience I can assure you that you will be asked this question. Again, be honest and brief.

You may of course discuss the fact that you got smart and analyzed your job skills and desires as well as researched potential employers in order to pursue a life-long career.

You can tell the interviewer that you have in the past, just taken the first job that came along, if this is truly the case.

You can make the statement that your job hopping days are over. However, we would suggest that you avoid any reference to 'Job Hopping' if you can. The less said of this the better.

In your own words discuss why, if this is the case, you were a 'Job Hopper'; though you may want to avoid using this word. Given the trend to restructure, downsize, and right-size, many persons have found themselves in this situation.

_____

_____

_____

_____

13. SUPERVISORY EXPERIENCE

The employer is always on the lookout for individuals with management and supervisory experience. If you have little, draw from your personal experience with groups and organizations. You may have experience in clubs, churches, or sports groups. Perhaps you have supervisory skills from the military, if so, state it.

If you have direct business management or supervisory experience, you will want to inform the interviewer.

In your own words, write about your management or supervisory experience.

_____

_____

_____

_____

14. REVIEW THE LAST INTERVIEW

This will be a valuable exercise and will be a powerful tool on your next job interview. Write town all of the questions that you were asked during your last interview. Believe it or not, the more you interview the more powerful and better applicant you will be. It is essential that you write down the questions that were difficult for you. This is the debriefing once you reach your car. Take time to recall, and write the questions down.

30

15. ANY OTHER INFORMATION NOT ALREADY MENTIONED

AFTERTHOUGHT

Think before answering any questions. Why is this question being asked? Try to understand what the interviewer is trying to disclose. Answers can often reveal things about you that are better left unstated.

<u>WHAT EMPLOYERS CAN NOT ASK YOU</u>

Today, the laws are very clear as to what specifically an employer or interviewer can ask an applicant. The following are questions you do not have to answer. However, let me point out that not answering the question may lead to <u>not</u> getting a job. I am totally aware of labor laws, but ask yourself these questions, do you want the job, do you have the time to go to court, and how valuable is keeping the information 'confidential'. Here is my point - you be the judge. I am only going to point out what they can not ask. I can recall one interview where the General Manager asked, "How long are you going to work before you retire?" Clearly an illegal question, however the job was not only wanted, but needed. I used the answer in a positive way, one that would sell me as the applicant and suggested that I would be with the firm for many years before retirement. I make sure that the answer could only put me in a positive light.

7001 Resumes-Plus Second Edition

It is illegal to ask the following of you:

1. Your sex, marital status, if you are divorced or separated, when a divorce would be final, if you live with anyone, etc.

2. If you have children, how many, how old, who cares for them, if you are planning on more children, whether or not the children live with you.

3. Physical information such as height, weight, physical/mental handicaps, etc. unless the job has specific health requirements.

4. If you have ever been arrested, jailed, or convicted of a crime (unless a security clearance is a requirement for the job). You will find these questions on job applications in the Education community.

5. If you have military background, which branch of service you were in, if you received an honorable discharge.

6. Any reference to age other than, 'Are you over 18'?

7. If you own a home, rent, etc.

8. Any question pertaining to your religious beliefs.

RESPONSE TO ILLEGAL QUESTIONS

As I suggested on the previous page, you must use your common sense when dealing with illegal questions.

- If you believe the interviewer has no other motive other than finding the best applicant, and do not feel an honest answer can cause you difficulty in being employed, go ahead and answer the question. Ignore the fact that this is an illegal question.

- If you are concerned that an honest answer could knock you out of the running for a position, try to tactfully turn the situation around and ask the interviewer, "How is this information important in selecting a new employee?" You could suggest to the interviewer that you have never been asked that question. It is not a good idea to simply remind the interviewer that the question is not legal.

- Telling someone that 'you are wrong,' especially the interviewer can be very costly for you. It could cost you the job. Finding out why the question was asked may not be worth the consequences, and you may as well answer the question

- If you find that the interviewer is persistent in asking illegal questions and it is obviously unreasonable, then you might state. 'I do not believe that these questions are relevant to the requirements of the position for which I am interviewing'. Remember, this could cost you the position, but you may be better off not working for this company or organization.

RESARCH RESEARCH RESARCH

Before you go of and write that 'glowing' and meaningful cover letter and résumé, I am going to recommend that you take some time to find out about the potential employers that you are thinking of working for. This is a more intelligent way of selling yourself. In addition, it is the only way that you will learn the procedures, policies, and attitudes of the prospective employer. Simply stated, if you do not do this you will be essentially whistling in the wind. This is your future you are dealing with so you be the judge as to what a little research is worth. What I am asking you to do is not all that easy and of course it will be somewhat time consuming.

By answering the following question you will have a significant advantage in developing a winning cover letter and résumé. Do you have sufficient feelings for the employer to make an intelligent decision as to whether or not you would want to go to work for them?

If after research you have decided that this is not the employer for you, you will not have to waste your time developing application materials. You now have saved yourself time to devote to other potential employers. Not only have you saved postage but perhaps time wasted working for an undesirable employer.

On the lines below indicate what you have discovered about each employer you have researched. Indicated who you would work for, who the interviewer might be, problems within the company, particular problems related to the job you are looking at, company contacts, and any other important information you have learned.

Employer:

_____

_____

Employer:

_____

_____

Employer:

_____

_____

By completing this exercise you have discovered many of the things a 'headhunter' would learn from the same exercise. You may have discovered that the person or persons who will be making the final hiring decision is not the person conducting the interview.

Do you have the facts, figures, information about the size of the firm, annual sales, officers of the corporation, industry, plans for future growth, policies, procedures, prodigality, position in the market place, competitors, etc? Every one of these items will have an effect on your future if you take a position with the firm.

Company:

_____

_____

Company:

_____

_____

Company:

_____

_____

Job descriptions are very important. If a firm or organization is in the process of hiring, this information is usually published. However, it can be a verbal description. The job description is invaluable as it will provide you with specific information which can be used to customize your résumé and cover letter point by point. Government agencies (state & federal) as well as school systems routinely print their job descriptions, this information is available at your local employment office, it's also found at county libraries, and school district offices. You may go in and find this information on display.

In the private sector, information is of course available from each potential employer. This information may be a little more difficult to obtain and will vary from employer to employer. However, private sector job descriptions are often posted within the employment offices of the employer and may also be posted with private job search firms. Today when you do job searches you may use the internet, which I will discuss later, but you will find job descriptions on the internet with the posted job.

On the lines be low write down job descriptions for those companies you are interested in. (You may need to place this information on a separate paper)

1. _____

2. _____

3. _____

CHAPTER THREE

EFFECTIVENESS VS. EFFICIENCY

It is important for you to understand the difference between effectiveness and efficiency. It is also important to understand how effectiveness and efficiency plays out at the company you were/are working for, and the one you are possibly going to work for.

Effectiveness means that you are doing the right things the right way. Efficiency means you are doing the most amount of work for the most optimal amount of money. You are getting the most **'bang for your buck'.** Both you and the company you are working for must be both effective and efficient or there will be major problems. You will be effective by doing the right thing. You are following this book so you are probably doing the right thing in order to get a job. You have to keep trying until you are successful.

You have to be efficient also by conducting cost effective procedures. As you know your money is limited. You have to evaluate what responses you are getting to maximize them. Do not continue any methods that have failed or that you feel uncomfortable with. You are the **'captain of your own ship'.** You have to keep the ship off the rocks.

7001 Resumes-Plus Second Edition

The company that recently 'downsized' you (or that you are not happy with) probably believes they can get someone to replace you for less money, or that your job can be eliminated. You will often find this very true with small firms; as one of their methods of reducing overhead. We might find that a firm will not keep an employee for 80K a year with benefits if they feel that they can hire three (3) new college graduates for 20K with no benefits for the first year. You may be 'damned' if you are quailed or un-qualified for the job. This is something that you are going to have to contend with as you interview for your next position. Here is a **'catch 22'**, You want to earn more money but the more money you make may set you up to be the next one to go.

Here is the problem. An organization may not hire you as a new employee for 80K a year because it is too much, but on the other hand, if you agree to go to work for 20K, they are more likely to not hire you because they know that as soon as you find a better-paying position you would leave. They will have wasted money training you only to find out that they must find someone to replace you if they do hire you for the lower salary and have you leave.

Many companies will always try to do the right thing by being in the right industry and bringing the right product to market. A firm will go broke if it fails to do this. However, a business may want to retain the best possible employees but not necessarily pay them the best possible wages. I am aware of a firm (President) that recognized that it was doing a number of things wrong in running the business, but when he interviewed a qualified individual for Sales Manager with new ideas that would possibly save the company and improve the business he was unwilling to pay a reasonable salary to break the status quo. It is believed that by doing this it will ensure that the organization can make the maximum profit for the owners and stockholders. You can see how this might not be true. This 'Greed' in the long-term could cost the company profits down steam.

If the company isn't effective and efficient it is very possible that they will go out of business. As above it was recognized that the company was not being effective or efficient; the President was cutting corners and suffering from short term 'greed' and not looking at the bigger picture. If a competitor or the market does the right things that forces their competitors hand, it may be too late. Once the 'wolves' are at the door the company can be wiped out. This is the law of business today.

A person must always be looking for opportunity in the ever-changing climate of business today. The firm will seldom tell the employee where the opportunities lie. Also the company will seldom tell the employees about future 'downsizing' plans. The reason for this is the good employees would look elsewhere for work and bad employees would be downsized anyway, either way the company losses. Politically, no boss/managers will wait until the last possible minute and then blame someone else, even if they are the ones responsible for the downsizing. The bosses/managers will always take credit when things go right but avoid taking blame if things go wrong. This is like many politicians. You must always have your 'ear to the ground'. This is how you can be the most efficient and effective employee to yourself.

You will find that most employees are in the dark at all times, so you can see why the smart employee should always be ready to go out the door at a moment's notice. Have your résumé ready and polished and you should not be in a panic. As they say in the Boy Scouts, **'be Prepared'**. Have feelers out at all times. Be aware of what is out there in the marketplace. Float your résumé out to your industry all the time because you never know when the 'ax' may fall. At the same time take care to protect the identity of the document; we do not want to be discovered for looking. Go to trade shows (if possible) to make contacts and see what the competition is doing, if the ax should fall your way.

CHAPTER FOUR

SPECIALTY APPROACHES TO JOB SEARCH

Looking for a job is a serious undertaking and you may find it very challenging. Statistics tell us that in today's economy you are fortunate to get one interview out of over 100 attempts. Your range may vary, if you recall we touched on this earlier. I know that at first glance you might want this to be a lot easier and simpler, but unfortunately it just does not work that way. As an example, an applicant had an inside lead that a 100 million dollar California company was looking, or would be looking for, a marketing manager. Now for several reasons the applicant wanted this position. Remember all of us have several motivations as to why we want to work for a firm. For that matter, I would hope that for every decision we make we have several reasons why we want to make the change or move. These reasons are influenced by economics, working conditions, ego, location, money, need, or whatever, but I would suggest that you use logic to make your decision. This company in question offered the applicant a good income, good location, and the applicant saw some challenges.

Well, the applicant did the traditional thing. He sent the firm a cover letter and résumé. He followed-up with a phone call and sent his employment package to several people with in the organization, but to no avail. So, not giving up since he really wanted to interview was to come up with some 'gimmick' to get the attention of the president. At this point he felt that he had nothing to lose and it would show that he would go the 'extra' mile. So he decided to design a five foot long poster with his computer wishing the President a Merry Christmas. Of course it was in color and well done.

The results, I would like to say, was that the President was impressed, and called the applicant to offer him a job interview or the position. Not so. The applicant never heard from the President at all and was never acknowledged for his innovative approach in getting some recognition. The message here is try anything! What he did do was to set himself apart from others. He was sure no one else had done this before, at least not at this company. Remember, we have decided that there are two kinds of employers, one that will hire you and ones that will not. For what ever the reason this President was not able to recognize the creativeness of the applicant and was not able to relate it to the needs of his company. Maybe another President would have.

Are you going to try this with every firm you apply to; probably not but understand, more than likely you will not be the only applicant to apply to a firm so one way or another to get consideration you are going to need some special approach that sets you apart from all those other applicants. Anyone can send a cover letter or a résumé. True creativity is harder to come by. You can fax, E-mail, or send a telegram to express your interest in a company. You may use a designed newsletter, which you will find a sample here in this workbook, or Special letterhead. You may be required to put together a mini-marketing plan to show your interest as well as skills to capture the position.

Within the last two years you may have seen employment ads requesting that you design a mini-marketing plan along with the cover letter, application, résumé, and salary history. This may be the wave of the future; it is a pre-test on the part of the employer to see if you really know what you are doing and it screens out some candidates who are not serious about the position, or who do not have the background or skills to make the job work. You should give it a try.

Also most everyday you can see the need to be able to use a second or third language. It is to your advantage to take courses in other languages in order to enhance your skills and qualifications. As you peruse the newspaper you will run into ads that are seeking applicants that speak and understand Spanish, Japanese, and Chinese. Some positions require a second language and others suggest that it would be a good idea to know a second language. I recall a few years back when I was still in sales and marketing, I interviewed with this firm and I am sure I would have been a 'shoe' in if I would have been able to speak Spanish and Chinese. Besides the Sales and Marketing experience, this was a major component of the position. This is another way we can set ourselves apart from other applicants. It also offer a degree of employment security since not everyone applying can offer a second or third language skill.

This is the same with becoming computer 'savvy'. This fact cannot be overemphasized. Want Ads today have many requests for not only Computer skills, but they in some cases are asking for specific knowledge of programs. You will find that companies want you to have experience in Word, Excel, Access, and of course other programs. So again, these Computer Skills will set you apart. Understand that the employer wants to get the most 'bang for his buck'. It is very simple, you as an applicant want to have and offer as many skills as possible; the employer is not hiring you because you're another pretty face.

You may prepare a job description which discusses your duties, and compensation sheet outlining in detail how much you want to make, which should include expenses and all related compensation and benefits. You should be able to sit down with an employer and go over this document line by line. Some managers are impressed and others will not be. I myself would be impressed with an applicant that has it together, and on the other side I would want to work for someone who appreciates the presentation; I believe it cuts both ways.

In job hunting you should be ready for anything, like the old Boy Scout motto, 'Be prepared'. Especially for the curve balls the interview may throw your way, and it will. You must be ready and flexible.

CHAPTER FIVE

TRACKING

So what is tracking; it is a concept that may be new to some of you. You may recognize the term 'pigeon-holed'. In either case, the basic rule is that once you enter a 'track', or get 'pigeon-holed' it is difficult of not impossible to get out of. Example: You're a Teacher so you can't be a Sales Manager.

You may be tracked in many different ways but most people are tracked in at least two, these are by job type and company type. If you have done one type of a job for awhile you can't do another job. Or you have worked for one kind of a business, industry, or sold one kind of product, so you can't sell another product or do another type of job.

You can choose what track you are on but you should choose carefully. Especially so you can move early in your working career. Human relations people always want you to return to your track because it is easier for them even though you may or may not want to go back to where they think you should be. For example: You once sold soap but now you want to go into industrial sales, or once you were a welder; it may be difficult for human relations to recognize that you have other attributes or skills that would allow you to be of benefit to the firm in another department.

7001 Resumes-Plus Second Edition

One of the first questions that you should ask yourself is, 'Do I want to work in a large or small organization'? There are advantages and disadvantages to both. A large organization may be able to offer you a higher salary, better benefits, better resources to get the job done, and more upward mobility than a small firm. On the other hand the larger company can be cold, impersonal, have more competition, it may even be hostile especially if you later discover the job to be a bad fit for you, or you my find yourself 'pigeon-holed'.

A small organization may give you a better overview of what is going on. You may get the chance to have more assignments and experiences within the firm. You may quickly move from job to job. If you opt to go to work for the small firm, you may be the Marketing Manager, Advertising Manager, and maybe even have an opportunity to get involved in product development and manufacturing. This kind of experience may have many benefits to you throughout your career.

You may be able to move up faster in a small organization because everyone would know that you are doing a great job. You may also have a more important role from the start. The small firm may be less bureaucratic, and less political than a large organization.

On the other hand a small company may give you experience that is a mile wide but an inch deep. You may not be able to move to a large firm once you are tagged as a small company person. Large organizations want people with a lot of experience in one small area. This can be frustrating.

You may also find that in the small firm often family members are integrated within the firm. This can thwart promotional opportunities. Promotions or management positions may automatically go to family members regardless of their ability, qualification, or attitude.

The next key decision for you is what areas to go into. Be careful on this one. There are a lot of areas you might like or have an interest in. Most people take the first job they are offered and wind up staying there for their entire career. The reason for this is that it is hard to move from being a salesperson to a production manager as the company may want or need you to handle this opportunity. Your best bet is to try some type of management trainee program and rotate through different areas before you select the one that your career makes the change for you. You will probably want to do this early in your career. The most significant thing is to look at all the advantages and disadvantages for each area before you set down your roots in any one as you may be here for a long time.

Remember, once you are tracked it may be hard to change to another area once you gain experience. You may want to move or change but you will be unable to get position because of where you are. Tracking can either help you to get a new job or it can destroy any chance you may have had to get a new job. You should always endeavor to use tracking to your advantage when you are out looking for another job.

Make sure you tell the interviewer that the job you are interviewing for is like the position you have had before. This might make it easier for the employer to see that the transition to the new job will not be too difficult. At the same time it will give you a better chance to get the new position.

CHAPTER SIX

CAREER PLANNING

Career planning is somewhat of an 'oxymoron' in today's world. Real career planning is not established, and the opportunity may vary from individual to individual. There are some attempts in many schools throughout America but no real cohesive programs, and most Educators 'pew pew' vocational education. Sure there are piece meal programs but administrators and government officials have graduating and going to college stuck in the heads of all students. Don't get me wrong, there is nothing wrong with being a college graduate, but only if you want to be one. I know that we are somewhat beyond career planning since it should start when you start going to school, but to say it is over because you never started before wouldn't be fair.

So from this point forward you should try to do something (planning) for yourself long-range. To see how you are doing you will need to check yourself from time to time to see if you are on track with your plan. Your best plans may 'go up in smoke' at a moment's notice so you must be flexible. You must 'adapt' or 'die', like the dinosaur. The quicker you do the job, the better off you will be and the faster you will recover from being unemployed. Unemployment can bring a loss in face as well as money. It can lead to all sorts of problems, including death, I am sure you have found some of this out already.

7001 Resumes-Plus Second Edition

Truly, opportunities are everywhere and at the same time, no where. They are like the mirrors in the fun house at the museum park. You may see them but you might find yourself bumping into many other mirrors before you find the right path to follow. You should not turn down opportunities to talk to anyone at any time that might be willing to help you. This is not to say you need to take any job offered. Always go to the interview even if you must schedule it for after hours or weekends. I am going to say this here and you may hear it from me again; job search is a real job. You need to treat it that way. Don't take the position that 'now that I am unemployed I have time to paint the fence'. You never know what will happen in an interview or what might be offered. You do however have the right to say 'no' once a job has been offered. As an example: I interviewed with the Vice President of a 35 million dollar firm here in Southern California. I, at the time, was interviewing for Sales and Marketing Manager, when I got to the interview the Vice President wanted me to help his company move 3 million dollars worth of product, work as a consultant, and my performance was to be evaluated for future employment. The Vice President did not want to pay me salary, but receive a commission on the entire product I helped the company move. So I considered the offer, acknowledging the fact that the President indicated it would be difficult to move the product, and that I, at the time, wasn't interested in being a consultant but since he brought it up counted it with the offer. The point here is, I had a chance to do some career planning and modified my plan. It is not necessary that you accept every offer, or any offer for that matter. The job should fit you and your needs. I have also turned down several teaching and business positions due to the need to relocate which would have caused undue stress on my family as well as economic considerations. It is important to know how far you are willing to commute (or move) to get a job. I am going to inform you that this question will be asked on many applications and during the interview and your answer or lack of one may cause you to lose the job. A job may be 'GUD' (geographically undesirable) but it may have other things or factors that are worthwhile (like pay). You will never know unless you go to the interview to see what is offered. Some employers may allow you to telecommunicate (work at home by computer) 2 or 3 days a week. This could cut down your traveling.

Your employer may give you the opportunity to gain additional and educational training at his expense. You will want to be sure that you take full advantage of any of these offerings. You will never know when this training will benefit you in your current firm, or a career move outside your present position. There is no question it will be helpful within your company. If your employer will pay for Adult Education, Junior College or University courses, take full advantage of this opportunity also. Sometimes the employer will pay a percentage of the cost of the classes or training and as you complete the work, may offer other incentives.

You may have heard this before and I am sure that I will continue to repeat it over and over, 'Knowledge is power'. It is simple in today's economy as we continue to see new technologies come on the scene and old ones disappear, so it is prudent to quickly continue to expand our education to stay competitive in the market place.

You should try to expand knowledge of 'cross-training' if it is available. Cross-training will help you to stay employed by expanding your horizon thus allowing you to be more flexible and available to fill more than one employment slot for the employer. Cross-training may include areas you like as a hobby. You may be able to adopt a hobby in to a full-time job. Your vocation can be you avocation. At your work you should do your best to 'cross-train' to other departments. This will give you more experience, make you a more valued employee, and add some fun in the work place. It may also give you a greater contacts and options in case something goes wrong on your current job. This is great opportunity to do **'networking'** on the job. The more people you know, the better off you are. More jobs are gotten by networking than just by you sending out résumés and trying to job search.

My recommendation to you is to continue to go to school the rest of your life. The old saying **'You can't teach an old dog new tricks'** is not true. This is what I am going to suggest to all of my students. You will be a better person for it. Of course, I can only suggest and recommend it, you will have to be the one who makes the final decision and commitment; it is up to you. And of course you will be the one who benefits from your commitment.

CHAPTER SEVEN

YOUR ASSETS

Ok, now get out your notebook or a sheet of pager. You are going to do this for you, not because I am telling you to. The following is to be used in the development of your cover letter, résumé, newsletter, follow-up letter, and your interview. It is important that you take some time and write down what you believe you have to offer an organization. People almost always under-value what they can offer and bring to a company. Believe me, the most important asset to most companies are it people. There is a quotation to this effect somewhere out there. You face serious competition, look around. You are competing with, in some cases, not only new upcoming college graduates, but adults returning to the to the labor force, emigrants coming to this country, and jobs being filled off shore. You are competing with a lot more people than you realize; you are in competition with the general population, individuals within your organization, and people from other businesses or companies. You can also be in competition with friends, relatives, and friends of people within your organization. You must get a grasp on your assets. Remember, there will always be competition for any worthwhile job including working for your self. Competition is a fact of life, which is good, and it will not go away. It is there and you can use it to your advantage. It can help you to land your ideal job.

One more thing, I would like you to think about what the second place applicant earns or gets in the job interview? Nothing! Like in a horse race there is only one first place winner and I want that to be you. And you will want to be the first place winner in the job interview so this means you must beat out all the other competition. That is, if you want to work at the place you have selected as your next place of employment.

Note: This is only a partial list, so your list of assets may be much longer than mine and will vary with your background.

List Everything You Have:

You will want to make sure that you recognize your foreign language and computer skills.

Example:

IBM   B3900 HP FORTRAN IV   Dell   GateWay   Photoshop 5.5   INS/DLI

GEM   XP Professional   Illustrator 8.0   PageMaker 6.5 plus   Acrobat 4.0   Office 2000

ADF   Windows 95   Windows 2000   WordStar   Word Perfect   Access   Excel   PowerPoint

QuickBooks   JAVA IMP   Pascal   Basic, and so forth.

You should identify degrees, certificates, special course work, seminars, and workshops. In addition list all skills, tools, machine knowledge, licenses, hobbies, interests, clubs, and positions held. All of us have notable information that could be valuable, such as: awards, books, articles, papers, etc.

Marketable Facts & Notable Information

Sometimes in the game of job search and interviewing questions will come up concerning your preferences. At this time I would like you to identify your choices here. This will give you a chance to think ahead. The fact is you may be asked this question not only during the interview but on the job application itself.

If you were to relocate where would you prefer to be:

City	State	Country

1st Choice

2nd Choice

3rd Choice

4th Choice

Business Assets:

<u>Note:</u> This is a list you can use (please fill in with your own information)

General Management	Research and Development
Manufacturing	Packaging
Personnel/Human Resources	Administration
Marketing	International Operations
Finance and Accounting	Etc., Etc.
Procurement	

Under each one of these categories you will indicate your function and experience. In front if you have experience (business or personal), place a '+'. Next, place a double plus '++' in front of each function for which you would like to be responsible in your next position. Place a triple '+++' in front of the functions you want to be involved with on a hands-on day-to-day bases (minimum of 3, maximum of 5).

Primary Experience

Note: The key is to know what you have to offer! You should list your functions and discuss them with an associate, friend, or a family member. Have them circle words that most closely describe your primary experience and background. You will also want to circle the words that you feel describes your experience and background:

Example:

Sales	Organizational Management
Sales Management	Financial Management
Engineering	Marketing
Manufacturing Engineering	Senior Management
Senior Executive	Graphic Design
Management	Computer Applications

<u>You Can Add More Items:</u> Remember we are discovering our assets. This information will be used in our interviewing, résumés, and cover letter.

Accomplishments, Duties, Experience, and Background

We now want to list and circle each work area that describes your overall accomplishments, duties, experiences, and background. Remember this is a workbook and the more you get involved in understanding your assets the better you will able to convey them to potential employers. The whole point of this book is helping you to obtain that **'new'** job!

Example:

Financial	Projects	Media
MISS	Design	Promotion
Operations	Proposals	Projects
Management	Negotiations	Administration
Franchise	Start-up	Training & Development
Public relations	Analysis	Electronics
Liaison	Purchasing	Business development
Account Executive	Manufacturing	User Interface
Sales	Import	Account Retention
Research	Sales Training	

You Can Add More Items

CHAPTER EIGHT

DEVELOPING YOUR INTERVIEWING SKILLS

The Interview

The interview is the key to getting a job. You cannot rest until you have this 'key' in your pocket. There may be conflicts between your ideas and the goals of your future employer. You should always be evaluating the situation for any possibility of conflict. This can happen as you are interviewing. In a few chapters back I was telling you about an interview I had with the Vice President of a 35 million dollar firm in Rancho Cucamonga, California. During the interview there seemed to be a sore spot about a definition over what he saw the job with his firm was and what I was interviewing for. At that time, I was wearing my Sales and Marketing Manager hat. So, to get back on the right path during the interview I had to concede to his view and reword my response. What I am suggesting is that you examine your options many times, and above all, remain flexible. Do not 'panic' or become disappointed. You should try to resolve any conflicts if you can, but you should be ready to take another position or job if you can't resolve these conflicts associated with the company or organization you were interviewing with. There are gray areas you should carefully examine before your interview. In the example I gave you I attempted to document the gray areas before I accepted the position.

You should have a ready answer for any question on the 'gray' areas in your background. Do not attempt to invent an answer during the interview. This will almost always go badly. I myself was recently asked 'If we contacted your principle, how would they view how you teach in the classroom?' 'Would I find that you spend most of your time behind your desk?' Since I had the principal in my classroom and had discussed my method of teaching, I knew he would tell anyone inquiring that I employ a great deal of individual instruction and work with each one of my students at their individual computer workstations. The important thing here is I am aware of my teaching techniques and how others would perceive me and can convey this information to an interviewer. You need to be able to do this too! The example I gave you here was in Education, you will find that there will be similar questions coming out of the private sector. Some companies will ask a series of these types of questions. I will give you a number of questions you may be asked. What I would like for you to do is make sure you have good solid answers for them and that you can recite them from memory.

Other questions could deal with periods of unemployment, underemployed, being out of the country, or when you were in jail. There could be a bad experience or company that would not enhance your résumé or give you a good recommendation, but you have worked for them. I have worked for firms that wouldn't look good on my résumé, I am sure everyone has, but they did provide me with a means to an end by providing short-term employment. You may have to adjust your résumé to put yourself in a good light.

Be aware that employers/interviewers already have an image in their mind of what they want for an employee. Your job is to fit as best you can to their image. The first impression is the most important thing. The first minute usually determines if you get the job. You should make it the best minute you can!

60

THE JOB SEARCH TOOL TO GET YOU THAT JOB

Your selling task is to attract favorable attention from the interviewer. You do this by being well-groomed, ready, poised, and friendly. You know you have succeeded when they return your smile. During the interview answer the questions directly and truthfully.

Use correct English and avoid slang. Do not interrupt the interviewer while they are asking you questions. Be prepared to answer questions about why you want to work for this organization, your hobbies, interests, books and magazines you read, education, part-time work experience, training, short-term and long-term goals. Remember to stress your qualifications for the job. Your responsibility in this meeting includes selling yourself and your goals. Be definite, not wish-washy, be interesting and interested! Try to fit into what the employer is looking for. Show them you can do the job.

The interviewer will give you a chance to ask questions in most cases. This is your opportunity to lean more about the nature and requirement for the job or organization you are interested in. You could clarify some questions or information that has been given. You may want to formulate some questions in advance to ask the interviewer. This is something that I always do the night before the interview; I develop a list of questions. You might find that during the interview many of the questions will be answered, however, if they are not answered during the dialog of the interview you can try to get answers during the question portion of the interview. You have the right to ask more questions about the job. If you are offered the job, don't ask about salary, benefits, vacation policy, etc. immediately. You will find that this information will be presented to you. If you start asking about vacations, salaries, days off, the interviewer may not offer you the job if they think this is all you are interested in. Remember that the interview may continue until after you walk out the door and to your car (be on guard).

You may lose a job on the way to your can by saying something 'stupid'; by being asked a question out-of-the-blue and not being prepared with the right answer. Also, avoid giving opinions about other individuals.

61

One thing that you must keep in mind is that you are not the only applicant. Very often there may be 20 to 50 applicants for each job you may be going for. In talking to many young people, they often do not understand that they are not the only person in the universe; you're not. But like the Army use to say: **'Be All You Can Be'**. Certainly have confidence in yourself and interview as if you really want the job, but bear in mind that you do have competition.

I am going to make the following recommendation and since you spent good money to purchase this book I am hope you are willing to take full advantage of it by doing the excises and suggestions. You should, whenever possible, do a **'dry-run'** interview. If you practice baseball before playing a game, then you should practice for the most important day in your career, getting that new or better job. In the beginning you might 'drop the ball' a few times, but better during practice then in the game; and your cover letter (letter of application)/ résumé, have a friend or family-member look it over before submitting the real thing. If you are married your spouse can be helpful in this area. In addition, you can get valuable feedback from your friend or spouse if you discuss what occurred in the practice interview; as well as review what takes place in your 'real' interview. I want you to act like the military by doing a **'debriefing'**. Like the military debriefing, the material from the interview is fresh in your mind and may not omit 'key' details of what was said in the interview. Before you drive or walk off try to write everything you said in detail on a piece of paper in order to review what happened for future interviews. Always try to improve on what you say. Sometimes what sounds good in practice does not come across in a real interview. So if this is the case, after interviewing, the review will help to prepare you for your next interview. The more you practice the better you will become.

In doing your résumé and cover letter you should be comfortable with them. Let me say this before I go any further; **'rule of thumb',** you can send a cover letter (letter of application) to an employer alone, but never send a résumé without a cover letter. My advice to you would be, unless the employer asks for a résumé don't send it. In job search you may send out a series of cover letters to try to create interest.

THE JOB SEARCH TOOL TO GET YOU THAT JOB

Your résumé should always be written to show the future employer how your experience can be a benefit to him and how your background will help improve his business. During your interview you can follow-up on these points. You are not there so you can get a great pay and benefits. Of course the reality is that it should be a win win situation for both you and the employer. Try to write your résumé so your experience relates to the job the employer wants to fill. Show them that your work experience and transferable skills can be a benefit to the organization. You must convince the potential employer that you are the most qualified person for the job. You have to sell yourself!

The first few minutes, perhaps seconds, the interviewer spends with you are probably the most important in the entire presentation. This cannot be said too many times! Unless you, the interviewee, can get the favorable attention of the interviewer at the start of the interview, it is very hard to gain lost ground later. You may be able to feel in the air, positive or negative vibes.

Remember, a good beginning is important. The approach you use requires preparation and attention to detail on your part. As I stated early on, develop a script, questions, and details. I want to make sure that you get your message across. Make sure you are aware of specialties, the industry, company, and products, before the meeting. In other words do your **'homework'**. If possible try including specific characteristics of the personality traits of the interviewer. This information may be hard to come by, but do the best you can. The more you know the more power you will have. Sometimes it is possible to talk to customers, suppliers, competition, other managers, and an administrator to gain insight and information.

As an interviewee you have an excellent opportunity to gain some knowledge of the company and to develop a relationship with the interviewer. Also, by reviewing what is in the interviewer's office, you can get some idea of what the interviewer is interested in. There may be pictures, objects, or trophies which indicate what the interviewer is interested in and will give you some ideas of a few things to talk about. This is an old **'marketing and sales trick'**. It can be an **'ice breaker'** and a way to find common ground.

No matter how well the interviewee has prepared his/her presentation for the interview or how well he/she knows the possible questions, you can't expect to conduct a successful interview unless one can gain a favorable impression. You must get the interviewer on your side. The interviewer must believe that you are a good candidate to spend time with.

Avoid name-dropping or phony compliments; these are excellent ways to blow the interview. Remember, be sincere and sell yourself with humility. If the interviewer mentions he is proud of his 68 golf score, you may have a great anxiety growing inside of you to tell him you shot a 67 – but fight the tendency. Say nothing and simply respond. 'That's very good!' If he asks you if you golf and what is your best score, of course, you can say so, but add, 'I think that I played at a much easier course, as I ordinarily am not that good'. For most of you golf, will be the conversation, but I am just illustrating the fact that you do not want to get into a contest with the interviewer. The fact is you need to stay close to the truth. So if you do not play golf, don't make something up. If I was in that situation I would say something like, 'I live on a golf course, but as of yet have not taken up the game'. This is pretty must a true story and then I would change the subject.

Evaluating If You Have Sold Yourself Well?

1. When the interviewer says, 'You remind me of myself'.

2. When he/she calls other members of the company or organization to step into the office to meet you.

3. When he/she starts selling you on their company, division, business, or organization as hard as you sold yourself.

4. When he/she gives you a tour of the plant, or business, introducing you to people as you progress.

5. When interview lasts more than thirty minutes.

6. When the interviewer asks, 'When would you be available to start work'?

7. When he/she goes into great detail explaining the fringe benefits of the organization.

8. When he/she asks, 'What kind of a starting salary are you looking for'?

9. When he/she starts talking about the position you can advance to after you have been with them for awhile.

Questions You May Want To Ask Once You Are Sure They Are Interested In You

First, you might preface your questioning by stating. 'Before I throw by heart and soul into this position, I'd like to make sure this is the right job for me, so if it's OK with you, I'd like to ask you a few questions.

May I point out that by asking sound, intelligent, well thought out questions, you will enhance the probability of your getting the position. A candidate who has no questions to ask conveys the idea that thinking is not one of his/her strong suits.

➢ Is this a new position?

➢ Has there been a high turnover in this job?

➢ Is the person who had this position last still with the company? If so, would it be possible for me to talk to him/her.

➢ Are openings for the better positions in this firm generally filled from within?

➢ If I do an exemplary job, when might I expect to be promoted?

➢ Are there problems with this position which need solving?

➢ Is there a written job description for this position that I might take a look at? (Ask this question only if you have not obtained one.)

- What is the average workweek of the individual filling this position?

- What does the future of this firm look like to you?

- Do you feel that most of the employees who work here enjoy coming in everyday?

- Will I be responsible to answer to one person, or will I have a multitude of bosses?

- Are there any chances I will be asked to relocate or travel? How much, or where?

- Is there any probability the company will be sold?

- Are there any serious problems that the company is experiencing now?

- Do you have any questions or concerns about my ability to do this job?

- When do you expect to make a hiring decision relevant to this position?

<u>If you have other questions you want to ask the interviewer – write them here.</u>

_____

_____

_____

_____

_____

_____

_____

_____

Before any interviews I develop my question list the night before and I would advise you to do the same.

THE JOB SEARCH TOOL TO GET YOU THAT JOB

Your Conduct During the Interview

The following are tips which will assist you during your interview. How you act is very important and can make or break whether or not you are going to be hired.

1. <u>Arrive on time</u> No one single thing can affect your chance of getting the job as this one single factor. Promptness is extremely important. As we have been suggesting if at all possible get to the interview early. I always try to get to the interview as much as a half an hour early. This gives you a chance to find a place to park, go to the restroom if necessary, and review your notes. You will also get a chance to checkout the company or organization, and some of the dynamics.

2. <u>Greet the interviewer with a smile</u> As I have suggested in some of the previous paragraphs smile on the phone, and smile at everyone you meet. Keep up this courteous attitude throughout the interview.

3. <u>Shake hands</u>   At the beginning of most interviews you will be called upon to shake hands; do it with a firm grip. Later in this book I will review with you some of the dos and don'ts of handshaking, please review this section.

4. <u>Try to be relaxed</u>   In most cases the interviewer will do everything in his or her power to make you feel at ease, so try to relax – but do not slouch, sit up, be attentive, and be aware of your posture at all times.

5. <u>Address the interviewer</u> Always address the interviewer as 'Mr.' Lambert, 'Mrs.' Dodds, or 'Mr.' Thomason.

6. <u>Be a good listener</u> Always allow the interviewer to take the lead in the conversation.

7. <u>Look at your interviewer</u> When the interviewer is speaking to you, look at him/her, this will indicate poise and a strong sense of interest on your part.

7001 Resumes-Plus Second Edition

8. <u>Let the interviewer terminate the interview</u> At this point, thank him/her for the privilege of having talked with them, and as whether you will be given further consideration for the job. (If this has not already been indicated).

9. <u>Leave additional personal information and data</u> This is where you get the chance to leave your résumé, and cover letter (letter of application). This will provide valuable supplemental information about your background and experience for the interviewer.

10. <u>Give to the interviewer</u> Whenever the interviewer asks you a question give a response.

11. <u>Follow up your interview with a thank you letter</u> As a 'rule of thumb', always follow job interviews with a thank you letter.

<u>Body Language</u>

There are many important components associated with getting a job; the résumé, cover letter (letter of application), and newsletter; these alone unfortunately are not going to do it for you. These items working in concert hopefully get you in front of the interviewer or interviewers. Once you are in front of the person or persons that hold the 'Key' to your future of getting a position in their company or organization, you must use additional job seeking tools:

<u>Notes</u>

ı   Have a pleasing facial expression!

ı   Smile!

ı   Have good eye contact!

ı   Appear friendly!

ı   Walk with confidence!

ı   Have good gestures and mannerisms!

ı   Do not be annoying!

Yes, the message you send as you enter the room without saying a word is selling you as is the shine on your shoes or the crisp paper your résumé is printed on.

Often applicants will drift into the interviewer's office, plop down on a chair, begin to slouch, cross their legs, fold their hands behind their neck, chew gum, and say, 'ok let's interview! Make sure this isn't you!

If you really want someone to hire you, you must make them feel you are a worthy applicant, someone they would be proud to have on their team or working with in their organization. In many cases the interviewer is going to have to recommend or sell you to other members of the company, organization, or school district. The only way they are going to be enthusiastic about selling you is when you come across that way to them. This gives them the ammunition to take you to the next level if necessary.

On the other hand, you body language can suggest disregard, immaturity, foolishness, disorder, gloom, apathy, stupidity, or much more. If this is the case you will be hard pressed to get the position that you are interviewed for.

Everyone's body movements tell a story so you need to practice in front of a mirror or in front of a video recorder until your body movements and gestures convey the appropriate message that is right for the job and projects the image of the organization you want to work for. No gum, and do not smoke, these two items will quickly get you shot down.

Video Taping

What I am going to suggest here is if you are unsure with how you look during an interview take some time and practice in front of a video camera. Have a friend or family member ask you the basic interviewing questions. You will find these questions here in your workbook. You will find that most of these questions are the same but may vary slightly. After the taping review and discuss the tape. You may discover some habits you might want to modify for your job interview.

Often a person can do things that may not be good in an interview and not even know it. You may be able to help your overall appearance and correct any bad behaviors or mannerisms by using the camcorder. The interviewer will judge you on your résumé, application, references, cover letter, and your appearance at the interview. They generally do not have anything else to go on. This is really very little information on which to base such an important decision. You must look as good as you can. Think about the fact that these impressions are made in the first few seconds of an interview, not minutes. And if you are going to try to go for a position, wouldn't it be worth a little time in from of a camcorder polishing your skills.

I am going to suggest that you practice video interviewing as much as you can. The more you do it, the better you will become. Would you ever see a professional football player or tennis player not continue to polish their skills? After every football game, and certainly before the next game, the 'pros' watch a video of how they played their last game, and also the videos of their competitors. You are going to play an important game that you want to 'win', and that is getting the job. So do as the pros do, watch and polish up for each game (interview), and the game of getting that job!

Talking To the Interviewer

Over **40** percent of your first impression will be from what you say, how you talk, or what is heard. Therefore, your communication is still another component in getting that job. So, we have to be careful of what we say and how we say it to be successful in our quest.

Notes

Many of you may fight the idea of doing a mock interview, but you need to remember it's your future we are trying to change. From being unemployed or underemployed, it is you who will benefit form this exercise. Besides you have paid good money for this book so if you want to get the maximum from the book and get the most out of it, you need to put in the maximum by doing your part.

(How is your voice projection? Do you sound self-assured?

(How is your voice inflection? Do you talk in the monotone to much?

(How is your enunciation? Are you understood clearly?

(Do you talk to fast or to slowly?

(How is your expression? Do you sound warm, friendly, interesting, or enthusiastic?

(Do you sound knowledgeable? Do you sound scattered?

(Do you talk too much?

(Are you a good listener?

Good Listener The last question, 'are you a good listener' needs to be discussed in more detail. As a teacher over the years, I have talked to college students and high school students about the importance of listening. I can't tell you how important this one trait is. There are courses on listening. But like these students, many applicants may be outstanding in all other aspects of the interview, less one, they fail listening. They talk too much, not allowing the interviewer a chance to conduct the interview.

These applicants believe that they have to spit out as much information as they can. It is hoped, that somehow, they finally learned to listen and that they are not still out there looking for a job and wondering why no one will hire them. Someone once said about listening, 'if God wanted us to talk more he wouldn't have given us only one mouth, and not two ears'.

<u>Be A Good Listener</u>

If you know little to nothing about the subject, do not try to impress the interviewer with your stupidity! No matter if it is policies, hunting, car repair, history, or gardening. If a discussion comes up, just listen. To keep it interesting you can occasionally add "that's interesting", "fascinating", "amazing", or "that's great".

You should try to gain acceptance and break the ice as soon as possible. This is a good skill to use when interviewing. It may be a set of golf clubs in the corner, a photo, an airplane

71

picture on the wall, or a fishing trophy. This is a good and useful technique, but do not go in to depth.

The Touch

<u>What not to do when shaking hands!</u>

- o Do not be a Ring Squeezer or a <u>McBone Crusher</u>. No one likes a person who tries to show off by breaking another person's hand. This type of handshake could close the door on you.

- o The Clam hand or <u>Mr. McFish</u> Shake. This limp handshake will send you limping out the door. The message here is a lack of self-confidence.

- o The <u>McPumper.</u> The person that keeps cranking and pumping up and down. Another you are out the door exercise. You may think I am kidding, but I am not! Remember, the interviewer is looking for the best applicant and the best application is one who they are most comfortable with. McPumper suggests fake enthusiasm and that means you are not sincere.

- o The <u>McJerker</u>. You know those who give you one short 'jerk' and quickly pull the hand away. This tells everyone that you could care less and you don't like people anyway. You can be assured that with this attitude the interviewer does not want you on the team. You have no real chance of ever getting the job.

- o Mr. <u>McCool hand</u>. This might be 'slick' Saturday night when you are greeting your 'buds'. But it isn't to cool in a business environment. So avoid the closed fist, hammer shake, high 5's, slapping hands, or any other non-conventional handshake. If not you will be shaking the unemployment stick!

If you do not have much experience shaking hands find a friend, your partner, your dad, and do some handshaking before the interview. This is also true for you women out there. I do not want to leave you out. It will help you to do a few dry runs to see if there are any problems with how you shake hands. You must be able to do it at any time during the interview because other persons may walk into the office while you are interviewing and you will be introduced to these people. As funny as it might sound, I would like to suggest that you practice, because this one physical touch can end your interview before it begins.

Note: You may shake hands with a woman if you are a man, but let the interviewer offer her hand first. This gives her an option to shake your hand or not. In the business community it is acceptable for a woman <u>not</u> to shake hands with a man.

<u>References</u>

Take some time and develop a list of references you can give to a potential employer if you are asked for it. Your references should be old family friends, teachers, co-workers, business people, employer, supervisors, or clergy who know your work and/or habits. You should always call and/or visit with these references to be sure they are willing to be a reference for you. In most cases you will be asked to supply the names, addresses, and, phone numbers of at least three (3) people on the job application and three (3) current letters of recommendation that out lines positive attributes you may have. In the private sector your references should be from people that know of your work and performance. Also, if you work in the education community, letters from your principal, department chair, and/other teachers that know of your work as a teacher would be beneficial. Make sure your letters are no older than three (3) years. For best results periodically talk with these people, have them observe the way you conduct your business and have them prepare recommendation letters before you need them. One thing I would like to say here is that references and letters of recommendation are based on past history so understand you are earning your reputation everyday.

7001 Resumes-Plus Second Edition

Type of Interviewers You May Meet

A section on interviewing would not be complete without a discussion on some personalities of the interviewers you maybe meeting while you are job hunting. By knowing some of the general characteristics, you should be better prepared to talk with them.

There are some interviewers that are cooperative, friendly, and very much willing to help to bring out the very best in you and make you feel that you are a fine person. Then there are the cold hearted, formal individuals who are apparently to busy to take the time to get to know you. These people make it miserable, if you let them get to you. There are some of these people who would appear to regard your call (interview) as an intrusion, even though the appointment was granted and there is a job opening. This person may even appear so indifferent that at the end of the interview you will feel you have made a poor impression regardless of how well you have done. When you meet this type of individual, and you will, you must be patient and courteous. Do not let him intimidate you, this can delight him, but you can assemble at least the appearance of composure, you may win his approval. This type of interview is called a **'Closed Interview'**, and this interviewer will do most of the talking.

There are interviewers that believe that the applicant should be made to do most of the talking; this is known as an **'Open-end interview'**. The theory behind this is not to embarrass the applicant but to make him/her feel at ease, and to see whether he/she will talk more freely when answering questions. If the interviewer is not skillful, there could be embarrassing **'gaps'** in the conversation while waiting for the applicant to **'talk freely'.** If you realize the interviewer's goal, it will help you adapt to this situation. The experienced interviewer will gently bring you back on the right track if you begin to talk about something inapplicable to the interview.

The Job Search Tool to Get You That Job

Your job is to know and recognize which type of interviewer and what kind of interview you are involved in and react and perform the best you can. As I have suggested before, the best way for you to be come competent in job interviews is to practice. In fact, the more interviews you participate in the better interviewee you should become.

Questions Frequently Asked By Interviewers

No matter what type of interviewer you may encounter, you can expect to be asked some or all of the following questions. What I would like for you to do is on the lines provided below develop your own responses so you are prepared if you are asked to respond to these questions by the interviewer. It is often the way you answer, and your hesitation that is evaluated.

1. What are the five (5) biggest accomplishments in your life or present job?

_____

_____

2. Why should we hire you?

_____

_____

3. Can you work under pressure, deadlines, etc.?

_____

_____

4. How long would it take you to make a contribution to our firm?

_____

_____

5. How long would you stay with us?

_____

_____

75

7001 Resumes-Plus Second Edition

6. What are your short-range objectives?

_____

_____

7. What do you look for in a job?

_____

_____

8. What is your philosophy of management?

_____

_____

9. What kind of starting salary are you looking for? Why?

_____

_____

10. Why didn't you do better in college?

_____

_____

11. Why are you leaving your current job? Or why did your business fail?

_____

_____

12. What business, character and credit references can you give us?

_____

_____

13. What can you do for us that someone else cannot do?

_____

_____

14. How good is your health?

_____

_____

The Job Search Tool to Get You That Job

15. How do you reel about people from minority groups?

16. If you could start again, what would you do differently?

17. How do you rate yourself as a professional, as an executive?

18. What new goals or objectives have you established recently?

19. How have you changed the nature of your job?

20. What do you think of your boss?

21. What are your feelings about: Alcoholism, Divorce, Homosexuals, and Women in Business, Religion, and Abortion?

22. Why haven't you obtained a job so far?

7001 Resumes-Plus Second Edition

23. What features of your previous jobs have you disliked? Why?

24. What features of your previous jobs did you like? Why?

25. Would you describe a few situations in which your work was criticized?

26. Would you object to working with a woman/man?

27. How would you evaluate your present firm?

28. Do you generally speak to people before they speak to you?

29. How would you describe the essence of success?

30. What was the last book you read? Movie you saw? Sporting event you attended, etc.

The Job Search Tool to Get You That Job

31. In you present position, what problems have you identified that had previously been overlooked?

_____

_____

32. What interests you most about the position we have? The least?

_____

_____

33. Don't you feel you might be better off in a different size company? Different type of company?

_____

_____

34. Why aren't you earning more at you age?

_____

_____

35. Will you be out to take your boss's job?

_____

_____

36. Are you analytical? Give an example.

_____

_____

37. Are you creative? Give an example.

_____

_____

38. Are you a good manager? Give an example

_____

_____

39. Are you a leader? Give an example.

40. How would you describe your own personality?

41. Have you helped increase sales, Profits, Reduce costs?

42. What do your subordinates think of you?

43. Have you fired people before?

44. Have you hired people before? What do you look for?

45. If you had your choice of jobs and companies, where would you go?

46. What other types of jobs are you considering? What companies?

47. Why do you feel you have top management potential?

48. Tell us about yourself?

_____

_____

49. Where do you expect to be in 5 years, 10 years?

_____

_____

50. What makes you think you will enjoy this type of work?

_____

_____

Interview Questions – Associate Principal (Education)

If you have the good fortune to interview for a school district you will find there methodology somewhat different than that of industry. While in industry you may have several interviews it is quite common that a school district will select a team of interviewers made up of administrators, union representatives, staff members, board members, and so forth. Each member of this team will ask you one or two questions in a round robin format.

(Tell us how your experience and background qualifies you for this position?

(Explain how you would handle a teacher that was reported that he/she was not doing his/her job as a teacher.

(How would you handle a classified employee showing up late daily for his/her job?

- ➤ We are expecting a large number of inexperienced teachers, how would you go about helping these teachers to be more effective in the classroom?

- ➤ One of our major problems here at this high school is attendance, what would you do or suggest that would improve it?

- ➤ We find that our test scores are low in English and Math, what would you suggest that would help to improve these scores?

- Why do you want this position?

- Do you have any questions for us?

- It is found that at the last moment the master schedule has a mistake and it is a Friday night, what would you do?

- Have you read any books that would help improve Education in our school? Tell us about them.

Note: These are just a sampling of some of the questions that are asked in a typical job interview for an Associated Principal applicant.

Interview Questions – Teacher (Education)

(Tell us about your experience and background that qualifies you for this position?

(Explain the various methods of discipline you employ in the classroom?

- If we came into your classroom what would we see?

- Are you willing to sponsor clubs 'FBLA,' 'VICA'. Yearbook? Drill team? Or others?

- How do you motivate your students to do their work?

- Do you have experience working with culturally diverse students?

- What classes would you prefer to teach?

Note: This is a sample of some of the question asked of teacher applicants as they interview.

CHAPTER NINE

NETWORKING

Today, and perhaps forever, Networking has been the best way for you to get a job or at least to get a favorable interview. You must get in front of the 'herds' of other applications that are out there for nearly every job. There are several types, levels, or categories of networking. It is safe to say that seventy –five percent of jobs, maybe higher, are gotten this way. Many jobs are given out by word-of-mouth. Some employers will ask their employees if they know someone like themselves that is looking for employment. This is considered the best way to get a job. An employer may go to the outside if there are no candidates for an available position. This process is done in large and small companies as well as government agencies. Most jobs are filled before the positions are posted. Employees will find the people (their friends) to fill an opening if they can. School Districts may contact teachers who might know candidates in other districts that might be interested in making a move. Hospitals will query nurses to recommend potential nurses from other hospitals, or from within the institution that could be hired or promoted.

So, what is the best type of networking? The best, of course, is 'networking that works for you'. The closer you are, the better it is recommended, that you have someone who knows personally of your abilities and experience to make direct contact on your behalf. I will call this type of networking 'Net 1'. Any networking is better than no networking. You should try

83

to keep in contact with your network (the person or persons who are assisting you in your job search). You do not want to lose what may be an important contact, you may need them later. You should keep in touch at least once a year perhaps more. People forget who you are if they don't hear from you for a long time. Keep in close contact.

<u>Example:</u>

An individual I know called a friend of his who he had worked with for nearly four years as a sales representative within the same company. His friend's father owned fifty percent of the firm at that time and it was a 5 million dollar company. Today the company has grown to 12 million dollars in gross sales in the compressed air distributorship in California. During the time the individual was employed with the company he was a top salesperson for several years in a row. When going to lunch with his old 'buddy' (now president) and current sales manager, they discussed old times and he mentioned the fact that he had been 'downsized' from his recent Sales Manager position and was looking for employment.

The President stated that when his company places an ad for staffing they would get from 100 to 150 responses. So after discussing the challenges of getting a job and it being a tough job market the President mentioned that he had an acquaintance that was looking for a regional Sales Manger in Southern California. It was suggested that the individual contact the acquaintance at the other firm, to which the individual suggested that it would be much better if he (his friend) contacted the 'key' person on his behalf. It was explained that the recommendation would have more weight then his call and would place him in a better light with the company. The company and the product were very well known. The individual provided the president with a <u>business card</u> and he stated that he would call in the following week.

This was a great level of Networking, and once the recommendation phone call was made it would be very important that you follow up with your own phone call. Your networking might not go down this way, but once you get the lead you do not want to hesitate to make you own phone call using the Presidents name as your lead in.

THE JOB SEARCH TOOL TO GET YOU THAT JOB

It goes without saying, you should always carry your personal business card to hand out at any meeting, you never know who you will run into, or who your contact might know. The cost for business cards is very reasonable, but as an alternative, or get yourself some 3 x 5 cards. You can write down names and phone numbers of people you meet or provide your name and number if you do not have business cards.

Networking can be used offensively or defensively. <u>Offensively:</u> When you are attempting to use you contacts to assist you in getting a job or interview. You will be asking your 'network' to assist you in finding leads to job opportunities, or better yet, suggesting to an employer that they have a friend who would perhaps fit the job opportunity. <u>Defensively:</u> Your 'network' may call and let you know of a rumor about major changes at your company which may involve lay-offs. This advance notice can be great for you as it gives you time to get your résumé out on the street. It would be wise to try to confirm this information if at all possible.

Networking is critical to your success in any job search. The more people you know the more networking you can do. Remember: NETWORK, NETWORK, and NETWORK. The people you know are your number one asset. Make sure you start there first.

Before you start calling everyone, it is important that you <u>plan</u> your personal contacts carefully. Before you go for the phone try to think of everyone you know who might be worth while contacting. Only after you have identified the people you might call, can you determine whom you should call and in what order.

If you know the Chief Executive, president, or owner of a company in the industry you would most like to work for, this should be the number one priority and contact. This person in all likelihood controls at least one job, and it could be the one you want. If you met someone at an Industrial Show a few years ago they probably will not remember you. If this is the case then you had better reintroduce yourself. You may want to write them a letter as you would an important stranger. What you are going to hear from me is if you want a good job you need to be proactive. As you can see I am asking more of you than just stuffing your résumé into an

85

7001 Resumes-Plus Second Edition

envelop. I am asking you to do some preliminary work first. And I can assure you that it will seem to take more work up front, but you will have more success long-term.

Now, if you know a first-class former subordinate who was always considered a genius, 'go-getter', or a dynamic individual who now is a department manager, chief engineer, or owns a small business in your industry of interest, they, might also be a high priority contact. There may not be a spot in his/her organization for you but he may know someone in your field. Caution, be sure that any of your network contacts have a positive opinion of you, are enthusiastic about you, and eager to help. Also be sure that the contact is intelligent, respected, and discreet; not a negative person that would potentially tarnish your image simply by affiliation with them.

Be careful, avoid the tendency we all have to get in touch with the people we know best and are most comfortable with rather than the one who can do us the most good. You can make the relevant contacts enthusiastic, but it is difficult to make the enthusiastic contacts relevant. Make sure you allocate your time accordingly, as we have said, you have only eight hours in the day to do the job search, make the best of your time.

<u>LEVELS OF RELEVANCE</u>

1. <u>Power People</u> These are the persons that can hire you, or have influence in getting you into the position in which you are interested.

2. <u>Advantage Position</u> Not the same level as above, but still a valuable contact. These people can be your **'spy in the sky'**; your extra eyes and ears. They could be middle management people in companies or organizations that you are interested in. They could be in your field, i.e., teachers, suppliers, parents, administrators, engineers, etc.

3. <u>No Power or Advantage</u> This is the lowest level of relevance and are probably people outside of you field altogether. Some may be widely connected and you may be interested in their 'bird-dogging' or off-the-wall ideas and suggestions. These are low priority, but occasionally come up with something that could be very useful.

The Job Search Tool to Get You That Job

Now you must ask yourself some questions before you use each one of these resources. How well and how favorably does the contact know your achievements and how well does he/she like you personally? You must build this network before you become unemployed. Part of this equation is that you have to earn and maintain their friendship.

ENTHUSIASTIC AND KNOWLEDGEABLE CONTACT

The next level of contact is the one who is enthusiastic and knowledgeable. They might fall into the following categories:

1. <u>Co-Worker</u>   Your former supervisor, associate principal, subordinate, or your peers. In most cases it is necessary to sell them. Just update them about what you are currently doing and what you are trying to achieve, and usually they will automatically became enthusiastic. However, if they are negative and not excited for you do not even bother with this person. Years ago when I left Proctor and Gamble one of my co-workers, I will call him 'Bob', was very negative about me leaving the company and was hostile, so hostile he called me 'a quitter' to my face in a very negative tone. We were friends before this, even though we were in different divisions as we would often work together with various customers. There was nothing that could be said or done to change his thinking. So if this is the case with you, just walk away from this person and carry on.

2. <u>Contact by Reputation</u>   People you may not know but who have heard of you and your reputation. You may have been involved in a trade association with competitors, other educators in your field, a trade magazine, etc: people that you have met at industry functions, suppliers who have solicited you as a customer, school conferences, and customers that you have solicited. In this situation there is a little more going for you than if the person was a stranger, but not much.

3. <u>The non-business contact</u> These are the people on the street, or the people you know very well but are not in your circle of friends. They may be 'long shots' but maybe the shot you are looking for.

SCORE THE CONTACT

Since' time is money' and the longer you are out of work the more it is costing you, it is important that you develop a scoring system for your contacts. The point of scoring is to make sure that you spend your valuable time with the contacts that are most likely to be helpful. It might be easier to spend time with those whose company you enjoy, that is understandable, but these people may not be as beneficial to the advancement of your career. You may use '10' as being the most valuable contact and '1' for the least valuable. It is hoped that this scoring system will keep you on your job seeking target.

After you have completely depleted your ideal business contacts you may want to try a few selective social contacts. You will need to use good judgment in your selection. Make sure that you neglect the ones that are least likely to help you and pursue the ones that are most productive.

In job-hunting it is very important that you keep up-to-date on what is going on in your industry of interest. You cannot get this information if you confine yourself to a desk. Only a few of the people you meet will give you suitable and valuable career information that you will really find useful. Be careful and remember, Networking is your #1, winning the job, search tool. Use it wisely, and to your best advantage.

Pursue your contacts in such a way that they remain an asset and do not become a liability. Do not be overly pushy or aggressive or you networking may backfire on you. It must be obvious to you that you do not want to portray yourself in a negative light. You will also not want your contacts making calls to people disclaiming their connection with you. Also, always assure your contacts and friends that when you use their name that you will never use it inappropriately.

CHAPTER TEN

THE CHAMPION

It can easily be said that today is like no other time in history when it comes to job search. I believe this to be true. I have been told that the United States has the lowest level of unemployment in history, but at the same time, I am aware of the fact that there are over five million Americans being put out of work through 'downsizing'. I have identified that it is necessary to send out as many as 1,000 résumés before one can realize any interest. You will be fortunate to see 3 – 5 interested parties and perhaps get one interview.

It is difficult and there are times that you will find that you cannot do it with out help. I want to tell you a short story to confirm what can happen to you. Before I decided to not go back into industry after retiring from teaching for over 14 to 15 years, I started a campaign to enter the world of work. Now understand I have move than twenty years of experience. I sent out hundreds of applicant letters. I applied to the Newspaper, Jobs on the Internet, Companies I researched, and more. I not only did this to find a position, but as research for this book. The point I want to make is even with experience, training, and education it can be a lot of work with a limited amount of results. Some of you may have better luck; others might have a worse experience.

7001 Resumes-Plus Second Edition

At this time you could turn to your **'champion'** for help. A champion can do things you cannot do. Should there be a reason why you need to conduct a job search anonymously (perhaps your employed and want this search confidential for now), your 'champion' could help you by sending your anonymous résumés out with the responses being sent to a post office box, though you would need to explain the reason for your secrecy in your cover letter. This approach has been used many times successfully.

The 'Champion' is a real live respectable person who can openly send your name-omitted résumé out and state why he/she is doing so. The 'champion' can also have any responses sent to him/her. It is a big help if the 'champion' is known in the industry as someone who would know a qualified individual when they came across one. It will more than likely enhance your image.

"Who can I get to do this for me?" We can safely say it cannot be the President, or Bill Gates, Lee Iacocca, or Captain Kangaroo. There is no question that these people are well known and prominent in their own right. They may or may not know who would make an ideal employee in a specific industry. A business acquaintance can become a 'champion' on your behalf. Getting the help of an individual like this should not be beyond your reach. Enlist someone who could begin his/her letter with a good deal of credibility, "As the president of a six million dollar stamping company, I know the importance of having employees that I can count on".

Your 'champion' should have some first-hand knowledge of your outstanding on-the-job performance. He/she should be a former employer, boss, or subordinate. I believe that if you have a customer that is keenly aware of your skills, they might make a good 'champion'. You may be able to enlist a prominent business person you know socially or a member of a non-profit institution you may know. I can think of several presidents and production managers of firms that I had extensive business dealings with as well as several educators in the education community that could also qualify as a 'champion'. You probably have similar contacts. Use them if you can.

You will want to be careful not to select too powerful of an individual within a corporation. The reason for this is that the information in the letter must be believable. It has to sound reasonable as to why they cannot use you in their own organization. A president or executive of a major national or international company would have a hard time explaining why they cannot find a slot for you within their own operation. They may not have any jobs at this time. This will need to be addressed up front.

IMPORTANT ELEMENTS OF A 'CHAMPION'S' LETTER SENT ON YOUR BEHALF

1. The champion's credentials must make him/her a valid judge of you skills and abilities.

2. The individual must have a vantage point that enables him/her to evaluate and endorse your on-the-job performance.

3. The recommendation is critical

4. There must be a believable reason as to why your champion cannot hire you.

5. Justify the reason for secrecy if you send an anonymous version of your résumé.

6. There has to be a commitment to you by your champion to keep in touch with the interested party

THE ENDORSEMENT

The advantage of the 'Champion's' endorsement allows him/her to say positive things about you that you cannot say about yourself. This type introduction is far more believable coming from someone else especially coming from your boss or a senior individual. It if comes from a headhunter, it is less believable since there is a compensation attached to the endorsement.

In some situations, the 'Champion's' direct mail promotion may be the only method to resolve a highly sensitive problem. This approach becomes a highly persuasive marketing process when done well. The endorsement provides a great cover and at the same time heightens you introduction and problem solving. The Champion's letter should always tell the prospective employer why you would be a great employee. The letter should close with a statement such as 'Please call me (phone number) if you have any questions. I highly recommend you hire (your name here)'.

CHAPTER ELEVEN

THE COVER LETTER (LETTER OF APPLICATION)

Perhaps one of the most important **(tool)** documents you will be sending out to a potential employer, if not the most important, is the Cover letter. What I want to point out here is this is the very first thing that the employer sees on your behalf. It may be the only thing that he or she will see. This is how important this document is. The reality is you have just a few seconds to gain the interest and attention which can make the difference as to whether or not you will get an interview. The cover letter (letter of application) is your introduction to the specific person who may be hiring you. Remember, the average employer will spend only 10-15 seconds on your cover letter and about the same time on your résumé which we will be discussing later. You must hit them fast or you will miss the opportunity. You will not get the job if your cover letter and résumé is placed in file 13 (the trash can).

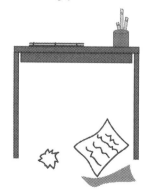

The contents of the cover letter should tell the employer that you have knowledge of the company or organization and that you are qualified to meet the challenge of the position for

7001 Resumes-Plus Second Edition

which you are applying. It is also to your advantage to mention that you are a team player even though you may need to work independently.

As your cover letter needs to grab the interest of the reader, it will need to cover areas about you and your qualifications that are not directly included in your résumé. It is my opinion that the cover letter is an excellent spot to sell special things that you can bring to the employer as well as review your character strengths and attributes. This is where you can **'toot'** your horn.

I would hope that I would not have to tell you this, however, a reminder never hurts; handwritten letters and résumés are <u>not</u> appropriate. Your letter should be typed and by all means make sure the grammar is perfect and you spelling is without error. A word about copies, do not mail self made, cheap appearing copies. This can be interpreted as insincere and lacking true interest. First quality copies can be made at your local copying business (Kinko's, Copy Max, or Office Depot). It is crucial that you always present your <u>very best effort</u> every time you send a letter and résumé.

All cover letters should be on 8-1/2' x 11' white or light color bond paper. Whatever you do, make sure that you get the name of the person and his/her title spelled correctly. Sending letters addressed To Whom It May Concern, Dear Sir, Gentlemen, or Madam, have little chance of reaching anyone except the wastebasket. You will probably be wasting your time. If you are answering a blind ad the name of the individual may not be provided. This is the best you can do in this situation so address the cover letter to the department, or how instructed in the ad.

Develop your résumé first then your cover letter. Make sure that you are selling yourself with everything that you have. In many cases, you may be in competition with up to 100 or more people with every ad you respond to. You will want to prepare a new cover letter that directly correlates to every position you respond to. What I like to do is touch on related experiences that can be directly related to the employers business.

In the last paragraph of your letter state that you will be contacting the company or organization on a specific day if you do not hear from them, you want them to know that their company and their position are the most important priorities to you. I would also suggest that you offer your phone number by which the employer could contact you. I often leave my Cell phone number and my E-mail address. Today this seems to be in 'vogue', I have also included my Fax. If you do not have these options, you will want to make sure that the employer can contact you easily.

STRUCTURE POINTS

1. Make sure your grammar and spelling are correct.

2. Keep the cover letter on one page if at all possible but do not sell yourself short. Use two pages if necessary, as long as it is as concise as possible.

3. Avoid 'bold' or 'fancy' paper. Use 8-1/2 x 11' bond. White, light blue, light gray, buff, or ivory are acceptable. Paper weight between 16-25 lbs is neither too thin nor too thick and presents well for this purpose. Paper texture can be linen finish or rag paper, the choice is your personal decision.

4. Avoid using the personal pronoun 'I'. Simply leave it out of each sentence if at all possible.

5. Use a layout that has good spacing, margins and headings. A little creativity can shout 'Read Me'. Experiment with your paper design until you are confident that you have an 'eye catching' format.

WORD PROCESSING SERVICE

Many of us are not competent behind the typewriter or computer. If this is your case you will want to hire a professional typist or data processing person to prepare you cover letter

7001 Resumes-Plus Second Edition

and résumé. You can look in your local newspaper or local yellow pages for persons or businesses that specialize in cover letters and résumés.

One of the nicest features of word processors versus typewriters is that the word processors have the ability to store typed information on a disk. This of course allows for the checking of spelling, grammar, or needed modifications. You will be able to tailor your cover letter and résumé to the specific jobs. This modification process can be done in a matter of minutes.

The sharpest print is obtained from a laser printer which most word processing services generally use. We would suggest that you do not accept type formats known as dot matrix or thermal as this will not offer the sharpness you will want for your letter and résumé.

Word processing services come and go. Therefore, you will want to obtain several copies of your letter and résumé, and also ask for the disk so that another service can modify your paperwork if necessary. Unfortunately things can happen to your disk so you will want to have a copy or two of your cover letter and résumé as backups. The most common word processing programs in use today are Microsoft 95, Microsoft Office 2000, XP Professional, and so on. These programs will be around for some time and are very popular therefore you should be able to find more than one word processing service to assist you if necessary.

You will have a superior quality cover letter (letter of application) and résumé comparable to those found in books, magazines, and newspapers. You can expect to be charged $25 - $75. Insist on a font (print type) that is easy on the eye and clear. Avoid fancy script. Your cover letter and résumé must say **BUSINESS DOCUMENT**

Font types (print types); the type size for each of the following is # 12

Times New Roman: Easy to read and clear type.

Centaur: Appears like this a little less clear

Arial: Easy to read and clear type

THE JOB SEARCH TOOL TO GET YOU THAT JOB

Most of the time you will be able to see the style that best suits your taste; select that one, and then once you have decided on a font stick with it. A letter with more than one font is unattractive to the eye and appears confusing. To line up the visual impact you can use a variation of this font by changing regular to bold or to italics. You can vary the importance of keywords with italics, underling important phrases, or bold and /or capitalize titles for additional emphasis.

Once your cover letter and résumé is completed please take the time to proofread them. The typists are not perfect. Check everything from beginning to end. This is also a perfect time to make any modifications to your paperwork. It never seems to fail that once you see your letter and résumé in print that you feel it will look better in a different format or you have forgotten to include something or would like to delete something.

- Is the layout and set-up the way you want it?

- Are all typographic errors corrected?

- Is the punctuation correct?

- Have the high-lighted, underlined, capitalized, bolded, italicized, and indentations been done appropriately and to your satisfaction?

You may want to have a second person review your cover letter and résumé. You too can write dynamite cover letters like the ones enclosed. You can use them if you would like. However, be sure to modify them to fit your needs specific to the job you are applying for.

Examples:

Klay Dodds
1234 Home Town Road
Corona, CA 92883

June 21, 2006

Personnel Services
Cerritos Community College District
11110 Alondra Blvd
Norwalk, CA 90650-6298

RE: Full-time/Part-time, Business Education instructor

Dear Colleague,

A few years ago I taught up to three nights a week for Riverside Community College as an adjunct instructor when I was informed that my services were deleted due to a down-turn in student enrollment. I am continuing my search for teaching positions at the junior college level by applying for the above position at Cerritos Community College District.

You will find that I have taught at four (4) junior colleges, seven (7) adult education programs and at the university and high school levels. In addition, I have twenty-six (26) years of Industrial and Business experience. During my educational career I operated one of the most advanced programs in the teaching of Distributive Education in the Western States and was appointed as a consultant for the California Department of Business Education.

I would welcome an opportunity to once again teach full-time or part-time for your Community College. I may be reached at my office at 310-263-7446 Monday through Friday, or at my home 714-514-4567, you may also contact me on my Cell phone 714-222-9131.

Sincerely,

Klay Dodds, MS

Anita Haviland
3322 Blank Road
Riverside, CA 92507
June 21, 2006

Mr. Dick Gregory
Personnel Director
Madness, Inc.
331 Block Drive, Suite 24
Los Angeles, CA 92325

Ms Mimi Fashion, manager of Fabulous Fashion Boutique in Riverside, suggested that I get in touch with you. She says you are now staffing three new shops in Los Angeles County and need experienced, capable, and enthusiastic sales people. I think I qualify for the Madness team.

I have worked for Fabulous Fashions for almost two years selling and modeling. My familiarity with the Freidan stock control system may be especially valuable to you since your new store will be using that equipment. I've been responsible for training all new employees since last November in the Freidan system as well as in selling techniques.

Details of my experience, training, and other qualifications are summarized in the enclosed résumé.

May I meet with you personally to answer any questions you may have? You can call me between 8:00 a.m. and 11:00 a.m. at 951-222-5656. I can also be reached after 5:30 p.m. at 951-324-8342.

Sincerely,

Anita Haviland

Henry Worthington   June 21, 2006
1345 La Cienega Blvd
Los Angeles, CA 92676

Mr. Bell, President
Bell Communications Company
56454 West Circle Road
Corona, CA 92883

Dear Mr. Bell,

Recently I have been researching the leading local companies in data communications. My search has been for companies that are respected in the field, and who provide on-going training programs. **Bell Communications** keeps coming up as a top company.

I am an experienced voice and data communication specialist with substantial background to IBM environments. If you have an opening for someone in this area you will see that my résumé demonstrates a person of unusual dedication, efficiency, drive, and I'm a team player.

My experience and achievements include:

- The complete redesign of a data communications network is projected to increase efficiency of the company by some **22** percent.

- The installation and troubleshooting of a Blue Boy II call back security system for a dial-up network.

I enclosed a copy of my résumé and look forward to examining any of the ways you feel my background and skills would benefit Bell Communications. While I prefer not to use my employer's time taking personal calls at work, with discretion I can be reached at 310-332-5433.

Yours truly,

Henry Worthington

Joe Brooks
1500 Main Street
Brea, CA 90638
June 21, 2006

Mike Johnson, President
Jet Way Engineering
4531 California Street
Bell Gardens, CA 98732

Dear Mr. Johnson,

I am interested in seeing you about a job.

My objective is to utilize my 12 years as an engineer (and an equal amount of in-depth business experience) to contribute to the one area that has always been the most satisfying for me, manufacturing.

My departure from the engineering field was one of mutual reluctance; I had been a business unit manager and was asked to join the staff at another company. I possess strong people skills so I decided to move on.

I have been an associate engineer, engineer, and engineering manager. I have never lost my love of engineering but I must move on.

Please call me at 714-665-4322 to further discuss how I might be a positive addition to your company. I look forward to hearing from you to further exploring your opportunities.

Yours truly,

Joe Brooks

Enclosure

DIRECT MARKET PENETRATION LETTER

Date

Addressee
Address

Dear Name,

Recently, I have been conducting research to identify (COMPANIES, ORGANIZATION, FIRMS) to which I thought I could make a significant contribution in/as (POSITION, RESPONSIBILITIES, OR TARGET). During the course of this research I identified you (COMPANY, ORGANIZATION). I feel that you would want to be aware of my interest and availability as much as I am interested in learning of your needs.

I offer proven background, experience, and ability which will provide specific competencies including:

- INSERT KEY CONCEPT

    OR

- STRENGTHS, ABILITIES, OR TRANSFERABLE SKILLS

I am confident that you will agree that a personal meeting will be of mutual interest and benefit.

While you are reviewing my qualifications, please note that I will contact your office. I will discuss any questions that you have at that time. I am most desirous of setting up an introductory meeting. (Enclose a phone number where you can be reached)

I look forward to speaking with you.

Sincerely,

(Note: This is a 'stand alone' letter. Do not enclose or attach anything to this document)

Dr. Ferris E. Merhish
24213 Owl Ct.
Corona, CA 92883

Mr. Joe Brown, President/CEO
Westside Enterprises, Inc.
5432 Main Street
Salt Lake City, Utah 52522

Dear Mr. Brown,

I would appreciate the opportunity to talk to you regarding an employment opportunity with your organization. I am excited about the possibility of applying my education experience and marketing background to any position you have available.

I would be happy to provide you with additional information. I look forward to hearing from you soon. You can also reach me at my home by calling 951-277-3233.

Sincerely,

Ferris E. Merhish

THE BROADCAST LETTER

The broadcast letter is just a quick variation of your cover letter. The information is gotten from your achievement section of this book and your résumé. It is designed to get you quick feedback from potential employers, perhaps a phone call or two. At some point if you are successful you will have to forward a résumé, but this is the whole idea. While a broadcast letter might have a place in you job search campaign, do not use it as your only medium or a substitute for your résumé.

(Addressee)   June 22, 2006

(Company name)

City

State

Dear Sir,

For the past ten years I have pursued an increasingly successful career in the sales profession. Among my accomplishments I include:

SALES

As a Compressed Air Equipment Salesman I contributed $500,000, or about 25% of my company's annual sales. I was **'Top Salesman'** my first year.

MARKETING

My marketing skills (based on a B.S. in Business & PhD in Marketing Management) enabled me to increase sales 25% in my economically stressed territory at a time when colleagues were striving to maintain flat sales. Repeat business reached an all-time high.

PROJECT MANAGEMENT

Following the above successes, my regional model was adopted by the company. I trained and provided project supervision to the entire sales force. By following this, your company showed a sales projection increase of 12%.

The above was based and achieved on my firmly held zero-price discounting philosophy. It is difficult to summarize my work in a letter. The only way I can think of providing you the opportunity to examine my credentials, is to talk with each other. I look forward to hearing from you. You my reach me at 951-277-2884

Yours truly,

Bob Smith

MARKETING YOURSELF TO AN EMPLOYMENT AGENCY

(Addressee)   June 22, 2006

(Company name)

City

State

Dear Recruiter:

The enclosed profile should be of interest to you as you review your client assignments. My outstanding background will assist you when selecting an individual for opportunities in the areas of:

(INSERT POSITION, RESPONSIBILITY, OR TARGET)

Please, take just a moment while you still have my documents before you and give me a call. We can set up an exploratory meeting convenient to your schedule. At that time I will also be happy to answer any questions concerning my background and experiences.

You may reach me at my home at 951-277-3533 or on my cell phone at 714-412-4433.

I look forward to hearing from you.

Sincerely,

Enclosure: Résumé

DIRECT MARKET 'NO TIME RESEARCH' COVER LETTER

(Addressee)   June 22, 2006

(Company name)

City

State

Dear (contact name and/or title goes on the envelope only)

I am using this informal but personal note to contact you as I wanted to get my résumé into your hands quickly.

Recently I have been conducting research on (COMPANIES, ORGANIZATIONS, and FIRMS) in your industry. I have identified yours as one to which I feel I can make a significant contribution in a position that is key to your activities in:

(INSERT POSITION, RESPONSIBILITY OR TARGET)

Therefore, I am letting you know of my interest, experience, and availability. As you review my profile, I am sure it will stimulate your thinking as to areas in your organization that would profit through my (TECHNICAL, MANAGEMENT) skills.

While you still have my profile in hand and its contents in mind, why don't you give me a telephone call? I will be happy to discuss any concerns or answer any questions. We can also explore the desirability of an initial introductory meeting. You may reach me at 714-514-6543 between 9:00 a.m. and 12:00 p.m. Or you may call me on my cell phone anytime 714-513-433.

I am looking forward to hearing from you in the near future.

Sincerely

Enclosure: résumé

BLIND ADS AND POST OFFICE BOXES

(Addressee)   June 22, 2006

(Company name)

City

State

Dear Advertiser:

I feel that my profile is one that you will want to review in detail. It appears that I have all

of the qualifications mentioned in your advertised position:

(MENTION QUALIFICATION/SKILLS THAT WERE IN THE AD)

I am looking forward to hearing from you to answer any questions or clarifying any

issues you may have. I can be reached at 714-555-5555 anytime. We can also explore the

feasibility of setting up an introductory meeting.

Sincerely,

Enclosure: Résumé

<u>RE-ACTIVATION OR FOLLOW-UP LETTER</u>

(Addressee)   June 22, 2006

(Company name)

City

State

Dear (Name of contact)

I am following up my earlier letter to you suggesting that we get together to discuss the way

in which my experience, knowledge and skills could be combined to benefit your organization. I

continue to be very much interested in your (COMPANY, ORGANIZATION, or FIRM) and

possible opportunities where my abilities would increase your sales/revenue and/or reduce your cost,

expenses, and overhead while increasing your profits.

Included in the personal profile of a successful (RÉSUMÉ POSITION) is a reluctance to give up

easily. It is for that reason that I am contacting your again.

(CHOOSE ONE OF THE FOLLOWING)

A. Not having heard from you, I wanted to follow-up as every professional must, to be certain

that no be certain that no worthwhile opportunity has been missed.

B. I am disappointed that your response was not more encouraging. Perhaps a number

of considerations prevent a positive reaction at this time. There may be someone else

however, who might be able to review my credentials. I would appreciate that opportunity.

I believe strongly that my talents, transferable skills and capabilities are relevant and that I would make an immediate and profitable contribution to your firm. Please take a moment to review the enclosed accomplishments and results overview.

(CHOSE ONE OF THE FOLLOWING)

A. While you have this letter in hand, why not call at (Phone).

B. As a follow up to this letter, I will plan on calling you.

I will be happy to clarify any issues you may have or answer any questions. We can discuss a mutually convenient meeting.

Sincerely,

(your name)

Letter writing Guidelines

I think that this is a good spot to some letter writing guidelines that can be used in several areas as you correspond with potential employers and others.

1. Use the name of the person or firm in the letter. For best result use the contact name otherwise you risk your letter not getting where you desired it to go.

2. Good letters are fast moving. They read like you speak. Before you mail the letter read it over to see how it sounds.

3. Always be enthusiastic about your subject. Again read your letter over to determine you reached this goal.

4. If you have related industry experience, mention it early in your correspondence.

5. Keep sentences short and paragraphs to five or six lines.

6. Communicate potential benefits if possible.

7. Don't oversell. 'If this guy is so good, why the hard sell.

8. Never begin a letter by asking for a job.

9. Letters are warmer if you use pronouns such as 'I' and 'we'.

10. When answering ads, tailor your response to the requirements.

11. When possible, offer to share some beneficial 'ideas'.

12. Use action words and direct brief descriptions.

13. Edit your letters and read them out loud. If you lose your breath, the sentences are too long.

14. Avoid income and don't explain why you are looking.

15. Commit yourself to a follow-up with a date and time.

16. When writing to employers who have been undergoing change, cite the opportunities implied by your information that relate to your experience.

17. Sign letters with your full name (never initials).

18. If you are addressing an influential person, recognize their position in a complimentary manner and be brief.

19. Having a third party send your letters can be powerful. Their statements can act as a strong endorsement. You don't have to be a close friend to ask for third party assistance. Just make it easy for the third party to assist. Offer to prepare a letter for their signature.

20. Follow-up letters must show continued enthusiasm.

CHAPTER TWELVE

THE RÉSUMÉ

What I would like to do here is review several types of résumés, but please, you will not find 7,001 résumés in this book. I will however give you a cross sampling of Chronological, Functional, and Combinational résumés that will be designed to give you a number of ideas on how to put your own résumés together from the data and information that you discovered about yourself during the Asset part of your personal research. Keep in mind that results count when it comes to designing your résumés.

The standard guideline for the length of a résumé is that it should be no longer than one page. If you are a senior individual, what I mean by this is that you have been in the workforce for say ten years or more so you might have a longer job history, but keep in mind you may not want to have more than the past ten years, and make sure the information is relevant. Usually, an employer or interviewer will not spend a lot of time reading your résumé. If your résumé is complicated or appears confusing the employer may spend even less time with your work and proceed to the next applicant. Make sure it as easy as possible for the prospective employer to review your résumé.

The résumé is just a thumbnail sketch of you, you should know this. Many details can be filled in later during your interview with you potential employer. You must grab the reader's attention quickly and hold it until the decision to interview or not is made. It is quite a challenge to get the prospective employer to like you from your résumé. Here are some tips.

You need to be very clear on what you are saying. Do not use abbreviations as they can be confusing to the reader. Use short clear sentences. Make your résumé something that you would like to read. A busy employer may look at hundreds of résumé a week; make yours the one the reader will remember. Your résumé will need to stand out from the others. Show this employer that you have what they want. One thing I believe and I want you to think about it, if your résumé sounds too hard to believe, well like they say, it will not be believed. You want it to be as exciting as it can, snappy, and memorable, but not a 'fairy tail'.

Whether you use the examples that are provided in this book or develop your own, you should keep these things in mind. First, companies do not hire people, people hire people. Your résumé will need to be designed to influence one or more persons. You will want to indicate on your résumé what your career objectives are in relation to what the company is looking for in this specific job opportunity. Last but not least, say nothing that you cannot back up. Do Not Lie. If you do, this may very well cost you the job. The employer may check up on every word you say.

CHRONOLOGICAL RÉSUMÉ

When people think of a résumé this is the format generally thought of. This style is very useful for (Individual just entering the job market). Your job history is listed chronologically from the most recent to your first job (or ten years back). This format works well for persons who have had only a few jobs and can represent your growth within a specific industry as your responsibilities have increased. You can now see why this type of résumé may not be in your best interest if you have had no or only one or two jobs to list that have been for **short** periods of time. This will indicate to the employer that you have limited experience in the real work force, perhaps in this specific industry, and may not be the best candidate for the position.

Job Counselors seem to prefer the **chronological** résumé; however, I do not believe that there is only one kind of résumé that works. Would you take the word of only one doctor if you needed major surgery? Of course not! What I am going to recommend is that you present your assets and qualifications in the format that best sells you and your skills.

If you select the chronological format you will list your work and educational history in a chronological order putting the most recent experience first. Employers want to see not only what you did but how well you did it (if appropriate), i.e., 'I increased the sales of my territory by 20%', or 'I was able to reduce expenses and improve the bottom line for the company by 15%'. Review your strengths and versatility, use statements that detail the depth your skills and responsibilities took on. Most importantly, emphasize your most notable accomplishments in each position held.

FUNCTIONAL RÉSUMÉ

For job seekers who are 'new' to the work force or for veterans, this format can work very well. The focus of the functional résumé is on the skills, abilities and qualification which would be specific to the job you are considering. In order to make this type of résumé work for you, you must identify a specific job/employment goal or objective. Your target skills in this résumé will focus toward this objective. If you cannot identify an objective you will have to generate a résumé that does not appear to meander or be too general. Even though your work history is not represented you will be able to present your specific skills.

It might be feasible to leave out specific dates of employment in the functional résumé as the emphasis is on skills. Employers are able to make certain assumptions based upon your employment dates. If included in your résumé, you may want to de-emphasize the dates by including the dates on a second page or a using smaller font.

7001 Resumes-Plus Second Edition

COMBINATION RÉSUMÉS

The **combination** résumé combines aspects of the chronological and functional résumé. This type of format might best be used to illustrate a career in progress. A summary of career accomplishments can be followed by a summary of acquired skills. The next section of your résumé can incorporate that chronological employment history. You can use each section to emphasize the skills or achievements acquired on each step of your career ladder. This résumé may or may not have an occupational goal stated. However, if it is not stated on your résumé it must be included in a cover letter. There are advantages and disadvantages to this type of résumé:

Advantages	Disadvantages
May be personalized	No standardized format
Emphasizes achievements	May not be recognized as a résumé
Quickly makes a point	You must have strong work skills to use it effectively

TAILOR-MADE RÉSUMÉ

If you are responding to a newspaper ad you will want a cover letter (letter of application) and a résumé tailor made specific to the ad. On a piece of paper write down the specific skills and functions of the position mentioned in the ad. Study the ad carefully. Next write down your specific skills and experiences that you have or are transferable to this position. Organize your skills into positive terms. Now draft you résumé. Once the résumé is completed develop your cover letter. Directly respond to the needs of the company. Your points must be made quickly and correctly. You will not get another chance to respond to this ad for this employment opportunity. You must get the reader's interest right away.

The Job Search Tool to Get You That Job
OTHER TYPES OF RÉSUMÉS

As stated earlier, any combination of the parts of various résumé types put together to create a unique and effective résumé is fair game in getting you that job. If you want to combine components of a Functional Résumé with that of a Chronological Résumé, go ahead. My advice is that you maintain a log of what type or résumé you are sending and to whom. I can tell you that most people do not do this, but this will give you information that you can fall back on and evaluate. This information can be invaluable for use in developing future résumés. When developing you résumé make every effort to learn something about the person who will be receiving your résumé – this will give you some clues perhaps as to the best format to use. You might also produce a résumé of each type and critique it for your own comfort. You also might invite a friend or an associate to review your résumé for further input.

I can assure you that the résumé that shows the most originality will most likely get the most action. Many résumés look the same and become a 'blur' to the individual reviewing them; often these résumés appear as though they came out of the same résumé mill. If from your research you have determined that you are the ideal person for a specific job, you owe it to yourself to break away from tradition and be a little creative. Bear in mind, if you determine that the person who will be reviewing your résumé is a conservative person you may want to approach this situation with a more traditional format

On the next few pages you will find samples of various types of résumés, however your will not find 7'001, which is the title to this book. What the title relates to is the number I once sent out during a period of my life when I was doing 'job search'.

The Chronological résumé

Robert Myers
555 Wishingwell Road
Placirita Canyon, CA 92251

SUMMARY: Twenty six years of experience in contracts and procurement of various equipment and supplies. Major focus has been Aerospace with significant transferable skills.

EXPERIENCE:
Broker, Employee Benefits Contracts, 7 yrs.
Douglas Aircraft, Administrator: Aircraft Parts & Systems purchasing, 7 yrs
Northrop Aircraft, Contracts Manager Aircraft Systems, 3 yrs
Boeing Aircraft, Administrator: Procurement of aircraft parts, 2 yrs
Seattle First Bank, Development & Purchasing, 2yrs
U.S Navy, Procurement Administrator, 5yrs

SKILLS:
Contracts management with knowledge of second language helpful
Negotiation skills
Team Leader
Report and procedure writing

EDUCATION:
JD   Pacific Coast University
MBA   National University
BA   University of Oklahoma
Certification: Computers and Computer Networking

Debi Dodds, 3434 Warm Springs, Corona, CA 92883 (951) 277-2891

SUMMARY: Ten years of increasing responsibility in the employment service industry Concentration in the high technology markets.

EXPERIENCE: Harvey Systems international, Inc.   1985 – Present

Responsible for recruiting and managing consulting staff of five. Set up office and organized the recruitment, selection and hiring of consultants. Recruited all levels of MIS staff from financial to manufacturing markets.

Additional responsibilities
- Coordinated with outside advertising agencies
- Developed P.R. with industry periodicals – placement with over 20 years magazines and newsletters
- Developed effective referral programs – referrals increased 32%

EXPERIENCE: Technical Aid Corporation   1977-1985
              National Consulting Firm: MICRO/TEMPS Division

Division Manager	1983 – 1985
Area Manager	1980 – 1983
Branch Manage	1978 – 1980

As Division opened additional West Coast offices, Staffed and trained all offices with appropriate personnel. Created and implemented all divisional operational policies responsible for P & L, Sales Increased to $20 million dollars from $0 in 1978.

- Achieved and maintained 30% annual growth over 7 year period.
- Maintained sale staff turnover at 14%.

As area Manager opened additional office, hiring staff, setting up office policies and training sales and recruiting personnel.

Additional responsibilities:
- Supervised offices in two states.
- Developed business relationships with accounts – 75% of clients were regular customers.
- Client base increased 28% per year.
- Generated over $200,000 worth of free trade journal publicity.

As Branch Manager: hired to establish the new MICRO/TEMPS operation. Recruited and managed consultants, hired internal staff, sold service to clients.

EDUCATION: Boston University
            B.S Public Relations, 1977

On the next few pages I am going to present the Functional/Skills Résumé. You are going see several examples of résumés, choose the one that best meets your needs. This format is recommended for the following types of applicants.

(Moms, wives, and partners re-entering the world of work

(Retired persons re-entering the world of work

(Caregiver attempting to re-enter the workforce

(A long-term volunteer returning from an assignment

Note:

The assumption is that you have been unemployed for sometime, perhaps a year or more, which would require re-writing your résumé because of the changes from the Chorological style of résumé. We are now focusing on skills and qualifications, and not employment work experience as in the Chronological Style of résumé.

Focus:

Remember the focus on Functional/skill résumé is on your skills, qualifications, project, highlights, and achievements. The purpose is to bring the readers' attention to your experience, knowledge, and value you can bring to their business or organization. It is important that you downplay the fact that you have been out of the workforce for sometime.

FUNCTIONAL/SKILL RÉSUMÉ

Kirk Smith

2345 Deer Valley Road
Riverside, CA 92885
home/msg. (915) 279-4638
mobile :(714) 515-2365
e-mail: K.Smith@comcast.Net

OBJECTIVE

**Receptionist/Office Assistant, Qualified by extensive
Administrative experience in professional settings.**

SKILLS SUMMARY

Customer Service	**Administration**
Oral & Written Communications	**Microsoft Word**
Proofreading & Editing	**Problem Solving**
Research & Analysis	**Shorthand**

CAREER HIGHLIGHTS

- Answered calls and scheduled appointments for a busy dental office. Listened to and addressed concerns of the patients.

- Created a charting system to track international shipments of bulk chemicals for Shell. Oil

- Communicated with freight forwarders, chemical inspectors, overseas affiliates, and foreign vendors to ensure that Shell Oil bulk chemical shipments were delivered on time.

- Coordinated orders and bills of lading for bulk chemicals.

- Ensured that current shipping regulations for countries were updated in an international Documentation Handbook.

- Reduced risk of late-payment fees with prompt processing of domestic and international bills.

- Converted international currency into U.S. dollars to accurately determine invoice amounts from overseas vendors.

- Prepared export documentation and reports.

- Established and maintained department filling system.

- Managed two high school reunions: found missing classmates, arranged radio and newspaper announcements, chose location and menu, and updated database.

WORK HISTORY

Receptionist (P/T) Dr. Jack Kelly, Riverside, CA (2 years)
Assistant Manager – Accounts Receivable, Shell Oil Corporation,
Brea, CA (6 years)
International Coordinator, Shell Oil Corporation,
Brea. CA (11 years)
Secretary, Shell Oil Corporation, Brea, CA (7 years)

7001 Resumes-Plus Second Edition

EDUCATIONAL-EMPHASIS RÉSUMÉ

This format is recommended for the follow situations

(The completion of your college degree, advance degree, or other type of educational training and/or certification

(Coming back from a sabbatical or other type of academic or research leave of absence

Focus

In this résumé your focus is on your recent academic work, training, and educational background. This is your greatest selling point to your prospective employer therefore make sure that you bring them to the attention and forefront of your résumé.

Mary Berry

492 Green leaf Lane
Orange, CA 98234

M.Berry@Comcase.Net

Home 714-223-7723
Mobile 714-543-3311

MARKETING

Product Management (Product Development - Packaging

Track record of revenue growth, profit enhancement, and successful product-line management during 9 years in progressively challenging marketing-management roles. Strong foundation in marketing research and technology paired with creativity and the ability to innovate. Talent for leading and inspiring teams to top performance.

(**Set new business directions** by recognizing and seizing market opportunities
(**Improved performance in all products and brands managed**; grew revenue, cut cost, developed unique retailer programs and packages, and improved brand image.

(**Effective prioritized multiple projects** to align results with business objectives.

EDUCATION

2002   MBA – Concentration Marketing Management   San Jose University, San Jose, CA

(**Key Projects**:
--**Case Study / Marketing Strategy for United Airlines,** identifying marketing opportunities in a post – 9/11 travel environment. Pinpointed competitive issues, market advantages, and financial strengths. *(Project Leader)*
--**Balance Scorecard Study**: Analysis of corporate culture and practical application of balanced-scorecard system to the 4 business perspectives. *(Capstone Class Project)*
(**Graduate Research Assistant / Teaching Assistant**
--Taught Marketing Research to undergraduate business students, bringing real-world perspective to theoretical class learning.

2000   **BS** – Computer Information Systems   Chapman University, Orange, CA

1990   BSBA – Concentration Management   San Jose University, San Jose, CA

EXPERIENCE

JAY CORPORATION, INC., Orange, CA   1995 – 1999
($180MM public company manufacturing and marketing consumer comfort products. Marquee brand is HappyFeet; buy accounts include Wal-Mart, Federated, and other national retailers.)

Senior Marketing Manager,   1997 – 1999

Drove marketing strategy and programs for 3 product lines totaling $150MM sales. Held P & L accountably and coordinated the efforts of design, product development, manufacturing, and other departments to deliver products for seasonal deadlines. Managed $2MM marketing budget, and also directed the development of sales brochures and marketing materials, developed and gave sales-force presentations on seasonal product lines, and managed national sales meetings for upper management and national sales organizations.

Mary Berry
M.Berry@Comcase.Net

Home 714-223-7723
Mobile 714-543-3311

Increased sales and profitability in all 3 brand segments:

(Value Brands:
--Boosted profit margins from 25% to 39% through continuous improvement efforts that removed cost from every point of production – souring, production, packaging, distribution.
--Grew Wal-Mart program from **$3MM** TO **$7MM** by identifying and capitalizing on sales trends and market opportunities.

(HappyFeet ™:
--Identified growth opportunity, then created and launched Premier Collection with light-end retailers. Increased brad-segment sales **60% -- $5.8MM** to **$9.3MM**.
--Initiated licensing partnership and developed proposal that included entry into nontraditional markets and projected **100%** increase in men's product line.
--Spearheaded redesign of product displays to accommodate **20%** more product without increasing costs.

(CoreComfort™:
--Challenged to redesign product packaging to improve visual appeal and create distinct brand image. Worked with designers on new packaging and with manufacturing on technology-based line restage, **31%** increase in product sales.

(Additional Business Contributions:
--Developed new packaging that increased inventory flexibility and saved $95K in the first year of implementation.
--Managed the company's market-research function, critical to product-line development, and increased understanding of industry dynamics, competition, and target customers.
--Stepped in as interim Visual Manager for 8 months and managed a complete packaging restage from concept through implementation. Worked with outside agencies on the development of new packaging line, displays, and advertising.

ABBY FIBERS, Santa Ana, CA
$5MM apparel and materials manufacturer

1990-1995

Assistant Product Manager, 1992 – 1995

Promoted to manage more than $11MM in private-label and branded product for accounts such as JC Penny and Sears, with responsibility for pricing, promotions, advertising, forecasting, and product/packaging development. Performed yearly budgeting/planning activities for private-label and branded product lines.

(Spurred **40%** year-over-year sales increase for product lines under management

(Instrumental in developing new markets for an existing single-market product line that has become the company's signature product and currently generates **55%** of total revenue.

(Aggressively pursued a key catalog retailer (Land's End), spearheading product development, developed what became one of its best-selling catalog promotions ever – and was the first step in a key business relationship that culminated in Abby being selected as the primary supplier for a major new Lands' End (today an **$188MM** account).

Marketing Assistant,

1990 1992

Recruited out of college based on strengths in statistics, mathematics, and analysis.

(Created a forecasting system that, for the first time, included sales history, inventory turns, and planned account expansion. Increased forecasting efficiency and improved on-time/complete shipping from **89%** to over **95%**

Page 2

FUNCTIONAL/SKILL RÉSUMÉ

Jerry Lewis
546 Deer Valley Road
Riverside, CA 92884
(915) 277-3041

OBJECTIVE: A position in Employment Service where my management, sales and recruiting talents can be effectively utilized to improve operation and contribute to company profits.

SUMMARY: Over ten years of Human Resources experience. Extensive responsibility for multiple branch offices and an internal staff of 40+ employees and 250 consultants.

SALES: Sold high technology consulting services with consistently profitable margins throughout the United States. Grew Sales from $0 to over $20 million a year.

RECRUITING: Developed recruiting sourcing methods for multiple branch offices. Recruited over 25,000 internal and external consultants in the high technology professions.

MANAGEMENT: Managed up to 40 people in sales, customer service, recruiting, and administration. Turnover maintained below 14% in a 'turnover business'.

FINANCIAL: Prepared quarterly and yearly forecasts. Presented, reviewed and defended these forecasts to the Board of Directors. Responsible for P & L of $20 million sales operation.

PRODUCTION: Responsible for opening multiple offices and accountable for growth and profitability. 100% success and maintained 30% growth over a 7 year period in 10 offices.

**WORK
EXPERIENCE:**

1985 to Present   ROBERT SYSTEMS INTERNATIONAL, Riverside, CA
National Consulting Firm
Personnel Manager

1978 to 1988   HIGH TECH AID CORPORATION Orange, CA
National Consulting Firm
Division Manager

EDUCATION   B. S., 1977, Santa Clara University

REFERENCES: Available upon request.

7001 Resumes-Plus Second Edition

Experience-Emphasis Résumé

You are going to find this format good in the following situation:

(If you have been unemployed or laid off for sometime (six months or more).

(If you are re-entering the work force after owning your own business.

(If you are re-entering the labor force if you have been out of country.

Focus

Remember here you are going to focus on your work experience. The selling points that you are offering point to what you have done and how valuable you can be to a prospective employer. Do not try to cover up what you have done or your work history because you are not currently in the work force.

Steven Meyers, CFA

2145 Orange Wood Road
Orange, CA 92345

smeyer@xyz.com

Home (714) 514-5551
Cell (714) 514-7899

PROFILE

Hard-working and versatile Investment Analyst experienced in performing economic analyses and evaluating market expectations. Proven ability to develop accurate and efficient procedures and to meet tight deadlines. Team player and able to work well independently. B.A. in Economics with strong knowledge

- Competitive Analysis
- Marketing Presentations
- Risk Management

- Asset Allocation
- Portfolio Recommendations
- Forecasting

WORK EXPERIENCE

Investment / Financial Analyst – Eagle Investments Corp., Stanton, CA   **2000-2002**
(San Francisco based company that has designed financial planning software for the B2B market.)

- Constructed, calculated, and maintained capital-market expectations and portfolio recommendations for a family of global asset-allocation portfolios of varying levels of risk.
- Collaborated with Vice President to determine methodology for the design of a questionnaire to determine investors' risk tolerance / risk aversion.
- Managed competitive analysis process as part of strategic planning effort and company valuation process.
- Led the creation of marketing and business development strategies and presentations.

Institutional Marketing Manager – American Savings Funds, Los Angeles, CA   **1998-2000**

- **Managed** product-comparison process of separate accounts and mutual funds for presentation
- Conducted performance attribution, style, and portfolio-composition analyses for various products.
- Coordinated and managed responses to consultant databases and maintained internal records
- Managed the new-business proposal-production process.

EDUCATION AND TRAINING

BA, Economics, University of California at Riverside, Riverside, CA   1998

- Minor in Entrepreneurship and Management.

Association for investment Management sand Research

- **Chartered** Financial Analyst – 2001

COMPUTER EXPERIENCE / SKILLS

+Lotus 1-2-3, Excel, PowerPoint, Word, and extensive Internet research and database development.

7001 Resumes-Plus Second Edition

The Importance of Format

The choice of the right format is important to the success of your résumé as well as your job search.

When you have been out of the labor force for some time, this information can suggest to the potential employer that your job skills are some what out of day. Therefore you should place your professional qualifications and skills near the top of the page so that the hiring manager or recruiter gets a better impression. Also integrate key words throughout with a strong presentation.

We want the interviewer to be impressed with your qualifications and not the period out of the labor force. It is hoped that you are not eliminated because of your gap in employment.

I also want to point out that today the addition of an E-mail address has been added to your résumé as a method of communication with you interviewer. You can also add a fax and cell number.

Take a look at the following two résumés as you will see in the first résumé the fact that the individual was a homemaker was placed close to the top of the page and has a good chance of eliminating the applicant before the manager or recruiter gets a chance to review the professional qualifications and skills.

Remember what you want is to give the individual who is reviewing your résumé a chance to develop a positive impression about your skills before you disclose information that might suggest that your skills are somewhat dated.

Penny Gardner

4532 Foster Drive

Rancho Cucamonga, CA

Home: 951-278-4432

Email: pennyone@hotmail.com

Objective

Interested in a full-time Office Administration position where my past experience, education, and interpersonal skills can be valued.

Summary of Qualifications

Possess knowledge and skills in the administrative field as well as in customer service. Duties also extended to postal regulations and procedures to include maintaining security of personnel and sensitive equipment within a 24/7 shop. Currently hold an Associate's Degree in Computer Science / Networking Systems Administration. Experience with supervising and teaching techniques to personnel in a classroom environment as well as training in the field.

Experience

Homemaker   January 1992 - Present

San Jose, CA, and Santa Clara, CA

Coordinated spouse's career movements by being flexible and supportive. Maintained family finances in an efficient and successful manner. Managed children's education, school activities, and extracurricular activities by volunteering within the community. Supported the family's interests by preparing and distributing reports for multiple associations of which we were members.

Tool Team Member   January 1991 – December 1991

Apex Printing Services, San Jose, CA

Provided first-level print support for the company's global print servers and systems. Used a variety of troubleshooting procedures to resolve customers' complaints involving print issues, location of files, and MPE/ UNIX print-server management. Used various electronic tools such as Batchnet, Maestro, Spool, and Spyvision to investigate and quickly solve customer complaints to the satisfaction of team members as well as management officials. Developed and wrote processes and procedures for team members to use as a reference to identify and resolve problems and improve customer service.

Computer Lab Technician

San Jose State University, San Jose, CA

Assisted the Network System Administrator in the installation, maintenance, troubleshooting, and repair of personal computers and workstation on NT network environment, Configured network cards, printers, and other hardware peripherals for use in a technical-training environment. Software installation included, but was not limited to, disk imaging and ghosting methods as well as loading various software programs onto several different operating systems. Assembled a new computer lab to include CATS cabling.

Nuclear, Biological, Chemical (NBC) Specialist   October 1987-December 1989

U.S. Army Mannheim, Germany

Supervised, trained, and advised the operators on the maintenance and use of NBD detection and decontamination equipment. Provided supervision and training on the proper use and maintenance of personal protective gear and equipment. Established and administered the training and application of NBC defense measures in an aviation organization. Maintained accountability and security of all NBC equipment assigned to approximately 150 personnel.

Nuclear, Biological, Chemical (NBC) Specialist   August 1986-October 1987

U.S. Army, Fork Polk, LA

Maintained, operated, and trained on variety of vehicles and equipment used to launch the Lance missile. Team participated in and won a competition regarding the live firing of missiles into the Mediterranean Sea. Handled additional duties as an Administrative Specialist as well as Mail Clerk. Prepared personnel action requests and provided customer service in a professional and timely manner. Collected, distributed, and re-addressed misdirected mail. Maintained the physical security of the mailroom and all individual unit mail, stamps, equipment, and the cash drawer.

Education

- Associate of Computer Science – Networking Systems Administration, Foot Hill Community College, Mountain View, CA 1998

- Graduate, Basic Leadership and Management Course, 4 weeks, U.S. Army, Fort Sill, OK, 1987

- Graduate, Intermediate Chemical Supervisory Management Course, 11 weeks, U.S. Army, Fort McClellan, AL 1986

- Certificate, Lance Missile Training Course, 4 weeks, U.S. Army, Fort Still, OK, 1982

Penny Gardner

4532 Foster Drive

Rancho Cucamonga, CA

951-278-4432 Email: pennyone@hotmail.com

OBJECTIVE	Interested in a full-time Office Administration position where my past experience, education, and interpersonal skills can be valued.
SUMMARY OF QUALIFICATIONS	Possess knowledge and skills in the administrative field as well as in customer service. Duties also extended to postal regulations and procedures to include Maintaining security of personnel and sensitive equipment within a 24/7 shop. Currently hold an Associate's Degree in Computer Science / Networking Systems Administration. Experience with supervision and teaching techniques to personnel in a classroom environment as well as training in the field.
ADMINISTRATION	Prepared professional documents upon request as directed by guidelines set by the company. Operated various automated devices within an office and workstation environment. Maintained various security levels of personnel information, correspondence, and personal mail. Proficiently handled collection, distribution, and redirection of company mail as well as maintained the security of such items.
CUSTOMER SERVICE	Listened and responded to customers' complaints, requests, and questions with professionalism and respect while on the phone as well as in person. Provided routine customers with solutions that were within my level of expertise and handled priority requests and complaints appropriately and in a timely manner.
NETWORKING	Managed print for a large company using various operating environments such as MPE and UNIX. Used the utmost respect and caring in handling time-sensitive print issuers for clients. Assisted the Network Systems Administrator with the installation, operation, maintenance, and repair of more than 200 networking transmission problems. Handled upgrading procedures as specified by management officials by applying personnel knowledge, training, and professionalism.
COMPUTER MAINTENANCE	Install, maintained, and repaired computer hardware components and peripherals for more than 175 communications devices and systems. Assembled a new computer lab to include hardware and peripherals, software packages, and physical setup of workstations such as 486 and Pentium processors, network interface cards, modems, memory, floppy/hard/jazz

drives, mouse, keyboards, motherboards, and power supplies.

TRAINING Planned, coordinated, and taught various subjects and tasks for use in training subordinates on nuclear, biological, and chemical operation. Subject matter included detection, use, and decontamination of personnel and team chemical equipment. Applied teaching and management techniques in both the classroom and training environments.

EDUCATION

- Associate of Computer Science – Networking Systems Administration, Foothill Community College Mountain View, CA, 1998
- Graduated Basic Leadership and Management Course, 4 weeks, U.S. Army, Fort Sill, OK, 1987
- Certificate, Lance Missile Training Course, 4 weeks, U.S. Army, Fort Sill, Ok, 1982

EXPERIENCE

- Homemaker, San Jose CA, Santa Clara, CA, 1992 – Present
- Tool Team Member Apex Printing Services, San Jose, CA 1991
- Nuclear, Biological, Chemical (NBC) Specialist, U.S. Army, Mannheim, Germany, 1987-1989
- Nuclear, Biological, Chemical (NBC) Specialist, U.S. Army, Fork Polk, LA, 1986 – 1989
- Lance Missile Crewmember, U.S. Army, Fulda, Germany, 1992-1996

THE JOB SEARCH TOOL TO GET YOU THAT JOB

AVOID BASIC MISTAKES

Before we go on I would like to take a few moments to discuss some basic mistakes to avoid. Which one of the following is incorrect?

(You have 'framed' and leveraged all your disparate job experiences to fit the job you want.

(You use the same résumé for all job applications but customize with a cover letter.

(You virtually copied your résumé from one of our sample résumés because the sample looks neat and professional (and everybody cribs).

☞ The answer is: When you virtually copy your résumé out of this sample book, or for that matter any sample book, you're selling someone else's idealized strengths rather than your own. Résumé books are designed to reveal standards to which you can aspire, not patterns to plagiarize.

The idea is that you can take or lift a phase here and there, but start from scratch using your experiences and data. Also if your cover letter is separated from your résumé it can look like you took a shortcut. To fix this, an ideal approach is to focus on what you bring to the specific employer's table.

It is also important to do a wide job search using all sources at your disposal. Do not just do your search on the Net. Don't be afraid to cold-call people because they might hang up on you.

For some of you this may hit home; don't work in your job search between going to the beach and going to the gym.

I hate to tell you, but all of these are classic. You need to do a job search that covers every source; it is your career you may be playing with. You need to think of cold calling as concentric circles, each call ends with a request for a referral to someone who can move you on to someone who could hire you.

133

You will want to make sure that your cover letter explains in detail what you can do for the employer; waging a comprehensive job campaign. And you need to prepare diligently for interviews, mapping out where the jobs that you are searching for are. Remember, that searching for a job is a full-time job!

CONTACT INFORMATION

Before we go on I would like to address something that you would think was simple. This is the top section: your name and contact information.

YOUR NAME

How simple could this be? Well there are several factors that you might want to consider.

- Most people choose to use their full, formal name at the top of the résumé, but you can use the name that you are normally called or that you prefer to be called.

- It is to your advantage that you give the option to the interviewer to call you the name that you are both comfortable with. Their comfort level may decrease if your name is gender neutral, difficult to pronounce, or very unusual, they don't know who they're calling (a man or woman) or how to ask for you. You can make it easier for them by following these examples:

(Ms.) Michael Wilson

(Mr.) Lynn T. Collins

Tahisha (Jean) Johnson

Johova (Bill) Kline

YOUR ADDRESS

No matter if you use a Post Office box for mail or not, it is important that you include your home address on your résumé.

YOUR TELEPHONE NUMBER (s)

Make sure your home telephone number is included on your résumé; this allows the employer to call you immediately. In addition, you can also include your Cell phone number (refer to it as your 'mobile' number and not 'Cell phone', to keep up with current terminology) or pager number. The pager number is less desirable because it requires you to call back. You may also include a home fax number if you have one, if it can be accessed automatically.

YOUR E-MAIL

I have to tell you that this seems to be in 'vogue' so without question you will want to include your E-mail address on your résumé. What we are seeing today is that the E-mail usage is often the preferred method of communication in job search, particularly in the early stages of job search and contact. If you do not have an E-mail address you can obtain a free, addressable anywhere address from a provider such as www.comcast.net, www.yahoo.com, or www.aol.com .and there are others.

ARRANGING YOUR CONTACT INFORMATION

Take some time going through this book looking at how the contact information has been arranged. Notice the top of each résumé to see how the information has been arranged and use these samples to present your own information. The most important point is that we want the employer to have a simple and easy way to contact you!

YOUR PAGE TWO

Make sure you include you name, phone number, and E-mail address at the top of your second page and any additional pages. The point here is that we want to avoid the chance that these pages get separated, and you want to make sure that company can contact you even if they only have one page.

7001 Resumes-Plus Second Edition

YOUR CAREER SUMMARY

Your Career Summary will be placed at the top of your résumé, which summarizes and highlights your knowledge and expertise. The trend is to move from the 'Career Objective' which is often too specific, while the 'Career Summery' is much more powerful as an introduction. The Career objective statement may be somewhat self-serving by indicating what you want rather than suggesting what you can do or offer the employer.

Your Career Summery allows you to position yourself as you want to be perceived and immediately you are 'painting a picture' of yourself in relationship to your career goal. You will want to focus on specific skills, qualifications, and of course the achievements of your career that are related to your current objectives. The summary is not a historical overview of your career. It is rather a concise, well-written, and sharp presentation of information designed to sell you into your next position.

You can give this section different names, or titles:

Career Summary	Highlights of Experience
Career Highlights	Management Profile
Career Achievements	Professional Qualifications
Career synopsis	Profile
Executive Profile	Professional Summary
Expertise Profile	Summary
Skills Summary	Summary of Achievement
Executive Profile	Summary of Qualifications

Or, as you may see later your summary does not have to have a title at all.

Your 'Career Summary' section of the résumé you will find to be very highly important for you the job seekers who are now trying to return to the world of work, because it allows you

136

to present all your key skills, achievements, technology, proficiencies, project highlights, and more. It is your goal to capture the attention and immediately communicate the value you bring to their firm. As such, when they arrive at your listing of employment experience, they're already impressed with you. The fact that you are currently unemployed will be of lesser consequence in their decision making.

I am going to offer a few examples of summaries; take a look at the examples and if you decided to use one of them design your skills, achievements and so forth around the format.

Paragraph Format

CAREER SUMMARY

ENGINEERING TEAM LEADER with extensive experience in lifecycle project management – from design, development, and testing through final product delivery commercialization, and market launch. BSCE Degree. Recipient of numerous awards for engineering and project-management excellence.

Core Competencies Summary Format

QUALIFICATION SUMMARY

CUSTOMER SERVICE
Staff Training / Employee Supervision / Sales Support

(**Customer Satisfaction & Retention**   (**Purchasing & Auditing**
(**Customer Relationship Management**   (**Sales & Marketing**
(**Employee Relations & Leadership**   (**Quality & Cost Control**

Bullet List Format

PROFESSIONAL QUALIFICATIONS:

Sales Professional / Account Executive with a Chicago – based Fortune 500 company

- Consistent record of over-quota sales with an average **25% sales increase** for the past five years.
- Effective relationship builder who is personable and caring; aggressive in **pursuing and capturing new business.**
- Outstanding **presentation, negotiation,** and sales closing skills.
- Excellent **communication, organizational,** and **project – management abilities.**

7001 Resumes-Plus Second Edition

YOUR EDUCATION, CREDENTIALS, AND CERTIFICATION INFORMATION

In this section you will include your college, certifications, credentials, licenses, registrations, and any continuing education. This section can become particularly important if this data is most appropriate for your situation in the main selling point in your résumé. If this is the case you will want to display this information prominently on your résumé to make sure that the interviewer can immediately see your educational qualifications.

YOUR PROFESSIONAL EXPERIENCE

If you find your Professional Experience the real selling point of your résumé you will want to take the most time here to develop it and write it. In this section you will need to take the time to make sure that it has the meat and depth in it. If you have been in the same job you are going to ask yourself 'how do I consolidate all that I have done over the years'. If you have had several jobs over a period of time you are going to ask yourself 'How do I consolidate these various experiences into a substantial and noteworthy section. For all these experiences you will need to approach it very careful answering the how, when, where, and why.

Answering these questions isn't easy, since it depends on you. What are your experiences, what have you achieved, what are your career goals, or objectives, and why were you unemployed? As you develop your résumé you will have to carefully address these by enhancing the positive areas and deemphasize those problem areas. I will give you a few examples of how to approach this concept.

YOUR ACHIEVEMENT FORMAT

When you use the Achievement Format the emphasis should be on each position, overall scope of responsibility, and the resulting achievement.

138

THE JOB SEARCH TOOL TO GET YOU THAT JOB

PROFESSIONAL EXPERIENCE

Riverside County Fire Department, Riverside, CA   1999 to 2001

(DIRECTOR OF EMERGENCY MEDICAL, SERVICES (1998 TO 2001
(SHIFT COMMANDER – (1994 TO 1998)
(ENGINE COMPANY OFFICER – LIEUTENANT (1982 TO 1994)
(EMERGENCY MEDICAL TECHNICAL – ENGINEER (1990 TO 1992)

Supervised Emergency Medical Services comprising of 45 EMT's and paramedics at three fire stations. Participated in the direction of all aspects of personnel relations including hiring, disciplinary action, training, development, and evaluations. Served as incident Commander at medical emergencies and structure fires. Coordinated all phases of EMS and served as Chairman of EMS Operations Committee. Wrote and implemented EMS protocols.

<u>**Achievements**</u>

- Planned, organized, and executed EMS training, testing, and recertification for 75 EMT's. Served as Emergency Medical Services Training Officer.

- Catalyst in the concretization of paramedic program for Riverside County Fire Department, creating a model for the state licensing for other fire departments.

- Instrumental in developing a medical director contract that became the model for other EMS agencies.

- Established and launched Fire Cadet Program (page internship) to allow 7 to 21 years' olds to participate in fire service through a comprehensive training and mentoring opportunity.

- Streamlined process to provide medical oxygen to EMS through small cylinders elimination renal fees and saving 50% on oxygen costs.

<u>YOUR CHALLENGE, ACTION, AND THE RESULTS YOU TOOK</u>

You may want to Emphasize the challenges you had in each position, the action you took, and of course the results or outcome that occurred.

<u>PROFESSIONAL EXPERIENCE</u>

Your job title, dates   Company name and location

Challenge – State your challenge

Action – State the action you took to resolve your challenge.

Results – State the results of your action. Be very detailed.

<u>YOUR EXTRAS</u>

The 'of course' focus of your résumé is on your background and professional experience as well as your academic work and credentials that are directly related to your career goals.

However you should include information that set you apart form other job searchers. Your goal is to demonstrate to the employment prospect your value. Interesting enough, it is the 'extra' that may get you that interview.

You will want to be careful however because what is important to you may not have the same effect on your potential employer.

I will give you a list of categories that you might want to use in your résumé, depending on your particular background and experience, as well as your career objectives. Take a moment to review these categories. To get more attention you may want to include your Career Summary if it is truly impressive. If you do this it is not necessary to include the same information at the end of your résumé.

YOUR TECHNOLOGY SKILLS AND QUALIFICATIONS

Depending on the extent to which the importance your technology is to the job, it is recommended that a separate section be developed to present your technology skills and qualifications. It is here that you will summarize all the hardware, software, operation systems, applications, networks, and whatever else you know that is relevant to your current career objective.

You will find that placement of this information is important. So if the job that you are applying for has a strong requirement for technical skills, it is suggested that you place your technology skills section right after your Career Summary, however, if your technology is more of a 'plus' or 'extra' than a specific requirement, place this information later in your résumé.

In any event these skills are important in any technology related position. Since this is extremely important make sure you display this data prominently.

Here I am going to give you two different ways that can display your technical qualifications.

THE JOB SEARCH TOOL TO GET YOU THAT JOB

Technology profile — ▪ — ▪ — ▪ — ▪ — ▪ — ▪ — ▪ — ▪ — ▪

**Operating
Systems:** XP Professional, Windows 98/95

**Protocols/
Networks:** TCP/P, NetBEUI, Ethernet 10/100 Base – T

Hardware: Hard drive, printers, scanners, fax/modems, CD - ROM, Zip, and Jazz drives

Software: Microsoft Office Modules, FileMaker Pro, and ARC serve,

---

TECHNOLOGY SKILLS SUMMARY

XP Professional	Window 98/95	Mac
Novell	MRP	Ethernet 10
NT 4.0	DRP	IPX/SPX
Microsoft Office	MS Exchange	ARC serve
Project Manager	PC Anywhere	FileMaker Pro

Note: If you want to inform your potential employer that you do in fact have skills you can state this in a line at the end of your Career Summary or the bottom of your résumé.

<u>Your Equipment Skills</u>

If you find yourself as one of those applicants that has equipment skills in manufacturing, construction, engineering, and other related industries, you **are** going to have special equipment skills and knowledge. It is of course important that you convey this information to a potential employer. If so, place this information as you did in the previous format. If you have experience in pharmaceutical products you may also want to display this important information again in this same format.

141

7001 Resumes-Plus Second Edition

Your Honors and Awards

If you have won awards or honors you can place them in the format that I have been suggesting at the end of your résumé, or you can integrate them in with your Education. If you believe that this information is noteworthy and related to your current career objective place this information in your Professional Experience section.

Your Publications and Public Speaking

This information can be very valuable to you, not only setting you apart from other applicants you could be a valuable addition to any company. And by having this experience you could be considered an expert and this information will be complimentary information in your résumé

Your Teaching and Training Experience

Regardless of the industry, or profession your teaching and training, experience can be a valuable asset to any organization or corporation. There is no doubt that you will want to include this skill on your résumé, since paid or not, to speak to an audience communicates a strong message about your skills, qualifications, knowledge, and expertise. Use the basic format that I have exhibited throughout this section.

Your Serving on Committees and Task Forces

Your serving on Committees and Task forces further shows your commitment, strengths, credibility, and perceived value to a potential employer. Consider using the standard format that we have been discussing. Place this information next to the end of your résumé.

Your Professional or Civic Affiliations

Your Professional Affiliations such as being a member of a professional, leadership, business, or educational association, are valuable information that should be included in your résumé. This information projects a level of professionalism; and if you have held a leadership role you will want to indicate this too. If you have Civic Affiliations this is also noteworthy and should be indicated in your résumé. However, the ones more relevant to your current career objectives are of greater importance to indicate. Use the basic format that has been illustrated throughout this section.

Your Personal Information and Consolidating Extras

It is not necessary nor is it recommended that you include your personal information such as your birth date, marital status, or how many children you have in your résumé. In a rare case if this information would give you a competitive advantage then go ahead and include it.

You want to be careful when adding extra information to your résumé; you do not want to make it too long. Therefore you will want to consolidate it at the end of the résumé. There is one thing that you do not want to do and that is to overwhelm the reader. Only include that information you think is important and has merit.

Writing Your Résumé

Your résumé at this point does not need to be 'perfect' the first time since you are still putting it together: As you complete your first draft you will surprised how close you are to your final document. As you develop your résumé try to follow these points.

- **Start with the easy stuff first** – Professional Affiliations, Technology, Education, Public Speaking, Publications, and any other extra information you want to include. This information is easy to complete and requires little time to develop it.

- **Develop short job descriptions for your older positions** – These are the jobs that you held some time ago. Make the statement brief and focus on the important points such achievements, professional honors, or employment with companies that are well-known.

Note: No matter what type of résumé you plan use, develop the job descriptions in a chronological format. This format will be easier to recall what you did as you take each of your jobs in order. Once you have done this you can regroup each job and the related skills and abilities, and your employment history will be left as a simple job list, or short description.

- **Next write the job description for your most recent positions** – This should take more time for you to write. You need to remember to focus on the overall scope of your responsibilities, major projects, and any significant achievements. You will be presenting to the reader of your résumé what you did and how well you accomplished the task. It is at this point that you can use any of the suggested formats to be creative and unique in presenting something about you and your career.

- **Your Career Summary** – It is at this point that you can develop your career summary, however you will want to remember what objective is in this section. Your summary should be designed to highlight the skills and qualifications you have that are closely related to your current career objectives, but not just rehash your previous experience. It is the responsibility of your career summary to capture the attention of the reader and sell you as a valuable individual.

At this point you should be done, and if you followed this outline you should have found the process of developing your résumé a lot easier.

You Are Selling

I want you to remember that your résumé is a sales tool. It is important that you understand and appreciate the importance and value of the résumé as it brings you and the prospective employer together. This document communicates your achievements to the company. It is important to remember, companies don't want to hire just anyone they will hire the individual that can be an asset to their firm. And it is your résumé that conveys this information to the reader.

Your Job Application

I want to take a few moments to touch on the Job Application. As you go from company to company you will discover that each firm will require you to fill out one of their company applications. In some cases you may receive one before the job interview, and maybe you will get one after. No matter when you get it, it will be your responsibility to fill it out. I would recommend that you do take the time to fill out the sample application here in this workbook, make a copy of it and take it with you as you go out on your job search. Make sure that all the information is correct and that all the words are spelled right. You will find that the samples I have provided are from familiar firms that you could have a full-time or part-time job with. By filling out one of these applications in advance, it will make it simpler to fill out other applications as you come across them.

7001 Resumes-Plus Second Edition

EMPLOYMENT APPLICATION
This application is considered active for ninety (90) days.

> **DRUG FREE WORKPLACE**
> All employees are subject to the
> drug and alcohol testing procedures

PERSONAL DATA   WOTC Registration # _____

Name (Last, First, Middle)	
Street Address	Social Security Number
City State Zip	Home Phone Number

Position(s) Interested In? _____ Are You Under the Age of 18? ☐ Yes ☐ No
If Yes, state your age. _____

Salary Requirements _____ Hour / Week (Circle One)
How were you referred? ☐ Newspaper ☐ Friend ☐ Other

Have You Ever Worked For Any Odd Lots, Big Lots, Mac Frugal's, Pic 'N' Save, All For One, ITZADEAL, Toy Liquidators, Toys Unlimited, Amazing Toy Stores, K•B Toys, K•B Toy Outlet, K•B Toy Works or other Consolidated Locations Before? ☐ Yes ☐ No

If Yes, When & Where _____

If Hired, Can You Supply Proof That You Are Legally Entitled To Work In The United States? ☐ Yes ☐ No

Do You Have Friends or Relatives Working For Us? ☐ Yes ☐ No

If So, Whom? _____

Can You Work: ☐ Anytime   ☐ Days   ☐ Evenings   ☐ Weekends

Are There Any Times Or Days You Cannot Work? _____

If in Hawaii Do Not Answer
Have You Ever Been Convicted Of A Felony Or Retail Related Crime (i.e., shoplifting, credit card fraud, robbery)?
Note: A "Yes" response will not automatically disqualify you from employment.   ☐ Yes ☐ No

If Yes, Please Describe: _____

MILITARY SERVICE

Have You Served In The U.S. Armed Forces? ☐ Yes ☐ No

If Yes, Please Complete The Following:
What Principal Duties Did You Perform While In The Service?

Branch Of Service

Are You Enrolled In The Military Reserves? ☐ Yes ☐ No   Expiration Date Of Reserve Status

If Yes, Check One: ☐ Active Status   ☐ Army   ☐ Air Force   ☐ Coast Guard
                   ☐ Inactive Status ☐ Navy   ☐ Marine   ☐ National Guard

EDUCATION   Have you ever attended school under a different name? _____

Type Of School	Name Of School	Location Of School	Area Of Study	Last Year Completed	Did You Earn A Degree or Diploma? Describe
High School				1 2 3 4	☐ Yes ☐ No
College				1 2 3 4	☐ Yes ☐ No
Graduate				1 2 3 4	☐ Yes ☐ No
Other				1 2 3 4	☐ Yes ☐ No

AN EQUAL OPPORTUNITY EMPLOYER
an Equal Opportunity Employer and does not discriminate in making employment decisions based upon race, color, sex, religion, national origin, age, disability, marital status or sexual orientation.

Length of your Résumé

I am going to suggest that your résumé be one to two pages long as a rule of thumb. It has been suggested that readers of résumés do not have a lot of time and get disinterested quickly. However, if you have been in the labor force for a long time or you have extensive or educational training with numerous credentials and certifications that are important, you may want to this information on a third page or an attachment to your résumé.

146

Enhancing your résumé or Cover letter

You might want to 'highlight', underline, **Bold,** *italicize*, or CAPITALIZE certain words, phrases, achievements, projects, numbers, or other information that you want the reader to pay special attention to. This may be a good idea; however, you do not want to overdue this to the point that you clutter your documents with these special items. Remember too many of these special items may result in nothing standing out.

What color paper should you use

The traditional approach is to be conservative, therefore using, white, ivory, and light grays are recommended. However if you are in marketing or some other highly creative industry, your creativity and design could be part of your way of setting yourself apart from other applicants. It is my feeling that whatever it takes to get you in front of a potential employer is fair game however at the same time you may not want go over the top, the choice is yours.

White Space

The rule of thumb here is that be careful to leave plenty of white space. Readability is important. White space does make a difference.

Accuracy

You have put a lot of time into developing your résumé. You want to take the final step to make sure that your résumé is well-written, free of all errors, and of course pleasing to the eye. Take time to make sure that you have found all typographical errors, and miss spelled words. I am going to recommend that you proof-read your résumé very carefully several times. And if possible try to get someone that you trust to read your résumé for you. Many times you may not recognize your own mistakes. Remember that the reader is evaluating your résumé as to the

7001 Resumes-Plus Second Edition

quality you will be doing for his firm. A résumé with errors and inconsistencies communicate to the prospective employer that you are careless and this is going to kill your job search.

Your Stationary

You should always use the best stationary that you can afford. All correspondence to any organization may result in either you getting a job or losing it. It can go either way. You never know.

You could be judged on your stationary. You should always type any response to any question on good stationary. They may tell you just write a quick note. There is no such thing as just a quick note when you are applying for a job.

Whatever you submit may be put in your file and stay there for a long time. Anytime anyone sees that file they may be judging you based on whatever they see. This may or may not be your best work. Always remember to use the best to impress!

Times New Roman	Tahoma
Arial	Bookman
Book Antiqua	Garamond
CG Omega	Century Schoolbook
Century Gothic	Lucida Sans
Gill Sans MT	Verdana

Your Typestyle and size

Your typestyle known as (font) should be clean, conservative and above all easy to read. Here are recommend fonts or typestyles that are good to use.

Note: You will find that most résumés are word processed in Times New Roman however it is the least preferred (font) because this style is overused. As I have suggested through-out this

148

workbook your job is to get the attention of the reader by being creative. To do this, use a font that achieves this goal.

It is important that your résumé be read, or the important parts skimmed, if the font is too small, it will be difficult for this to be done. Therefore the reader could discard your document and proceed to the next document. Also it could have too large a font size. So after you complete your résumé, review your document. Make sure the font is not too small or too large. And pick the font that best presents your work. Remember that boldface type takes up more space so be conservative with its use. The general rule is to use from 10 to 12 point size when doing the body of your document. A lot depends on the typestyle or font.

CHAPTER THIRTEEN

THE FOLLOW-UP LETTER

After every interview or contact with a potential employer it is your responsibility to send the interviewer a Follow-up letter. This document is designed to do two things. First, you need to express your appreciation for being allowed the time to interview. If, for some reason, the interviewer has not decided upon a finalist, the follow-up letter may continue to persuade the interviewer to at least select you for a second or third interview. A good follow-up letter can be an effective marketing tool if used correctly. It is hoped that, at his time, you have a better understanding about the job you are interviewing for so you can now design this document around this new information. It gets your name, ideas, and qualifications in front of the interviewer and decision maker again.

As an example, keep in mind that there may be more applicants than just you out there. Sometime ago I am aware of an applicant who was interviewing for a management position with Staples. This applicant was told that he was selected from 80 applicants for the initial interview. For the second interview he was one of nine. May I suggest that for any good job there may be many applicants. So you want to take every opportunity to continue to sell your case. Remember you are the most valuable applicant therefore you want to do the most you can to present your skills. Each time that you talk to the employer, interviewer, or decision-maker you should send your follow-up letter discussing what transpired during the contact and continue to sell how you would be a benefit to the organization. In fact, if you have several contacts you will want several different letters that present your skills and qualifications in different ways.

Try to give a brief review of what you can do by using key points that were from your last meeting. This will remind the interviewer who you are and what was discussed. It will at least keep you in the in the interviewer's mind. This is important. You should remember that old adage, 'Out of sight, out of mind'.

Your thank your letter - Teaching

Dr. Kirt Harper
Santa Ana Unified School District
1601 East Chestnut Ave
Santa Ana, CA 92701-6322

Re: Teaching in your Horizon Program

Dear Kirt,

I want to take this moment to thank you for the time you and your colleagues spent with me discussing employment opportunities with the Santa Ana Unified School District; also to assure you that I enjoyed our meeting and conversation.

If you select me to teach in your district, I will bring the following attributes, experience, and benefits:

- I am a fully qualified Business Education teacher.
- Experience working with at 'Risk' students.
- Over ten (10) years of teaching experience at all levels, University, Adult Education, Junior College, High School and Junior High School.
- Operated a Demonstration Program for Hayward Unified School District, ROCP, and recognized by the State of California Department of Business Education.
- Taught in two (2) Juvenile Court Programs, Riverside County Department of Education and Orange County Department of Education.
- Worked with disadvantaged and culturally diverse students.
- Computer trained and competency.
- World traveled.
- Flexible and a team player

I would extremely enjoy the opportunity to teach in the Santa Ana Unified School District and look forward to continue to talk with you in the future. You may reach me at 714-996-4421.

Sincerely yours,

Gene Merhish, PhD

Sample of a Thank you letter - Teaching

Dr. Kirt Harper
Santa Ana Unified School District
1601 East Chestnut Ave
Santa Ana, CA 92701-6322

Re: Teaching in your Horizon Program

Dear Kirt,

I want to take this moment to thank you for taking the time to
talk to me on the phone, Tuesday, August 11, 1998.

I understand your concern about communication with parents however, as I pointed out, I
have been working with culturally diverse students since 1972. Plus, last year I operated
and developed a program that was identified as 'SWIFT' School with a Future, a program
designed for students who were truant, educationally handicapped, and who have behavior
problems.

I worked very closely with parents to maintain contact, indicate behavior, student
attendance, and report progress. The results were very positive, and many parents were
pleased with the improvement of their students. I have little to no problems communicating
with parents and getting their cooperation.

As I indicated, I am very interested in teaching and/or working for Santa Ana Unified
School District. If you can at all use my skills or know of any other program that could
benefit by my Business, Industrial, and Educational experience, please have them contact
me.

You may reach me almost everyday from 0800 to 1800 hours by calling at 714-966-4221, or
my Cell phone at 714-514-3434.

Sincerely yours,

Gene Merhish, PhD

Sample of a Thank you letter - Business

Mr. Larry Hill, President
Space Stampings, Inc.
5454 Circle Road
Corona, CA 92880

Dear Mr. Hill:

I want to express my appreciation for the time and consideration you extended to me during our meeting on July 7, 2006. Following our meeting, I took the opportunity to review our discussion.

I am excited about my potential association with Space Stampings, Inc. and my interest and enthusiasm continue to be high. It seemed to me that the qualifications I possess are a good match with the specifications for the position. Important strengths which we discussed include:

- REMINDER TO IDENTIFY SPECIFIC AREAS OF IMPORTANCE ONLY: i.e. THE THREE (3) MAJOR RESPONSIBILITIES, SUBJECT OR TOPICS DISCUSSED DURING THE MEETING

- INCLUDE ONLY THOSE THINGS THAT SEEM TO BE MOST CRITICAL AND IMPORTANT TO THE INTERVIEWER FOR YOUR SUCCESS IN THE POSITION.

(The following paragraph must be modified to match the outcome of the meeting.)

I will be contracting you (AS DISCUSSED DURING THE MEETING – DAY OR DATE OR BY PHONE, WHICHEVER APPLIES) and look forward to a positive response or establishing the time and place of our next meeting.

Sincerely yours,

Joe Applicant

Sample of a Thank you letter - Business

Mr. Bruce F. Reichenfeld, Vice President
West Coast Rubber Machinery
P.O. Box 2159, 7180 Scout, Ave
Bell Gardens, CA 90201

Re: Position of Responsibility Sales, Marketing Manager and/or VP Sales

Dear Bruce:

I was delighted we had the opportunity to meet Saturday, July 10, 2006. This letter and enclosures are a response to your interest in me to fulfill future managerial requirements for your firm.

My purpose: to encourage you to initiate an action that will enable me to meet with you in the near future to further discuss opportunities with your firm.

My objective: to quickly relate my experience, skills, and capacity to accept and respond to significant, continuing responsibility (requirements you may be looking for in staffing as you move your company forward.

I have functioned in/as:
Sales/Marketing/Manager/Educator/trainer in companies and organizations requiring above dedication and effort in order to achieve desired results. In the course of meeting company objectives, I have identified and improved upon opportunities that resulted in increased market share and profitable sales growth.

You may be interested in the following:

- 1987 System Salesman of the Year, Top Territory of the Year. Increased sales by 35 percent at times.
- 1986, 1987, and 1988 managed a five Million dollar sales territory as salesman.
- 1991 as a Manager, developed National sales force and increased marketing penetration, increased target Marketing and sales force training. Worked nationally and internationally.

(As a General Manager, maintained gross profits over 75% UNICO rotary repair company.
(Consultant for the Department of Business Education, State of California. Distributive Education

Conducted seminars, set goals, and orchestrated many industrial shows nationally, also budgeting, forecasting and administration.

The enclosed résumé will support the above and more. As an exploratory meeting with me will confirm it!

Although I would like to call you next week to determine if a meeting can be scheduled, I believe that to be impractical and disruptive. Rather than take your time with repeated phone calls, please call me to arrange a meeting at your convenience. I am available for interview after 9:00 a.m. everyday. And I will be available for employment after July 15, 2006 on a full-time or consulting basis. You may reach me at 714-996-4221. Or you may contact me by cell phone 714-996-3235.

Sincerely yours,

George Martin

Enclosure

Sample of a Thank you letter - General

Date:

Your address

Addressee
(If possible, use individual's name)

Dear (Addressee)

I appreciated the opportunity to talk with you on (date). The information you shared with me about (company name) was excellent, and I am excited about the possibility of applying my education and experience to the position we discussed.

If I can provide you with any additional information, please let me know. I look forward to hearing from you soon.

You may contact me at 714-541-5432 my home, or 714-541-3232 my cell phone.

Sincerely yours,

(Written Signature)

Your name typed

<u>Sample of a Thank you letter – For Plant/Office Visit</u>

Date:

Your Address

Addressee
(If possible, use individual's name)

Dear (Addressee)

Thank you for your letter on (<u>date</u>) suggesting a plant/office visit at (<u>time</u>) on the following dates (<u>list dates</u>).

The most convenient date for me would be (date). I will arrive at your office at (<u>time</u>) on the following date: (<u>list date</u>).

Enclosed is a copy of my résumé along with the application for employment (if necessary).

I appreciate the opportunity to visit your plant/office. I am very interested and eager to learn more about possible employment opportunities with (<u>organization name</u>)

Best wishes,

(Written Signature)

Your name typed

Your Letter of Acceptance - General

Date:

Your Address

Addressee
(If possible, use individual's name)

Dear (Addressee)

I am very pleased to accept your offer (state the offer) as outlined in your letter of (date). (Include all details of offer – location, starting salary, starting date.)

(Mention enclosures – application, résumé, employee forms, or other information and any related commentary.)

I am looking forward to meeting the challenges of the job and I shall make every attempt to fulfill your expectations.

Sincerely,

(Written Signature)

Your name typed

<u>Your Letter of Rejection - General</u>

Date:

Your Address

Addressee
(If possible, use individual's name)

Dear (Addressee)

After considerable thought, I have decided not to accept your offer of employment as outlined in your (<u>date</u>) letter. This has been a very difficult decision for me. However I feel I have made the correct one for this point in my career.

Thank you for your time, effort, and consideration. Your confidence in me is sincerely appreciated.

Sincerely,

(Written signature)

Your name typed

<u>Your Thank you letter – Teaching</u>

F. E. Merhish, PhD
789 West Oak Drive
Westbury Park, CA 92345

Dr. Kirk E. Seemore
Santa Robles School District
4221 Rim Dive
Santa Robles, CA 92346

RE: Instructor position in the Horizon Program

Dear Mr. Seemore:

I am taking this opportunity to thank you for the time you and your colleagues spent with me discussing employment opportunities in the Santa Robles School District. It was a pleasurable meeting for me and I trust it was informative for you.

If I am selected to teach in your district, I will bring the following attributes and experiences. All of which I feel will benefit the students in your district as well as your school district.

- ☛ I am a fully qualified Business Education instructor
- ☛ I am experienced working with 'At Risk' students
- ☛ I have over 15 years of teaching experience at all levels of teaching
- ☛ I have taught in two Juvenile Hall Programs

I look forward to hearing from you or your staff in regards to my application and interview. I am most easily reached after 6:00 p.m. at home. My home phone number is 310-555-1135.

Sincerely,

F. E. Merhish (Gene) PhD

CHAPTER FOURTEEN

SOURCES FOR JOBS

There are a great many sources for jobs. In this chapter I am going to discuss some of them here in this workbook. Before I go on I will want you to recall an earlier statement; I suggested that over 80 percent of jobs are gotten by the technique of networking. But, a point I want to make is that you do not rely on only one source. This section will not be a priority, but it will suggest areas and how they may work for you.

The first thing that comes to mind, one that you may have used in the past, is the National Job Newspaper published by the The Wall Street Journal. The cost for this tabloid is around $36.00, so it is a little pricey in my opinion, but if it works for you, then it is worth the investment. This tabloid covers jobs nationally, so you have to make the decision that you are willing to relocate. You should not restrict yourself, but this needs to be a decision you will have to make. The tabloid is much like a newspaper Help Wanted Section of your local newspaper. One thing that I want you to think about is that it will generate many applicants for few positions. Yes, the jobs in this document are upscale, but the tabloid is reaching many people seeking employment form all parts of the country. You will have to realize that this paper has a circulation

163

7001 Resumes-Plus Second Edition

of thousands of job hunters. However the Wall Street Journal tabloid also provides very valuable job search tips and other timely material, so you may find it a worthwhile investment.

I would advise you to your local newspaper, the Los Angeles Times, Orange County Register, New York Times, Press Enterprise, Long Beach Press, Des Moines Tribune, Denver Post, or what other major paper that may be circulated in your community. These papers bring not only local, but national, and some international positions; each can count on having many competitors for each position you might apply for. You may be a salesman, accountant, truck driver, engineer, teacher, or manager. You are going to want to apply for the position that is looking for your skills. But what if you are a sales manager and you answer an ad placed for an Engineer? No you are not applying for the Engineering position you are going to apply for a Marketing Management, or Sales Management position. First, you are applying for a position that is not being advertised. You are using the ad as a lead to a firm that seems to be active and growing. Therefore you automatically eliminated over 60 to 100 applicants. That's right, your have a chance to be 'Johnny on the spot' or maybe not. What I am going to suggest through out this work book is that you be creative and also 'think out of the box'. You are also going to answer the ads that request your experience and job title, and so is everyone else.

Which is better; neither! The best one is the one that gets you the job. I am going to ask you to do whatever it takes to get your career on track as quickly as you can. And that is what it's all about.

Most industrial or trade magazines have job search sections in the back where they have several job openings for various companies. These jobs are much like the ones in the newspaper in that they are open to everyone and anyone to apply for. The truth in this case, you may have a fewer number of applicants because the magazine is normally read by people in the field that the trade magazine has been created for, but you will have a large number of competitors for each job. But no stone should be left unturned. You will find these magazines published by nearly every product, association, and industry.

At your local University, Public Library, State Unemployment Office, or County Office you should find many sources for job search. There is the Thomas Guide or State Business and Manufactures directories that you can get information on companies' addresses, what the company does, and often officers within the companies'. The California Manufactures Directory is available on disk. This directory has around 36,000 manufactures in it. You can purchase this directory, but it is somewhat price at around $800.00. And I would suggest that you can purchase similar directories in your state. But you can use these books 'free' at your local city library, the only limitation is you can not check them out. With the aid of these Manufactures Directories you can identify the size of a company, what they make, officer's names, address, phone numbers, and a lot of history that assists you in determining if this is the kind of company you would like to be associated with. However, it doesn't tell you the personality of the company or business orientation attitude, but neither does the newspaper. It is a fact that it is very difficult to get attitude of business orientation. This is an important issue and will or could determine if this is the company you would really like to work for.

If you are in sales and marketing, you would most likely want to work for a firm that favors the importance of this area. It is not as simple as it seems. Some companies believe that marketing and sales are the most important elements within the firm. Others may lean another way, that sales and marketing are a necessary evil but not to be taken to seriously. I was once on a plane with a president of a middle sized company in Orange County California and during our conversation he stated that he does not have a Sales or Marketing department and really did not need one. And this is the way that he has done business for years. So if given a chance, you can ask, are you a production-oriented, or marketing-oriented firm? Does the company have a business plan, Marketing plan, 3 or 5 year plan, what is the mission or goals of the firm? We will deal with more of these questions later. But the point is to get a good fit, the personality of the company and yours, need to be close for you to be successful.

Some companies are run by engineering and for engineering. A company in aerospace may be like this. You should plan to go get an engineering degree if you get a job at this type of firm. Chances are you will not advance without an engineering degree.

If you don't know by now, more than 80% of the jobs are gotten though networking. You may not have the luxury of totally networking. You should be networking at all times. Spend some money and buy yourself some business cards. You should hand out two types of business cards – one that represents the firm you are with, this is assuming you are employed, and the another one that presents you. So if you are unemployed you need to have your own cards and give one to everyone you engage in conversation with. This is the beginnings of your 'Networking'. Or you can carry around some blank cards, but which is more professional it is up to you! As you hand out your personal business card, or the blank card with your name, phone number, and maybe a short note you are planting seeds, Networking, making it known that you are looking for employment.

Another source of information which is 'free' is your Business to Business, or Yellow-page phone book. This resource will have just about every company that is in business in your area or region that you would like to work for. However, what these directories can't do for you is give you the size of the organization, or the names of important contacts or officers within the business. You can add this source to your inventory of potential employers, and you will have a large inventory of companies to choose from.

You do not want to forget the Wall Street journal itself as a source of job search. I don't know anyone that has gotten a job out this media, but this is not to say that people don't. Depending on the degree of your pursuit, you can get every major newspaper in the country. I have found that most of these papers can be located at major bookstores and in your nearest library.

There are also local tabloids, as an example, Orange County has a business newspaper where every week besides business news, they 'showcase' a number of businesses. The tabloid identifies the president, size of the firm, what they do, address, and the phone number. The reason I like this medium is that you are getting a good source with key contact persons identified and limited competition for employment. Some of these companies may not be in the field of your expertise but the cost of this resource is right; it is 'free'. Look in your area for such a business tabloid.

While you are out looking for sources of employment information, and depending on the level of employment, you will also run into what I will call employment tabloids, these papers are circulated in Supermarkets, you will also see them in free standing newspaper dispensers. Usually these tabloids offer more entry level positions, as well as a various number of training schools. But here again, the document is 'free'.

Two other areas of references that may be overlooked by many are the 'Health Care Reference Sources & Buyers Guide' and the 'Directory of Manufacture's Sale Agencies'. The Health Care References has companies and services in the Health Care Industry. You may get this resource from Medi-Pages, Inc. 757 Cayuga Street Lewiston, New York 14092. Their phone number is 1-800-554-6661. It will give you another place to look up companies to apply too.

The Directory of Manufacturer's Sales Agents could offer a completely new source of places to send your résumé to. This book has independent sales and marketing companies that from time to time are looking for people to bring into their organizations to help expand their business, marketing, and sales. The benefit to you is that it is generally an unknown area of job opportunities. You can contact

7001 Resumes-Plus Second Edition

the Association of Manufacturers Agents at P.O. Box 3467 Laguna Hills, California 92654. The book sells for around $30.00.

Another source is the 'net', Internet, or the Web. Whatever you want to call it, it seems that there are many companies looking for qualified applicants. You must remember however, that when the call goes out for a job on the Web, that often this call is exposed world wide in scope and that these job vacancies are reaching thousands of applicants.

The net can be used both offensively and defensively. The net is used offensively when you put your résumé out on various web sites. This has the advantage of being able to get your résumé out to a lot of companies. The disadvantage is that your employer may also see your résumé on the web and lay you off. There is some protection however but you must be careful. One applicant was laid off after his boss 'discovered' the applicant's résumé on the 'web'. He then told him that he might be more comfortable looking for another full time job.

The web can also be used defensively by going out to various web sites and seeing what jobs are out there. You will be able to see what the companies are about so that you can decide if you want to send them your résumé or not. The major disadvantage to this method is that it takes a lot of time. Time is one thing that most job seekers don't have a lot of. In another chapter I will review more in depth as to how to use the Internet for job search.

If you are running out of places to send your résumé you can contact one of the many mailing list firms, like the Mailing list of Southern California, 1-800-352-7450. This company can provide you with thousands of company names and addresses.

INFORMATION SOURCES FOR MAJOR EMPLOYERS

If you are considering relocation for employment opportunities you will find the Chamber of Commerce a great source of information about potential employers. Request that the Chamber of Commerce send you a membership catalog.

The Job Search Tool to Get You That Job

Do not overlook the libraries. Go to your public or University library and talk with the head librarian or the business reference librarian. The librarian's job is to help people and they do enjoy finding solutions. The following list of directories and references can be found at your community library or University library in your area.

The Fortune Directory of U.S. Corporations

Published by Fortune Directories

229 West 28th Street, New York, NY 10001;

prepaid copies for $10.00.

This directory includes the Fortune 500 list of the largest industrial companies and the Fortune Service 500 list of top non-industrials. The lists can only help you with standings within these top 500 companies. Corporate names and addresses are not available.

Moody's Industrial Manual

Published by Moody's investor Service (A subsidiary of Dunn & Bradstreet)

99 Church Street, New York, N Y 10007

Phone 212-553-0300.

This manual is a good source of financial and business information on every industrial company listed on the New York Stock Exchange and over 500 companies listed on the regional exchanges. The manual will provide and service principle plants, management and names of resources, and directors. You will find this manual to be a very good resource in your job search.

International Directory of Corporate Affiliations

Published by National Register Publishing Company

3004 Glenview Road, Wilmette, IL 60091

This directory lists foreign companies with U.S. holdings and 1,400 U.S. corporations which have overseas affiliates, subsidiaries, and divisions. This will be helpful if you are looking for employment in a foreign country. You will also find the complete names and addresses of 95 consulates in the United States.

Directory of Leading Private Companies

Published by National Register Publishing Company

3004 Glenview Road, Wilmette, IL, 60091

This is a unique directory in that it lists invaluable information about our countries top 3,500 privately owned corporations. You will find names and title of key contacts, number of subsidiaries, numbers of employees, assets, liabilities, net worth, types of computer hardware, addresses, and phone numbers.

American Society of Training and Development Directory

Published by the Association of the same name

6000 Maryland Avenue, Suite 305, S.W. Washington, D. C. 20024

This directory covers 'Who's Who in Training and Development' throughout the United States.

Thomas Register of American Manufacturers

Published by Thomas Publishing Co.

1 Penn Plaza, New York, NY 10007

You will find this book at your local library. The register contains information about thousands of businesses, large and small, in just about every field. This is a twelve volume set of books. These books contain names, locations, phone numbers, and the products that each company is manufacturing and marketing.

Standard and Poor's Register of Corporations, Directors and Executives

Published by McGraw Hill, New York, NY 10007

This is a three volume set of books. The first volume lists all of the major companies by industry and geographic locations. The second volume gives details and contact information on these companies, and the third volume represents personal data on many corporation executives.

Dunn's Employment Opportunism Directory / The career Guide

Published by Dunn & Bradstreet, New Your, NY 1007

This is an excellent guide for the job seeker as it lists over 4,000 companies with names, titles, addresses, and phone numbers. It also provides a projection of career opportunities within each company and the educational specialties each company hires.

The National Job Bank

Published by Bob Adams, Inc.

840 Summer Street, Boston, MA 02127

In this book you will find a comprehensive directory providing information on over 8,000 major employers. The employers are listed by state. Data includes a description of each business, contact information, educational background requirements, common positions, and fringe benefits offered.

<u>OTHER HELPFUL BOOKS</u>

- Who's Hiring Who, Author: Richard Lathrop
  Published: Ten Speed Press, P.O. 7123, Berkeley, CA 94707

- What Color is Your Parachute? Author: Richard Nelson Bolles
  Published: Ten Speed Press, P.O. Box 7123, Berkeley, CA 947007

- Rites of Passage at $100,000 +, Author: John Lucht
  Published: Viceroy Press, Inc. New York, NY

- How to Teach Anyone Who is Anyone, Author: Michael Levine
  Published: Price Stern Sloan
  410 North La Cienega Blvd., Los Angeles, CA 90048

7001 Resumes-Plus Second Edition

- Jobs '97, Author: Kathryn & Ross Petras

  Published: Simon & Schuster (Fireside)

  Rockefeller Center, 1230 Avenue of the Americas, New York, NY 10020

- National Survey of Professional, Administrative, Technical and Clerical Pay

  Published annually by the Bureau of Labor Statistics (97 Pages)

  Available Government Printing Office, Bulletin 2208 S/N 029-001-02826-1,

  $4.75 Summarizes an annual survey of selected professionals, technical, and clerical

  occupations in private industry. Includes occupational definitions used in the

  survey and a table which compares salaries in the private sector to those in the

  federal government.

- The American Almanac of Jobs and Salaries, Written: John W. Wright

  Published: Avon Books (774 pages), $12.95

  Includes job descriptions, salary ranges, and advancement potential.

- The Almanac of American Employers, Written: Jack W. Plunkett

  Published: Contemporary Books, Chicago. (340), $15.95

  A guide to America's 500 most successful large corporations, profiled by rank in the

  area of salaries, benefits, financial stability, and advancement opportunity.

- How to Sell Yourself, Author: Joe Girard

  Published: Warner Books, Inc., 75 Rockefeller Plaza, New York, NY 10010

NEWSPAPER

It goes without saying that you will always want to consult the 'Help Wanted' ads in your local newspaper aspiring to the philosophy of 'not leaving any stone unturned'. It might be possible for you to find the opportunity of your dreams in a local paper. I will have to confess that a few years ago I found one of my most memorable and interesting jobs in the Press Enterprises which is the local paper in Riverside, California. You must start reading the newspaper with a different slant than you have in the past.

You could come across the opportunity of a lifetime on the front page, in the business section, editorial, sports section, and or course the want ads. You may come across an article about a new company forming in your area; a large corporation setting up a branch office, a new store, a new restaurant, a new sports stadium, or a new product. With this information you should immediately begin to think about ways that you might become involved or contact these companies. Take advantage of the information you have read.

You can be assured that there is not a day that goes by here in America that a new product is not announced or a new opportunity is presented by a company or individual. The more you read the more opportunities will make themselves available to you. Besides the local newspaper, you will want to start reading journals and publications in the area in which you are interested. There is probably a trade journal or publication in just about every industry in which you might be interested, and of course you can read newspapers from other parts of the United States.

MAGAZINES

As with the newspaper, you will find many stories about interesting and profitable companies in magazines. You will have to keep your career in mind when you are reading these publications. No matter what your interests, there is probably a magazine on the newsstand that appeals to you. The only thing I can say here is to get these magazines and read them. You could find ideas and opportunities that could offer you insights in to the 'Ideal Job' for you. This just might be the turning point in your life. Here are some magazines that may be helpful in your job search: Success, Fortune, Small Business Opportunities, Inc., Selling Power, Forbes, Time, Newsweek, Business Week, Money, and Entrepreneur.

7001 Resumes-Plus Second Edition

THE YELLOW PAGES

The Yellow Pages are another source of potential employers. You may look for 'Trade Associations' in your area of interest or specific field. The next step will be to contact the Trade Association for a membership directory. You may also want to review the category titles to find companies or products of interest and then contact employers that seem interesting.

THE INTERNET

Although I am going to spend additional time later in this Workbook discussing job search, applying for various jobs, and using job search sites on the internet, I want to suggest that you can use the internet to explore various companies and industries in your area anywhere you would like to go, by city, state, or for that matter world wide if you so desire. Last year I found an interesting company and product line in India, and explored some opportunities with the President and Vice President as a result of a product search on the Net. You can get detailed information about these firms from company Websites, product information, or by using various Search Engines such as www.yahoo.com. In most cases you can get addresses, phone numbers, contacts, products, and locations. The internet will allow you to reach out to new horizons. It is a very valuable tool that is available to you, use it.

ED-JOIN ON THE INTERNET (In California)

If you are a teacher doing job search in the state of California, you are very fortunate to be able to participate in a system called **ED-Join** (EDjoin.org). This system, found of course on the Internet, is a program developed and set up by the California County of Superintendents Educational Services Association **'ACCSESA'**. This is a premier education job search website where you can be exposed to up to 10,000 teaching jobs from k-12 for public education. So if this is your 'bent' this is a great resource for you to explore and develop your career. If you are interested in a position at the community college level you can visit **CCCJobs Registry** – Plus, or if it is an Administrative or Supervisory position you can go to **ACSA Job link page**. Outside of California look for similar sites on the Web. One Website that you can go to is **Teacher.Net**. Here you can post your résumé, do job search, and much more.

STATE EMPLOYMENT SERVICE

Every state has a Department of Employment or Labor. These services are offered at no cost to you. You will find jobs or employment opportunities for all levels. In addition there are counseling, testing, and placement services available. Consult the white pages of your telephone directory under state government listings in order to locate your local Employment Office. If you are a Veteran you will find special services available to you; so, this is 'another stone for you to overturn'.

Use the space below to list the agencies you are interested in contacting:

1. _____
2. _____
3. _____
4. _____
5. _____

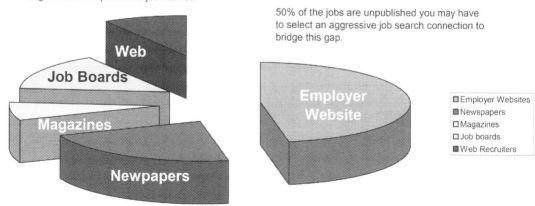

Published openings (50%) openings you can find

The market consists of employers who make public their openings. And those who don't. There are five segments to the publsihed job market.

50% of the jobs are unpublished you may have to select an aggressive job search connection to bridge this gap.

The vast majority of the published positions of the job market is available through these sources.

7001 Resumes-Plus Second Edition

ASSOCIATION INDEX

100,000 Employers	3,000 Newspapers	2,500 Trade Mag's	300 Job Boards	3,500 Recruiters

FEDERAL JOB INFORMATION CENTERS

The Federal Government employs over 1.5 million workers here in the United States and has employees in most foreign counties. The average income for this work force exceeds $30,000 a year. One important thing to keep in mind about government employment, once you go to work for the government, it is next to impossible to be fired or laid off. In addition, it is not hard to advance up the ladder.

Additional information about government employment can be obtained from your nearest library. Look for the U.S. Government Manual. The book is lengthy but it offers information about every division of the government as well as lots of names of high level officials you can contact. You will need to take some time with this book.

To purchase the U.S. Government Manual, contact the U.S. Printing Office at 1-202-783-3238. You may want to visit the Federal Job information Center of the U.S. Office of Personnel Management in your state. I am going to provide you a list of state offices, however, please check for current phone numbers and addresses as they change too fast to be 100% accurate.

Institute for Financial Education
122 Route 111, P.O. Box 728
Smithtown, N.Y. 11787
631-979-6161

National Association of Bank Women
500 N. Michigan Ave., Suite 1400
Chicago, IL 60601

American Society of Microbiology
1752 N Street N.W.
Washington, D. C. 20036
202-737-3600

Academy of Television Arts and Sciences
5220 Lankershim Blvd.
North Hollywood, Ca. 91601-3109
818-754-2800

American Sportscasters Association
225 Broadway, Suite 2030
New York, NY 10007
212-227-8080

American Women in Radio and Television
1760 Old Meadow Road, Suite 500
McLean, Va. 22102
703-506-3290

National Association of Broadcasters
1771 N Street N.W.
Washington, D. C. 20036
202-429-5300

American Business Women's Association
9100 Ward Parkway
P.O. Box 8728
Kansas City, MO 64114
800-228-0007

American Society of Professional and Executive Women
3280 Sunrise Hwy
Wantagh, N.Y. 11793
215-563-4415

Industrial Chemical Research Association
1811 Monroe St.
Dearborn, MI 48124
313-46-4555

American Institute of Chemical Engineers
3 Park Avenue
New York, NY 10016
800-242-4363

7001 Resumes-Plus Second Edition

National Association of Executive Secretaries
900 South Washington St., #G-13
Falls Church, VA 22046
703-237-8616

National Association for Legal Secretaries
8159 East 41st Street
Tulsa, OK 74145
918-582-5188

National Association of Secretarial Services
22875 Savi Ranch Parkway Suite H
Yorba Linda, CA 92887
813-823-3646

Association of the Institute for Certification of Computer Professionals
2350 E. Devon Ave
Des Plaines, IL 60018-4610
847-299-4227

Association for Computer Machinery
2 Penn Plaza, Suite 701
New York, NY 10121-0701
212-869-7440

National Cosmetology Association
401 N Michigan Avenue
Chicago, IL. 60611
866-871-0656

National Shorthand Reporters Association
118 Park Street S.E.
Vienna, Virginia 22180
703-281-4677

International Credit Association
243 N. Lindbergh Blvd.
St. Louis, MO 63141
314-991-3030

National Association of Credit Management
8840 Columbia 100 Parkway
Columbia, Maryland 21045-2158
212-947-5070

The Job Search Tool to Get You That Job

**Data Processing Management Association
(Association of Information Tech. Professionals)**
401 North Michigan Avenue, Suite 2400
Chicago, IL 60611-4267
800-224-9371 / 312-245-1070

American Dental Assistants Association
35 East Wacker Drive, Suite 1730
Chicago, IL 60601-2211
312.541.1550

American Dental Technicians Association
444 North Michigan Ave
Chicago, IL 60611
312-440-8900

American Dental Association
211 East Chicago Ave
Chicago, IL 60611
312-440-2500

American Institute for Design and Drafting
966 Hungerford Dr., Suite 10 B
Cleveland, OH 44122
216-464-7986

National Association of Business Economists
28349 Chagrin Blvd.
Cleveland, OH 44122
216-464-7986

Institute of Electrical & Electronics Engineers
345 East 47th Street
New York, NY 10017
212-705-7900

Electronics Technicians Association International
5 Depot Street
Greencastle, IN 46135
317-653-8262

Society of Women Engineers
United Engineering Center, Room 305
345 East 47th Street
New York, NY 10017
212-705-7855

7001 Resumes-Plus Second Edition

International Association for Financial Planning
2 Concourse Parkway, Suite 800
Atlanta, GA 30329
404-395-1605

Women in Film
6464 Sunset Blvd.
Hollywood, CA 90028
213-463-6040

American Institute of Floral Designers
13 West Franklin Street
Baltimore, MD 21201
301-752-3318

International Chefs Association
P.O. Box 1889
New York, NY 10116
201-825-8455

National Restaurant Association
1200 17th Street N.W.
Washington, D.C. 20036
202-331-5900

Geological Society of America
P.O. Box 9140, Penrose Place
Boulder, CO 80301
303-447-2020

Graphic Arts Technical Foundation
4515 Forbes Ave
Pittsburgh, PA 15213
412-621-6941

American Institute of Graphic Arts
1059 Third Ave.
New York, NY 10021
212-752-0813

American Home Economics Association
840 N. Lake Shore Dr.
Chicago, IL 60611
312-280-6000

The Job Search Tool to Get You That Job

American Hotel and Motel Association
1201 New York Ave, Suite 600
Washington, D.C. 20005-3917
202-289-3100

American Society for Personnel Administration
606 North Washington St.
Alexandria, Virginia 22314
703-548-3440

Industrial Relations Research Association
7226 Social Science Building
1720 I Street N.W.
Washington, D.C. 20006

American Academy of Actuaries
1720 I Street N.W.
Washington, D. C. 20006

Independent Insurance Agents of America
100 Church Street, 19th Floor
New York, NY 10007
212-285-4250

American Society of Interior Designers
1430 Broadway
New York, NY 10018
212-944-9220

American Bar Association
750 North Lake Shore, Dr.
Chicago, IL 60611
312-988-5000

National Association of Legal Assistants
1601 South Main, Suite 300
Tulsa, OK 74120
917-587-6828

Environmental Management Association
1019 Highland Ave.
Largo, FL 33540
813-586-5710

7001 Resumes-Plus Second Edition

American Telemarketing Association
5000 Van Nuys Blvd. Suite 200
Sherman Oaks, CA 91403
800-440-3335

American Marketing Association
250 South Wacker Dr., Suite 200
Chicago, IL 60606
312-648-0536

American Society of Mechanical Engineers
345 East 47th
New York, NY 10017
212-705-7722

American Association of Medical Assistants
20 North Wacker Drive, Suite 1575
Chicago, IL 60606
312-899-1500

American Medical Association
535 Dearborn Street
Chicago, IL 60606
312-645-5000

American Society of Metals, International
Metals Park, OH 44073
216-338-5151

National Association for Practical Nurse Education
1400 Spring Street, Suite 310
Silver Springs, MD 20916
301-588-2491

American Optometric Student Association
243 North Lindbergh
St. Louis, MO 63141
314-991-4100

American Society for Training and Development
P.O. Box 1440
1630 Duke Street
Alexandria, Virginia 22313

THE JOB SEARCH TOOL TO GET YOU THAT JOB

American Petroleum Institute
1220 L. Street N. W.
Washington, D.C. 20005
202-682-8000

Student American Pharmaceutical Association
2215 Constitution Ave. N.W.
Washington, D.C. 20037
202-628-4410

Associated Photographers International
P.O. Box 4055
22231 Mulholland Highway, # 19
Woodland Hills, CA 91365
818-888-9270

National Free Lance Photographers Association
10 South Pine Street
Doylestown, PA 18901
215-348-5578

American Psychological Association
1200 17th Street N.W.
Washington, D. C. 20036
202-955-7600

Public Relations Society of America
33 Irving Place
New York, NY 10003
212-995-2230

International Association of Business Communication
870 Market Street, Suite 940
San Francisco, CA 94102
415-433-3400

National Association of Purchasing Management
P.O. Box 2210
2055 East Centennial Circle
Tempe, AZ 85285-2160
602-752-NAPM

7001 Resumes-Plus Second Edition

Institute of Real Estate Management
430 North Michigan Ave
Chicago, IL 60611
312-661-1930

National Retail Merchants Association
Statler Tower, Suite 458
Cleveland, OH 44115
216-771-6640

National Association for Professional Saleswomen
P.O. 255708
Sacramento, CA 95865
916-484-1234

American Society for Industrial Security
1655 North Ft. Meyer Drive, Suite 1200
Arlington, VA 2209
703-522-5800

International Union of Tool, Die and Mold Makers
71 East Cherry Street
Rahway, N.J. 07065
201-388-3323

National Association of Business and Educational Radio
1501 Duke Street
Alexandria, Virginia 22134
703-739-0300

American Society of Travel Agents
1101 Ring Street
Alexandria, Virginia 2202
202-965-7520

International Association of Tour Managers
North American Region
1646 Chapel Street
New Haven, Connecticut 06511
203-777-5994

International Television Association
6311 North O'Connor Road, Suite 110
Irving, TX 75039
214-869-1112

The Job Search Tool to Get You That Job

American Society of Radiologic Technologists
15000 Central Avenue S.E.
Albuquerque, N.M. 87123
505-298-4500

American Society of Travel Agents
4400 Mac Arthur Blvd. N. W.
Washington, D.C. 20007
202-965-7520

American Welding Society
P.O. Box 351040
550 N. W. Lejeune Road
Miami, Fl. 33126
305-443-9353

OFFICE OF PERSONNEL MANAGEMENT

FEDERAL JOB INFORMATION CENTERS

ALABAMA: Huntsville
Southerland Building, 806 Governors Dr. S. W., 35801
Office Hours, M-F 9:00 a.m. for 4:00 p.m. (self-service)
205-544-5802, 24 hour recorded message

ALASKA: Anchorage
Federal Building, 701 C St. Room B 118, 99513
Office Hours: Tuesday, Wednesday, & Thursday, 11:00 a.m. to 1:00 p.m.
907-271-5821, 24 hour recorded message

ARIZONA: Phoenix
U.S. Postal Service Bldg. 522 W. Central Ave, 85004
Office Hours: M-F 9:00 a.m. to 12:00 p.m.
602-261-4736, 24 hour recorded message

ARKANSAS: Little Rock
Federal Building, 700 W. Capitol Ave, Room 3421, 72201
Office Hours: Monday, Tuesday, Thursday, 12:00 p.m. to 4:00 p.m.
Wednesday & Friday, 8:00 a.m. to 4:00 p.m.
501-378-5842, 24 hour recorded message

CALIFORNIA: Los Angeles
Linder building, 845 S. Figueroa, 3rd Floor, 90017
Office Hours: M-F 9:00 a.m. 3:00 p.m. (Closed 12:00 to 1:00 p.m.)
213-894-3360, 24 hour recorded message

7001 Resumes-Plus Second Edition

Sacramento
1029 Q Street, Room 100, 95814
Office Hours: M-F 9:00 a.m. to 12:00 p.m.
916-551-1464, recorded message

San Diego
889 Front Street, Room 4-S-9, 92188
Office Hours: M–F 9:00 a.m. to 12:00 p.m., (12:00 p.m. self serve)
619-293-6165, 24 hour recorded message

San Francisco
211 Main St., Room 235, 94105
Office Hours: 9:00 a.m. to 12:00 p.m.
415-974-9725, 24 hour recorded message

COLORADO: Denver
P.O. Box 25167, 80225
12345 Alameda Pkwy, Lakewood, CO
Office Hours: M-F 9:00 a.m. to 3:45 p.m. (self service)
Personal assistance 12:00 p.m. to 3:45 p.m.
303-236-4160 or 303-236-4161, 24 hour information
Request forms 24 hours a day, 303-236-4159

For the following states: North Dakota 303-236-4163, South Dakota 303-236-4164, Montana 303-236-4162, Utah 303-236-4165, Wyoming 303-236-4166.
Request forms 24 hours a day, call 303-236-4159

THE JOB SEARCH TOOL TO GET YOU THAT JOB

CONNECTICUT: Hartford
Federal Building, 450 Main Street, Room 613, 06103
Office hours: Monday – Thursday, 9:00 a.m. to 2:00 p.m.
203-722-3096, 24 hour recorded message 203-722-2320

DELAWARE: See Philadelphia, Pennsylvania listing.

DISTRICT OF COLUMBIA: Metro Area
1900 East Street, N.W. 1416, 20415
Office Hours: M-F 8:30 a.m. to 2:00 p.m.
202-653-8468, recorded message M-F 8:30 a.m. to 3:30 p.m.

FLORIDA: Orlando
Commodore Building, 3444 McCrory Place, Room 125, 32803-3712
Office Hours: M-F 9:00 a.m. to 4:00 p.m. (self-service)
305-648-6148, 24 hour recorded message

GEORGIA: Atlanta
Richard B. Russell Federal Bldg
75 Spring Street S.W., Room 960, 30303
Office Hours: M-F 9:00 a.m. to 4:00 p.m. (self service)
404-331-4315, 24 hour recorded message

GUAM: Agana
Pacific News bldg., 238 O'Hara Street, Room 902, 96910
Office Hours: M-F 9:30 a.m. to 4:00 p.m. (self service)
404-331-4315, 24 hour recorded message

HAWAII: Honolulu (and other Hawaiian islands and overseas)
Federal Bldg., 300 Ala Moana Blvd. Room 5316, 96850
Office Hours: M-F 9:00 a.m. to 12:00 noon
Oahu, 808-546-8600, 24 hour recorded message
Other Hawaiian Islands and Overseas, 808-546-7108

IDAHO: See Washington listing

ILLINOIS: Chicago
175 West Jackson Blvd., Room 519, 60604
312-353-6192
Office hours: M-F 8:00 a.m. to 4:30 p.m. (self service)
M-F 9:00 a.m. to 12:00 p.m.
312-353-6192, after hour telephone recorded message

7001 Resumes-Plus Second Edition

INDIANA: Indianapolis
Minton-Capehart Federal Bldg. 575 North Pennsylvania Ave, 46214
Office Hours: M-F 7:00 a.m. to 6:00 p.m. (self service)
Telephone service M-F 9:00 a.m. to 1:00 p.m., 317-269-7161
312-353-7161, recorded message after telephone hours

IOWA: Des Moines
210 Walnut Street, Room 191, 50309
Office Hours: Monday, Wednesday, Friday 8:00 a.m. to 11:00 a.m.
515-284-4545, recorded message
Scott County 312-353-5136
Pottawattamie County, 402-221-3815

KANSAS: Wichita
One Twenty Bldg., 120 South Market Street, Room 101, 67202
Office Hours: M-F 9:00 a.m. to 12:00 p.m.
Recorded Message: M-F, 9:00 a.m. to 3:00 p.m., 316-269-6106
In Johnson, Leavenworth, and Wyandotte Counties, 816-374-5702

KENTUCKY: See Ohio listing

LOUISIANA: New Orleans
F. Edward Hebert Bldg, 610 South Maestri Place, Room 802, 701130
504-589-2764, Office Hours: M-F, 10:00 a.m. to 2:30 p.m.
(closed 12:00-12:30) Recorded message after hours 504-589-2764

MAINE: See New Hampshire listing

MARYLAND: Baltimore
Garmatz Federal Bldg., 101 West Lombard Street, 21201
Office Hours: M-F 9:00 a.m. to 4:00 p.m.
Recorded message: 301-962-3822

D.C. area: See District of Columbia listing

MASSACHUSETTS: Boston
John W. McCormack Post Office and Courthouse (Lobby), 02109
Office Hours: M-F 9:00 a.m. to 4:00 p.m., 617-223-2571
617-223-1775 or 617-223-1776, 24 hour recorded message

MICHIGAN: Detroit
477 Michigan Ave., Room 565, 48226
Office Hours: M-F 8:00 a.m. to 4:00 p.m.
Telephone Service, M-F, 12:00 to 4:00 p.m., 313-226-6950
Recorded message after telephone hours, 313-725-4430

THE JOB SEARCH TOOL TO GET YOU THAT JOB

MINNESOTA:
Twin Cities
Federal Bldg. Ft. Snelling, Twin Cities, 55111
Office Hours: M-F, 9:00 a.m. to 12:00 p.m.
Telephone Service, M-F 12:30 p.m. to 3:30 p.m., 912-723-4430

MISSISSIPPI:
Jackson
100 West Capitol Street, Suite 335, 39269
Office Hours: M-F 9:00 a.m. to 1:00 p.m.,
Telephone 601-965-4585
Recorded message after office hours: 601-965-4585

MISSOURI:
Kansas City
Federal Bldg., 601 East 12th Street, Room 134, 64106
Office Hours: Monday, Wednesday, Friday, 8:00 a.m. to 11:00 a.m.
Recorded message: 816-374-5702

St. Louis
Old Post Office, 815 Olive Street, Room 400, 63101
Office Hours: Monday, Wednesday, Friday, 8:00 a.m. to 11:00 a.m.
Recorded message: 314-425-4380

MONTANA:
See Colorado Listing

NEBRASKA:
Omaha
U.S. Courthouse and Post Office Building, 215 North 17th Street
Room 1010, 68102
Office hours: Monday, Wednesday, Friday, 8:00 a.m. to 12:00 p.m.
Recorded message: M-F, 9:00 a.m. to 3:00 p.m. 402-221-3815

NEVADA:
See Sacramento, California listing

NEW HAMPSHIRE: Portsmouth
Thomas J. McIntyre Federal Bldg, 80 Daniel Street, Room 104 03801
603-433-0763
Office Hours Monday – Thursday 9:00 a.m. - 2:00 p.m.
402-223-3815, 24 hour recorded message

NEW JERSEY:
Newark
Peter W. Rodino Jr. Federal Bldg. 970 Broad Street, Room 104, 07102
Office Hours M-F 9:30 a.m. to 4:30 p.m.
Recorded message M-F, 8:30 a.m. 5:00 p.m., 201-645-3673
In Camden, 215-597-7440

189

7001 Resumes-Plus Second Edition

NEW MEXICO: Albuquerque
Federal Bldg., 421 Gold Ave, South West, 87102
Office Hours: Monday – Thursday, 8:00 a.m. to 12:00 p.m.
505-766-5583, 24 hour recorded message
In Dona Ana, Otero, and El Paso Counties: 505-766-1893

NEW YORK: New York City
Jacob K. Javits Federal Building, 26 Federal Plaza, 10278
Office hours: M-F, 8:30 a.m. to 4:00 p.m.
Recorded message: M-F, 7:30 a.m. to 4: p.m., 212-264-0422

Syracuse
James N. Hanley Federal Bldg., 100 South Clinton Street, 13260
Office Hours: M-F, 9:00 a.m. to 3:00 p.m., 315-423-5660

NORTH CAROLINA: Raleigh
Federal Bldg., 310 Bern Ave., P.O. Box 25069, 27611
Office hours: M-F, 9:00 a.m. to 4 p.m. (self service)
919-856-4361, 24 hour recorded message

NORTH DAKOTA: See Colorado listing.

OHIO: Dayton
Federal Bldg., 200 West 2nd Street, 45402
Office hours: Monday, Tuesday, Thursday, Friday, 10:00 a.m. to 2:00 p.m.
Telephone service: M-F, 8:00 a.m. to 11:00 a.m., 513-225-2720
Record message after telephone hours: 513-225-2720

OKLAHOMA: Oklahoma City
200 N. W. Fifth Street, Room 205, 73102
Office hours: Monday – Thursday, 10:00 a.m. to 3:00 p.m.,
(Closed 12:00 to 1:00 p.m.)
405-231-49498, 24 hour recorded message

OREGON: Portland
Federal Building, 1220 South West Third Street, Room 376, 97204
Office hours: M-F, 12:00 p.m. to 3:00 p.m.
503-221-3141, 24 hour recorded message

PENNSYLVANIA: Harrisburg
Federal Bldg., Room 168, P.O. Box 761, 17108
Office hours: Monday, Tuesday, Thursday, Friday, 8:00 a.m. to 12:00 p.m.

THE JOB SEARCH TOOL TO GET YOU THAT JOB

Philadelphia
Wm J. Green, Jr. Federal Bldg. 600 Arch Street, Room 1416, 19106
Office hours: M-F, 9:00 a.m. to 3:30 p.m., 215-597-7440

PUERTO RICO: San Juan
Federico Depetau Federal Bldg., Carlos E. Chardon Street
Hato Rey, P. R. 00918
Office hours: Monday, Wednesday, Friday, 8:30 a.m. to 12:00 p.m.
Recorded message, M-F, 7:30 a.m. to 4:00 p.m., 809-753-4209

RHODE ISLAND: Providence
John D. Pastore Federal Bldg., Room 310, Kennedy Plaza, 02903
Office hours: Monday – Wednesday, 10:00 a.m. to 1:00 p.m.
401-428-5251

SOUTH CAROLINA: Charleston
334 Meeting Street, 29403
Office hours: M-F, 9:00 a.m. to 4:00 p.m. (self service)
803-724-4328, 24 hour recorded message

SOUTH DAKOTA: see Colorado listing

TENNESSEE: Memphis
100 North Bldg., Suite 1312, 38103
Office hours: M-F, 9:00 a.m. to 4:00 p.m. (self service)
901-521-3956, 24 hour record message

TEXAS: Dallas
1100 Commerce Street, Room 6B4, 75242
Office hours: M-F, 10:00 a.m. to 3:00 p.m. (closed 12:00 to 1:00 p.m.)
214-767-8035, 24 recorded message

Houston
701 San Jacinto Street, 4th Floor, 77002
Office hours: Monday, Tuesday, Thursday, Friday, 8:00 a.m. to 12:00 p.m.
713-226-2375, 24 hours recorded message

UTAH: See Colorado listing

VERMONT: See New Hampshire listing.

VIRGINIA: Norfolk
Federal Bldg., 200 Granby Mall, Room 220, 23510
Office hours: M-F, 9:00 a.m. to 4:00 p.m. (self service)
804-441-3355, 24 hour recorded message

7001 Resumes-Plus Second Edition

D.C. area See the District of Columbia listing

WASHINGTON: Seattle
Federal bldg., 951 Second Ave., 98174
Office hours: M-F, 9:00 a.m. to 12:00 (self service)
12:00 p.m. to 3:30 p.m.
206-442-4365, 24 hour recorded message

WEST VIRGINIA: Charleston
Federal Bldg., 500 Quarrier Street, Room 1017, 25301
Office hours: Tuesday – Friday, 12:00 p.m. to 4:00 p.m.
Recorded message 304-347-5174

WISCONSIN: Counties of Grant, Iowa, Lafayette, Dane, Green, Rock, Jefferson, Walworth, Waukesha, Racine, Kenosha, and Milwaukee, call 312-353-618 All other Wisconsin residents refer to the Minnesota listing.

WYOMING: See Colorado Listing

FUNCTIONS OF THE JOB INFORMATION CENTERS

Here is how the job information Centers work. The Federal Job Opportunity List publishes a list on the 1st and 15th of each month. The Federal Job List has job openings in local areas as well as selected positions nationwide and worldwide.

You will find that these lists are very lengthy so they will only be posted. A copy will not be available. Review each listing and make notes on the jobs that are of interest to you. Each job description will tell you how to apply, the grade level, pay, location, number of vacancies, and how to get the forms to apply for the position.

The starting grade level is GS-1 which as a pay level is about the same as minimum wage. A GS-12 grade level pays approximately $16.00 an hour. It is possible, with experience and time on the job, to be promoted to a GS-18 grade level which pays approximately $68,000 per year or higher.

The Job Search Tool to Get You That Job

After you have checked the list and found something interesting, you can also contact the State Employment Service. They have a copy of the Federal Job Opportunity list. Find the nearest State Employment Service location to obtain a copy.

No one agency of the government does the hiring. You will have to apply to each division that has a job of interest to you. The application process is similar to a private sector job. You have to interview and sell yourself. 'Networking' can help you get your foot in the door. Like the private sector, many times knowing someone will help you get the job. You may want to consider visiting the offices of your U. E. Representative and/or your U.S. Senator. Inform your representative or Senator that you would appreciate any help that they may be able to give, for example an introduction to anyone they might know in the agency that you are interested in working for. You may be surprised with the help you may get. Be sure that you have the name of the agency, location, and name of the hiring authority before you ask for such favor.

It is necessary when you apply for a Federal job that you submit form SF171 which is essentially a government application form. The forms are available where you find the Federal Job Opportunity List. The form must be completed before you go to an interview. You will also want to take your résumé which reflects your skills and experiences toward the job description you are responding to. Like responding to a private sector job, you will want to show how your job experience and qualifications make you the best suited for the position.

For every position you find of interest from the Federal Job Opportunity List, you will want to fill out a separate copy of the 'Prospective Employer Information and Follow-up Form'.

NOTE: For additional information about Federal Jobs, read the **Directory of Employment Opportunities** in the Federal Government by Stephen E. Vogel. It is published by Arco Publishing, Inc., 215 Park Ave. South, New York, NY 10003

7001 Resumes-Plus Second Edition

WARNING WARNING WARNING

You may find ads in the newspapers throughout the country which may read something like the following:

'Government Jobs' $15,400 to $72,500, now hiring'

These ads are not placed by the Government agencies. They are placed by people selling information. They have no authority to hire, and you can get all the information you need about Government jobs from the agencies' addresses provided in earlier pages.

IDENTIFYING THE SPECIFIC JOB OR THE IDEAL JOB

I have asked you to do some research to find out information about a company or organization you have heard about or read about in the newspaper or other source. I am now going to give you some ideas as to how to proceed after you research the job and company.

1. First, contact someone you might know in the company or organization. Get on the phone and talk with everyone you know. 'Networking,' right? Then get the name of an employee. Let me say this; I can see you saying to yourself, "What is this nut talking about, this is a lot of work", Right! Think for a minute how many others out there are going to do this. Not many. No one said this was going to be easy. Not me! The only one who is going to benefit from this is YOU!

2. After you have gotten the name, call the contact / person and introduce yourself. Tell him or her who suggested you call them. Then ask if he/she knows the name of the person who is the decision-maker on hiring. It would be to your advantage to discuss the job description. If this person does not know, get another contact within the organization and continue to do your networking until you get the answers to all your questions. It would be beneficial if you record every name and all comments.

The Job Search Tool to Get You That Job

3. Next you will want to visit the organization if at all possible. We are aware of the fact there may be limitations as to logistics, time, and money. But if at all possible, you want to know if you will fit in. Are the people you meet the kind of people you would like to work with? Are they friendly, receptive, and smiling? Do the employees look happy to be employed there? Is the overall environment inviting.

While you are there, you can confirm what you know or get answers to questions you do not know, discuss the job description, get financial reports and product brochures, and see the company's business. If possible, find out if the position is a new one or if it is replacing a terminated employee. Find out the name of the person if you can so that you might contact him/her.

You might ask, 'Well, who should I talk to'? Talk to everyone from the 'gatekeeper' (secretary) to the janitor. Ask them if they are happy with their job. Be a good 'listener'. This can be invaluable in getting people to respond to you.

Listening makes people feel important. People also enjoy helping others when given the opportunity. The receptionist can be a very good source of information. They are out in front exposed to a lot that is going on in the organization. They normally have the position because they are very outgoing and willing to talk.

If you still come up short in regards to information about the company you are interested in, ask the receptionist for the name of the nicest person in the Personnel Department. Next, go to the department and ask for this person. Tell this person you were told that he/she was identified as the nicest person in the department. You have given the individual a reputation to live up to, hopefully they will. Inform him/her that you are applying for the _____ position. Ask if there is a written job description, or if someone could explain what the organization is looking for. You can also ask about the person that had the position before. Was this person promoted, downsized, or did they quit? What you learn about the ex-employee, such as punctuality and absenteeism, you can incorporate these issues in

195

7001 Resumes-Plus Second Edition

your cover letter. If you do contact the employee, you can compare their story with those that you heard. You may decide after your research that you may not find this job to your liking. On the other hand, you may indeed discover that this could be your 'ideal job'.

4. You can go to the library and check out the company, its financial strength, ownership, offices, products, time in business, branches, and other valuable information. Consult Dunn & Bradstreet Directories, Fitch Corporation, Moody's Industrial Manual, Standard and Poor's Register of Corporations, Thomas' Register of American Manufacturers, and Who's who in Finance and Industry. You may find the name of the contact in your search listed in one of the Who's Who books.

Any time you have trouble finding information at the library, see the reference librarian. He/she works with this information everyday and will be able to direct you very quickly.

5. If you are to work for a national company at a new branch, take the time to visit and talk to the employees as I indicated above. Of course, it is necessary to locate phone numbers and addresses of branches in other cities or states. You can call and talk to people who hold the position you are applying for in other areas to gain their help and information. Before you call, make sure that you have all the questions written down to save their time, and of course your time too, your trouble and phone costs.

6. You can visit competitors of the firm you intend to interview. Tell them your intent, be honest. Ask them their opinion of the firm. I would say that in most cases they will be truthful although some of the information may not be totally objective. You will find out things you did not know.

7. A lot of work, right? It sure is, but I would not want to do this again if I could help it. Go home, take the information you have and put together a 'knock-em-dead' cover letter and résumé. You will have some valuable experience to take forward. You will get better and better the more times you do this.

196

The Job Search Tool to Get You That Job

You will have discovered a networking system, and the employer may delay running an ad or contracting an employment agency in lieu of discussing future openings with you as a result of your phone call.

CHAPTER FIFTEEN

IS THERE A JOB INTERNET FOR YOU?

Today a new media has come on the scene, this is the Internet. It professes to bring us everything from financing our home to finding us a new career. But just what does the Internet do for us as far as career development and job search? One thing we can quickly find out is there is a vast **sea** of information, and places to spend a lot of time looking for answers.

The first thing we need to understand is how to use the Internet. The internet can be confusing. It can be used to get information on many sources and topics. The person who knows how to find the right route to what they need will be able to find what they are looking for quickly.

One of the most important tools you need to learn would be terms like '**Search Engine**'. There are other methods you will need to learn in the performing and refining of your Internet searching skills.

To get started you will need to get online and get a Browser. But before we go any further you need to be acquainted with:

(Web directory   (Search Engines   (Metasearch tools

(Off-line   (Personal Web Agents   (Push Technology

(On line Data bases

7001 Resumes-Plus Second Edition

You also need to be able to use a **Web Directory** to establish your topic, and in this case we want to explore **'Career and Job Search'.** The Web Directory is a no-nonsense tool that gets the job done. However, remember that Web Directories cover only a small fraction of the pages available on the World Wide Web.

The '**Search Engine**' will cover much more than the Web directories can. So know how to use them if you do not want to waste your time.

For **General information**, start with a Web directory. Use Yahoo or Magellan. So let us see what we can find on these sites that could help us.

As you will see on YAHOO.com you can '**click**' on Careers, this in turn will open up windows that will give you information on building and storing your résumé and Job listings, also a browser will allow you to select various career areas that will have postings on jobs titles, companies, locations, and in some cases pay levels. Since this information is so voluminous and dynamic, and changing all the time, I am only going to show you a Web site and a few selected windows so that you can experience what is available on this Web site.

Let me say this, and I am sure I will repeat it many times throughout this book. Getting a job is a '**job within itself**'. You will have to find this Web Site and explore it to determine if it has the kind of information you can use. One thing I must point out is that I believe the information is valuable, but the jobs are all over the country, if not the world and the information is viewed by thousands of job seekers. So understand you are in a great deal of competition with any of the jobs that you would apply for on any of these sites.

Today we discover, according to the data on **YAHOO.com,** that the most popular jobs are Data Entry, Management Trainee, Entry Level Communications, Receptionist, Administrative Assistants, Pharmaceutical Sales, and Customer Service. These are '**hot**' today, but what about tomorrow. Well, it is your duty to explore various careers and watch to see what doors are opening and closing. Many jobs are popular today, but as trends change, jobs come and go out of '**vogue**'. Recently it was announced on the television that individuals today will have as many as ten (10) jobs during their career.

What you are going to find on the following pages are some samples of Web pages which by filling in the various blanks you can get started on your job search on the internet. I am going to share with you some of the '**hottest**' places on the Web where you can find jobs of all kinds. And also place your résumé.

As you will see Yahoo.Careers is one of many job sites. However, you need to get familiar with the format. You will find that most of these sites are similar.

You can go to www.4work.com – You'll find opportunities listed under such categories as: Jobs, Internships, Volunteer, and Part-time. You can register your own 'job Alert Profile.' You will find an e-Mail based matching system for you, the job seeker, and potential employers,

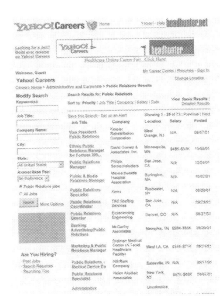

or search listings of job opportunities all over the U.S. I tried several searches and found a great deal of success with sales and sales Management positions in California. Also there are many technical jobs in big cites. Of course, I am talking about finding job announcements. I can't say if one could really get a job here. I have no real evidence of that at is time. However if it evolves I will include this information later in the book. For example: there were a lot of Sales Management positions in Northern California around San Jose and San Francisco. Also Sale Management jobs in the Los Angeles and Orange county areas. For 'Technical' there seemed to be more opportunity in the Atlanta and New York areas.

One thing I want you to remember, the downside with this site is that you are getting a lot of competition as well as getting the opportunity to see what is really out there over the horizon. Here also, is a place for the Internet volunteer and non-profit organizations to find one another. No matter how competitive this site might be when you're looking for a job, you owe it to yourself to check it out.

Another site to seek out is www.6figurejobs.com. This is a good site for executives, as its name suggests, CEO's, consultants, attorneys, physicians, financial analysts and other **'big hitters'** will probably benefit most from this site. For you who are just starting out this isn't a site you. You don't want to spend a lot a time on this site but it will give you some idea of what you might be looking toward in the future.

For an individual that is searching in big cities or in coastal states this would be, more than likely, a good place to get the best results. The site includes secure résumé and cover letter posting capabilities, a service that broadcasts résumés to recruiters, and information about featured companies.

Career resources are excellent on this site. They include an executive library of helpful books and magazines, advice columns, a newsletter, a learning center for career development and further education, a salary guide and more. So for information on www.6figurejobs.com this site is worth reviewing as the information provides a career resource.

If you are a high-tech computer or engineering person www.americanjobs.com is a good place for you. This site is recognized by Fortune magazine, CareerXroads, Weddles, and The Recruiters Bible as one of the most cost-effective sites on the Internet. For you entry level folks this may <u>not</u> be the site for you, but for you guys that are more qualified you can post a résumé, read employer profiles which are posted alphabetically, search for jobs by state, industry and job title; and take advantage of a large number of links to career resources for everything from reference checks to the best restaurants for your power lunch. This is a good web site as it is fast and easy to navigate.

An interesting designed site is www.preferredjobs.com. This site is linked to websites of companies posting jobs. You will also find a search engine also linked to **Careerbuilder.com** for 'mega search' capabilities. You will search by area, job type and other criteria, or go straight to the company you would like to work for and see what jobs they have available. You will find an advanced search function that supposedly picks up keywords within a company's ad, but may not work as well as it should. In addition you can go to an online career bookstore and job fair. You will also find a **'job wanted'** forum where you can link your résumé. What I like about 'Careerbuilder' is that if you have an email account you can set up with them to post to the site jobs you might be interested in, they will do this on a daily bases, or you can program how often you want the data delivered to you, job types and locations.

One of the problems with these types of links is the fact that it is hard to know if they get much exposure to potential employers. And like other sites, you will be able to get lots of advice from the Career Center which includes help with writing a résumé. For you guys out there that might be interested in getting involved in internship programs, which I would suggest many of you take a very close look at. You will find exposure to these programs here. Internships are a good way to get your feet in the door. You will also find salary surveys, newsgroups and other career links.

For an excellent site that lists nearly one million jobs go to www.ajb.dni.us. This site has jobs from state unemployment agencies and directly from employers. And since it is free for both job seekers and employers, for you entry level individuals this site may provide you with a good source of jobs. The site also provides nationwide job listings from the U. S. Department of Labor and can be searched by job title, keyword, military code or job number, or your zip code.

The jobs listed can be checked off if you're interested in compiling a list of possibilities. When you see a job you like, you can click on the links. The **JOB BANK** also offers a profile of your state, wage and trend information related to your job type, outlook on the U.S. job market and other career resources. This is a very comprehensive site which also links to state

7001 Resumes-Plus Second Edition

employment service websites. And you will find it a fast and useful site. There is no question; I would suggest that the entry level individual spend some time searching this site.

One thing I have always suggested is that job search is not an easy undertaking and is very time consuming. I am going to suggest that a 'rule of thumb' on job search is six (6) hours per day. My slant on it is that it is your job and you owe it to yourself to do your best at it.

If we have resent college grads or folks that are moving onto a new career track you will find that www.analyzemycareer.com an excellent site. I like this site; you can take aptitude, personality, occupational and entrepreneurial skills tests to discover your skills, abilities, and attitudes. I personally think that you should take the time to do some self evaluation. I am of the opinion that at different points in your life, your career needs will change and these self evaluations my help you in determining your new direction.

You will find an extensive database that lists thousands of careers, job outlooks, salary, work requirements and other statistics. If you are involved in training, this part of the site may provide valuable information as to where or what training you may need to get that job of choice. A job search engine provides links to other sites that offer searches for specific careers. You will also find a college search feature. On this site there is no place for the posting of your résumé and no employer search.

A career alternative which you might want to consider is opportunities working for the Army in a civilian capacity. You can go to www.cpo.army.mil and can enter a job number if you know it or click on a map of the 50 states to target opportunities in your area or area of interest. Be it at this site or any of the others, if you are willing to relocate, it will give you a great job opportunity selection. After you have selected your area of interest you can narrow it by field and other criteria. Special occupational categories include morale/welfare recreation, entry-level civilian careers, career programs positions, reserve military technician positions and hard-to-find medical positions.

204

THE JOB SEARCH TOOL TO GET YOU THAT JOB

Also you will find a résumés builder, employment opportunities in Europe, government-wide vacancy announcements, salary calculators and a wealth of information on other opportunities available in the army.

Now we go to this site which identifies itself as the best jobs in the USA www.bestjobsusa. com. Bestjobs' seems to be better for business and professional searches than careers in art, teaching or social work. The site also seems to be geared to people looking for jobs in specific geographic locations. There is employment information, job listings and career links for each state. You will find on the site information on local companies and insights from hiring professionals. You will find links to other career resources, job fairs, best employers, best places to live and work salary surveys and career-related publications. The site will provide security by providing **RÉSUMÉ MASKING**. This will protect your contact information if you post a résumé.

For work-at-home categories, headhunters, and résumé postings lets go to www.bigjobs. net. You will also find many links to other sites but you may go to a help site or a site that is trying to sell you something so you will have to screen the information. However, you can post your résumé here but there is no information on how you can keep your résumé secure. To do your searching you can search by keyword, company, U.S. or international locations. Some of the career tools include relocation information, benefits, job tips, a salary wizard, and salary news. All this comes however with pop-up advertising and flashing stuff. This is not the easiest site to navigate or to find what you are looking for, but there is some good information.

For a fun and friendly, easy-to-use job site go to www.brassring.com. Here we will find a job site targeted for the 'twenty-something' in the high tech industry, but it is also good for any age. You will find the site well organized with a lot of reliable and first-rate information related to job-hunting. You will find much needed information on self-presentation, also résumés, career events, information on featured cities, and links to international sites. The JOB SEARCH function will yield the best results for high-tech careers, but the career advice you may find invaluable for all fields. You can post your résumé on this site with confidential blocking functions to make sure that your identity is secure.

For first-rate articles and an excellent career center go to www.careerexchange.com. This site is Business Weeks magazine. You will find career tools such as a career Newsletter, a question and answer forum, and links to companies hiring MBAs. It is apparent that the site is not for the entry level job searcher but it is worth talking about. You will find a company research tool that includes a career news letter, and a question and answer forum. There are some cost of living comparisons for different cities, salary comparisons, MBA programs, education information and forums. Also an executive recruitment search tool, Leaders Online, matches you to companies seeking middle managers and executives in the $75,000 to $180,000 salary range. I would recommend that the entry level person spend much time here as you can see the emphasis is on individuals with post graduate degrees.

How about a site with emphasis on the student about to graduate and enter the world of work! If this is for you, then www.campuscareercente.com is it. This site works as a resource to match the students' background and interests with opportunities at major companies. The recruitment services include résumés posted and extensive information about top businesses worldwide. You are to fill out a profile that can be searched by participation companies using keywords and job titles. A bulletin board is also available in the STUDENT CENTER which features lists of jobs and internships available. There's also a library, career resources, and lots of helpful advice.

As the information provides, this site is designed for the student graduate entering the world of work. It is clear to me that this would be one of my sure stops if I were a new or upcoming graduate. I also try to tell the students that I teach that if they plan to enter the world of work anytime soon that they start now. There is no time like the present. You have got to remember that you are not the only 'fish' in the sea. If your goal is to get a job my advice to you is like the saying says 'The early bird gets the worm.'

The Job Search Tool to Get You That Job

We have another site that is geared for the recent college graduates and entry level positions. This may be for you, www.career.com. This site offers several different types of search methods. You can search by company, discipline, locations or keys words. There are special databases for new graduates, hot jobs, and international jobs. Also you will find that you can respond online to job postings or post your own résumés in a database. You will find resources on writing résumés, tips, links to other jobs postings, and special advice. Besides a job fair, this site provides a location where the job searcher can talk to potential employers. Forums are also available for advice and feedback.

I am always encouraging my students to contact and talk to potential employers. I have suggested that they ask various questions about their training. This site is one of very few that provides this opportunity, I strongly suggest that you seek it out and spend some time asking questions about future employment.

Build that career with www.careerbuilder.com. This site offers three different kinds of searches. There is a search by company, or perform an advanced MEGASEARCH, this is a consolidated search of your other job sites. This site offers career advice – including help with cover letters, résumés, job interviews and general tips about working life. Many individuals have trouble making the transitions and balancing their work and their family.

What is interesting on this site is that you will get a personal agent that will notify you of new jobs that match your job search criteria. If you post your résumé online, Career Builder.com offers you the ability to block specific employers from seeing it. You may find this very helpful if you already have a job and you do not want your employer to know.

Here is a site for the young crowd of twenty-something's, www.careerbuzz.com. This site is for the 'play hard, work hard'. Is this you? This site contains categories, BUZZWORDS, and offers thousands of current job postings, daily career articles and links to related sites. This site will offer a good cross section of jobs from the technical and business sector, but is mostly oriented towards liberal arts. You can sign up for 24/7 **JOB SEARCH**. Here again you will have

7001 Resumes-Plus Second Edition

a personal search agent which e-mails potential jobs to you. This site will offer constant up to date articles on the job market.

I would suggest that this is a good site for you to visit to see if you can find it to be valuable to you. I like the interaction of the personal agent e-mailing potential jobs to you.

For another real user friendly site I would suggest that you visit www.careercast.com. So if you can not get past the almost unreadable introduction, check out this great hub, portal network for other sites. This site can hook you up to about 150 career sites, 122 newspaper career sites and active job listings from 3812 newspaper employers nationally. The site's database receives over 14 million job and résumé searches every month and lists over a million jobs. It's also a host for many well-known and helpful sites including USA Today, The Boston Globe, The Wall Street Journal, www.Salary.com, Seattle Times, the Nature Publishing Ground, and Altavista.com.

By the sheer volume of activities and exposure I must suggest that you use this web hub. The question may come up 'just how do I use so many sites, hubs, networks and such.' Well, the best way I can explain this is that you must use discipline. Before you get started, have a good idea where you want to go. What kind of job you want, what industry, and of course the location. Then start your search using one system at a time. You may even want to set more than one goal or plan, such as my very simple A, B, & C plan.

Let us take a look at another very comprehensive site www.careercity.com. This is an excellent site and from the publisher of the book 'JobBank'. This site searches for a job by category and location. You can find a job fair (by city), and you can find an employer (by industry, location and keyword). Also, you can access other career and industry research information. Résumé's posted are not secure unless you make them, protecting confidential information.

You will also find lots of advice on career planning and management from résumés and interview tips, to self-assessment and special tips for women. Also a large and helpful section on healthcare and biotech careers, government and education.

I can't say that this site is for the entry level individual, but it does have some special interests that need to be explored, especially by women. I would recommend some time in a learning mode here.

Another website specializing in high-tech jobs in the U.S. and Canada is www.careerexchange.com. This site allows the job seeker to search jobs in the U. S., Canada, overseas, or by category. To register you must fill out a form then you will be contacted by a recruiter who will customize your search. You can post a résumé, or a computerized search agent will match your résumé to jobs in the job bank and notify you via e-mail. Career exchange is linked to many other job sites, including: www.Yahoo.com, www.altavista.com, www.jobfactory.com, www.jobnext.com and www.employment911.com.

For the entry level job seeker this may <u>not</u> be the site for you, but you can gain valuable information for jobs in the U.S., Canada, and overseas. If one had the qualifications, I am impressed with the way this site will match your résumé with jobs in the job bank and notify the applicant.

The **Wall Street Journal** has a job site known as www.careerjournal.com. However, this site is for executives, professionals, and managers; it includes salary and hiring information and columns by career professionals and journalists. This site offers a large job advice section which includes how-to on résumés, networking, changing careers and search strategies on the net.

Let us continue by looking at another Web Site. In this case let us take a look at **www. MSN.com.** As you do this you will see there is a great deal of what I call **'stuff'**. It is not bad, but you have to sort out what you are looking for to get to what you are after. You will want to go to the '**Career**' area and '**Click**' on it to proceed.

7001 Resumes-Plus Second Edition

The first page or site you are going to come upon is a general guide or table of contents of what you are going to find on this Web site. Narrow your search to jobs or careers. You will move toward the '**CareerMart**'; on this page you can select a number of articles written about careers and job search. After you have read some or all selected reading provided you may decide to go on. You may want to visit the Career Recruiter. This is a one stop recruiting area. You can Create and/or edit your job postings, search the résumé database, and review other information.

This site also offers a one-stop **Human Resource Center**. You can set up an account which gives you access to job stats and job reports.

See: **www. Careeremart.com/Companies/Employers/ENaccnt.htm.**

I can not commend nor '**pan**' the benefits that you may or may not get from this site, but I can only suggest that the site is here and **MSN** has taken a great deal of pains to try to provide sources where by one could do job search. However, one also must continue to realize not only do you expose yourself to perhaps greater opportunity, but at the same time you open yourself up to world wide competition. Not for a minute would I suggest that you not use this site. No, on the contrary, my recommendation to you is to use any and all leads that you can generate.

Next let us look at www.careermosaic.com; this site is a subsidiary of Headhunter.net, which features an easy-to-use job search engine including a 'Quick Search' using keywords, city, and state. **A COMMUNITIES SEARCH** categorizes jobs by discipline. An **INDUSTRY SEARCH** offers targeted results by business. **A COMPANIES SEARCH** features a specific organization's list of available jobs. Career Mosaic's ONLINE CAREER FAIRS allows you to search jobs targeted by specific job functions, geography, or industry. Also check out employer profiles; a college connection to help the graduates find entry-level employment, and a career resource center full of good advice. Job-seekers can search by job description, post their résumés or use the **10 MINUTE JOB PERFORMANCE APPRAISER.**

The Job Search Tool to Get You That Job

It is my advice to check out this web site. Remember, not every site is <u>good</u> for everyone, but this one looks as if it would have advantages for the entry level individual. I have used www.careermosaic.com and I found it easy to use. I went ahead and put my résumé on the site, and as I have indicated, this was simple to do. Also there were a lot of jobs to pick from. Not to say that I could get a job from this site, that has to be seen. But there is an old religious saying that I happen to believe and it's as follows: 'You must cast your bread on the water.' The more you expose your résumé the better your chances of finding a job.

For a well-organized source you can go to www.careers.org, it contains over 7500 links to jobs, employers, businesses, educational, and professional career services on the Web. You can search for specific sites using dozens of different criteria. Search sites devoted to individual states, employers, types of jobs, and internships. Or search employer Websites, federal job openings, and classified advertising in newspapers. Jobs in higher education and social services are also featured. This excellent site is highly recommended to get you started on your search. It has a lot to offer an individual so it would be my advice to spend some time here to determine if this site can help you in your job search.

For free résumé posting, plus some automatic matching service, I would like to suggest that you swing by www.careershop.com. This site is an **AUTOMATIC HIRE**; it will automatically match your résumé by scanning its database for employers looking for candidates with your background. If a match is found, your résumé is mailed directly to the employer. There is also an automated system that sends matching jobs to your e-mail address based on your confidential information. A job search engine searches by job locations, job category, and keywords. This site also offers career advice, a descriptive list of employers, and training information. My advice with regards to this site is this is one that you should not pass up. Spend some time here and post your résumé on this site.

How about www.careersite.com; this site has been named the **Top Mega Job Site** in 'The Complete Idiot's Guide to Finding Your Dream Job Online'. Careersite.com offers an easy-to-

7001 Resumes-Plus Second Edition

use array of services. You can retain control of contact information and résumé disclosure. You receive automatic notification of matching jobs, or you can click to match jobs to your profile immediately. This service also allows you to apply for jobs online and forward your résumé. One interesting feature is the way their search engine works. You can enter several **SKILLS CONCEPTS** (management, oral communication, etc.) that are then matched to employer searches. With the features that are offered here I would suggest that you spend sometime here to determine it this site can assist you in your search.

Here at www.abracat.com is a large classified ad site that lists jobs and contains a job search engine. To use the site you type in a Key-word, choose from several categories – including location, experience and type of position – and click for results. The search system is a little difficult and a little hard to use as compared to some of the other sites I have been discussing.

The listings come from classifieds pages in the area you choose, so this engine can search for a wider variety of jobs – from sales, to entertainment, to professional jobs. You can also post your résumé here.

I happen to like the fact that you can post your résumé, but on this site there is no guaranty of privacy for your résumé, so you will have to take this under advisement. Since there are a wide variety of jobs this site is worth a visit.

I can see where you might believe that with all these sites you could be seemingly overwhelmed in doing your job search, and perhaps it is, but it is your future and career, and as it has been said, **'I never said it would be easy.'** And job search isn't. Set up a plan for yourself and work the plan. Let us continue to see what other Web sites are available to do our job search on.

www.careertrust.com is a reliable recruiting service that serves specific areas of the country, mostly the Northeast, California and Chicago areas. So if you live or want to move to these areas this is one site you would want to explore. The job search engine here, SEARCHLINES, allows you to search by job type, location, or keyword. Anyone can search, but in order to apply for

212

a job, you will need to register to become a member. This is not unlike other sites where you may in some cases supply your name, address, and e-mail address. This site has a search agent that looks for matches to your profile or résumé. The service focuses on technological, library and records-related jobs, but also lists legal, clerical, accounting, banking, and management jobs. Also the Career Trust's **CORESTAFF** services deal with temporary, flexible, short-term, or temp-to-hire jobs in accounting, information technology, and information management.

I can see some benefit here if you are interested in the areas that this site concentrates on and the job focus. Also if you are interested in temporary employment or short-term work swing by this site to see if it has opportunities for you

For you college types www.collegecentral.com is for you. Here you will find a **CAREER CORNER** for you job-seekers, also you will find a **RÉSUMÉ CENTER** where you can build and post your résumé. This is a special function that allows you to see which employers have reviewed it. You will also find internship postings at the college or university that you currently attend. Also you can read employer profiles, and visit virtual job fairs, get tips and explore career resources. You can also take advantage of question-and-answer services. There are various wizards you can utilize that deal with salary, relocation, and so forth. You will find this site fun and user-friendly. If you are a college student or recent graduate this could be a site for you, and one you want to explore.

For you entry-level or recent college graduates this is another site for you, check-out www.collegegrad.com. This site is easy to use and it will help you with your résumé. You will find job postings, new listings, and interviewing tips for you neophyte job seekers. I found this site interesting with its videos on interviewing and résumé preparation. There is a question and answer forum. This site has received several net awards.

Go to www.collegerecruiter.careercast.com; if you are a recent or not-so-recent college graduate this is a site for you. This site explores other job databases as you do your job search. The purpose is to give you better results than you might get using just one search engine. There

7001 Resumes-Plus Second Edition

is a wide list of fields and you can narrow your geographic location search too. You can post your résumé and there is a search agent. In addition to these there is career advice available from experts and you can learn how to apply for college loans and scholarships. Again this site does not provide a confidentiality option when you post your résumé or personal information and it will be available to companies as you do your search. So be careful.

Let us now take a look at what **www.FlipDog.com** has to offer; it's a place to go designed to help people who are looking for a change or those who are unemployed. This site is designed to help individuals who need help with their résumés, or to help provide job seekers with better insight as to where to look for that job.

It is suggested that the sites are updated daily with new opportunities everyday. These sites provide you with job descriptions, salaries, and/or benefits (if available). In addition, these sites will provide you with information on how to jazz up your résumé and suggestions on the cover letters that you send to the potential employer.

It is suggested that if you are really striving to improve your career or are unemployed that this site will hopefully help you to develop a new chapter in your career.

What you will find at this site:

- A list of great sites where you find updated listings of jobs

- Resources – tips on where you can find sample résumés or cover letters

- Entry Level – listing of sites to find a junior level position. Great for college graduates

- Cover Letters – guidelines and tips to writing a cover letter

- News –

- Freelance jobs – those with specific talents and skills who are looking for a career

What I am going to suggest is that you spend some time on the Internet and discover the various sources that will be of benefit to you in your job search and career development. I am not going to find every web site that you can use to do your job search on, but to provide you

214

with some samples and locations to indicate that the Internet is another emerging source that can help you in finding the job of your dreams. But I will caution you not to rely on any one source when you are doing your job search. The bottom line in search is how well you use the various sources to your benefit, and the education and training that you have to offer a potential employer once you find that job opportunity.

You want to find the **'coolest'** jobs? Go to www.cooljobs.com. This is a good site for the eccentric and outside the mainstream job seekers. You will choose from a large list of categories and your search will take you to other job sites that relate to your specific dream job. As an example, if you wanted a job as a clown this would be your site. There is also a mailing list that you can subscribe to which will give you updates and other information not on the site. You can post your résumé or a position-wanted notice, or explore other links. This site may prove to be interesting to you so it is worth taking a look.

If you go to www.dice.com this site is evaluated as one of the best sites for jobseekers who specialize in Information Technologies (IT). I have been told by my Son-In-Law that he was impressed with the site. He is in his late thirties, and has been working in Information Technology for a few years. This site has an advance search engine and it allows the applicant to search by keyword, job title, skills, state or area code. There is a geographic search for a number of major cities. Candidates may set up a personalized collection of password-protected job tools. It is suggested that there are 5,400 companies available to the job seeker. Also there is a system that will notify you via e-mail if there is a job match after you have posted you résumé. This site does provide privacy-controls. Also there is certification preparation testing available for purchasing for various IT skills. As you can see this site is designed for Information Technology people so unless you're trained in this area this site is not for you.

How about a one stop shopping site for employers, recruiters, and the job-seekers specializing in Sales/Marketing, Computers/IT, Engineering/Technical, Executive/Professional, Medical/Health Care and other professions. You will go to www.employersonline.com; you can

7001 Resumes-Plus Second Edition

post you résumé here. It isn't the simplest site to work and it is not clear if your résumé will <u>not</u> be protected if posted. This site does offer question and answer tips on how to answer interview questions, and what your résumé should include. This is for the entry level applicant or job seeker; it may not be for the neophyte job seeker.

How about an awesome site www.employment911.com, this site lets you search 350 major job sites and three million jobs at the click of your mouse. You can do geographical location searches and also have your résumé go to thousands of employers free of charge, and I like **'free.'** There are articles, stories, relocation tools, and media videos too. There are also other services that you will be pleased with, so based upon what this site offers you will want to spend time here.

www.careerweb.com offers a search engine, résumé posting, and services and career advice. This site is a little hard to manage and there is a fee; though it does offer a fresh perspective on the market, there is a service that distributes your résumé to recruiters and employers who might be interested in hiring you.

You may want to swing by this website and see if there is anything that can be valuable to you.

www.employementwizard.com is an interesting site; it combines classified ads from national newspapers with jobs posted by individual employers so you may find many jobs that aren't online anywhere else. With this one point in mind, there is no question that it is worth your time to visit this site. You will find over 60 newspapers, you can search current openings at the local, regional, or national level, and you can apply instantly to the jobs via e-mail. In addition, the job-seeker can access details about the companies, get advice about managing a career, or conduct job search. You can develop and post your résumé on line. You can obtain advice on getting a job and get reprints of career advice articles from various newspapers. The site will provide invaluable information and advice.

THE JOB SEARCH TOOL TO GET YOU THAT JOB

As you can see on one of the previous web pages, **'FlipDog'** is going to help you select various locations in the United States and identify the jobs that you could find in these areas. If you are serious about finding a job you may want to move to a location that has more employment going on.

Here is another option, www.excite.com/career.com. You will find that this site includes career planning, continuing education, and it lists industries and occupations. The focus of the site is high-tech, legal and pharmaceutical jobs. I would suggest that if you are entry-level you may not find what you are looking for here, but on the other-hand, since the site has occupation and continuing education components you my want to visit it. You can post your résumé though there is no guarantee that you will get protection of your personal data. The job search engine is simple to use but doesn't offer an advanced search function, however, there is an option to broaden your advance search function if you wish. This would be a good site if you are getting started in your job search, though not for the serious minded career-seeker.

If you go to www.classifieds2000.com, this site allows you to search classified ads. It also has a function that will notify you when a classified ad appears to fit your description of the job you would like. You might find this site worthwhile.

At www.usajobs.opm.gov there is everything you wanted to know about finding a job with the federal government. This is a friendly and informative site and makes working for the government look good. It has a one step application that gets jobs sent to you by email; I hope you can see how important it is to have computer access. You will find all kinds of jobs here including salary requirements, but the information can be extremely slow.

The first area that this site is exploring is location, which is step one. As I suggested you may want to move because there are more jobs in an area. Or you may want to move because of an interest in some geological preference, or you have finished school and now you want to settle down.

7001 Resumes-Plus Second Edition

The second step is to determine the categories (jobs) you would consider. If you are an experienced applicant your interests and considerations would be different than a job seeker that is looking for work for the first time. But, in any case what you would like to do is very important to you, and of course it would be important to determine how many jobs there are available in your vocational interest.

The third step helps you to determine what companies out there are in fact looking for applicants.

Keep in mind that you will quickly generate a number of jobs to go after by having this system so visible and easy to access. You are not going to be the **'Lone Ranger'** out there ringing door bells and doing job search. As I have said before, you are going to be in competition with a lot of individuals. Let me share a number or two with you. I myself went after a Regional Management position for **Staples;** I was told that there were 80 applicants. Today that number may be 3 times what it was then. This information in not given to discourage you, but only make you aware the job market is truly competitive.

What we have done in this Chapter was to give you a taste of want the Internet has to offer you in your quest for a new career or just a job. You will find that if you 'Click' on Yahoo. com and select **'Advanced Search'** then type in **'Job Search'**, you will come up with over 695 sites to go to.

Each site will require time, research, and evaluation to determine if the particular job search site is useful to your set of circumstances. If so, of course, you will then have to process the information, data, and plug in the information that will lead to the employment opportunities offered by the particular Web site.

You might find www.funjobs.com an interesting site for some fun loving jobs such as skiing or tennis instructors, or camp counselors. You will find a list of some 107 fun jobs which are all resort-related. You will find this site easy to navigate and it includes a job search engine.

Some career planning and advice, and a special section for women will be found on this site. You will also find a good selection of toots and information about job-hunting.

How about www.gojobs.com; this site allows employers to select multiple boards to post jobs on. So when you use the search engine you will be getting employment opportunities from up to 500 boards. You will find jobs in the following areas: banking, engineering, computer technology and architecture. So if you find a job you like, you will apply directly for that specific job by posting your résumé onto the selected page and 'click' to send.

Post your résumé and do your search on www.headhunter.net. Here we are going to search more than 250,000 job postings by keyword. Also you will be able to search geographic locations, salary range, and many other criteria. This site will allow you to apply online and you also have control over employers seeing your résumé.

There is an area for graduates to find entry-level jobs and there is good job advice. You will have up to 13 different criteria to narrow and/or maximize your search. This is a good general site for technical and management jobs but you will run into flashing pop-up advertisements which can be distracting and annoying. I would suggest that you spend some time at this site, you may benefit by the time spent.

How about www.hotjobs.com, it's one of the top job sites. You will find thousands of jobs and it features good job search options. You can fine-tune your search by choosing a Career Channel. You can control the privacy of your posted résumé and you can also set up automatic job search agents and tracking of you job applications. You can produce over 1000 jobs. Drop by this site to see how it might benefit you and your job search.

America's first and oldest online career guidance service, www.iccweb.com, has been in operation since 1989. It has a wide range of services that are well-organized and a database of 650 best career and employment websites on the Internet. There is an extensive library of advice articles and a database of career coaching and much more. Also there is a distribution system that will expose your résumé to thousands of recruiters and companies. Since it is the oldest site they're doing something right so take the time to check it out.

One of the largest and most popular sites geared towards women is www.ivillage.com/work. This site offers an excellent array of services in their **JOB RESOURCE CENTER**.

Next we are going to go to www.jobbankusa.com; this site specializes in providing career information including a job and résumé database service for candidates, employers and recruitment firms. The **JOB BANK USA** also offers a unique free service, **INSTANT REFERENCE CHECKING** which allows job seekers to improve their chances of getting hired by letting potential employers check references instantly. Other services include a **RÉSUMÉ BROADCASTER**, a list of featured companies, an occupational guide, a list of Fortune 500 companies, a section on **HOT COMPANIES**, newsgroups, career fairs, assessment and relocation tools, articles, and résumé samples. This is an excellent all-around site for professionals.

> **What I want you to know that besides giving you this list of job search sites, I am researching most of them to really see how they work, and their benefits and shortcomings. What I want this book to be and my others books to be are real 'tools' that offer practical applications for you the reader, not a philosophical document leaving you to rediscover the 'Wheel.' If you are looking for a job, and you are serious, you more than realize by now that it is serious business and you need all the help you can get, and this is just what I want to provide you.**

If you have not discovered it, you soon will. Many of these job search sites have the Résumé Broadcasting feature, but there is a cost in most cases. As an applicant you may be tempted to sign-up for each one. My advice is to be very careful. I can't tell you not to select one or two, but I will ask that you take your time and make sure that you are not paying for duplication and not getting your moneys worth.

Let us look at www.jobdirect.com. Here is another site geared toward college students and recent grads, so this site may be valuable to you. It offers information on internships, co-

THE JOB SEARCH TOOL TO GET YOU THAT JOB

ops, summer jobs, and contract work. Internships are a good way to get into a business. Some colleges will give college credit for this option. The site includes interviewing tips, a list of employers, and articles related to job-hunting. A list of **HOT EMPLOYERS** includes Boeing and American International Group.

You can create a personal profile, post a résumé, and search for jobs once you've registered with the service. The site claims to make over 150,000 job matches per-week. The process of registering is rather elaborate and somewhat confusing and no information is available about how to guard your privacy if you do post your résumé.

For a real amazing site you can go to www.jobfactory.com. This site offers nearly two million job openings collected by the **JOB SPIDER**. This site is searchable by job title and geographic locations, you can see every job of any type listed everywhere in the U.S. from Atlanta, GA to Fairbanks, AK. The **SPIDER** links to 23,000 plus job sites on the Internet that post employment openings. If you will recall, this is one of the reasons I suggested that you checkout the sites carefully for overlap and try to select the one the does the best job for you. Resources on this site include listings of employers' e-mail addresses and fax numbers that are set up to accept résumés. What is interesting is to see this new trend where more and more companies are having you e-mail your résumé to them. It was just a few years ago where faxing was the in thing. Today there are those firms that still have you fax in or mail in your résumés, but more and more, as I stated, are turning to e-mail for this function. The site automatically creates a list of related employers for you to consider in your job search, and you can search for employers either geographically or alphabetically. In addition, the site offers links to the classified job advertisements at 1067 newspapers in the United States, Canada, Asia and Europe. There's also useful information including the number of miles between cities, Internet disability resources, and links to the 220 best job sites categorized by industry. This is a highly recommended site.

In your surfing the Internet you may stop by www.job-hunt.org. This site is a mega-list of online job-search resources and services. The site is maintained by Stanford University.

You will find that www.joboptions.com offers some unique options for protecting the privacy of your résumé while allowing employers to search through your experience and employment history without seeing your personal information. For those of you who are not employed this may not be an issue for you, but if you are employed this approach will not put your job at risk if you are looking for a new job. At this site you can search through job postings by locations, industry/profession, and keyword. You can also search through the **EMPLOYER DATABASE** by location, industry, and keyword. You can register for Job Alert to find out when a new and interesting opportunity hits the database, and Job Alert will contract you by e-mail.

I have not discussed it with you yet and this may be overdue, but if you have not realize it yet I will now point out that to really use these job search sites not only do you need a computer, but you need to be connected to the Internet. You will be receiving e-mails everyday with good or bad news. If you decide to do this, I would highly recommend you explore 'Cable,' 'Wireless', or 'Satellite.' I assure you I get no **'kickback'** from these people, and I know little to nothing about 'Satellite,' I have both. I am connected to the Internet 24/7, and yes I am getting e-mails everyday about various jobs so it makes sense to me. But I also do a lot of work on the net in research and such. The choice is yours and there is a cost for this privilege. If you are not aware, cable will cost you from $30 to $50.00 per month. This is not an inexpensive enterprise. I should expect that you could deduct some of your expenses from your income tax, that's if you have income. If you get a job in part using your Internet, I would suggest that you share this information with your tax person some of this should be deductible.

The site www.thejobresources.com is a free service for college-educated job seekers and recent graduates. As you know this book was designed for High School Students and Adults entering the 'World of Work' for the first time, but I do hope that there is a broad enough field of information that it can be used by college grads too. Your résumé can be posted and you can search for jobs from over 1000 top companies. There is an area where you can take a survey to determine your interest and abilities, and also search for jobs. There is a list of **HOT**

COMPANIES! This is a good site for general research on companies, but the search engine is not as good as it could be. You may have trouble coming up with a job. For example, if you were looking for jobs in accounting in California, there is nothing that comes up. And management jobs in California are limited.

> As you go though each one of these sites you will have to register your Username and Password before you can use the site. You may want to write them down or use the same ones on every site.

You will find that www.jobcareer.com is a very simple site that you can use. It includes a search engine, but not much else. You can search employment opportunities in Accounting, Contracting, Sales, Pharmacy, Engineering, and Management. You just type in the key word and the location you want. There are a couple of links to human resources, products, and a chat room. Stop by and check it out.

When you go to www.jobsonline.com you have to register to use their services; including the job search and résumé posting functions. Like other sites the registration takes a few minutes. This site, like some other sites, wants date of birth, but the information is supposed to be confidential and not available to employers.

The next site is www.justtechjobs.com. This is a wonderful job site for Information Technology Professionals. It works a little different than many other sites. The site leads you to technology job sites searchable by skills and geographic locations. So for this site to be valuable to you, you will need of course salable skills in information technology.

The next site I will explore is www.justwebjobs.com. On this site it works a lot like JustTechjobs.com. It features employment opportunities in a wide array of technologies in the internet industry. You can click on one or more technologies to move to a sub-site that is dedicated exclusively to the technology you've chosen. However I will suggest that this site is for Web Professionals. So, if you are at entry-level this site is really not for you, you will find that every job posted is for a Web position. This site, if you have the qualifications gives you a unique ability to get the right position.

The next site, www.manpower.com is a nationwide recruiting company. It also offers job search capabilities. You choose a state, and then choose either the **PROFESSIONAL** or **ADMINISTRATIVE** category then use the advanced search function to find suitable jobs in your area based on key-words. The search function is rather unconventional in its setup and takes some brainpower to figure out. I hope you have discovered that I explore each one of these websites to be able to talk knowledgeably about them. In the case of this website it takes some work to get the full benefit from it, and in the case that you are still entry-level this is <u>not</u> a site that will be of full benefit to you.

One of the biggest and best known general job sites is www.monster.com. You will discover that it is the countries hottest advertising site for companies. You can search job openings by location, category, and keywords. You can post your résumé with fairly good privacy protection, although reports advise that you need to use caution in protecting your identity. On this site a Résumé Agent lets you know when a new opportunity that meets your criteria appears. You can also research local companies. The **MONSTER BOARD** offers an overview of employers and a helpful interactive database that supports job searching by company name, location, discipline, industry, and job title. Most of the jobs are technical, but you will also find positions in other disciplines. There is no question this is a site worth spending some time on.

If you are a college or university student or recent graduate www.monstertrak.com is a good site for you. MonsterTrak is in partnership with their career centers. So to find a job you will need to get a student or alumnus password that is issued through the college career center. You can search your university's job board or do a special entry-level search for jobs and internships. As you know in most cases you do not get paid for internships, but not only is it a way to get your foot in the door, you also get experience. Also, in some cases, you can get college credit. You will also find chat rooms and message boards hosted by professionals giving advice on topics ranging from career planning to internships. Also available is tutoring help, a database of career-related articles, and a scholarship search.

At www.nationaljob.com it includes a network of Specialty Sites ™ promoting jobs in specific employment categories which are listed alphabetically and can be searched individually. The site also offers **CUSTOM JOBS** pages set up by employers and **COMMUNITY PAGES** for individual companies and communities. The community pages list jobs by city or area, and employers by area. The job search engine, P.J. Scout ™, finds job openings of specific interest to you and sends a detailed job description via e-mail, including **HOW TO APPLY** information. Your personal information is kept confidential on this site. Resources include links to training sites, contract payment calculators, and career assessment tests. I like this site and I believe you will too!

Here we go, let us take a look at www.net-temps.com; this is site is specifically designed for contract and temporary employment. The search engine here will allow you to choose an employment category and geographic locations. You will find a good cross-section of job types on this easy-to-use, fast site.

> As you work your way through the various Job search sites you will discover those that are of a benefit to you and you will of course make them your favorite sites. You will also discover that some are easier to use and more helpful then others, while others will ask you to invest varying amounts of money for extended services and most will require varying degrees of time to master. Many of you will be able to post your résumé on a site. Last but not least, you will find varying degrees of success using them. My advice is very simple: do not <u>rely</u> on any one job search method. What works for one may not work for you. And of course remember, this job search <u>is</u> a job. I know some of you will not put in the time as others will, but I can assure you the <u>more</u> time you dedicate to job search the more success you will have finding the position of your dreams. Work smart!

Here at www.opportunitynocs.org is one of the very few sites devoted exclusively to jobs and careers in the non-profit sector. This site allows you to do a quick keyword search or an advanced search to see job listings by city, state, organization or position. Currently, Opportunity Noc's lists around 700 non-profit jobs. Not every state is listed. The site does offer links to related sites, career resources and a non-profit library with excellent mega-indexes for researching jobs in the industry. I did not spend much time here so I can not tell you about results.

This well-organized site, www.recruitersonline.com by Purdue University Placement Service, has a listing of over 1000 online job search resources and services. You will need a number from the Placement Service. I would suggest if you are entry level this may not be a site for you.

The next site is heavily weighted toward tech jobs, but you will find that it has hundreds of listings and the site is easy to use. You can build and post a résumé but it's hard to say how well your privacy will be protected. The service does allow you to customize your profile and edit your résumé to hide personal information. This site is www.recruiters-online.com. The site has

THE JOB SEARCH TOOL TO GET YOU THAT JOB

few resources beyond the job search engine, résumé posting service, and recruiters' contracts – no articles, chats, contacts, quizzes, etc. I happen to like not having that stuff. This site is a place to do your job search quickly.

You will find that www.worktree.com is the largest job-search portal in the world according to the site but there is a catch, you are going to have to pay for the service. The current cost is $49.00 for a three-month membership. **Worktree** allows you to search thousands of job sites depending on your interests. There's a job-seeker's toolbox of helpful advice for résumé building, interview advice, writing cover letters, negotiating your salary and much more. My opinion is this; if you are unemployed $49.00 for three months may be a valuable investment. However much of the services offered by this site you can find free in many other sites as well as in this book. I did not invest the money at this writing to use the privilege of this site.

I am going to suggest that you take a close look at Cybercode jobalert, the website is Jobalert@Cybercoders.com. This is a professional website that does a very good job of providing a variety of jobs for you to look at. You will have to sign up providing a user name and password; this is for your security and control. You can post your résumé on the site and when a job comes up that you are interested in your résumé can automatically be sent. There are provisions to modify your résumé, and adding and customizing your cover letter for the job you are applying to. The site allows, in some cases, to apply directly to the firm of your interest. In addition, the site provides you with feedback and confirms that your résumé and cover letter has been received. It is important that you have email capability to facilitate this function. I like this site, and I think you will too. What you can do is tell the site what types of jobs you are interested in and locations and the site will automatically seek out these jobs and send them to your email. You can also select how often you want this done. You can select several jobs to review everyday if this is your choice. There is also a system to send jobs that might be of interest to your friends. There is no cost to you for this service.

7001 Resumes-Plus Second Edition

> **The following is a sampling of some additional websites you can assess by simply making the one inquiry as indicated in the first paragraph!**

The following is sampling of some additional Web sites you can asses bymaking the one inquire as indicated in the first paragraph

1 <u>Education Canada Job Search</u> – This site provides searchable listings by location and specialty. If you're a teacher and you're looking for a job in Canada this might be the site for you. Go to www.jobsearch.edcationcanada.com. You will find more sites in this area for educational opportunities and employment in Canada.

2 <u>The ultimate job search survival guide</u> – Here, the author Paul Dryer, provides job search links to many career related web sites. You need to go to www.pauldyer.com. Paul, you'll find, has been quite hard at work in the area of job search so I would suggest that you give his suggestions a great deal of consideration.

3 <u>Networked libraries in the job search guide</u> – This is another site dedicated to finding librarians, employment.pw2.netcom.com.

4 <u>Physician job search (PJS)</u> – what you will discover here are listings for medical jobs throughout Canada, organized by specialty, region, and employment duration. You'll find this information at www.physicianjobsearch.com.

5 <u>Job Search Online</u> – On this site you will find employment resources for drivers, and owner operators of trucking. Also other related information for job search in this area. www.jobsearchonline.com

6 <u>Irish Job Search</u> - This site is for people who are looking for work in the Ireland's hospitality and leisure industry. If this is for you go to www.ishjobsearch.com.

The Job Search Tool to Get You That Job

7 <u>ESL Job Search</u> – This site lists vacancies and provides a forum for people that are looking for employment in English as a Second Language. So if this is your need check out www. esljobsearch.com, it may be for you.

8 <u>Media Job Search Canada</u> – Here is another link to Canada, it connects you to companies and industries in News and Media business and related employment opportunities. Go to www. mediajobsearchcanada.com.

9 <u>Pittsburgh.Net job Search</u> – If you are interested in a job in Pittsburgh, or Pennsylvania you may want to go to this site.

What you have here is just a sampling of what is available on the internet to help you with your career and job search. The fact is that here on www.Yahoo.com you will find nearly 700 different sites and links that you will be able to gather job search information. There are more sites and links that you might find valuable such as www.headhunter.net. This one I would call full service, it gives you job exposure for Job Seekers, Employers, and Third-party employment recruiters.

In many cases in major cities such as in Los Angeles or Orange County California you will find sites like MyOC.com, www.ocjobjinder.com/job_fairs.shtml. This site offers the jobseeker:

- Job Search

- Search Companies

- Post Résumés

- Career Fairs

- Register Classifieds

- Much more

7001 Resumes-Plus Second Edition

Also, sites like www.lacareers.com help the job seeker to find employment in the Los Angeles area. This site will link you to employment career pages of local companies. You will find that this is a 'free' resource and it lets you send your résumés, research salaries, take surveys, and it has lifestyle and relocation resources. This site will give you free links to major employers in the area. You will need to check the employment sites offered your major city or state.

I would suggest that you not over look **'Job Fairs'** that may be offered in your areas. These fairs bring together companies and organizations that are looking for people with experience and education who are looking for employment. Usually you will find that you have to have a minimum of one full year of work experience and a four-year degree.

But do not overlook job fairs in your area, you will find them a good source of career information. Information about these fairs will be found on these web sites.

You will find in many cases today that you will be encouraged to email your résumé to participate in one or more of these on site hiring departments. I would suggest that you take the time to prepare your résumé and place it on a computer disk, be it 3-1/2" floppy, Zip, or flash memory which will allow you to automatically email it as the need requires.

State Employment Agency Websites

To provide you with additional help and continue with my philosophy of leaving **'No Rock Unturned',** I would like to provide you with another very important source of jobs and help. It is your state employment agency Websites. You will find that each state has its own Web site. These sites feature current job listings. In addition you'll find almost unlimited resources, advice, helpful hints and links. I found with the California web site that you can post your résumé and use the search engine just like the Internet job sites we have been looking at. You will discover that the Employment Agency in your area will also provide similar options.

The Job Search Tool to Get You That Job

What is good about these sites is that they are not trying to charge you money for the help, and you will find a **Varity of jobs**. If you are a new job searcher there is special help for you, this is also true if you are a veteran.

Alabama – www/dir.state.al.us/es/default.htm

Alaska - www.job.state.ak.us/job-seeker.htm

Arizona - www.akb/prg/az

Arkansas - www.ajb/org/ar

California - www.edd.cahwnet.gov/findjob.htm

Colorado - www.ajb.org/co

Connecticut - www.venet/default.asp

Delaware - www.ucnet.net/default.asp

District of Columbia - www.does.ci.washington.dc.us/main.shtm

Florida - www2.myflorida.com/job-seeker.html

Georgia - www.dol.state.ga.us

Hawaii - www.ajb.org/hi

Idaho - www.labor.state.id.us

Illinois - www.ajb.org/il

Indiana - www.ajb/org/in

Iowa - www.state.oa.is/jobs

Kansas- -www.kansasjobs.org

Kentucky - www.desky.org/jobsrch/jobsrch.htm

Louisiana - www.ajb.org/la

Maine - www.mainecareercenter.com

Maryland - www.ajb.org/md

Massachusetts - www.ajb.org/ma

Michigan -www.michigan.gov

Minnesota - www.des.state.min.us

7001 Resumes-Plus Second Edition

Mississippi - www.ajb.org/ms

Missouri - www.work.state.mo.us/mu2a.htm

Montana - jsd.dli.state.mt.us

Nebraska - www.ajb.org/ne

Nevada - www.detr.state.nv.us

New Hampshire - www.nhworks.state.nh.us

New Jersey - www.ajb.org.nj

New Mexico - www.ajb.org/nm

New York - www.labor.state.ny.us

North Carolina - www.esc/state/nc.us

North Dakota - www.state.nd.us/jsnd

Ohio - www.stateofhiojobs.com

Oklahoma - www.oesc.state.ok.us/jobnet/default.htm

Oregon - www.emp.state.or.us

Pennsylvania - www.ajb.org/pa

Rhode Island - www.det.state.ri.us

South Carolina - www.sces.org

South Dakota - www.state.sd.us/dol/.htm

Tennessee - www.state/tn.us/labor-wfd

Texas - www.twc/state.tx.us/twc/html

Utah - www.dws.state.ut.us

Vermont - www.detstate.vt.us

Vermont - www.vec.state.va.us

Virginia - www.vec.state.va.us

Washington - www.wa.gov/esd/employment.html

West Virginia - www.dwd.state.wi.us/jobnet/mapwi.htm

Wisconsin - www.dwd/state.wi.us/jobnet/mapwi.htm

Wyoming - Onestop.state.wy.us/appview/wjn_home.asp

Privacy issues and the internet

Once your résumé is posted on the any number of major internet job boards, you have no idea the number of people who may have access to viewing your material. Almost all major job boards make use of some form of résumé scanning software. They sell access to their database of résumés to employers looking for candidates. Since every word in your résumé is scannable, someone who uses their service might uncover *your* résumé. This is one more reason for using short résumés on the internet; they don't review any unnecessary material.

CHAPTER SIXTEEN

PREPARING YOUR RÉSUMÉ FOR POSTING

You have taken the time to research and write a 'knock them dead' résumé, now your next challenge is to make sure that the design, layout, and the presentation looks good. Unfortunately it is not enough that the document reads right it also has to look right. Now we have to be concerned with cosmetics. This one thing I tried to explain to my students when I was teaching; 'It is extremely important how good your work looks'. You must always remember that you're in competition with many other applicants, and just as with everything else you have done in your job search, there is no one simple answer. What appears good to one employer doesn't appear good to another; you must make the final decision about how your final résumé will look and its final presentation.

Today there are four basic types of Résumés

In the job market today applicants are using four types or résumé presentations:

- Printed

- Scannable

- Electronic (E-mail attachments and ASCII text files)

- Web

I will try to review for you in the following section, plus detail on when you should use each type. I will also suggest how to prepare each type of résumé.

The Traditional Printed Résumé

As you know the printed résumé is known as the 'traditional' résumé, this is the one you put in the mail to send to a company, recruiter, take to a job interview, or respond to a want ad in the newspaper. As you put together your printed résumé you will want it to be good looking, professional, and sharp. It is also important to remember that the type of paper conveys a message and makes the first impression so it is important that you take full advantage of this opportunity. As I have tried to suggest from the beginning there are many applicants for each job, it is also important to note that you may not be the most qualified in your industry. The way your résumé looks matters a great deal. You want every 'tool' in your arsenal to work to the maximum for you

Your Scannable Résumé

Your scannable résumé needs to be simple, straight forward simple. Here are the things that you would normally do to make it look attractive: sharp-looking font, bolding, italics, multiple columns, and so forth; you want to leave off the 'scannable résumé'. You want have a document that is easy to read and easy to scan. If your résumé is longer than one page make sure that you print each page, have your name on each page, be sure to have your phone number and e-mail address on the top of page two, three, and so forth. And do not staple your résumé together. I know that some times companies will ask you to fax your résumé, try to avoid this if you can. Send you résumé unfolded in a 9 x 12 envelope.

Your Electronic Résumé

The electronic résumé can be in two formats, the e-mail attachment and ASCII text file. If you send your résumé as an attachment with an e-mail you are going to 'click' on the attachment option in your e-mail program to access the document from your word-processing file. Since you will find that most business use Microsoft Word, this is a very acceptable format and offers the fewest problems or difficulties when attached.

On the other hand because there is a variety of software and operating systems, it is possible your well designed résumé can look different once sent. So to try to insure that there be a minimal amount of problems use generous margins all around and as I said earlier avoid fancy forms, and fonts.

Before you send you résumé to a prospective employer e-mail a sample of your résumé to some of your friends and have them view it and run it through their printer. If you use another program besides Microsoft word, consider saving your résumé in more than one program. For best results make sure you test what you have done by sending your résumé to a friend.

<u>Making an ASCII Text File</u>

You can go the 'extra mile' and possibly avoid formatting problems by placing you résumé in the body of an e-mail rather than sending it as an attachment; this method reduces the chance of a virus.

<u>Creating a text version of your résumé:</u>

1. The 'Save As' feature of your word processing program will create a new version of your résumé. Select 'text only' or 'ASCII' in the 'Save As' option box.

2. Close this new file.

3. Reopen the file and you'll find that your word processor has automatically reformatted your résumé into the Courier font and removed all formatting, and left justified the text.

7001 Resumes-Plus Second Edition

4. Now to promote the maximum readability when you send your résumé electronically, reset the margins to 2 inches left and right so that you have a narrow column rather than a full-page width. (This margin setting will not be retained when you close the file, but in the meantime you can adjust the text formatting for best screen appearance. For instance, if you choose to include a horizontal line {perhaps something like this ++++++++++++++++++++} to separate sections of the résumé by working with the narrow margins you won't make the mistake of creating a line that extends past the normal screen width. Plus, you won't add hard line breaks that create odd-length lines when seen at normal screen with)

5. It is important that you review your résumé for errors and mistakes, such as odd looking characters that may have been inserted to take the place of your quotes, dashes, accents, and other nonstandard symbols.

6. It may be necessary to add extra blank lines to improve the readability.

7. You might want to add horizontal dividers to break the résumé into sections for improved readability and skim ability. It would be ok to add or use any standard computer symbols such as an *, ( ), =, +, or #.

    A sample of such résumé will appear on the following page:

Your Web Résumé

Here is a new approach; because of the new technology you can easily post your electronic résumé on the Web. You will host your own website (with your own URL) to which you would refer prospective employers or job recruiters to. Instead of showing the 'traditional' ordinary version of your e-mail résumé, with just a 'click' they can access, download, and print your Web résumé – that is well done, nicely formatted, and presenting your qualifications in a positive way.

THE JOB SEARCH TOOL TO GET YOU THAT JOB

This approach is such an efficient and simple way to manage your job search tool. This offers you the opportunity to include more information than you would with the printed scannable résumé or the electronic one. You can have a separate page for your achievements, your techno local qualifications, equipment skills, honors, awards, management skills, and so on, if you believe that these items will enhance your chances of employment. The thing I want you always to keep in the front of your mind is that you are selling yourself and you want to put yourself in the best light.

Not only can you present your résumé but you could create a virtual multimedia presentation that can present and demonstrate how talented you are. This could be especially beneficial for you Technological oriented types. The Web résumé is an outstanding tool for people seeking employment in technology-based industries.

Mel Goodman

560 Cloves
San Jose, CA 89034
408-914-3033
Mel.goodman@comcast.Net

SALES PROFESSIONAL

Dynamic, motivated, award-winning sales professional with extensive experience. Troubleshooter and problem solver. Team player who can motivate self and others. Excellent management and training skills.

RELATED EXPERIENCE

Quick Chemicals, San Jose, CA
Sales/Customer Service   1995-2000
- Advised customers to purchase products that best met their needs, while focusing attention on products more profitable to company.
- Troubleshot and solved customer problems, identifying rapid solutions and emphasizing customer satisfaction and retention.
- Oversaw shipping and receiving staff.

Freeway Ford, San Jose, CA   1990-1995
General Manager
- Consistently in top three for sales in district; met or exceeded sale objectives.
- Supervised, hired, and trained staff of 100.
- Converted a consistently money-losing store into a profitable operation by end of first year.
- Focused on customer satisfaction through employer satisfaction and training.
- Built strong parts and service business, managing excellent interaction among parts, service, and sales.
- Instituted fleet sales department, becoming top fleet sales dealer four years running.
- Built leasing portfolio from virtually none to 35% retail.

Day's Ford, Sunnyvale, CA   1988-1990
General Manager
- Reached top-ten volume dealer five years straight in Northern California.
- Managed all dealership operations including sales, parts, service, and administration.
- Profitably operated dealership through difficult economic times.
- Met or exceeded parts, sales, and service objectives.
- Maintained high-profile used car operation.

ADDITIONAL EXPERIENCE

California State, San Jose, CA   2000-2002
Computer technology
- Built customized computers for the state office.

EDUCATION

BS, California State University at Jose, CA   Major: Business Studies

JERRY BROWN
1492 Blossom Hill Road
San Jose, CA 89899
408-277-9871
JerryB@comcast.Net

SALES PROFESSIONAL
Dynamic, motivated, award-winning sales professional with extensive experience.
Troubleshooter and problem-solver. Team player who can motivate self and others. Excellent
management and training skills.

RELATED EXPERIENCE
Clearwater Pool Products, San Jose, CA
SALES/CUSTOMER SERVICE, 1995-2000
- Advised customers to purchase products that best met their needs, while focusing attention
  on products more profitable to company.
- Troubleshot and solved customer problems, identifying rapid solutions and emphasizing
  customer satisfaction and retention.
- Oversaw shipping and receiving staff

Funny Ford, San Jose, CA
GENERAL MANAGER, 1990-1995
- Consistently in top five for sales in district; met or exceeded sales objectives.
- Supervised, hired, and trained staff of 100.
- Converted a consistently money losing store into a profitable operation by the end of the
  first year.
- Focused on customer satisfaction through employee satisfaction and training.
- Built strong parts and service business, managing excellent interaction among parts,
  service, and sales.
- Instituted fleet-sales department and became top fleet-sales dealer four years running.
- Built lease portfolio from virtually none to 35% retail.

Downtown Chevrolet, Santa Clara, CA
GENERAL MANAGER, 1988-1990
- Reached top-ten volume dealer four years straight Northern California
- Managed dealership operations including sales, parts, service, and administration.
- Profitably operated dealership through difficult economic times.
- Raised customer satisfaction to zone average.
- Met or exceeded parts, sales, and service objectives.
- Maintained high-profile used car operation.

ADDITIONAL EXPERIENCE

State of California, San Jose, CA
COMPUTER TECHNICIAN, 2000-2002
- Built Customized computers for the state offices

EDUCATION
BS, California State University at San Jose, CA   Major: Business Studies

JERRY BROWN
1492 Blossom Hill Road
San Jose, CA 8998
408-277-9871
JerryB@comcast.net

SALES PROFESSIONAL

Dynamic, motivated, award-winning sales professional with extensive experience.
Troubleshooter and problem-solver. Team player who can motivate self and others. Excellent
management and training skills.

RELATED EXPERIENCE

Clearwater Pool Products, San Jose, CA
SALES/CUSTOMER SERVICE, 1990-1995
- Advised customers to purchase products that best met their needs
  while focusing attention on products more profitable to company.
- Troubleshot and solved customer problems, identify rapid solutions
  and emphasizing customer satisfaction and retention.
- Oversaw shipping and receiving staff.

Funny Ford, San Jose, CA
GENERAL MANAGE, 1990-1995
- Consistently in top five for sales in district; met or exceeded sales
  objectives.
- Supervised, hired, and trained staff of 100.
- Converted a consistently money losing store into a profitable operation by the end
  of the first year.
- Focused on customer satisfaction through employee satisfaction and training.
- Built strong parts and service business, managing excellent interaction among parts,
  service, and sales.
- Instituted fleet-sales department and became top fleet-sales dealer five
  years running.
- Built lease portfolio from virtually none to 35% retail

Downtown Chevrolet, Santa Clara, CA
GENERAL MANAGER, 1988-1990
- Reached top-ten volume dealer four years straight Northern California.
- Managed dealership operations, operations including sales, parts, service,
  and administration.
- Profitably operated dealership through difficult economic times.
- Raised customer satisfaction to zone average.
- Met or exceeded parts, sales, and service objectives.
- Maintained high-profile used car operation.

ADDITIONAL EXPERIENCE

State of California, San Jose, CA
COMPUTER TECHNICIAN, 2000-2002
- Built Customized computers for the state offices

EDUCATION

BS, California State University at San Jose, CA
Major: Business Studies

The Job Search Tool to Get You That Job

A Comparison Chart of the Four Types of Résumés

This chart points out the differences between the four types of résumés presented in this chapter.

	Printed Résumés	Scannable Résumés
Font Style	Sharp, conservative, and distinctive, see recommendation	Clean, concise, and machine-readable: Times New Roman, Arial, Helvetica.
Enhancements	Bold, *italics*, and Underline to be only type. Good for transmitting	CAPITALIZATION
Font Size	10, 11, or font best...larger font size (14, 18, 20, 22, & even larger, depending on font style) will effectively enhance your name and section headers.	11, 12, or larger
Text Format	Use centering and indentations to optimize the visual presentation	Type all information to align left.
Recommended Length	1 to 2 pages, maybe 3 if essential	1 to 2 pages recommended, length could be longer, not the main issue
Recommended Paper Color	White, Ivory, Light Gray, maybe light blue, or make sure conservative background.	Basic white best, other may not scan. Make sure there are no flecks, or shadings that might affect the scannability.
White Space	For best results use appropriately and be generous to maximize readability	Always use generously to to maximize scannability

7001 Resumes-Plus Second Edition

Electronic Résumés	**Web Résumés**
Courier	Sharp, conservative, and distinctive -- attractive Onscreen and when printed from an online document.
CAPITALIZATION is the only enhancement available to you	**Bold**, *italics*, <u>Underlining,</u> and color for Emphasis.
12 Font	10, 11, or 12 font recommend -- larger font size (14, 18, 20, 22, and even larger depending on font style) will effectively enhance your name and section headers.
Word process all information. Align left	Use align, center, and indentions to optimize the visual presentation
Length 1 to 2 pages recommended. Can be longer or as long as you want, but your résumé to text will make it longer.	Length 1 to 2 pages recommended. Can be longer, make sure your site is well organized to make it simple for the viewer to find it interesting and able to find the important material.
N/A	There is no paper, but make sure you have the right background to maximize the readers' ability to read it.
Use white space to maximize readability and break up any dense sections.	Use white space to maximize readability on the screen and for printing.

244

THE JOB SEARCH TOOL TO GET YOU THAT JOB

Lets Review to see if You Are Ready to Write Your Résumé

The following is a checklist; let us review to see if you are ready to write your résumé. Each item is an important step that you must take in the development and design of your 'drop dead résumé'.

- Are you presented clearly, and how you want to be perceived.

- Make sure you clearly document your important skills, knowledge, and qualifications.

- Clearly document your noteworthy career achievements and successes.

- Make sure you identify one or more specific job targets or positions.

- Clearly identify one or more industries that you are interested in targeting.

- From the list, or the industry, include your profession; make sure you have included key words that are specific to the target jobs.

- Select the appropriate résumé format that suits you and your career in the best light.

- Choose an attractive font that presents your résumé with maximum readability.

- Select the type of presentation you need; a printed résumé, scannable résumé, electronic résumé, a Web résumé, or a combination of all of them.

- If you do not have one, obtain for yourself a secure private e-mail address.

- Make sure that you review your résumé to make sure that all the data is current, of good format, organized, of good style, and of course with good language.

CHAPTER SEVENTEEN

SELF EMPLOYMENT

Self-employment is always an avenue that a person who is looking for a new career or job opportunity should consider. The best idea is to be very careful what business you are looking into. This is true whether you are looking to work for someone else, or yourself. It always pays to look before you leap. In the case of working for yourself it is important that you do your research before you put down any of your hard-earned cash. A great many individuals have been burned by going into a business for themselves with out doing product, or market evaluation. Be sure you are doing the right thing. Service businesses are the easiest to get going with limited finances.

The types of businesses out there are unlimited; however, considering some type of service business may be best since there is little outlay for inventory. Inventory can be expensive and can kill you before you get started. The scope of this book is not to examine going into business, however I will touch on a few details that may be helpful to you.

You may want to consider a franchise operation especially if the franchise agrees to train you and get you started in business for a fixed fee, but understand these good franchises can require a major investment. I am talking ten's of thousands of dollars, or more. However, in most cases franchises can be a very good approach. On the other side of the coin, ninety

7001 Resumes-Plus Second Edition

percent of all new small businesses will fail in the first five years. The reason given for this is usually money (or the lack of it), and not only the lack of money but also a lack of management, training, and experience. The management must not only need to know how to get funding, but to manage it. There is a great deal of money or venture capital out there if you are familiar with the business and have a great, well-developed and thought-out business plan. When I was teaching at the college and adult levels I would often run into people who would want to go into business for themselves, but I would have them come and ask me, "What business should I go into", or I had others who would ask me, "Why do I need a Business Plan or Marketing Plan?" Few businesses have made it without pre-planning. Many businesses that fail do so because they look good to the 'new' entrepreneur, but either he/she has not done their homework as to the feasibility of the business or he/she is totally lacking in management skills. Ninety percent of all franchises will survive the first five years. The reason for this is that they have: researched the target market, provided training, have a great product, and have outstanding and knowledgeable management.

You must stay in business for at least five years as a 'rule of thumb' before you can make any real money; this is called the 'break even point.' You must hang in there or you will be wiped out early in the game! You can expect to start making money after five years of hard work in almost any business. There are many franchises; therefore, you will want to investigate each one completely to determine which one is the right 'fit' for you. You will need to ask a lot of questions and get written answers to all of them to your satisfaction.

The hardest part of going into business is finding qualified customers who can buy or use your products and services. People must have enough money to keep their business afloat long enough to get proper marketing exposure. It has been estimated that to get a business going you have to be able to stay in business more than three years without making any profit. Other sources say it takes three to five years to get a business going. I am not going to tell you how long it will take you to get your business launched, but only to suggest that you need to be careful in this undertaking. There are too many variables to consider and each one of you has different needs and talents. Also, there are many different buying cycles among various customers that you have to deal with that will affect your business success. Having your own business does have many rewards which you may want to consider. The most obvious reward is money down the road; you are working for yourself and you control your own destiny.

With the 'Business Plan' and 'Marketing Plan', the business owner is in a better position to balance personal needs against the advantages and limitations of each type of organization. It is for this reason that I suggest that you take the additional steps necessary in the development of a small business that will help you in the quest for personal success. The 'Business Plan' along with a 'Marketing Plan', are important steps you should take to realize you goals.

Many millionaires were people just like you; most did not win the 'lotto' or inherit the money, they went into business for themselves. Bill Gates started in a small garage, so did Michael Dell. It is very difficult to make a lot of money working for someone else. The reason is obvious, the owner always get the profit not the workers who make it happen. You may make a comfortable living but usually you do not get rich. If you like to call the shots and take risks, you may want to have your own business. Remember, the down side is that the average millionaire has gone broke eight times before hitting it big. Having a 'good idea' and hard work pays off in the long haul. You must keep trying and follow your dream.

You must be ready to change your plans quickly as opportunities avail themselves. Opportunities come and go all the time, the door opens and closes. Remember, you are looking for the 'best' deal for your future. No one rings the bell announcing that a job or opportunity is available for you. You have to be creative, motivated, and willing to go the 'extra mile'.

No one will ever look out for your interests better than you, your family, and maybe your friends. Your place of employment will look out for its best interest which may not necessarily be your best interest. You have to look out for you! You can only trust one person every day to look out for you and that person is YOU!

7001 Resumes-Plus Second Edition

SELF ASSESSMENT

During your self-assessment consider the following 'personality profile' of the successful entrepreneur.

- Tough mindedness - the entrepreneur must be able to make and stick to decisions

- Willingness to work - You must work harder and longer than anyone else in the business

- Self-confidence - You must feel no threat to your authority

- Willing to take 'reasonable' risks - the entrepreneur must be able to take risks based upon intelligent limits

- Flexibility - As an entrepreneur, you have to be able to juggle many hats

- Creativity - You have to be able to see problems as opportunities

- Goal setting - The successful entrepreneur strives to make things come true

- Problem solving - Have the ability to chart a path to success

- Desire for profit - Remember, profit is not a bad word, be efficient with your resources.

- Enthusiasm - Avoid negativism

CHAPTER EIGHTEEN

TEMPORARY EMPLOYMENT

Sometime the only way you can get a job with the 'ideal' company or get that 'dream' job is by going to work as a temporary employee. There are 'Job Search' agencies that place temporary vacancies. Fact is, some companies have this type of hiring policy, and the way it looks is this is going to be a trend for a long while since it is working for many large corporations.

Here is why it looks good to many companies. First, the firm does not have to pay for any benefits or employee taxes. It the employees do not meet the expectations; he/she can be immediately replaced. Companies do not have to take as great a 'risk' when they are hiring, they are getting an unknown commodity. The companies can try any number of individuals on a given job until they find the individual that fits their needs. Then they can offer that person a full-time position.

This is ideal from the employer's standpoint. Are there any advantages for you? Sure, but you have to maintain an outstanding attitude and understand that you have to do your best on each assignment because you are being evaluated; and you will be developing a reputation, good or bad; if good you can use the employer as a reference. And, they could offer you full-time employment with benefits. In addition, this temporary assignment may provide you with

7001 Resumes-Plus Second Edition

additional experience, it gives you that all too valuable immediate income and a major advantage, it allows you to take a look at the workings and the operation of the 'ideal' company without making a major commitment. It may or may not be what you are really looking for and now you have a painless way to find out.

Remember, temporary agencies will test your skills at no charge, so it is also a means of checking the proficiency of some of your skills. This can be especially helpful if you have been absent from the job market for a while.

The temporary agencies earn their pay by performing a screening and placement service for employers. Their job of course is finding and placing qualified candidates for specific jobs. You must sell yourself to these agencies as much as you would if you were interviewing directly to the employer. Before you contact a temporary agency, make sure you are familiar with all phases of this job search.

Remember, be it a temporary assignment in a choice company or a 'stop gap job' that is helping you get over that unemployment hump of being low on money, you still want to do the best job you can because you never know when you will need a recommendation that with help you get the job of your dreams.

RECORD NAMES OF TEMPORARY AGENCIES

Agency _____ Phone _____

Address _____

Agency _____ Phone _____

Address _____

Agency _____ Phone _____

Address _____

Agency _____ Phone _____

Address _____

Agency _____ Phone _____

Address _____

Agency _____ Phone _____

Address _____

Other part-time or temporary work

If you are degreed, you can make money as a consultant, tutor, researcher, analyst, tax preparer, bookkeeper, or a variety of other business educational services. Or as we did, you might be able to substitute teach. Since it is projected that there will be a national shortage of teachers, this approach could offer you a fair part-time position or a new career. Most states are looking for degreed individuals as a minimum requirement. I would recommend that you discuss the requirement for an 'emergency teaching credential' with any local School District or County Office of Education. In California see **ED-Join.** Also if you check you local want ads you will also find school districts looking for people.

If you have vocational skills there are many small businesses that might be pleased to find a person who performs clerical services at home as an example. Typing and word processing can be an excellent source of income that you can do from your home. If you are skilled in the use of a computer you might start a training program. I have a long time friend who for years worked for a Doctor transcribing his notes. People in the health profession can make some very reasonable amounts of money working part-time in health care by caring for the aged, the handicapped or home care.

You may look for additional sources of income by perhaps turning your hobby into cash! You might be able to teach dance, photography, catering, art, or dog training. Do not leave any rock unturned. Talk to others to see how they did it. Make sure you write everything down. You are going to have to establish a budget so keep records. We will discuss the reasons for this later.

7001 Resumes-Plus Second Edition

In the past one of my best part-time jobs that I was able to develop was the teaching of Marketing and Business at several junior colleges and a private graduate school. Not only was it financially rewarding but personally rewarding. If you have some special training it is possible to turn this skill and experience into money. Most importantly, do not get into the bad habit of putting things off; do not waste your time. If you procrastinate, it could cost you your 'dream job'.

CHAPTER NINETEEN

THE SMALL BUSINESS: IT COULD BE FOR YOU (THE IDEAL JOB)

Your 'dream' job may be to work for a Fortune 500 company. The real fact is throughout the 1980's and into the 1990's, and even today, this country's giants like Ford, Xerox, IBM, Boeing, General Motors, and numerous others have been or are continuing to lay off hundreds and even thousands of employees; the total number of persons who have lost their jobs can be in the millions each year.

The fact is that small and medium-sized companies are now emerging as the **'key'** creative force in our nation's economy. Smaller-scale firms with less than 250 employees have climbed to employ seventy percent of the total workforce of the United States. It has been estimated that this trend will continue into the millennium.

If you are like most Americans, you may have a desire to have you own business someday. If so, pay your dues with the smaller companies, it could be exactly the apprenticeship you are looking for. When you work for a small company you often have the opportunity to learn every aspect of the business operation. When you work for a giant firm, you may get pigeon-holed and not have the same opportunities.

The entrepreneur is today's folk hero of modern business life. Not only do they provide jobs, introduce innovations, and spark economic growth, they offer many opportunities for employment and training.

The entrepreneur is no longer viewed as a dull purveyor of groceries or auto parts. Instead they are seen as energizers who take risks necessary in growing a productive economy. Each year, thousands of such individuals from teenagers to senior citizens launch new businesses of their own providing the dynamic leadership that leads to economic progress.

The entrepreneur may not only be the founder of the business but for definition it also includes all active owner-managers. This also includes second generation members of family owned firms and owner-managers who buy out the founders of existing firms. So not only can you learn and earn from working for a small firm, you might be able to purchase said company if the conditions are correct without starting from scratch to generate a new business for yourself.

No matter how or why you got to the small business you will get a chance to examine the kinds of opportunities that exist. You will also have an opportunity to explore how attractive the rewards of being an entrepreneur might be. This is true at least for the company or business you are associated with.

You must remember entrepreneurs possess special characteristics in order to succeed; you are going to have to do a lot of self-assessment to determine if you have these characteristics. Another important point which is often overlooked is to determine if it's the 'right time' to launch a new business. This point was brought up when I launched an oil field equipment sales company in the oil industry. As you know today, a barrel of oil is selling for around $70.00. Well within months of launching my business the price of a barrel of oil went to $10.00 in 1980. At that point it was impossible to give equipment away let alone sell it. Large established companies in the industry were forced to sell equipment, if they could, very cheap. Homes were being abandoned and foreclosed on in oil country; it went from a not to bad economy to a recession. It goes without saying a 'great idea' became a disaster and I closed the business after a few short months.

What kind of (small business) entrepreneurs are there and what types of businesses do they operate? I am going to explore these questions and see if I can put them into perspective. Lets look at a few individuals that have had successful ventures; this approach may give you a feel for the possibility that can be achieved in the dream of having your own business. These examples demonstrate the continued existence of opportunities and show the vast potential for new ventures. Remember, all business ventures may not be spectacular but can still provide highly attractive career options!

I have a friend named Vern, he and his brother were teachers but they got the entrepreneur itch and over time have started or been involved in several businesses to the point that they both have incomes way above average. Not that they have not had their ups and downs and failures. Today he manages and operates a Termite Inspection business in the Real Estate housing industry in Northern California. This of course is a multi-million dollar business. I have known Vern from the beginning, he new nothing about the business or industry but because of happenstance, luck, timing, or the 'hand of God', you make your own decision. He sold his home to a young man who was unhappy with the Termite firm he was working for, and they were off. They worked very hard and studied to get their license. Vern worked his tail off crawling under houses and making sales calls on Real Estate people to get there business, and they did. Not to take anything from them because I know that they worked very hard to build the business, but at the same time a major boom hit Northern California and houses were selling in days and not months as normal. So their hard work and the boom helped to build their 'dream job'.

The medical industry is a billion dollar business and there are many companies and organizations that have developed multi-million dollar operations such as hospitals, insurance companies, HMO's, etc. However, within this industry there are many entrepreneurial organizations and businesses. In Irvine, California a pharmacist established OSO Home Care,

7001 Resumes-Plus Second Edition

Inc., in 1983. OSO Home Care is independently owned and provides the highest quality of pharmaceutical products and services throughout Southern California. OSO was formed to meet the growing need for home intravenous therapy, medical surgical supplies, and medical equipment as an economic alternative to prolonged hospital care. OSO Home Care prides itself in their ability to stay on the leading edge to all the latest pharmaceutical developments. Currently, OSO offers a full range of intravenous and nutritional therapies for home use. OSO has grown from a Mom and Pop operation started in 1983 to more that a five million dollar operation today and is still growing. Both the pharmacist and his wife play an active role in the business to insure it continues to grow.

From a start-up business in 1973, Federal Express Corporation has grown to a $7 billion dollar company. It is a relatively new business as far as businesses are concerned. Federal Express originated in the mind of Frederic W. Smith, a student at Yale in 1965. He wrote a paper for an economic course proposing a new type of air freight service. According to his thesis, which later proved successful, a company with is own planes dedicated to freight distribution should be superior to existing freight forwarders who were limited by the shifting schedules of passenger airlines.

I want you to pay close attention here; this venture has been <u>unique</u> in many ways. The business was forced to start with a fleet of planes that could cover the entire country. The founder also came from a wealthy family and was able, as well as willing, to <u>risk</u> a substantial part of the family fortune, investing several million dollars. Nevertheless, the financing requirements were great and Smith found it necessary to obtain the major portion of the financing from the venture capital industry. As the business developed over a dozen equity groups participated in three major rounds of financing.

Although the start-up was unusual in many ways, it is especially significant in showing the ability of one person, a potential entrepreneur, to <u>conceptualize</u> an entirely new type of business, studying business methods and new trends. Smith's concept was implemented so successfully that it changed the very way in which business in America communicates and ships its freight.

THE JOB SEARCH TOOL TO GET YOU THAT JOB

Over the years we have seen a number of companies', large and small, move into the delivering of freight. Today there are several well known names in this industry.

After spending some time at a small Alabama college, Barbara Gardner Proctor found a job as an advertising copywriter in Chicago. As she gained experience in advertising, she also developed an appreciation for quality in advertising. One particular concept suggested for a TV commercial struck her as tasteless and offensive, this difference of opinion lead to her being fired. Following her dismissal she was able to get a loan from the Small Business Administration for $80,000 and she was on her way to opening her own business. She opened her agency in 1970. Today, still relatively small, she is well respected in her industry. She specializes in advertising, public relations, and event management. Serving accounts like Kraft Foods, Sears, and Chicago's big Jewel Food Stores she found her niche in which she can compete effectively and be true to her own values.

We have known a number of individuals with an entrepreneurial spirit, some in the industrial area, food industry, cosmetics, manufacturing, computers, and several other areas. Their personalities are all different but they all have one thing in <u>common</u> – they all were willing to take risks and preferred to be their own boss.

In a private enterprise system as we have here in America, any individual is free to enter into a business for himself/herself. At any time there could be opportunities existing in our environment. It is important that these opportunities be recognized and acted upon.

Here is a short list not necessary in time line order, but they are all well known and had or have the entrepreneurial spirit:

Mary Kay, Steve Jobs, Henry Ford, Michael Dell, Harvey Firestone, Dave Thomas, Bill Gates, Colonel Sanders, Howard Hughes; and the list goes on and on.

7001 Resumes-Plus Second Edition

Rewards and Drawbacks

There are a number of reasons why individuals are 'pulled' toward becoming an entrepreneur. These rewards may be grouped, for the sake of simplicity, into three basic categories: Profit, independence, and a satisfying life-style; if you have another reason that's ok.

Profit

The financial status of any business must compensate its owner for investing his/her time and personal savings in the business before any 'true profit' can be realized. The person who goes into business expects a return that will not only compensate them for the time, energy, and money they invest, but also reward them well for their risk and initiative taken in operating their own business. The profit incentive is the most powerful motivator for most entrepreneurs. The truth is in many cases, the dream of wealth and profit may never materialize. More than sixty-five percent (65%) of the companies that go into business are in bankruptcy after five (5) years. Even I have a long-range plan that my little book publishing and writing company be some what profitable in the near future.

Independence

It is true there are many of us out here that welcome the freedom to operate independently. For many this is an important motivating factor. In a survey of small-business owners, thirty-eight percent (38%) of those left their job because they wanted to be their boss. Many of these entrepreneurs have a strong desire to make their own decisions, take risks, and reap the rewards. Being one's own boss seems an attractive idea. I can recall working for a compressed air and pump firm in the 1980's where more than twenty-five percent (25%) of the sales staff spun off to start their own business.

Of course, independence does not guarantee an easy life. Most entrepreneurs work very hard for long hours and in many instances receive no pay in the beginning. However, they do have the satisfaction of making their own decisions within the constraints imposed by economic and other environmental factors. In talking to many independent businessmen across the county I frequently hear about the personal satisfaction they feel in regard to owning their own business. Some even refer to their business as 'fun'. As an entrepreneur myself, I can identify with this 'fun' attitude. There is an enjoyment derived from the independence as well as making the 'deal' or closing the sale, and writing your self that paycheck.

Drawbacks of Entrepreneurship

Although there are many rewards, there are also drawbacks and costs associated with business ownership. Starting and operating one's business typically demands hard work, long hours, and much emotional energy. Business ownership is described as exciting but at the same time you will find it very demanding. Then there are major strains on the family which needs to be taken into consideration. You may find that in the beginning that family members may be less then enthused and completely non supportive. You must understand your 'dream' can at least, in the beginning, be a burden on them. In some cases you may be asking them to make personal sacrifices and give up pleasures. You must take these strains on the family into consideration. And there is always the possibility of the business failing. This is a constant strain on the entrepreneur and the family. As I have indicated, the entrepreneur must assume a variety of risks; no one likes to be a loser. I recall how I felt when I had to close my sub-chapter 'S' corporation back in the 1980's. It was like I had lost a family member.

Characteristics of Entrepreneurs

The common stereotype of the entrepreneur emphasizes such characteristics as a high need of achievement, a willingness to take moderate risk, and a strong sense of self-confidence.

As we look at specific entrepreneurs we see individuals, who for the most part, fit this image. This author has known many entrepreneurs over the years and has found that most could be described as loners, had a difficult time working for others, and wanted the freedom to come and go as they please. In addition, most were money motivated and did not like to take orders from others. However, I must express words of caution, first, scientific proof of the importance of these characteristic is lacking, second, there are exceptions to every rule. Individuals who do not 'fit the mold' may still be successful as an entrepreneur.

Need for Achievement

Psychologists recognized that people differ in the degree of their need for achievement. Individuals with low need for achievement are those who seem to be contented with their present status. On the other hand, individuals with a high need for achievement like to compete with some standard of excellence and prefer to be personally responsible for their own assigned tasks. In a leading study on achievement motivation, there did appear to be a positive correlation between the need for achievement and entrepreneurial activity. It has been suggested that those who become entrepreneurs have, on the average, a higher need for achievement.

Willingness to take Risks

There is a risk that all entrepreneurs must take when starting and/or operating their own business. These risks will vary from business to business. The stress and the time required in starting and running a business will place the family as risk. You may be willing to make the sacrifice, but your family may not. This author can recall many evenings during which I enlisted the help of my children to lick hundreds of envelops and package products for mailing as I tried to get my business going. There is a point that these activities are unwelcome tasks especially in the beginning when there may be little to no rewards. You may be building your future business, while at the same time destroying your family. In some situations the outcome depends on timing and pure luck.

Self-Confidence

Individuals who possess self-confidence feel they can meet the challenges that confront them. They have a sense of mastery over the types of problems they might encounter. Studies indicate that successful entrepreneurs tend to be self-confident individuals who see the potential problems in launching a new venture but believe in their own ability to overcome these problems.

Entrepreneurial Opportunity

There is no substitute for education and experience as part of the necessary preparation for most entrepreneurs; although requirements vary with the nature and demands of the particular business. However, there is a requirement for some 'know-how'. Besides having experience, additionally prospective entrepreneurs must build their financial resources in order to make the initial investment. This author can recall when I was in your shoes, many friends and acquaintances were telling me 'why don't you go into business for yourself?' This sounded simple to my friendly advisers, however, without financial resources, research, experience, and motivation I couldn't easily 'run off' and start a business, and neither can anyone else.

There are no hard and fast rules concerning the right age for starting a business, although some age deterrents exist. Young people may be discouraged from entering an entrepreneurial career by inadequacies in preparation and resources. On the other hand, older people develop family, financial and job commitments that make entrepreneurship seem too risky. As much 'fun' as it was to have my own corporation this author would have to think long and hard about building a new business. For other older people, there is a stronger interest in acquiring retirement benefits and/or higher positions within their current organization with rewards of greater responsibilities and higher salaries with out taking the risk.

The ideal time for starting a business appears to lie somewhere between the late 20's and early 40's when there is a balance between preparatory experiences on the one hand and family obligations on the other. But I understand why Colonel Sanders did not really get going until he was 72 years old; obviously there are exceptions to this generalization. For other persons at ages 50 or 60 they walk away from successful careers in big business when they become excited by the prospects of entrepreneurship.

Anticipating the Event

Many potential entrepreneurs never take the fateful step of launching their own business ventures. Some, like this author, actually make the move stimulated by precipitation events such as a job termination, job dissatisfaction, or an unexpected opportunity.

Losing a job is only one of many types of experiences that may serve as a catalyst to 'taking the plunge' as an entrepreneur. Some individuals become so disenchanted with formal academic programs that they simply walk away from the classroom and start new lives as entrepreneurs. Others become exasperated with the rebuffs of perceived injustices at the hands of superiors in organizations and leave in disgust to start their own businesses.

In a more positive vein, prospective entrepreneurs may unexpectedly stumble across some business opportunities. A friend may offer, for example, to sponsor an individual as an Amway distributor. Or a relative may suggest that the individual leave a salaried position and take over a family business. What is interesting here is that I was offered to also go into business with my friend Vern, back in the 1970's, but because of my family pressure, and I was finishing my Masters degree, I declined. My point here is that opportunities present themselves all the time. It does happen. There is little in the way of precipitating events involved in their decision to become an entrepreneur. We cannot say what percentage of new entrepreneurs make a move because of some particular event. However, many who launch new firms or otherwise go into business for themselves are obviously helped along by precipitous events.

Preparing for the Career as an Entrepreneur

It is important that we mix the right amount of education and experience. How much or what kind of each is necessary is notoriously difficult to specify. Dave Thomas, President of Wendy's Hamburgers, at 15 years old was working in the restaurant industry. Later after meeting and helping to reestablish four Kentucky Fried Chickens with the Colonel, he 'spun off' and developed the Wendy's empire. Bill Gates with little to no money, but had a college education, developed Microsoft and we all know where he is today. Henry Ford was in the bicycle business and believed that he could build an automobile for resale, and he did!

Different types of ventures call for different types of preparation. The background or skills needed to start a company to produce computer software are obviously different from those needed to open an automobile garage. There are also striking differences in the background of those who succeed in the same industry. For these reasons, we must be cautious in discussing qualifications, realizing there are exceptions to every rule.

Some fascinating entrepreneurial success stories feature individuals who dropped out of school to start their ventures. This should not lead one to conclude however, that education is generally unimportant. Research tells us that new business owner's formal education is superior to that of the general adult public. In recent years we have seen college and universities greatly expanding their offerings in entrepreneurship and small business. Now thousands of students across the country are taking low-top-start-your business courses.

Business owners themselves identify three general factors that they regarded as important:

1. **Entrepreneurial value** – Intuition, extroversion, risk taking, creativity, flexibility, a sense of independence, and a high value of time.

2. **Managerial skills** – Niche strategy, effective management of cash flow, a simple but efficient budgetary system, pre-ownership experience, education, and a simple organization structure.

3. **Interpersonal skills** – Good relationship with a credit office or banker, good customer service relations, and good employee relations.

Types of Entrepreneurships

The field of small business takes in a large variety of entrepreneurs and entrepreneurial ventures. I am going to review a number of entrepreneurships by identifying various types of people and the firms that are out there.

New Wave of Entrepreneurs

The new 'wave of entrepreneurs' are women. Their presence has risen dramatically over the last two decades. We have seen a growth of 57.4 percent increase of women-owned businesses, the business receipts rising by 81.2 percent. In the United States women own 28 percent of the businesses and employ 10 percent of the nation's workers. Women are opening beauty shops, clothing stores, and the women ownership of construction firms rose by nearly 60 percent, also their ownership of manufacturing firms more than doubled between 1982 and 1997.

Women do face barriers; some women find limited opportunities finding business relationships with others in similar positions. It takes time and effort for these to gain full acceptance and to develop informal relationships with others in local, mostly male, business and professional groups. Women are attacking this problem by increasing their participation is predominantly male organizations and also by forming networks of their own – the female equivalent of the 'old network'

Franchises

Because of the constraints and guidance provided by contractual relationships with franchising organizations, the franchise functions as a limited entrepreneur. Franchising has many advantages and disadvantages to them. It is not within the scope of this book to go into great detail on the subject of franchising. However, since it may be an option to being self-employed, we do need to at least bring it to your attention. There are three shortcomings that you need to be aware of: 1. The cost of the franchise, 2. The restrictions on growth that may come with a franchising contract, and 3. The loss of absolute independence on the part of the franchisee.

If you have an interest in franchising take your time to investigate wisely the franchisor to make sure the business opportunity being offered truly meets you needs for the present and the future. The sources of the information to get answers to your question are, the franchisor themselves, government, and trade associations. Talk to other franchisees, they with have valuable input about the franchise; also look at business publications. You may also want to speak with a franchise consultant; when choosing a franchise you need to pick one that is reputable. A franchise consultant is not an attorney so you will want to consult an attorney also to review and evaluate all contracts or legal documents before you sign. You might want to attend a franchise seminar. There are many examples of good franchises out there, but there are some that do go wrong. I once new a young man that wanted to go into business for himself, so he found a well known tool rental franchise. The first thing that came up was he did not have experience with tools. The next he found was that to have the franchise he had to move from an area that he was well known in, he had to put his family in disarray by breaking them up; some of his children were in their senior year of high school and basically refused to move to the new location which was clear across the county. The franchise company selected an area that had a wide range of population swings, where in the summer time there were thousands of residents, but reduced to nearly a 1/3 of the population in the weather time which caused drastic sales and income swings.

And of course the entrepreneur was not known in the area. As we have suggested it takes time to get established when starting a business. So, do to the wide business swings, limited financial backing, limited support of his family, perhaps the wrong location, being unknown in the area; who know this entrepreneur dumped his business at a loss and returned to where he relocated his family from.

Make sure you explore all aspects of the franchise before you take the plunge. Had the above businessman started a similar business where he was well known, it might have been a success.

Growth of the Firm

The potential growth and profit of various small business ventures will vary greatly. Some of these ventures will create millionaires others will provide a modest return to the entrepreneur. Income from some of these small businesses can vary from $50,000 to $200,000 annually. In contrast there are firms that provide income that will allow the owners to barely survive. Recognize that there is an entire range of ventures along each point of the spectrum, each of them with varied problems and rewards.

The point of this chapter is to suggest that developing your own business is one opportunity to consider as you continue seeking ways to advance your career. In addition, as a small business owner, you have the possible rewards from just getting by to creating a multi-million dollar enterprise.

CHAPTER TWENTY

HOW SHOULD YOU DRESS?

The first few seconds may be all you get to make that lasting impression. This may be surprising to you, nevertheless, it is true. Think about when you see or meet a man or a woman; we all make judgments in the first few seconds when we meet them. The impression we get may or not be fair, but the judgment is made. We may adjust or change our opinion over time, and then again we may not. Dress for your success! People rarely change their opinion of you at an interview once it is set. They will not want to admit to an error.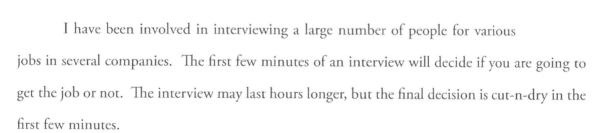

I have been involved in interviewing a large number of people for various jobs in several companies. The first few minutes of an interview will decide if you are going to get the job or not. The interview may last hours longer, but the final decision is cut-n-dry in the first few minutes.

The key question is why? The reason appears to be that if the interviewers like you and what they see, you will get the job. You will be shown the door if the interviewers don't like you.

7001 Resumes-Plus Second Edition

The way you dress or your cloths may help you get the job. I am sure you have heard the statement 'clothes make the man' well here we go!

A man should wear conservative clothes to the interview, and a woman should do the same. Do not wear outlandish or fancy clothing. You should be conservative in all respects.

You do not want to over or under dress. This is true of anyone. You should always be in good taste. Men can wear a 'power suit' like a three piece black suit with a coordinating shirt, tie, and black shoes. Women should generally wear a dark dress with little or no make up. Avoid oversized way out earrings, nose rings, or any way out accessories. Wearing too much make up may detract from you and the interviewer. Try to wear something which you would like to see if you were doing the interviewing.

Let's talk for a moment about smoking. You may or may not smoke, fewer and fewer people smoke today. Many offices and companies are non-smoking. There appears to be little to stop the no smoking movement. You should not smoke during an interview. This is true even if you see a smoking permitted sign. Let me point this out, more often then not people who do not smoke, do not like the smell of tobacco smoke. If you smoke before the interview it will permeate your clothing and a non-smoker can detect this and be irritated. You may not notice, but they can and this could cost you the interview.

Hair

Let's talk about hair. Many of you may like long hair and so may the interviewer, to a point. I was told a story about a salesperson that had grown his hair very long. The longer his hair got the less business he did. Now I do not know if this is a true story or not, or if it has happened to you, but unless you are interviewing for a 'Rock Band', keep the length in good taste.

For men, keep you hair trimmed neatly but not shaved; women should have neat hair for all interviews. Long hair to the floor may be great for the 'Believe it or Not' book, but it has no place in an interview; also multiple colors. The 'Rule of thumb' here is, keep it conservative.

Avoid gum, candy, and anything you could be eating during the interview. Any of this kind of stuff can get points taken away from your interviewing performance. It is distracting as well as being discourteous.

Just a word on drinks at or during an interview, try to get your coffee or drinks before or after the interview. Do not accept a drink of coffee (even if one is offered) at the interview. There are only three things that can happen with drinks at the interview and all are bad. Tell the interviewer thanks but you just had a drink. I can tell you, that here is where 'Murphy's Law' comes into play, 'if it can spill it will'.

And those 'black shoes' you are wearing, always shine your shoes before the interview. Some interviews are lost on bad shoes alone. Wash your hands, and keep your finger nails clean and well cut. If you never had a manicure, get one.

Notes

During your research, if you can, find out how the interviewer dresses and how much emphasis the company puts on 'proper business attire'. You might try to visit the company or office and observe what the dress code is at the firm. Follow the company's rules if you know them.

CHAPTER TWENTY ONE

THE MULTIPLE PARTY INTERVIEW

There will be times when you are going to be interviewed by a panel or more than one person. I have faced this situation many times. You may be warned in advance and sometimes not. Your position here is that you should be prepared regardless of how many people are interviewing you. If possible, try to find out if it will be a group decision in hiring you or if there will be only one person making the decision on the job you are applying for.

You will be asked questions by several different people, sometimes there will be a lot of questions coming from all directions at the same time. At other times, and normally in the Education community, each panelist may ask questions from a formal list or extemporaneous questions in a round robin format. Your task is to answer all the questions quickly, briefly, and as accurate as you can. Do not try to fake answers. If you don't know the answer, state so. Look directly at the person who is asking the questions. Try to make eye contact with all of the panelists in turn.

In the Education community you will find that the panelist arrangement is common place. You will generally have 5-7 panel members. In the business climate, more often than not, the interview will be one on one, but sometimes there may be more than one person involved.

7001 Resumes-Plus Second Edition

On occasion, I have seen multiple interviews taking place where the President and Vice President are both interviewing a candidate. There could be a HR person and a Sales Manager.

If a dispute arises between people on the panel, you should give your opinion if you are asked. A dispute may arise over one of your answers, but do not get into an argument with anyone on the panel. If necessary state your position, but if you argue, you will always lose. The panelists will always feel they are right. This will result in you possibly not getting the job.

You should generally side with the top-ranking person on the panel if you can, but do not tell this person that he or she is wrong. They will probably be important in deciding if you get hired. You want them on your side. Some times they have the only say in who gets the job. Try to get him or her to like you. Above all, always dress appropriately for the interview. See chapter 21 which discuss in detail appropriate dress.

If you can, try to get feedback on your résumé and presentation at the end of your interview. This may or may not happen, but if you do not ask, you can be assured you will not get a critique of your work or presentation. This may help you to improve your presentation on your next interview and make you 'shine' that much brighter. Remember, there will always be another interview.

Always ask what the next step is until you are hired and what the time frame is for these steps. More often then not after you have had the panel interview, school districts will give you a written set of questions that they will ask you to respond too. The newest approach is to have you answer these questions in written form in handwriting or by word processing on a provided computer.

I heard of a situation that an individual once interviewed at a company that was going to hire someone six (6) months in the future. This kind of situation can be a waste of your time and gas unless you are currently employed and looking toward the future for opportunities. You may want to find out when they are hiring before you go to the interview. This will avoid wasting

274

THE JOB SEARCH TOOL TO GET YOU THAT JOB

your time and efforts over non jobs. Companies have been know to conduct interviews merely to poll the market to see what is available and at what price. These polling exercise are a waste of time since they will never result in your getting a job because there is no job!

Attempting to get as much information as possible out of the panel is always prudent. This may include things like how many jobs are available and how many people have applied for the various positions. The more information you have, the better off you are. Remember, information is power. Ask how many people are ahead of you.

It is a good idea to be there at least 15 minutes early. Call if there is some reason you are going to be late. When I was interviewing in both Industry and the Educational community, I always tried to get to the interview 30 to 45 minutes early. This gave me time to check out the office, maybe talk to the secretary, and get a feel of the office climate and dynamics; collect your thoughts! You can also take care of restroom needs if any and make any adjustments to your personal appearance before the interview. You should never be late, and under no circumstances should you be late without calling. You should use your cell phone or a phone booth if you find yourself not on time for some unforeseen reason.

In Southern California, and I am sure in many other metropolitan areas, there are ever changing traffic conditions on our highways, streets, and thoroughfares, leaving early for a job interview will give you the opportunity to adjust to these conditions as well as allow you to locate unfamiliar addresses. Besides, you need to find a parking place, your papers, and so on.

It is generally not a good idea to ask for or get a coffee. There is a chance that in the process of moving from your seat to the interviewing room that you might spill it. I have seen this happen to someone with a 'coke'. This has happened to me and you need to understand this can distract you from the interview. You are now attempting to clean up and do the interview too!

I have provided for you a number of the standard questions that are asked by interviews both in the normal one on one situation and on the panel Education interview. I strongly

7001 Resumes-Plus Second Edition

recommend that you get a yellow pad and practice answering the questions before you go to the interview so that you will be prepared.

Here are some additional Teacher Interview Questions

1. How do you explain grades to your class (Students) and parents?

Answer: What I do is develop a grade sheet, with requirements that I make available to the parent and the student the first day of class. I send it home with the student and provide it to the parent during back to school night. I provide the student with a weekly assignment sheet. The student is required to develop a handbook around the requirement on the material I provide for them. **You need to develop your own statement.**

2. How do you determine if you have 'English as a second language' learners?

Answer: There are two basic methods, first, get the information from Counseling if you can, which might be slow, but try. Information can come from the classroom by talking to the students. You can speak with them and also evaluate from their English lessons. **You need to develop your own statement.**

3. Present a lesson: This you will need to have some practice with. Have several types that you can do.

Answer: Maybe a generic one, and one or two in your field. They need to be exciting, new, and creative. Give examples how you might address the students. Groups, teams, lectures, cooperative learning seems to be the most impressive. **You need to develop your own statement.**

4. How do you motivate students? This is an amazing question, since many of the people interviewing you may not be able to motivate anyone.

Answer: You will need to come up with your own answer; however I have talked about being truly excited about learning and the subject matter. Give examples of being able to advance from the knowledge. But I also discuss working with a student who was not interested in learning and finding out his or her interest and turn the student around. You may have to make up a story. **You need to develop your own statement.**

5. Explain why you might be a benefit to the school district or teaching organization or how you might contribute to the system. If you have any questions this is your turn to make sure you ask about the job you need to know. **You need to develop your own statement.**

If you are in business you may not have questions dealing with students, but you will have similar questions dealing with your employee-employer relations, how you might benefit the company, deal with other employees, such as dealing with an employee the is often late for work, or who might be drinking on the job.

CHAPTER TWENTY-TWO

THE COST FOR JOB SEARCH

Let's talk about the costs associated with job search for a moment of two. First, job search is a job, and a costly one at that. You should be spending 4, 6, 9 hours a day doing some sort of job search. It could be developing your résumé, research at the library, or interviewing. It is the most important function you should be involved in if you want to survive in our complex society. You will want to set aside time as well as money so you can to cover the cost of job search. Let's say that you want to send out 100 pieces of mail (letter of applications/ résumés) per week. Good paper use for résumés will cost around $.08 per sheet. Say you put three (3) sheets in one envelope. This alone is $67.00 a week; which includes the envelope and postage. You could spend more than $268.00 a month. There are other costs such as ink, phone calls, transportation, faxing, and so on. If you join one or more résumé mailing web sites you'll spend more than $30.00 just for that. A good job search program isn't an inexpensive task to say the least.

Let us share some additional thoughts about the cost of a job search campaign. I have a long-time friend of about thirty years. He was employed by a world renowned aerospace

7001 Resumes-Plus Second Edition

firm and was 'downsized' about two years ago or so. His approach to job search was to mail out perhaps 5 résumés per week or less. On the other hand, when I was 'downsized', I made out 25 to 30 résumés a day. Which one of us was 'right' about the choice you have to make. Nevertheless, there is a cost. As we have found out, it takes more than 100 résumés to generate one interview. So we have our work cut out for us. As the title of the book indicated, there was a time that over 7,001 résumés were sent out. The truth is that while developing this second book, I found myself still interested in getting back into the labor force so I developed and sent out more than 800 letters of application, a number of faxes, and dozens of E-mails. I generated a small number of interviews and fewer offers. The point I want to make is you have your work cut out for you and it is an expensive proposition. During the recession of the early 90's there were ten's of thousands of Americans competing for very few jobs. Today, with the economy 'boom', there are still thousands of job seeks out there looking for a good jobs and upward mobility. The fact is it is still competitive.

Take your time and set up a job search budget that works for you and meets your expectations. Do not forget your only going to get out of a job search program what you put in it. As the old saying goes 'Nothing ventured, nothing gained'. So if finding a job is important to you, do not take it lightly, to get a job you will have to pay whatever the price is. You must be willing to sacrifice to get there. This is something only you can do. No one can do this work for you.

Whatever you do-do not quit!

CHAPTER TWENTY-THREE

TAX DEDUCTION JOB SEARCH

Because of your job search you may generate large expenses as a result. In most cases you will be able to deduct some, if not all your job search cost. This includes the cost of your car mileage to and from your interview. Also, any related transportation costs. This includes picking up materials, copies from Office Max, cost for postage, paper, ink, air fare, meals, phone costs, tolls, gas, paying to place your résumé on the internet, and all associated costs. If you fax your résumé, special deliver it, or have any special preparation, make sure you get and keep all your receipts.

Develop the following list:

- Postage cost
- Paper cost/envelopes
- Stamps
- Typing/word processing cost
- Mileage
- Air fare
- Telephone cost
- Hotel cost
- Meals
- Résumé preparation
- Toll cost
- Ink cost/toner
- All associated job search costs

List here all costs associated to your job search:

7001 Resumes-Plus Second Edition

_____

_____

_____

_____

_____

For further tax information on tax deductions for job search please see your tax advisor or your CPA. This book is <u>not</u> intended to give you tax advice. These guidelines given are only to help you to evaluate your job search situation. Individual situations may vary.

CHAPTER TWENTY-FOUR

THE BEGINNING – NOT THE END!

To finally find a career position is not the end, it is only the beginning of rebuilding a career and hopefully it is your 'dream job'. If you have made it to the end of this book, I hope that your journey was rewarding. It was not too long ago that our grandfathers would work for a firm for thirty (30) years, receive the gold pocket watch, and retire. This story is happening less and less in today's economy. What we are seeing more and more is individuals working for more than one company. In fact some so called experts are telling us that we may have up to ten (10) job changes. And of course more than one career.

In my case over my some 30 plus years of work I have been in sales working for several companies working for a number of different firms, the military, in education teaching for several school districts, community colleges, a private graduate school and more. Not all my job changes were because I wanted to make more, and I was not a 'job hopper'. By the way I really never liked the term. I look back and see a lot of valuable experience and opportunities were gotten, but at times there were some challenges and hardships going through job search and unemployed periods. But on the plus side, I worked for some 'key' people, traveled nationally and internationally. No, I don't feel bad about changing jobs and moving around. There were times that I changed jobs because I had to, the company I was working for was having financial problems and I was laid off. It became a real battle getting my career going, and I can assure

7001 Resumes-Plus Second Edition

you I like to eat as well as the next guy, according to my wife maybe too much. That's another story and another book. As I said, doors sometimes open, but there is the other side; sometimes things are not as timely as they should be. Of course I was <u>not</u> in the 'crash' of '29, but I have seen some challenging recessions.

The point is this: more than likely some of you are going to see some good times and some bad times during your career. You will want to make the best of the good times and minimize the bad. You will want to do the best job of research you can to find the best position that fits you and affords you the opportunity of career growth that you are looking for. But today I am going to advise you that you need to keep honing your skills and keep your résumé up-to-date. New companies are coming at the same time industries are going or being moved offshore and by honing your skills, you will be in a better position to make that change if it becomes necessary. And the more your practice, the better you will get!

There are many experts out there who would suggest that in today's global economy you actively continue to keep looking for a job and interview any time and all the time you get the opportunity. This will keep your interviewing skills sharpened, besides the fact that one day you will come upon the 'job of your dreams'. You should remember this dream job may prove to be a mirage of organizational changes. As you know, every time we pick up the newspaper, turn on the radio or TV, some major company is 'downsizing', 'restructuring', 'reorganizing', 'right-sizing', it could be the firm that you are currently working for. I am not telling you to become 'paranoid'; I am suggesting that you are always prepared. As late as yesterday I was addressing a class of students explaining to them how today we will more than likely have several jobs in our career as well as several career path changes. Because of this, plus the fact that technology is moving so quickly, I suggested to them that I see myself going to school the rest of my life and suggested that they plan on doing the same. I believe that this is a wise path for you to follow. Since computers are becoming more and more a part of our lives it would be advantageous that you take additional computer training. I have over ten years of computer experience and training, but with the new programs coming out all the time I am constantly taking these classes and training. Then there are Management courses. I am sure you are getting the drift. Besides the apparent benefits, these courses are generally deductible as career enhancements and advancements from your taxes. You will need to consult your tax consultant for the details in this area.

Remember; find yourself a 'champion'; in fact if you can find a champion in several career areas you will want to do this while you have a job. This is not an easy task and this is why you want to do the development of the champion before you need them. It is a 'prudent' move on your part though. You will never know when you are going to need someone to go to 'bat' for you. Also 'network, network, network'. I can't overemphasize this point. Do this at your place of business, church, club, and everywhere you go. You want to talk to everyone. Again start 'network' before you need the help or support. I try to talk to everyone. Also, get yourself some business cards; this is one of the best $10.00 to $30.00 investments you will ever make. You can use the business cards from your firm; however I would suggest that you have your own card. If you do not have a company business card or you do not want to associate your firm with your job search, and I would suggest not, have your own personal business card made up. You can have your name, address, and phone number, or, offer some special service. Be creative. ALWAYS carry your business card with you. You should give it out freely to anyone who may help you on your job search. Since almost every restaurant has a 'Free lunch collection bowl' you might be able to pick-up a free lunch once in a while too. Now, I have my own business card with my Web site, and I pass it out, I am doing this today for a slightly different reason, but I do it. In my case, I want people to see my books, but nevertheless, I am doing my 'networking' and it does work. Why not set up your own Web site; put your résumé, cover letter, and special certificates on it so you can broadcast you résumé on demand.

Build yourself a job search portfolio or binder. In this portfolio place samples of your various cover letters, résumés, job applications, and other important documents that may be

7001 Resumes-Plus Second Edition

valuable and needed in you job search mission. One of the classes I taught at the High School level included a collection of all the computer work the students were doing. Copies of this type, or samples of this kind of work, could be placed in your portfolio.

Many times you may be required to fill out a job application, provide references, and letters of recommendation. If you are a teacher your placement file and transcripts can go in your portfolio. Your portfolio, binder, or Job Search Handbook, will provide you with a central location to store and keep this information in for quick reference. I also keep samples of some of my special work in my binder, such as Advertising material and samples of new letters I have designed. So my advice to you is to build your own binder, handbook, or portfolio; it will be helpful in your job search. One more thing here, many times I have seen individuals trying to fill out a job application requiring, names, addresses, and so forth; if you have already done this, you can take in your copy then quickly and easily fill out these forms.

If you start your own business as a career alternative, great, but do not try it alone; seek out advice and talk to people in a similar business you might be interested in. In other words, 'do your research'. If it means that you have to take special training, travel some distance to get the information, or invest a little money in the beginning, do it. Ask questions, get opinions. Seek thoughts, suggestions, ideas, and maybe on the job training. If you know what the business is you are going to go into, be a great 'listener' and write everything down.

When you have gotten an idea and it excites you by keeping you awake at night and it's on your mind all the time, you may want to proceed. At this point, talk to business people in the industry, the manufactures, and then start developing a business and marketing plan. You will also want to talk to your banker, and more importantly your family. Often businesses fail because the family fails to buy into the development of the business. There are approximately 15 million small businesses in America and over a million new ones start yearly, but only 10 percent make it beyond five years. So to give yourself and the business a better chance, follow the proven steps. Small businesses fail because of a lack of money. A lack of money caused solely by bad

The Job Search Tool to Get You That Job

management. The scope of this book is not to prepare you to go into business; that is another book. But I will suggest you seek out training and help from your local Community College, Continuing Education Program, and Small Business Administration. You may also take business courses at your local Universities. In addition, as I was suggesting, you can get a great deal of information from the U.S. Small Business Administration; they can provide you with complete sets of training handouts on starting and operating a small business.

This information includes:

- o Understanding the Nature of Small Business
- o Determining your Potential as an Entrepreneur
- o Technical Assistance
- o Types of Ownership
- o Marketing Strategy
- o Location

- o Financing
- o Legal Issues
- o Government Regulations
- o Business Planning
- o Management
- o Records
- o Other

For more information contact the Small Business Administration in your area, or write, U.S. Department of Small Business Administration Washington, DC U. S. Printing Office. Have them send you a list of their publications. You may also contact The National Center for Research in Vocational Education – The Ohio State University, Columbus, Ohio.

Know what problems you will face before you start out and get the information and training first. Good Luck!

CHAPTER TWENTY-FIVE

HEADHUNTERS AND RECRUITERS

Professional 'Headhunters' and Recruiters may work for you, I can say in the past they have worked for me but they can cost thousands of dollars. This is before they even get started and there is no guarantee of a job at the end. There are headhunters and recruiters that advertise themselves as 'free', then there are management and consultants who are set-up to 'redesign' and 'coach' you, to help totally recreate you. Now these guys are very expense. Depending on your circumstances though they may be worth the investment, I have to leave this up to you. My advice to you is, just be very careful. The paid consultants and management search firms paint them selves as being able to find you a better and higher paying position. I can not dispute this but you may have a less than satisfactory experience with them. One thing I will say here is that several years ago I was very pleased with an organization called Management Recruiters. On a couple of occasions they did help me find two very good Industrial Sales Positions. I have found over the years that generally Job recruiting organizations will do anything to get you to sign up for their services and many times they do very little thereafter. But I want to be fair, this has been my experience in more resent times. Or of course, come up with a whole lot of money for the complete make over, which I have never done.

7001 Resumes-Plus Second Edition

There are several types of headhunters, and in my opinion, are basically not your friends. I think you need to go in with that attitude. They generally only get paid if, one way or the other, they get you placed in a position. I am sure they want you to succeed, but for their welfare not yours. I am not going to tell you not to use them; on the contrary, they can be valuable to you. You may have good luck with them and they can expose you to that second job market that I referred to earlier in this book. As I have indicated, there were times in my career that I did advance my employment situation by using a search firm. You may find that it is important to understand how they work for you or against you. You will also want to know how they work for the employer and themselves. Headhunters may be offering services as an employment consultant, contingency employment, employment agency, retainer recruiter, management recruiter, etc. You should look closely at each one of these and determine if they can be beneficial to you.

If you are introduced to an employer by a search firm, you come with a price tag on your head. This may or may not be bad, but this price tag can be tens of thousands of dollars depending on the position being recruited for. If you come to the employer on your own, you will not have this price tag and the employer may overlook a particular skill you are lacking but can be taught if overall you are the type of candidate he had in mind and the large fee will be saved. With the price tag route the employer will want every skill or experience covered. The question is can you find this job without the recruiter, if not then it is worth the deal. This is a chance both you and the employer have to take.

Some employers, because of the volume of work they do with an agency, pay a retainer so it is safe to assume that this headhunter is going to present applicants that meet all criteria. The fact is, if you do not have all that the employer is looking for you are not going to be presented. If you are being presented, during this consideration process you will not be presented to any other employer until the first headhunter is done with you and you are back in the file.

The Job Search Tool to Get You That Job

The contingency headhunter might present you but he is also going to present other applicants. The contingency headhunter does not get paid unless the employer selects one of his applicants. Consequently, he has a loyalty to the employer and not you.

I discussed the job consultant that you pay $3,000 or more for their service; this type of headhunter will help you with your application, letters of introduction, even distribution of your résumé. These paid consultants will help you learn terms and refresh you on your interviewing techniques and skills. You must be careful in your selection as well as you must be able to afford this service. Be aware of the fact that they cannot and will not guarantee that they will get you a job.

I had a personal experience with this type of headhunter which resulted in my having to forfeit $1,500 to the consultant. Although I had started interacting with the consultant, I managed to find a Sales Management position on my own. I was unable to get any of my money back from the consultant even though the firm was only in the beginning phase of working on my behalf. I did like some of the stuff that the agency could do for me but was it worth the money, not at that point. Maybe I waited too long to get started with them, nevertheless I did not get any of my fee back.

There is nothing that these firms can tell you that you cannot do for yourself with the help of this workbook except perhaps introduce you to the invisible job market. That is a chance you will have to take. They can however be a waste of your time and money if you are of the opinion that they can not get you employment. As I indicated, these agencies cannot guarantee you employment. It is a real 'catch 22'. You may not be able to wait for them to perform, if time and money is not an issue for you this may be a viable resource. You should plan for over a month or two, perhaps longer, though keep in mind that it may never work for you. So never rely on one source, always have that ace in your pocket, and that ace is you.

One of the things that I have discovered in regard to 'free headhunters' is that if you are somewhat hard to place, or you do not fit any of their openings quickly, they will drop you. The

7001 Resumes-Plus Second Edition

contingency headhunter may be broadcasting your résumé without first letting you know where they have been sent. Should you, as an individual, approach one of these companies, remember you will have a 'price tag on your head' which may put you out of the running before you have a chance to present your special skills and talents.

Most headhunters will ask you to list every company that you have contacted. He will not want to waste time going to a company that you have already approached. Be sure to keep your list updated.

I can understand you may feel compelled to contact a headhunter for help out of frustration. You may be setting yourself up for trouble. You are now in the right position for the contingency recruiter to put that price tag on your head and rush your résumé to potential employers before you do, and at the same time, you are equally vulnerable to have the same price tag applied by a retainer recruiter. So now it is possible for you to wind up with a double price on your head.

You cannot tell when you are going to obtain the service of a recruiter or what type of recruiter you are getting as there is not a door sign indicating their type of business. The recruiter can also change roles from time to time. It will be very important for you to discuss the type of business this agency has and how you will fit into the picture.

It is only natural, when presenting your self to the recruiter, to want to present yourself in the most favorable manner. The problem here is that the contingency recruiter is inclined to 'blast' your résumé everywhere. He wants people, lots of people, coming in as 'the more bread upon the water', the better chance for him/her to make money. So if your appointment is easy to get and if you are rushed through the interview favorably, the warning bells and lights should go off in your head. You are probably working with a recruiter that sees you as the next highly marketable 'meal ticket'. Maybe worse if you are seen as unmarketable.

Be wary of the recruiter who tells you only what you want to hear. You do not want to be circulated unless the recruiter takes the time to get your approval to submit your résumé to a firm or organization.

Remember, when you communicate with recruiters, never be negative about your employer and never appear desperate. Also keep in mind that recruiters are 'assignment –oriented', they need to fill their active contracts or job listings. So, when you send them a résumé or register online, most of the time your résumé will simply be placed in their files.

What to Expect From Distributions to Recruiters

➤ People with recognizable 'tickets' do best (for example well-known schools, degrees, blue chip affiliations, etc.)

➤ People in popular occupations also do best. Some response is immediate, but most come in over months.

➤ Contacting recruiters is less effective for those in low demand specialties or for those making a career change.

➤ Also, as you go up the pyramid, since fewer jobs are available, the response will be lower. Overall, it's a low percentage game that is why you need greater numbers.

➤ A second distribution to the same list three to four months later produces about 80% of the initial response.

When responses come in and they engage you on the phone, be ready with your 30 to 60 second commercial. Also, keep in mind that you will be most popular with recruiters if you will explore attractive situations, but are not openly unhappy. Though timing is critical, luck can also play a role.

CHAPTER TWENTY-SIX

THE TOP 100 COMPANIES IN THE UNITED STATES

The following list is a list of 100 companies rated by their employees as being the best companies to work for. While you are doing your job search and career planning it might be to your advantage that you explore employment with one of these firms.

Rank Company	Job growth	Company size	U.S. employees
1. Genentech	20	Midsized	8,121
2. Wegmans Food Markets	7	Large	31,890
3 Valero Energy	5	Large	16,582
4. Griffin Hospital	2	Small	1,048
5. W.L Gore & Associates	6	Midsize	4,537
6. Container Store	16	Midsize	2,857
7. Vision Service Plan	-2	Small	1,915
8. J.M. Smucker	-13	Midsized	2,930
9. Recreational Equipment (REI)	9	Midsized	7,443
10. S.C. Johnson	0	Midsized	3,404
11. Boston Consulting Group	17	Small	1,356
12. Plante & Moran	9	Small	1,358

295

13.	Quicken Loans	60	Midsized	2,951
14.	HomeBanc Mortgage	9	Small	1.342
15.	Wholefoods Market	18	Large	33,248
16.	Edward Jones	3	Large	29,197
17.	Republic Bancorp	-9	Small	1,190
18.	Baptist Health Care	0	Midsized	4,003
19.	Alston & Bird	3	Small	1,509
20.	Kimley-Horn & Associates	24	Small	1,777
21.	QuikTrip	6	Midsized	7,819
22.	American Century investment	0	Small	1,778
23.	Qualcomm	23	Midsize	7,561
24.	David Weekley Homes	18	Small	1,361
25.	Cisco Systems	8	Large	26,644
26.	Goldman Sachs	3	Large	11,836
27.	NetworkAppliance	26	Midsized	2,712
28.	FourSeasons	-12	Large	10,625
29.	Starbucks	26	Large	91,056
30.	SAS Institute	1	Midsized	5,118
31.	Robert W. Baird	-1	Small	2,125
32.	Alco Laboratories	1	Midsized	6,227
33.	Nugget Markets	10	Small	1,091
34.	CDW	7	Midsized	3,948
35.	American Fidelity Assurance	1	Small	1,385
36.	TD Industries	-9	Small	1,297
37.	American Express	-3	Large	42,453
38.	Miliken	-3	Midsized	9,300
39.	Amgen	6	Large	11,374

40.	JM Family Enterprises	-3	Midsized	4,114
41.	Timberland	-2	Small	1,978
42.	Microsoft	1	Large	37,746
43.	Intuit	6	Midsized	6,516
44.	Pella	7	Midsized	8,758
45.	SRA International	23	Midsize	3,986
46.	Nordstrom	3	Large	45,112
47.	AFLAC	5	Midsized	4,034
48.	Perkins Cole	-4	Small	1.553
49.	Nixon Peabody	4	Small	1,583
50.	Northwest Community Hospital	1	Midsized	3,089
51.	Genzyme	9	Midsize	5,399
52.	Eli Lilly	-7	Large	21,898
53.	Hot Topics	22	Midsized	8,314
54.	Arnold & Porter	-4	Small	1.363
55.	Station Casinos	6	Large	10,967
56.	Publix Super Markets	3	Large	129,412
57.	Synovus	0	Larger	11,890
58.	Stew Leonard's	-2	Small	1,819
59.	Baptist Health South Florida	3	Large	10,706
60.	Vanguard Group	8	Large	11,070
61.	Sherwin-Williams	14	Large	27,938
62.	Memorial Hospital	2	Midsize	4,301
63.	Russell Investment Group	22	Small	1,092
64.	FedEx	7	Large	212,241
65.	PCL Construction	26	Midsized	2,543
66.	MITRE	4	Midsized	5,575

67.	Ernst & Young	5	Large	23,657
68.	Bronson Healthcare Group	6	Midsized	3,396
69.	Valassis	0	Small	1,803
70.	AG Edwards	8	Large	15,708
71.	Pricewaterhouse Coopers	11	Large	26,392
72.	Booz Allen Hamilton	9	Large	15,582
73.	Yahoo	29	Midsized	5,444
74.	Standard Pacific	22	Midsized	2,317
75.	Quad/Graphic	1	Large	10,399
76.	Children's Healthcare of Atlanta	4	Midsized	4,910
77.	National Instrument	4	Small	2,148
78.	Methodist Hospital System	6	Midsized	8,714
79.	East Penn Manufacturing	2	Midsized	4,082
80.	CH2MHILL	48	Large	17,770
81.	Autodesk	5	Small	2,098
82.	Bingham McCutchen	0	Small	1,542
83.	Texas Instruments	-8	Large	16,102
84.	Worthington Industries	-4	Midsized	6,233
85.	First Horizon National	11	Large	13,228
86.	Principal Financial Group	2	Large	12.723
87.	Washington Mutual	-7	Large	54,396
88.	Morrison & Foerster	3	Small	2,140
89.	Mayo Clinic	4	Large	38,085
90.	John Wiley & Sons	1	Small	2,090
91.	Granite Construction	6	Midsized	4,300
92.	Men's Wearhouse	9	Large	10,757
93.	CarMax	12	Large	11,400

94.	Bright Horizons	8	Large	13,551
95.	Wm. Wrigley Jr.	-2	Midsized	3,377
96.	IKEA (U.S.)	18	Midsized	9,499
97.	Intel	1	Large	48,655
98.	General Mills	-5	Large	17,992
99.	Marriott International	3	Large	128,704
100.	Nike	5	Large	12,502

> Note:
>
> N.A. (Not available). U.S. employees includes part-timers as of the time of survey. Job growth, new jobs, and voluntary turnover are full-time only. Average annual pay: yearly pay rate plus additional cash compensation for the largest classification of salaried and hourly employees. Revenues are for 2004 or latest fiscal year. All data based on U.S. employees.

PROFILE OF TOP 20 COMPANIES.

What makes these companies so great? Each one of these firm have unique characteristics which leads there employees to find them great. In this review I am going to discuss the top twenty companies. To get additional information on the other 80 firms you can go on line to CNN.com to get more details and further facts.

Genentech

Ranked number **four** in 2005; In the case of this company, right off the 'bat' we find that the employees get to be on a cancer-fighting team; so, how about having a great time while you are doing your work. And of course it does not hurt; the employees own 95% of the stock and are benefiting from soaring stock value. The company has seen a 79% rise in earnings because of it sales on cancer drugs. You will find the employee ratio is 42% minorities, and 50% women, of which 8,121 work in the United States. The most common job is salaried and the position is

7001 Resumes-Plus Second Edition

Research Associate, making $69,425 a year. The second most common job is hourly as a Mfg. Technician (Bio-Process) earning $47,817 per year. The company has had a job growth (1 year) of 20 percent, in addition a surprising low percentage of 5 percent (voluntary). You will find that Genentech offers Professional Training of around 51 hours per year. The company's headquarters is in South San Francisco, CA and their website is: http://www.gene.com

Wegmans Food Markets

This firm was ranked number <u>one</u> in 2005. Let's see why this company is so great. First, it is a privately held grocery chain. To get to know new employees before they opened a new store the CEO, Danny Wegman, charted a jet to fly them to Rochester to meet them all. The company has 31,890 employees working in the United States. Of these, 15 percent are minorities and 54% are women. The job growth was 7 percent with 723 new jobs. You will find that the company enjoys an 8 percent (voluntary) turnover. The most common job (salaried) is Store Department Manager at $46,741. The next most common job (hourly) is Customer Service at $28,047. The company does have Professional Training of about 40 hours per year. You will find the company headquarters in Rochester, NY and the company is in the Food & Drug Store business. The company does have a Website: http://www.wegmans.com.

Valero Energy

Here we have a company in the Petroleum Refining business. In 2005 this firm was ranked 23 so you can see something is happening here. From what I can see when hurricanes Katrina and Rita hit, is this company all pulls together. Valero dispatched semis filled with supplies, set up temporary housing for employees, fed volunteers, and donated $1 million to the Red Cross. So it seems when disaster strikes, this company is there. Valero Energy has 16,582 employees working here in the states, and 4,393 working outside the country. Forty percent of its employees are minorities and 40 percent are woman. The most common job (salaried) is Store Manager (retail) at $38,277, and the most common job (hourly) is Customer Service

Representative (Retail) at $16,651. You will find that the company has had 701 new jobs with a job growth of 5 percent. You will find that this firm has Professional Training of 67 hours per year. One thing that you have to look at is that the firm has a 26 percent employee (voluntary) turnover. The company is enjoying high profits from a high demand for motor oil. Company headquarter is in San Antonio, TX. You may find this firm at their website: Http://www.valero. com.

Griffin Hospital

Here we have an operation in the Health Care industry. They are a small organization. In 2005 they were ranked eight. The hospital employs 1,049 in the United States. There are 10 percent minorities with 78 percent being women. The hospital realized an 11 percent increase in new jobs with a growth of 2 percent. We can find that the hospital enjoys a (voluntary) turnover of 8 percent. The most common job (salaried) N.A. and the Salary is N.A. However the most common (hourly) is Registered Nurse at $64,454. It seems that money is not everything here at Griffin Hospital, since the pay scale is 5% to 7% lower than other hospitals in the area. The Hospital receives 5,100 applications for a range of 150 open positions in 2005, largely due to its top-notch reputation for patient care. You will find Griffin Hospital headquarters in Derby, CT. The hospital does have a Website: http://www.griffinhealth.org

W.L. Gore & Associates

With this midsize firm we can talk about some unique and innovative styles of management methods that encourage involvement in the company and gets tasks done. At W.L. Gore there are no bosses, job titles, or organization charts. The company sponsors team members and leaders. You will find W.L. Gore & Associates in the Chemicals industry. The company has 4,537 employees working in the United States and 2,247 working outside the US with 15 percent of the employees being minorities and 40 percent women. The company has developed 261 new jobs with a job growth of 6 percent. You will find that the company enjoys

7001 Resumes-Plus Second Edition

a (voluntary job turnover of 5 percent. The most common job (salaried) is Field Sales Associate with N.A. on salary. The most common job (hourly) is Medical Device Assembler, but here again I do not have salary information. The headquarters for this firm is in Newark, DE and they do have a website://www.gore.com. One thing I will add here is this company is reporting that they get around 37,926 applicants a year. The company is reporting about 18 hours per year of training.

Container Store

What we have here is a firm in the Specialty Retailer business. The company is a midsized organization with 2,857 employees working in the United States and 400 employees working out of country. One thing that is unique at this storage retailer is that even the part-timers can receive bonuses, and drivers are rewarded for long service and safe driving records. One interesting item I have to report is that in 2004 one driver took home $5,000 for ten years of perfect service. Here at Container Store 29 percent are minorities, with 62 percent being women. The company is reporting new job growth of 117 at a rate of 16 percent. You will find that this firm offers 108 hours of training. The most common job (salaried) is Store Sales with an income of $40,394 and a most common job (hourly) being Distribution Center at $28.227. The company is reporting a (voluntary) turnover of 18 percent. You will find this company headquartering in Coppell, TX. This midsized company has a website: http:/www.containerstore.com.

Vision Service Plan

This small firm is located in Rancho Cordova, CA. At this not-for-profit eye-care-insurance firm, managers get into the trenches and work rank-and -file jobs. The company has 1,915 employees working in the United States. You will find 30 percent minorities, and 68 percent women. New jobs are down at this company by a minus 44 percent and a minus 2 percent job growth. The most common job is (salaried) Application Developer at $91,699 and most common job (hourly) Customer Service Representative II at $33, 993.

J.M. Smucker

This 109-year old jam and food company has been a family business for a long time. At the helm are two bothers Tim and Richard Smucker. I have been to there well laid out plant in northern California. The company employs 2,930 here in the United States and 1,947 outside the country. They are reporting a minus 402 jobs with a minus 13 percent job growth. Twenty-four percent of the company's employees are minorities, with 44 percent females. The company is reporting a 5 percent (voluntary) turnover. You will find that the most common job (salaried) is Production Supervisor at $51,166 and most common job (hourly) is Customer Service representative at $32,527. You will find the J. M. Smucker headquarters in Orville, OH and you can contact them at their Website http:www.smucker.com.

Republic Bancorp

Moving from their ranking of 17 in 2005 to 3 this small commercial bank supports a rah-rah atmosphere. The bank is 20 years old and has offices in the Midwest. One thing that seems to make this company fare so well is that anyone can submit questions to the CEO's monthly TeleRap conferences or nominate a co-worker as a 'local hero'. The company has 1,190 employees in the United States of which 10 percent are minorities, and 75% women. At this point the firm indicates -109 new jobs and -9 percent job growth. However the company does offer 50 hours of professional training. The most common job (salaried) is Mortgage Loan Officer at $165,000, and the most common job (hourly) Customer Service Representative of $35,500. The company is showing a (voluntary) turnover of 15 percent. You will find the company headquarters in Owosso, MI. The companies Website is: http://www.republicbancorp.com

7001 Resumes-Plus Second Edition

Baptist Health Care

This midsized company can boast about its amazing ranking movement from 59th in 2005 to 18th today. The company is in the Heath Care industry and likes to have all their new hires at their Southern hospital group wear an ID badge sticker for the first 90 days so that co-workers can give them a helping hand as they need it. The hospital also promotes a culture brush by having after five months a day of skits, contests, and speakers. You will find 4,003 employees in the United States with 25 percent being minorities and 79% being women. At this point the company is showing 8 new jobs with a 0 percent growth. You will find approximately 60 hours of professional training per year. The most common job (salaried) Manager at a $43,000 per year and the most common job (hourly) is Registered Nurse at $52,727. The organization is showing a (voluntary) turnover of 18%. The headquarters for the company is in Pensacola, FL and their Website is: http://www.ebaptisthealthcare.org.

Recreational Equipment

This midsized firm is a Specialty Retailer who seems to provide a shared atmosphere where the employees and the consumers can share the same passion. This outdoors-goods maker regularly hosts environmental-service projects. Some employees see the company's way of doing things a way of life. The company employs 7,443 employees in the United States of which 12 percent are minorities, and 40 percent women. The company boosts 192 new jobs with a 9 percent job growth. The most common job (salaried) is Retail Store Manager at $80,144 with the most common job (hourly) being Retail Sales Specialist at $21,835. The company offers about 30 hours of professional training a year. The firm indicates that they experience a 12 percent (Voluntary) turnover. The company headquarter is located in Kent, WA and has come from the 45th ranking in 2005 to 9th today. The companies Website is: http://www.rei.com.

THE JOB SEARCH TOOL TO GET YOU THAT JOB

S.C. Johnson

What we have here at this midsized firm is a very devoted workforce which is witnessed by an incredibly low turnover rate of 2 percent. S. C. Johnson is a family owned consumer-products manufacturer. One of the reasons for the loyalty is that the company is a profit sharing organization that added 19 percent to the employees' paycheck last year. The company employs 3,404 employees in the United States and 8,596 outside the US. 15 percent of their workforce is minorities with 38 percent being women. Last year they offered 8 new jobs with a zero percent of job growth. The company indicates that they offer 40 hours of training. The most common job (Salaried) is Sr. Research Scientist at $102,161, and the most common job (Hour) Associate-Production at $58,300. The company is headquartered in Racine, WI. There Website is: http://www.scjohnson.com.

Boston Consulting Group

Is a small company that strongly supports education and commitment? If you show up at this management consultant company with a B.A. degree, they will send you to a top institution for your MBA and pay the bill if you agree to stay with the salary. At the same time they will double your income. The firm has 1,261 employees in the United States with another 3,868 working outside the county with 20 percent of their employees being minorities and 44 percent being women. The company has offered 167 new jobs with a 17 percent job growth. You will see around 106 hours of professional training per years. The most common job (salaried) Consultant $120,776 with the most common job (hourly) Executive Assistant at $56,477. The turnover here at this firm is (voluntary) 12 percent. The firm is headquartered in Boston, MA and it Website is: http://www.bcg.com/home.jsp

7001 Resumes-Plus Second Edition

Plante & Moran

Going from a ranking of 41 in 2005 to 12th improving its standing. This small company encourages the employees to 'Speak up' if things are not right and the company will try to change the problem. The firm offers consulting services with 1,356 employees in the United States. Minorities are 5 percent at this firm with 56 percent of the work force being women. The company has created 102 new jobs with a 9 percent job growth. You will find 60 hours of professional training a year with a job turnover of (voluntary) 14 percent. The most common job (salaried) is Auditor at $65,000 and the most common job (hourly) is Secretary at $32,600. The company is located in Southfield, MI, and has a Website: http://plsntrmoran.com

Quicken Loans

You will find this midsized firm in the Commercial Bank industry. There seems to be a supercharged mantra culture which rules at this mortgage bank. Saying such things as "EVERY CLIENT, EVERY TIME" and "NO EXCEPTIONS, NO EXCUSES" are plastered on posters, T-shirts, travel mugs, notepads, and portfolios. The company employs 2,951 employees in the United States. Nineteen percent of the employees are minorities with 52 percent being women. The company can boast about their 1,093 new jobs with a job growth of 60 percent. You will find a whopping 250 hours of professional training. The most common job (salaried) Web Mortgage Banker at $76,400 and the most common job (hourly) Loan Analyst $43,825. You will find this firm located in Livonia, MI and their Website is: http://www.quickenloans.com.

Whole Foods Market

What we see here is that the employees up and down the food chain have benefited by a rapid growth of the companies stock. It has tripled in the past three years. Another reason for the firm's movement in ranking from 30 in 2005 is that even part-time employees are eligible for stock options. The company employs 33,248 employees in the United States with another

The Job Search Tool to Get You That Job

1,120 out of county. You will find that 45 percent of the employees are minorities, with 43 percent being women. The company can boast of having 4,579 new jobs with a job growth of 18 percent. The most common job (salaried) is Associate Store Team Leader at $73,061, and the most common job (hourly) is Prepared Food Team Member at $25,451. The company offers about 112 hours of professional training a year. The (voluntary) turnover is 25 percent. You will find the company headquarters in Austin, TX. This large Food and Drug Store has a Website: http://www.wholefoodsmarket.com

Edward Jones

Here at this large Financial Service Company the education never ends. The company spends 2.5% of payroll on training. This brokerage firm has a mentoring program that pairs new brokers with veterans for a year. And a large number of employees take company subsidized business school classes. The company employs 29,197 in the United States and 2,048 outside the country. Six percent of the work force is minorities with 65% being women. The company is indicating 605 new jobs with a 3 percent job growth. You will find that the company offers 106 hours of professional training. The most common job (salaried) is Senior Programmer Analyst with an income of $74,323, and the most common (hourly) job is Branch Office Administrator with an income of $27,396. A (voluntary) turnover is 15 percent. The headquarters for this firm is located in St. Louise, MO. The company's Website is: http://www.edwardjones.com

Alston & Bird

Here we have a movement of ranking from 19th in 2005 to 9th. This small company in the Legal Services field believes in open discussions, and communication is vital at their national law firm based in Atlanta, GA. Everyone is kept in the loop via a monthly firm meeting, fireside chats, 'Town Hall' meetings, and a daily online newsletter. The company has 1,509 employees in the United States with 24 percent being minorities, and 56 percent of them being women. The company is showing 48 new jobs with a 3 percent job growth. Over the year the firm

7001 Resumes-Plus Second Edition

is providing 50 hours of professional training. The most common job (salaried) is Associate Attorney with a salary of $131,239. The most common job (hourly) is Legal Secretary with an income of $59,088. The company has a (voluntary) turnover of 12 percent. Their Website is: http://www.alston.com

<u>Kimley-Horn & Associates</u>

Here we have a small Engineering Construction Company which has grown in ranking from 46th to 20th. What makes this company so great, in part, are the rewards which seem to be plentiful at this employee-owned engineering firm. The company still pays the entire cost of health insurance premiums for both the employee and the dependents. They hand out up to 12 percent of pay bonuses. The firm funds a 401 (k). 1,771 of their employees are here in the United States. You will find that 16 percent of the firms employees are minorities and 31 percent of them are women. The company is showing a job growth of 24 percent with 325 new jobs. You will find approximately 28 hours of professional training. And they can boast about their low turnover (voluntary) of 7 percent. The most common job (salaried) is Project Manager with a salary of $100,745 and the most common job (hour) being Clerical with a salary of $38,874. The company is headquartered in Cary, NC. The firm's website is: http://www.kimley-horn.com

As I indicated for additional information on the balance of the 100 best companies to work for in 2006 go to: http://money.cm/meagaiznes/fortune/bestcompanies/snapshots/3943/html

CHAPTER TWENTY-SEVEN

NEGOTIATE TO INCREASE YOUR FINANCIAL PACKAGE

It is important that you know when to negotiate, what to negotiate for, and how to negotiate. The 'key' is to use common sense and selling. Since many applicants seldom face a personal negotiating experience it comes as no surprise that few of us are really any good at negotiating for ourselves. While at the same time we may be good negotiating in business situations, when interviewing for ourselves we may leave serious money on the table when it comes to negotiating our own employment package.

First of all, the first thing we need to know is when to start the negotiating process. The problem is some applicants mistakenly think negotiation is a continuous selling situation that occurs throughout their interview. However this is not the case, before you ever attempt to negotiate, it is important to make sure that the interviewer and/or the employer is 'sold on you' and that a job offer has bend extended.

Now, once you have an offer, you might be able to negotiate, however you need to be sure that you can get the employer to offer you new terms. This has to be determined on an individual level. It is important that your credibility and sincerity be sensed by the interviewer.

7001 Resumes-Plus Second Edition

What to Negotiate for

It is important to decide what you are going to negotiate for before you start the negotiation process, and this of course will differ for each one of us.

o Money

o Benefits – health insurance for yourself and dependents

o Stock options

o Company car

o Commission

o Money for relocation

o Holidays and Vacation time

o Retirement/company contribution 401 (k)

o Travel

o Exit severance pay

o Sign on bonus

o Other perks

Exploring Some Basic Considerations

When you make a change you want to expect a total package that is 20 percent more than where you were. Other elements include such things as commission, medical and life insurance, annual bonus based on meeting performance goals, profit sharing and pension plans. If you negotiate profit sharing, know the accounting. The truth is if you are employed you are in a stronger position to negotiate, but I do not want to suggest that you just take what you are offered either.

If you don't have any success in you negotiations, then try to shift from the 'present' and focus instead on down the road, like a review after a period of time, maybe a six month review; maybe an automatic increase in pay with a better title. These should be easy to do.

Contract

There are firms that do not like contracts, however you can ask. The contract should include the length of the agreement, your specific assignment, your letter, location, to whom do you report, your compensation, and what happens if there is a merger or if you rare fired. It should include everything that was negotiated as part of your employment package. Usually contracts are offered to upper executive positions. I personally never received a contract from the private sector but I have from the educational community. What I have gotten is however, a letter of employment listing the benefits, territory, commission rate, salary, vacation, and other benefits including the company car I was given. Very often this will be presented; it border lines a contract, but it is not a real contract. Any agreement you accept should cover all non-legal situations under which an employer may choose to terminate you. Signing bonuses and generous severance packages are moving into all income levels - especially when you relocate.

Whether or not if there is something that is important to you and if it is a contract or a letter of employment when you are trying to negotiate something you want included in your deal, you do not want to be intimidating or use an attacking strategy, it has no value. Remember you're setting the tone here for a long-term relationship. The best way to negotiate is to be prepared and never cause irritation. Make sure that you are sincere and reasonable.

As you approach your negotiations it is essential you have a clear idea about what you want; remember though, you are not going to get everything. Always keep in mind the main objectives and never risk the entire negotiation by coming on too strong about less important points.

Avoid Premature Discussion of Income

Premature discussion about money can be a real deal breaker. You will find sometimes, enthusiastic employers will begin an interview by asking you, "How much money do you want to start?" You need to come back with something like the following: "I could talk more intelligently about my circumstances after I know more about the position".

Or, "I would not take your time if I did have an idea of the range you could pay, but we need to agree that my experience fits your needs, if so, I believe we can come to a reasonable compensation'. If these statements fail, then give a range surrounding your estimate of what the job pays.

Once you are offered the job take the time to praise the firm and explain that you need some time to consider the offer. The standard period of time is a week before you respond. In some cases you may want to respond quicker. When you call back be positive about the job then you can raise the possibility of redefining it. Or, if you are happy with the job but would like to raise the salary, use the same technique, but show some vulnerability, then suggest that a dollar figure be added to the base. It is important to note that if the figure is within 15% of what you have been offered, the employer may not take offense and will grant you part of it. Of course, asking for more money is a negative, and needs to be balanced by positives.

Expressing a slight amount of vulnerability can be a power weapon. Just let the employer know that accepting the job as offered causes you some personal difficulties. When you use this strategy, it plays to their desire to make you happy. Be flattered by the offer but say that you may have to disappoint you family in order to afford the job.

For more power, use 'questioning rather than demanding' as the rule. We want to persuade through questions. This gives you needed information to gain control and gives you the time to think and not put all your cards on the table. Then follow up with questions so the employer can discover that their proposal is not quite enough. If your questions lead them to discover they were wrong then they are in a position to change the terms.

Let us talk about reshaping the job into a larger one, and the range will be higher. To get started, begin with a positive comment about the job and the firm and suggest they might benefit by adding responsibilities to the job. Then offer to share your thoughts.

This gives you a chance to talk about the areas where the firm might capitalize on your experience, telling them stories of how you made contributions before. If the interviewer agrees these are important, have them add this information to your job description. Believe it or not, reshaping the job can often be just that simple!

CHAPTER TWENTY-EIGHT

YOUR BACKGROUND CHECK

Having beaten out the other applicants for the job doesn't always mean you are going to get hired. Most candidates may think that once they have aced their interview they have gotten the job. In most cases this may be true, however there is a very critical wrinkle in the job-winning formula, and this is the background check.

Through-out history, to some extent, companies have always done some sort of background check. In the '50's background checks were little more than a routine procedure than a corporation's formality. Today, it can be job maker or job breaker.

Companies are fast learning that just because an applicant looks good on paper, and turns in a great interview, doesn't mean he'll perform well on the job. The fact is the applicant could be a complete loser, and this is all too common.

A recent study reveals that increasing numbers of companies are running background checks on prospective new hires. Since discrepancies on a job application can take you out of the race for your 'dream' job, preparing for a background check is now as important as updating your résumé. According to the results of Spherion Corporation's workforce Study report, 79 percent

315

of corporate respondents say they now run background checks on prospective employees, and more than half say they've increased their use of the pre-employment screening tool in the last five years.

Earlier this year, ACP Employer Service, a provider of integrated outsourced payroll benefits and human resource service, released its ninth annual Screening Index and reported a 12 percent increase in the use of corporate background checks over the previous year. Forty-nine percent of the education, employment, and credential verification revealed a data inconsistency compared with what the applicant reported.

"The consistent rise in the number of background checks performed year after year is evidence of the diligence employers are taking in the recruitment and hiring process," said Dean Suposs, general manager of ADP Screening and Selection Services. "Employers use ADP as a pre-employment screening process to reduce hiring risk, such as applicant's dishonesty, negligent hiring liability, and turnover."

The manufacturing industry, for example, like many other industries, makes good use of the benefits gleaned through pre-employment screening. Suposs adds, "Pre-employment screening is conducted in an effort to reduce turnover and help the organization remain productive."

What is a Background Check?

The background check is designed to verify what most employers deem critical and essential information for making a hiring decision. Along with your Social Security number, they can include an analysis of your work history, the people you know, and a full credit report. That's right, your potential employer could very well check your credit so it is important to make sure your credit report looks to maintain your buying power, but it also needs to look good so that you do not lose your 'dream' job.

They also include your credit payment records, driving record, and criminal history. All inquiries should be related to the job. For example, before you are hired to work in a financial service company (bank, brokerage or insurance firm), it stands to reason that the company would like to know if you have a history of embezzlement or theft.

Note: The Company is going to use your job application and not your résumé to run their background checks!

You will want to make sure that when you fill out that job application that all the information is correct. In 2005 companies ran almost 5 million background checks, so I can almost guarantee that the employer you submit your completed job application too will run a background check on you. So even if you are the best candidate in the world you are not going to get hired unless you pass the background check.

Corporations are not the only ones running background checks; the U.S. government has reported that they too have taken it very seriously for a long time. The fact is the government is so serious that a few months ago I had an investigator from the government personally interview me about a colleague of mine who had applied for a position with them. Another example, Laura Callahan, once third in command at the Department of Homeland Security, had a bogus diploma hanging on her office wall for 19 years, when just a year away from, retiring with a 20-year pension, she was discovered and fired, and forced to give up all rights to her pension.

Callahan had plenty of company, all of whom had powerful, high-placed jobs in the government. Topping the list was Charles S. Abell, appointed by President Bush. A presidential appointee confirmed by the Senate, he is the primary assistant of the undersecretary of defense for personnel and readiness.

Abell's résumé was incredible. His work history was exemplary, and his educational credentials were impressive too, particularly the master's degree from Columbus University. Abell also had a bachelor's degree from Pacific Western. But there was a big problem. Both schools were bogus, accurately dubbed 'diploma mills.' His degrees were worthless and signified nothing.

7001 Resumes-Plus Second Edition

The disturbing part is that the backgrounds check on Abell – which was supposedly very intensive because he was a top security clearance government official – failed to find out whether either school was legitimate. Columbus University, a Louisiana diploma mill, was shut down. The story made national news. Scarier still, Abell is still in office. Reportedly, there are other high-ranking government employees with diploma mill degrees at the Transportation Dept., Security Administration, the Defense intelligence Agency, and the Department of Treasury and Education. Let me say this, do you want to take a chance that you will lose that 'dream' job because of bogus information, well I wouldn't, but it is up to you.

Be Prepared For Your Background Check

I hope that the message I am trying to make here is loud and clear. Background checks are getting more, and more intensive than ever, and you'd be wise to prepare for them sooner than later the best you can.

First, get a copy of your credit report. I believe that you can get one 'free', you see it all the time on TV or on the internet that credit agencies are always offering a 'free' copy, so take them up on it and have them send you one. If you feel that some or all of the information is incorrect, dispute it with the creditor. You will more than likely have to send a letter to both the credit agency and the creditor. I find that by putting information in written form you will have a better chance of getting or making a change. Usually if you call the creditor or agency and then follow-up with documentation and a letter you will be more successful. Next, check your motor vehicle record by requesting a copy of it from your state department of motor vehicles. Ask your previous employer for copies of your personnel files. Make sure you know what your references are going to say, and the best way to do this is talk to the ones that you are going to put down to be contacted by your potential employer.

It is also important that you go over your résumé carefully and make sure all the information is accurate and truthful. If you lie and get away with it, there is a good chance it will come back to haunt you in the background check. So ask yourself if it is worth it.

Know your rights. Under the Federal Trade Commission's Fair Credit Reporting Act (FCRA), employers must notify you in writing and get your written authorization before running a credit check. If the employer is just conducting inquiries, he should also ask for your consent. This gives you the option of withdrawing your application if there is information you feel will work against you.

If an employer decides not to hire you because of this report, he must give you a 'pre-adverse action disclosure', which includes a copy of the report and a copy of your rights; it must also provide the name and address of the consumer reporting agency too so you can dispute the report if you want to.

<u>Tips For Filling Out Your Job Application</u>

1. **Tell the truth**. There is nothing that will disqualify you faster and cause you to lose your 'dream' job faster than a lie.

2. **Have complete information.** Provide as much employment and education history as you can. Put all the information on the application. Spell out and fit legibly all company and school names. Supply complete addresses and phone numbers for every employer that you list, and make sure the information is up to date.

3. **Account for all your time.** Hiring companies don't like to see unexplained gaps in employment. If the time between is three months or more explain what you were doing.

4. **Prep your references.** As I said earlier make sure that your references are willing to speak on your behalf. Try to find out, if you can, when and where they want to be

7001 Resumes-Plus Second Edition

contacted, and let them know what skills and attributes you'd like them to talk about. It is also important that you contact your former employers to make sure your records are available. Often your records may not be where they are supposed to be. If you find out that your records are not available or that a company has gone out of business. You will have to prepare an alternate way to verify this information.

It is important that you do your homework so you understand how the background process works. Most large employers, for example, don't do their own background checks on prospective employees. They contract with outside firms to do the job. Most of them go about the background checking process with the thoroughness of an FBI or CIA investigation. The bigger the job, the more thorough the investigation; and the more a company will pay for it. I have gone over the ins and outs of the background check and it is up to you to make sure that the information you present puts you in the best light and it is correct.

SAMPLE RÉSUMÉS

Jane E. Cannfield
951-277-1465

145 Sweetwater Road Riverside, CA 92883
janecann@comcast.net

RHIT / MEDICAL RECORDS / MEDICAL OFFICE MANAGEMENT

Skills
- (RHIT Certified
- (Customer Service
- (Insurance Company Relations

- (Billing / Claims Handling
- (Organizational Skills
- (New Program Set-up

Qualifications: Seven years' experience in **medical office management**

- Managed insurance claims coding, claims filing, payment-date entry and follow-up communications with insurance companies in a 7-person medical office.
- Created record-keeping system for new mammography service.
- Maintained quality assurance for mammography records.
- Established new Medicare and insurance payment database for a new women's health clinic.
- Processed medical-record requests while ensuring confidentiality of patients.
- Delivered quality customer services for scheduling, medical records filing, and patient check-in and check-out.

Employment History:

Los Angeles Women's Health Partners	Los Angeles, CA	
Medical Data Entry	1997	

Female Contemporary Health Care — Los Angeles, CA — 1995-1997
Medical Secretary
Hired by medical director based on work performed during internship from Los Angeles Nurses training school. **Collected $75,000 of previously unpaid Insurance claims.**

University of California Irvine Hospital — San Ana, CA — 1978-1981
Medical Office Front Desk Personnel

Kaiser Permanent — Riverside, CA — 1977-1978
Nursing Secretary

Certification: Registered Health Information Technician (RHIT) Through 12/2/03

Jane E. Cannfield	**Page 2 of 2**

Education: Los Angeles State College Los Angeles, CA
Associate's Degree – Health Information Management 1995
- Participated in 4-month internship with Female Contemporary Health Care
- With High Honor – 3.95

University of California Riverside, CA
Bachelor of Science – Medical Technology 1977
- With High Honor –3.65

Community Methodist Church – Summer Carnival Riverside, CA
Involvement Coordinator 1993-1997

Coordinated weekend fund-Raiser that netted the church $45,000 annually.
- Promoted the fund-raiser in the church and the community.
- Ordered all customer request rides and vendors.
- Coordinated volunteers for operating the carnival.

Methodist Church Riverside, CA
Treasurer 1994 – 1995
Administered the Parents' Association Committee Treasury with annual budget of $250,000.

References: Available upon request

<u>Note:</u> This is small for a person returning to work after raising a child. Minimize focus on dates by using the functional format. Focus on present skills and qualifications up front. Certification, education, and previous work experience.

Sandy Miller

2100 Warm Springs Corona, CA 92883

Telephone: (951) 277-8992

Profile

Human Resources / Team Leadership
- Expertise, qualifications, and experience encompassing all facets of HR – generalist functions.
- Plan, develop, and executed strategic HR recruitment, selection, induction, and training methodologies.
- Full accountabilities for staff payroll, work-care claims, and OH&S compliance.
- Team leader, trainer, and mentor: optimize staff performance and productivity.
- Communicate vision and facilitate team collaboration to surpass company objectives.

Interpersonal / Communication:
- Outstanding interpersonal and communication skills; interfacing with staff, clients, and vendors from diverse backgrounds.
- Exceptional negotiator, evaluating, implementing, and resolving union and staff disputes.

Office Management / Administration / Bookkeeping:

- Proven expertise in all facets of office management and bookkeeping, including financial and executive reporting utilizing MYOB and QuickBooks software.
- Excellent organizational, administrative, and time-and resource-management skills. Ability to Set and achieve priorities and manage multiple projects in tandem without compromise in quality. Perform well in busy work environments.

Education & Training

Diploma of Business (Human Resource Practice)	2002
Cert IV Human Resource Practice / Operations	2001
Cert III, IV and Diploma of Management	2001
Cert IV in Assessment & Workplace Training	1999

Professional Experience

NASH ENGINEERING, INC, Riverside, CA   8 years
Office Manager
Diverse hands-on management role performing HR, bookkeeping, secretarial, administrative, and clerical functions. Recruited and trained administration staff with on going direction, motivation, and supervision.
- **Payroll and personnel management**: Calculated hourly rates / overtime, pay reviews, work-covered claims, superannuation, and personnel file management.
- **Extensive liaison with clients**: Assisted with sales, and problem resolution, utilizing diplomacy and assertiveness to achieve mutually beneficial outcomes.
- **Accounting and administration**: Set up and trained on QuickBooks accounting software. Completed financial reporting; interfaced with accountant as required, Authored correspondence, quotations, sales / promotional material, and management reports.

Sandy Miller	Page 2

- **Evaluated, developed, and implemented office procedures.** Problem-solved computerized financial records requiring investigation and rectification of incorrectly recorded information. Organized managers' international travel and accommodation. Planned and prepared international Trade Show events, including promotional material, display products, and subsequent sales staff traveling arrangements and accommodation.

  (Spearheaded set-up of computerized financial information onto QuickBooks.

  (Effectively coordinated the entire office, maintaining operational efficiency.

  (Streamlined quotation department through development, preparation, and implementation of job-costing procedures.

  (Successfully mediated internal and external conflicts between staff, clients, and unions, demonstrating exceptional negotiation and communication skills.

  (Facilitated an encouraging work environment, which improved internal staff communication and cooperation.

  (Researched, planned, and authored job descriptions for each role within the organization.

Volunteer Experience

Treasurer / President   *3 years*

Fun in the Sun Kindergarten

Chaired monthly meetings, led, interfaced with, and provided direction for other committee members. Collected and banked fees; chased overdue accounts, organized and paid various vendor invoices. Reconciled and prepared monthly budget versus actual expenditure reports and presented at monthly meetings. Represented Kindergarten at various promotional events. Calculated and paid teacher and assistant wages and benefits.
- Collaborated with committee members in the recruitment and selection of a Kindergarten Teach Assistant.

Technology

- MS Word • MS Excel • MS PowerPoint • MYOB • QuickBooks

Professional references available upon request

Note This résumé sample is for individuals returning to the work force. Here as you can see we are displaying broad skills and diverse experience through a lengthy Profile section. Also follow up with your recently earned educational credit that relate to the job target. Notice we have eliminated date of employment and simply showed job tenure.

Sharon R. Robinson

19 White Tail
Corona, CA 92883

Phone 951-277-2234
SharonRRobinson@comcast.com

DATA • ENTRY • RECEPTION • CUSTOMER SERVICE • OFFICE SUPPORT

Conscientious professional exploring opportunities in a business environment where expertise
In customer service and office administration will contribute to company goals and objectives.

Skills

Data Entry	Reception	Microsoft Office
Office support	Multi-line console	Windows 95/98
Customer Service	Scheduling	Lotus 123

EXPERIENCE

- Prioritized and responded to high volume of inbound calls for professional businesses
- Identified urgency of calls and proceeded efficiently and effectively in a time-sensitive environment.
- Furnished detailed messages, scheduled appointments, and communicated effectively with professional col agues and clients.
- Recognized for providing excellent customer service resulting in advancement to lead sales Associate with specialty retailer.
- Researched and entered competitive marketing analysis data for retail advertisers.

WORK HISTORY

Big buy Discount, Santa Ana, CA   1993 –1994
State – Wide discount retailer
Petco Super Discount, Santa Ana, CA   1992 – 1993
Retailer specializing in supplies and service for domestic animals

EDUCATION

Santa Ana Junior College, Santa Ana, CA   Associate degree, 1988

References available

<u>Note:</u> This is another sample of a résumé designed for people returning to the world of work.

In this functional format the emphasis is on relevant skills that support the applicant's goal of a

mid-mid-level office-support job in a smaller environment with reasonable flexibility regarding

to hours.

Debi E. Dodds, C.T. M.

1235 Dear Drive ■ Corona, CA 92883 ■ 951-277-5454 ■ DebiETeach@comcast.net

---

Tour Manager ■ Special Events Coordinator ■ Airport Hospitality

TRAVEL EXPERIENCE
- Traveled in 7 European counties – Switzerland, Italy, Germany, Sweden, Finland, Norway, and extensively in France, Traveled throughout U.S. (Great Lakes states, New England, Colorado, Texas, and California).
- Completed independent study projects in Switzerland and Quebec.

LANGUAGES
Bilingual English/French; Taught Spanish I

TRAVEL MANAGEMENT
- Co-leader for high-school tour of France.
- Coordinator for annual student trips to Festival of Nations.
- Facilitated arrivals and departures for international exchange programs.

Education

- International Guide Academy, San Jose, CA   Certified Professional Tour Manager
- University of California Santa Cruz, CA   Bachelor of Arts in French Education, Summa Cum Laude
    Bachelor Arts in Sociology/Social Service, Cum Laude

COMMUNITY
- Area representative for international student-exchange program.
- Advisor, World Language Club.
- Host for international guests from France, Russia, and Scandinavia.
- Organized cultural programs for university and community.
- Performed administrative duties for volunteer organizations-youth cocker club, church groups, and Community Theater.

COMMUNICATION SKILLS
- Area representative for international student-exchange program.
- Advisor, World Language Club.
- Host or international guests from France, Russia, and Scandinavia.
- Performed administrative duties for volunteer organizations—youth soccer club, church groups, and community theater.

SPECIAL INTERESTS
- **Member**, Le Club Francais.
- **Certified** in crisis-intervention counseling.
- **Actress**, long-time member Fullerton Playhouse Community Theater
- **Member**, Las Angeles Symphony Chorus

WORK EXPERIENCE
Social Services, 7 years, Teaching 9 years

Kirk E. Merhish

5463 West Draper Ave
Draper, CA 78903
801-345-2244
kirkE@aol.net

CLASSROOM / TEACHER AIDE

Professional Profile:

Mature and caring individual with a commitment to working with children with special needs, over 7 years experience as a full-time stay-at-home parent caring for disabled children. Provide a nurturing, compassionate, and supportive environment while encouraging academic, physical, and personal growth.

Summary:

- Assist children with fitness, recreational, and academic activities.
- Ensure the heath and safety of children.
- Evaluate children's performance and keep track of progress.
- Utilize special skills in working with children with various disabilities, including autism and learning disabilities.
- Initiate and supervise activities to encourage learning and healthy, structured play.
- Proved exceptional care, assessing children's needs and resolving their problems.
- Encourage appropriate socialization and interaction.
- Create and carry out arts and crafts projects.
- Instruct children in math, language, and reading lessons.
- Demonstrate superior skills in making students feel comfortable and at ease, resulting in a trusting relationship.
- Convey a friendly, gentile, and positive attitude to children of all ages.

Experience:

Stay-at-home Dad, Salt Lake City, Utah (1995-2002)

Manager/Owner, Salt Lake City, Utah (1987-1994)

Manager, Hidden Valley Antiques, Draper, Utah (1982-1996)

Education:

University of California San Bernadine, California
Physical Education courses with a concentration in Physical Education and Special Education

Volunteer:

Chaperone and Parent Aide for numerous school field trips and activities. Coached AYSO Soccer for five years.

References:

Furnished upon request.

Note: This is a stay at home dad with 7 years experience raising disabled children, thus using his experience to pursue a career working with children.

Linda S. Bond

745 Main Street
Sunnyvale, CA 97335
LindaS@aol.com

<u>Customer Service Representative</u>

Experienced in providing direct customer support by answering inbound calls end providing in-person customer service. Solid customer-satisfaction and account-management skills that contribute to increased revenue and long-standing customer relationships.

Qualification includes:

- Timely assessment and understanding of customer expectations. Take a hands-on approach in clarifying customer expectations and resolving issues efficiently.
- Answer and follow up on customer inquiries, generate, sales, and handle complex discrepancies related to transaction processing.
- Described as courteous, patient, and respectful of client concerns.
- Portray a professional image and properly handle confidential information.
- Strong verbal, written, interpersonal communication, and data-entry skills, Focus on detail and accuracy.
- Solid computer skills including MS word, Excel, Access, and Outlook.

PROFESSIONAL EXPERIENCE

CUSTOMER SERVICE REPRESENTATIVE, Bankco Popular, 1993-1996, Sunnyvale, CA.

Service customers including processing and disbursing loans, opening, closing, and reconciling accounts; Processing payroll deductions and direct-deposit requests; processing modifications to existing accounts; and marketing additional banking services and products to customers.

CUSTOMER SERVICE REPRESENTATIVE, Bank of America, 1991-1993, Mountain View, CA

Provided information to customers on issues such as account balances, and CD and loan rates. Recommended services such as stop-payment orders, check cards, and fund transfers; processed on-line applications. Verified deposits and answered questions regarding products and services.

SUPPORT SERVICE REPRESENTATIVE, First Mortgage Homes and Loans, 1990-1991, San Jose, CA

Input member information in main system for easy, up-to-date access of data. Maintained files and documentation regarding member accounts. Performed various clerical duties including answering phones, distributing mail, and filing. Offered support to other members of Service Center team.

Education

San Jose State University, San Jose, CA, 1995

Note: In this résumé the dates of employment have been deemphasized and the qualifications are highlighted. Note education is listed without a degree.

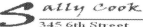

Sally Cook
345 6th Street
Riverside, CA 92894
Telephone 951-277-9873
Scook@aol.com

| Receptionist |
| Customer Service |
| Customer Relations |

SUMMARY

Outgoing, energetic individual liberated from the full-time demands of family and poised to enter the next round of professional and life opportunities. Excel in influential communications – listening to the customer, resolving problems, and recommending products and courses of action. Expertly restore order from chaos, manage multiple tasks simultaneously, and rise to the challenge of deadlines and pressure.

Never shirking from less-than-glamorous task, have demonstrated capacity to 'roll up the sleeves and pitch in' to ensure a task is completed on time, to high professional standards. Cited by past employers for being good-natured, has cooperative outlook, willingness to work hard, and team contributions.

Professional strengths include:

- Diplomatic & Expeditious Problem Solving
- Staff Supervision
- Dispute Mediation/Negotiation/Resolution
- New Product Development
- Continuous Improvement
- Quality Control
- Workplace Health & Safety
- Staff Rosters

- Stock Ordering/Inventory Control
- Staff Training & Development
- Customer Relationship Management
- Procedure & Process Streamlining
- Special Sales/Retail Promotions
- Telephone Communications
- Cost Containment Initiatives
- Cash Balancing

Software Knowledge: Microsoft Word, Excel, Access, PowerPoint, and email

EXPERIENCE SUMMARY

Organizational & Workflow Management

- Successfully settled staff unrest over rigid work roster system at a retail bakery. Revamped staff scheduling. To achieve a more equitable mix of skills that allowed for personal flexibility, while meeting the demands of peak customer periods.
- Commended by management and team members alike for ability to meet the challenges of high-pressure, fast-paced environments.
- Revamped storage areas to maximize space and provide easier and safer selection of frequently used supplies.

Sales & Communications

- Assumed role of staff mentor and trainer to enhance the knowledge base of subordinates. As Factory Outlet Manager overseeing the retail arm of a small manufacturing firm, translated and communicated retail sales policies, conflict-resolution techniques, and important occupational health and safety issues to staff.
- Developed outstanding relationships by individualizing and nurturing loyal/regular clients, remembering pertinent facts from previous sales and / or communications.
- Spearheaded several small-scale promotional competitions that invited proactive customer involvement, encouraged repeat business, and built business goodwill.
- As a senior sales assistant and team member, identified underlying tensions negatively impacting the work environment, steadily and quietly mediated conflicts between disgruntled staff and management that, when resolved, infinitely improved staff demeanor and productivity.
- Won back wholesale buyer, returning up to $1,000 a week to business revenues.

TRAINING
Receptionist/Front Desk Training Course (March 2002)
Introduction to Computer, (2001)

| Sally Cook | Page 2 | Confidential |

PROFESSIONAL EXPERIENCE

Happy Day Bakery, Riverside, CA   1988-1998
Popular pastry and bread bake-house family-owned with staff of 20

Senior Sales Assistant
As the longest-serving staff member, recognized for senior level knowledge of bake-house operations. Headed a small tight-knit customer service team. Multifaceted role touched several core business disciplines from sales and marketing through customer service, team leadership and training, inventory control, and new product development. Frequently acted as 'fire-fighter' mediating conflicts between staff and management to maintain workplace harmony.

Selected accomplishments
- Restored confidence of VIP client – a wholesaler buyer previously contributing up to $1,000 a week to the bottom line. Citing irreconcilable differences with the owner, the buyer was resistant to reversing decision yet responded positively to subtle maneuvering intended to re-open lines of communication. Mediated steadily between both parities to resolve areas of contention. This buyer returned to Happy Day Bakery and preferred product.
- Conducted revamped staff roster system, winning across-the board approval for initiatives in achieve more equitable time and skills mixes.
- Conducted formal and informal training to new recruits to ensure optimum customer service and promote workplace safety.
- Initiated several ideas for new products that served to stimulate customers' interest and prompt repeat business. Reduced food wastage by suggesting several new derivative product that could successfully utilize unsold items, turned a loss onto a revenue raiser.
- Refurbished stock area, restoring order to chaos, improving worker safety, and providing at-a-glace information on existing supply holdings.
- Instrumental in staging special promotions including customer competitions.
- Instrumental in staging special store promotion including customer competitions.

RALPH'S SUPERMARKET, Corona, CA   1994-1998
Chain supermarket with active lottery outlet

Sales Assistant

At the local level providing this supermarket with new customer service, performed counter sales,
processed stock orders, checked deliveries against order tickets for accuracy, and relieved staff in the adjacent tattles lotto area, selling lottery tickets, renewing memberships, and paying prizes.

STATER BROTHERS SUPERMARKET   1984-1988
Sales Assistant
At the local level providing this supermarket with new customer service, performed counter sales,
processed stock orders, checked deliveries against order tickets for accuracy. Stock shelves, administered daily banking, trained new staff.

PERSONAL

Leisure interest include reading, hiking, crosswords, jigsaw puzzles, computers, craft work, walking.
Served as Committee Member and AYSO soccer coach

| Sally Cook | Page 2 | Confidential |

Note: This résumé is designed to help this individual transition to a new field. As you can see (all of her experience was in retailing) the first page discusses her expertise and the second page gives support skills.

Donald A. Hess

3562 East Blossom Hill Road
Santa Clara, CA 94335

408-234-9872   Donboy@aol.com

ENVIRONMENTAL PROTECTION

Lifelong interest in and study of plants, wildlife, and environmental protection
Enhanced by educationally focused studies and experience at nature centers

- Skilled in collection, identification, cataloguing, and study of data from various biological and ecological sources, experienced in plant taxonomy, ethno botany, and botany.
- Proven ability in analysis, scientific theories, and procedures; strong laboratory and field-analysis skills.
- Detail-oriented, with ability to create scientific drawings.
- Confident communicator; comfortable providing tours.
- Member, nature Conservancy and Save the birds.
- Computer application skills using Microsoft Office and Windows.

EDUCATION

B. S. in Biology, Minor in Zoology, Santa Clara University, Santa Clara, CA
A. A., General Education, Western Wyoming Junior College, Rock Springs, WY.

<u>Relevant Curricula</u>

- Entomology
- Botany / Ethno botany
- Plant Taxonomy
- Plant Kingdom

- Local Flora
- Ecology
- Molecular Cell Biology
- Organic Chemistry

- Zoology
- Animal Physiology
- Herpetology
- Oceanography

RELEVANT EXPERIENCE

Biological Sciences

- Worked an in the arboretum and herbarium at San Jose Butterfly Haven and Garden for summer independent study credit.
  - o Assisted in relocation and replacement of herbarium – entire library of specimens.
  - o Maintained arboretum hothouse and grounds, handling transplanting, building of arbors, weeding, and identification and labeling of tree species.
  - o Performed wild-bird rescue, capturing, transporting, and splinting injured birds for Save the Birds.
  - o Researched and created scientific drawings of cellular organisms utilizing a microscope for class.
  - o Collected, preserved, identified, and catalogued different plant species, developed extensive knowledge of vascular plants with emphasis on the flora of the State of California for class.

Public Relations, Administrative & Coordination

- Performed extensive event coordination as a PTO volunteer and volunteer teacher at Spectrum.
  - o Handled program planning of student graduation and field trips to include selection location, recruiting and coordination volunteers, negotiation prices, securing donations, and setting up.
  - o Assisted students in the classroom and on field trips; designed and taught curriculum.
  - o Managed the diverse aspects of running a business to include management of inventory, development of customer relations, administrative control, human resources, and budgeting at Friday's.

WORK / VOLUNTEER EXPERIENCE

Biology Independent Study, Jose Butterfly Haven, San Jose, CA, 2002
Rescue Volunteer, Save the Birds, San Jose, CA, 1996-Present
Volunteer, PTO & Volunteer Teacher, Cupertino Elementary School, Cupertino, CA, 1994-1997
Manager, Friday's Restaurant, San Jose, CA 1989-1996

Note: This résumé demonstrates skills and knowledge gained through experiences and schooling completed. This is a functional style of résumé that presents strong credentials for applying to current job.

JACK WORTHINGTON, RN

4534 Pine Street • Orange, CA 94332 • JackWRN@aol.com • 714-514-5544

PROFESSIONAL OBJECTIVE & PROFILE

Dedicated health-care professional looking to utilize experience and education within an established organization. Skilled in medical, surgical, coronary, and critical-care environment.

- Demonstrated ability to remain calm and focused in high-stress/fast-paced environment while providing quality care and meeting patients' needs.
- Self-motivated, dependable, flexible, loyal, and quality team leader.
- Instrumental in building positive relationships with administration physicians, peers, patients, and families; genuine concern and sensitivity for others.
- Exceptional communication, organizational, time-management, and problem-solving skills.
- Proficient in all paperwork, documentation, and records management, with careful attention to patient confidentiality.
- Computer skilled in Microsoft Word and internet applications.

SUMMARY OF PROFESSIONAL EXPERIENCE

- Served as Head Nurse, Charge Nurse, and Staff Nurse in various health-care settings
- Skilled in MED, CCU, OR, Ortho, telemetry, and step-down care.
- Evaluated performance of Registered Nurses, Licensed Practical Nurses, and Certified Nurses' Aides.
- Developed, coordinated, and implemented comprehensive nursing assessments and care plans.
- Administered appropriated medication as ordered by attending physician.
- Monitored, assessed, and communicated patient progress to attending physician on a periodic basis.
- Participated in care-planning meetings with departmental advisors, clients, and family members.
- Taught and mentored fellow nurses, delivered orientation courses, and conducted in-service programs.
- Selected to serve on numerous health-care committees.

PROFESSIONAL EXPERIENCE

Medical-Surgical RN (Per Diem)	UCI Medical Center Santa Ana, CA	1995-1990
Coronary Care RN	Western Medical Center, Anaheim, CA	1979-1983
Telemetry/Step-Down Unit Head RN	Kaiser Hospital, Riverside, CA	1974-1976
Instructor RN		
Medical-Surgical-Ortho-ICU RN		
Internal Med-Cardiac Rehab Office RN	Los Angeles Medical Center, LA, CA	1974

EDUCATION & LICENSE

Master's Degree: Counseling Psychology, University of California at San Jose, San Jose, CA
Bachelor of Science: Dual Major: Psychology/Zoology, University of California at Santa Cruz, CA
Summa Cum Laude Graduate
Associate of Science: Nursing, Riverside Community College, Riverside, CA

State of California License

CERTIFICATIONS

Basic Cardiac Life Support • American Heat Association CPR Certified • Intravenous Certified Nurse

---

<u>Note:</u> In this résumé we show strong professional experience, and down play the fact that it is somewhat old experience. As you can see this applicant is trying to return to the same field.

Joyce Anderson

2106 S.E. 14th Des Moines, Iowa

Residence (508) 345-2345 • E-mail: Joyce2345@aol.com • Cell (508) 345-2346

MARKETING • ADVERTISING • STRATEGIC COMMUNICATIONS

Creative, self-motivated, and solutions-driven business professional offering 10 years expertise in marketing and business management. Expert communicator with ability to simplify complex issues, cultivate key relationships, and build cohesion across all corporate levels. Motivational leader inspiring staff to new levels of performance. Resourceful problem-solver with natural business savvy and proven ability to coordinate projects from inception to completion. Strength in planning, multi-tasking, organizing, and time management.

AREAS OF EXPERTISE

Tactical Marketing & Advertising Campaigns
Public & Media Relations
New Product Development
Corporate Branding
Agency / Contractor Relationships
Training & Development

Strategic Planning & Communications
Media Production
Direct Mail / Promotions / Special Events
Team Building & Leadership
Budget Administration / Fundraising
Market Research

CAREER HIGHLIGHTS

MARKETING COORDINATOR / ADVERTISING DEPARTMENT MANAGER / BANK OFFICER

Bank of America, Inc. – Des Moines, IA (7 years)

Fast-track progression from marketing coordinator to Bank Officer for $4 billion, statewide holding company with 42 bank locations. Controlled 4.5 million annual advertising budget, directed 5-member department. Selected primary advertising agency partnership. Identified and targeted new niche markets.

Piloted strategic and promotional plans for each division and member bank. Coordinated product development, internal and external communications, direct mail campaigns, public relations, research, training, collateral materials, and special events. Supervised production of television and radio ads.

- Built advertising department from ground up as company's first Advertising Department Manager.
- Reorganized and centralized marketing and advertising functions of 42 separate banks during merger, increasing budget efficiencies by as much as 35%.
- Created and maintained graphics standards for new organizations.
- Designed new corporate sales materials and brand image, achieving 63% increase in institutional recognition and 12% rise in tagline recognition.
- Developed, directed, and appeared in series of corporate training videos used to train employees in member banks on marketing objectives and strategies. Resulted in 14% decrease in training expenses.
- Nearly doubled market share in 5 years.
- Garnered statewide press coverage in *The Des Moines Register* for highly successful TV / radio / print corporate image campaign.
- Orchestrated several advertising and direct mail campaigns recognized with local and national Advertising Federation awards.

Note: As you can see here in this résumé the dates have been left out and the focus is on the experience and achievement. The goal of this résumé is to return the applicant to the field of marketing and advertising. Also the volunteer work is added because of its links to the target goal.

Joyce Anderson

Résumé • Page 2

CAREER HIGHLIGHTS CONTINUED.....

MEDIA PLANNER & BUYER

Acme News Media & Advertising – Omaha, Nebraska (3 years)

Recommended, coordinated, and executed media options for financial service, telecommunications, public-utility, and airline clients in sync with corporate marketing and sales objectives. Optimized diverse marketing venues including television, radio, newspaper, magazine, direct mail, and outdoors media.

Interfaced with market research to determine return on investment for media cost, Tracked sales increases to prove position, bottom-line results for wide range of client companies.

ADDITIONAL EXPERIENCE

Event Coordinator & Fundraising Sales Chair – Iowa Baptist School

Fully managed, highly demanding and time-sensitive sales project equivalent to a small business. Led PR, product distribution, database management, sales training, presentations, complex reporting of vendor and product expense control, incentives, and coordination of 75 volunteers

● Catalyst for fundraisers' most successful years in its 20-years history, generating $100,000 in funds over two-year span.

Registrar & Database Manager for 600 members – AYSO Soccer Club
Auction Chair & Fundraising Committee – Oakland Transitional School for the Homeless
Budget Committee – The Junior league Oakland
Advisory Board & Big Sister – Big Sister of America
Funds Allocation Committee – United Way of Des Moines

EDUCATION & TRAINING

B.S. in Business Administration / Marketing – Drake University, Des Moines, IA

Professional Development
Microsoft Office Training -- Fresno Community College
International School of Bank Marketing Graduate – San Francisco State, San Francisco, CA (2 yr. program)

Technical Skills

MS Office Suite (Word, Excel, and Power Point, Quick Book Pro

Jane Brown

P.O. Box 456
Anaheim, California 94334
Phone: 714-514-6543
Email: JaneB@Yahoo.com

SUMMARY OF QUALIFICATIONS

(Outside Sales
(Customer Service
(Account Management

(Staff Supervision
(Cashier Operations
(Conflict Resolution

PROFESSIONAL HIGHLIGHTS

01/02 to   Wick Industrial Supply – Anaheim, California
03/02   **Outside Sales**
Accepted the challenge of straight commission sales marketing industrial lubricants to residential and commercial property – management companies, municipalities, and businesses in Orange County California.

(Produced over $50,000 in new business, including $5,000 during training, in the first 7 weeks of employment. Added 25 new customers in the first 4 weeks after training,
(Gained expertise in account identification and qualification, cold-calling, needs assessment, presentation and closing, cold-called on the average 15 businesses daily.
(Oversaw account management: re-orders, customer service, and issue resolution.

2000 to   Kingarden Child Care – Santa Ana, California
2001   **Nanny**
Provided childcare and parenting services in a variety of environments, Assisted with homecare, nutrition, and transportation, Experienced in grief management, conflict resolution, emotional stress.

1980 to   Ralph`s – Orange, California
1985   **Service Manager (1982 to 1985)**
Oversaw the efficient operations of the 'front of the house', guiding the efforts of 12 cashiers and sackers. Prepared cash drawers, ensured check-out supplies, monitored work schedules, approved personal checks, and assisted customers with issuers.
➢   Established a five-year record of excellent dependability and consistent merit raises and promotions.

Cashier (1980 to 1982)

CIVIC CONTRIBUTIONS

YOUNG WOMEN SOFTBALL LEAGUE – 1997 To 2001
COACH   Municipal league for 15- to 20 –years-old
JERRY'S KIDS – 1997 to 2001
Referee
Assisted with athletic events for the physically challenged.

Note: This is a Chronological style résumé used to show recent work history. As you can see the applicant is seeking a sales position. As you can see success was shown by using numbers, this is important when seeking a sales position.

Vern Thomason

408-736-8972   4215 Sea Gull Lane Sunnyvale, CA 93454   VernT@hotmail.com

Customer Service Representative

RELEVANT SKILLS & STRENGTHS

(Dependable, flexible, resourceful and adaptable.
(Even tempered – able to calm the troubled client or dissatisfied customer.
(Organized and quick to prioritize.
(Communications, oral and written – one-on-one and in groups.
(Computer skills: Windows, MS Word, and Word-Perfect 5.1

EXPERIENCE

San Jose County Housing Authority, Sunnyvale, California   04/01-02.02
Office Assistant (VISTA Volunteer – stipend compensation through AmeriCops)
(Typed letters and memos, ordered supplies, sent faxes, made copies, and answered phones.
(Assisted housing residents with community resource referrals.
(Planned and secured door prizes for Career Fair and Community Day, and sent thank-you letters to all participating resources and donors.
(Facilitated after-school homework tutoring program.

Star Cleaning Service, San Jose, California, Part-time   04/99-08/00
Cleaning Technician
(Cleaned, dusted and vacuumed a large chemical company.
(Recognized by owner and given a merit raise for dedication to quality.
(Kept only master set of keys held by an employee.

ABC Corporation (Contractor for Municipal Utilities Department), San Jose, California   01/96-06/98
Customer Service Representative
(Calmly handled complaints and answered questions for disgruntled customers.
(Scheduled appointments for owner, supervised installation of utility meters.

Big brother Counseling, Reading, Mountain View, California
Office Manager/Client Services (completed as part of training in Office Assistant program)
(Scheduled appointments and maintained office supplies.
(Transcribed doctor's notes and recommendations.
(At reception desk sometimes dealt with difficult 'criminally mentally disturbed' clients.
(Commended for calm handling of difficult clients.

Community Service
Parent-teacher Association Volunteer – Homeroom Dad
President of Head Start parent group
Church secretary and Sunday school teacher
Organized Community Services Christmas parties for children with mental and physical disabilities – 3 years

EDUCATION
University of Oklahoma, Norman Oklahoma   Diploma, Office Assistant – 2 year program, 1997
San Mateo Community College, San Mateo, California   Completed 1 year

MILITARY
U.S. Army Reserves, 6 years – E-5 Honorable Discharge, 1990

Will continue education or training to optimize performance! Willing to commute.

Note: In this résumé the focus is on the job target using bold headlines even though there is limited experience in the field. Focus on experience.

Sandra Sliver

921 Palm Tree Drive
Riverside, CA 92334

Home: 951-277-5545
E-mail: SSliver@aol.com

*
MEDICAL TRANSCRIPTIONIST
*

Over ten years of medical transcription and secretarial experience in private medical, clinical research, and corporate office environments, Familiarity with medical terminology, skilled in Dictaphone use.

*
HIGHLIGHTS OF MEDICAL TRANSCRIPTION EXPERIENCE
*

Orthopedic Associates, Orange County, CA   1988-1993
Medical Transcriptions
Recorded physician observations / findings during patient evaluations for this orthopedic surgeon who specialized in Workers Compensation cases. Subsequently transcribed the information (compiling data from doctor's tapes and evaluations) for claim reports.
- Consistently earned annual merit bonuses based on volume and quality of work.

California College Research Center, Orange County, CA
        1981-1892
Medical Transcriptions / Word Processing Secretary, Oncology Department
- Typed patient protocol reports, working closely with residents, interns, and physicians in an n intensive, fast-paced office.
- Selected to assist the Grant Administrator in the preparation of annual NIH grant applications.

*

HIGHLIGHTS OF SECRETARIAL / ADMINISTRATIVE EXPERIENCE
*

Home Based Business, Riverside, CA   1994-Present
Administrator
Conduct all office administration and sales for a home-based business, using excellent organizational and time management skills and adhering to a high standard for quality work. Skilled in use of computer word-processing, desktop publishing, accounting, and spreadsheet applications on Macintosh and Virtual PC.

Professional Engineers, Riverside, CA   1984-1988
Secretary
Served six engineers and supported a 40-engineer department. Produced documents ranging from correspondence to technical reports. During automation of office, mastered this new software and trained the engineers in its use.

Executive Offices, Corona, CA   1983-1988
Head Secretary
At this innovative executive office suite, was selected to direct the workflow of three secretaries supporting office administration for ten tenant companies in a new facility. Typed, edited, and proofread correspondence. Coordinated conference calls, managed mass mailings, and maintained extensive customer databases.

*
EDUCATION
*

B.A. California State University at Riverside, CA   M.A. California State University at San Bernardino, CA

Note: In this résumé the applicant is show casing her most '**marketable**' skills and breaking it in two parts which is the medical transcription and the secretarial background.

Earl Rusher

456 Apple Road
Riverside, CA 93990

(951) 277-382-1456 Home
(951) 277-382-7546 Cell
ERusher@aol.com

Qualifications

(Fifteen years of progressive experience handling multiple lines of insurance claims.
(Experience in handling property claims, Commercial Auto Liability, Bodily Injury, and General Liability, Bodily Injury, and General Liability lines.
(Knowledge of applicable insurance contracts (commercial P &C), laws, and DUI regulations.
(Interfaced effectively with policy holders, claimants, physicians, medical providers, attorneys, and repair shops.

Work History & Summary of Key Skills

Claims Department Manager / Supervisor (15 years), AAA Insurance, Riverside, CA
Initial hired as a Claims Representative Trainee, quickly promoted to Senior Claims Representative, and ultimately selected as Claims Department Manager / Supervisor. **Prevented losses, contained costs, exercised initiative, and demonstrated independent good judgment.**

Effective Negotiation Abilities

Negotiated property damage and personal injury claims on both first – and third-party claims. Authority to **negotiate up to $1,000,000** per claim.

Evaluated settlement strategies and alternatives, Determined settlement value and analyzed the potential cost, benefits, and risk of litigation.

Attended mediation conferences and claim committee meetings to **achieve fair and equitable settlements**.

Keen Investigative Skills

Investigated commercial auto property damage claims. Acquired information and maintained accurate records regarding accidents from first to last step.

Conducted investigations of accidents, screened vehicles, researched missing information on claim forms, and processed claims from first to last step.

Arranged independent medical exams, reviewed reports, and followed up on inconsistencies and / or coverage issues.

Strong Leadership Qualities

Managed a staff of 10 claims representatives, 4 claims processors, and 4 appraisers.

Assigned incoming claims and **monitored process** to ensure accurate and timely handing of claims. Held biweekly claim-committee meetings to evaluate and delegate authority to settle third-party claims.

Interviewed and trained staff in technical software, company procedures, and claims, regulations/statutes.

Education

Bachelor of Arts, Finance, University of California Riverside, CA

Strong references available upon request.

Note: Here we have a résumé that hides the age of the experience by eliminating dates and shows only the length of employment. Take the time to emphasize your experience and not how old it might be. You want to put your best foot forward.

338

Ann Browning

4500 Sunnyshine Lane
Ontario, CA 96332

909-278-2599
909-278-2598 Cell
AB1967@aol.com

OBJECTIVE

FLIGHT ATTENDANT

EDUCATION

University of California at Los Angeles, CA
Bachelor of Arts degree in Communications

SKILLS SUMMARY

Organizer / Planner/Leader

(Planned activities for spouses/guest during international accounting
conferences — traveled extensively to U.s., Canada, England,
Scotland, Turkey, Mexico, Germany, France, Italy, Holland, Austria,
and Switzerland.
(Sat 2 year on gated community Architectural Review Committee
with 3 builders, the project developer, and 4 homeowners.
(Chaired and coordinated volunteers for successful Christmas Gala
including selection of wines and cheeses for wine-tasting event and
procuring items for a silent auction.

Sales/Marketing/Customer Service

(Contracted by furniture manufacturers to represent product lines
during Furniture Marketing Los Angeles, CA
(Marketed and leased personal home to executive groups for
restocking of lines and supplies.
(Assisted upscale caterer with serving of elegant sit-down dinners for
300-600 guests during Furniture Market or manufacturer show
room and *House Beautiful and Architectural Digest* groups.

Public Presentation

(Modeled and emceed in fashion shows in the community to raise
funds for charities.
(Studied and interned in radio and television journalism in college
(Entertained and hosted social events on behalf of largest CPA firm in
LA County, California.

Person Strengths

(Articulate and persuasive
(Energetic, flexible, and adaptable
(Exceptional interpersonal skills

Computer Strengths

(MS Word, Internet, E-mail

**COMMUNITY
INVOLVEMENT**

Board member, committee member, volunteer for children's liturgy
group, Children's Bible school, and nursery department for local
church.

Note: As you can see in this résumé it shows no real professional employment skills. Instead
it high lights extensive volunteer and community experience. In this case you would want to
highlight any key skills that would relate to the goal of being a flight-attendant.

Bob Gonzalas

2911 Snow flake Drive
Aguilar, CO 78909

Residence: 719-343-3522
Cell Phone: 719-343-3533
BigBobG@hotmail.com

Expertise

SALESMAN MANAGEMENT AND MERCHANDISING: A goal-oriented, dedicated, and sincere sales professional who is highly organized and analytical. New York markets buying experience. Familiar with Microsoft products including Word and Excel. Demonstrated expertise in the following areas.

(Client Relationship Management
(Target Market Development
(Consultative & Influential Selling

(Quality Product Assurance
(Personal Goal Setting & Sales Results
(Strategic Business Planning

Excellent communicator capable of working effectively with individuals from all backgrounds and levels of education.

MERCHANDISING EXPERIENCE

EDUCATIONAL BUYER – Tiger Hobby House, Denver, Colorado
Jewelry Buyer – Zales Jewelry Store, Denver, Colorado

Highlights: Accountable for product selection and purchasing of educational materials and trend items for a craft and hobby retail establishment. Identified trends and developed production assortment to meet needs of consumers within an affluent suburban community. Traveled to San Francisco markets to make product selections. Managed point-of-purchase and merchandising activities to drive sales. Developed marketing and public-relations campaigns to increase traffic and revenue.

(Achieved success with several product assortments that created tremendous interest and generated high sales volume.

MANAGEMENT EXPERIENCE

Medical Office Manager — Dr. James Bond and Dr. F. Bush Medical Offices, Denver, Colorado
Legal Office Manager – Dr. Peter Jennings, and Dr. Bob Green Legal Offices, Denver, Colorado

Highlights: As medical office manager accountable for ordering medical/dental supplies, managing patient scheduling, and providing patient assistance within medical practices offering OB/GYN and cardiac care. Met with suppliers and vendor representatives, organized product choices, and negotiated pricing. As legal office manager, conducted medical/medical/legal research for malpractice cases. Assisted with human-resources activities. Attended legal conferences and other public-relations/marketing events to promote business.

EDUCATION

(Bachelor of Education
(Colorado State University Colorado Springs, Coronado

(Bachelor Health/Science
(Colorado State University Colorado Springs

AFFILIATIONS

(Pi Bata Pi Colorado State University Alumni Association
(Young Men's Business Club

(Business Education Teachers Association
(Junior Circle K Club

Note: What we have is a résumé of an older individual that had not been in the labor force for sometime. What we need to do in this case is to pull together relevant work history that shows qualifications for a sales and merchandising position.

Linda Dove

951-277-8790 Home
951-277-7890 Cell

9001 North Compton Ave — Riverside, CA 93998

L.Dove123@aol.com

SUMMARY

Ten years of experience in insurance underwriting, customer service, and management combine with a background in community relations, event planning / coordination, fundraising, and administration. Recognized as a well-organized, efficient professional with a strong work ethic and leadership qualities. Proven ability to meet deadlines, reach goals, and deliver results. Excellent public / customer-relations skills. Computer literate.

Earned Charter Property Casualty Underwriter designation.

INSURANCE EXPERIENCE

FARMERS INSURANCE COMPANY, Des Moines, Iowa

Assistant Manager (1984-1990)
Senior Account Analyst / Account Analyst (1980-1984)

Promoted to supervisory role with increasing responsibilities in Commercial Lines Units for marketing, profitability, customer service, agency relations, and underwriting. Assisted District Manager in new programs-development and decision-making activities in the unit. Supervised, trained, motivated, and evaluated team of 10 underwriters. Recruited, appointed, and maintained positive relationships with up to 40 agents. Implemented new product programs and trained agents.

Accomplishments

- Assumed supervisor's role during leave of absence and ensured smoothly running unit operations.
- Consistently achieved / exceeded goals for production, new business development, and profitability.
- Reorganized District Assistant Program resulting in earlier renewal processing and issuance.
- Supervisor's evaluation: *'Linda continually distinguishes herself with hard work and dedicated effort. She is an extremely important part of the operation.'*

COMMUNITY RELATIONS EXPERIENCE

DES MOINES TECHNICAL HIGH SCHOOL, Des Moines, Iowa (1990-Present)
Board of Directors Member / Fundraising – Vocational Clubs of America (3 years)
- Contributed to event-planning, organizations, and administrative activities to benefit school programs.
   Created display posters to promote events, coordinated raffles and direct mail campaigns. Established sponsorships and led fundraising efforts that generated over $150,000.

Des Technical School Parent Teacher Association (10 years)
Various Leadership roles in the organization

- Co-chair/Committee Member – Cultural Enrichment (4 years) – Researched, planned, and coordinated cultural/educational programs presented to audiences of 700 students at the elementary and middle schools. Managed program budget. Earned 'Person of Character' Award in 1996 By Gov. Terry E. Branstad.

- **Chair** – Membership (2 years) – Coordinated efforts that increased new membership 25-45%
- **Chair** – Sale Homes (2 Years) – Compiled and distributed directories to parents.
- **Fundraising Chair** – Girl Scouts Award (3 Years) – Honored f or service and dedication.

EDUCATION

Bachelor of Arts (English), Drake University, Des Moines, Iowa

Note: As you can see in this résumé the first haft is split, with the first part of this chronological résumé show casing her insurance experience, which is career goal related. With the second half explaining why this applicant was away from the work force.

Tom T. Hall
2222 Warm Springs Drive
Bosie, Idaho 83245   303-554-1255   TTH42@hotmail.com

**EMPLOYMENT
BACKGROUND
+
(20 Years)**

LEADERSHIP TRAINING, INC
BOISE, Idaho
Administrative Assistant

Office Manager

KOLES DEPARTMENT STORE

BOISE, Idaho
Sales Assistant
Department Manager

ONE DAY PHOTO LAB

CALDWELL, Idaho
Sales Associate

FAST CUSTOM & ONE HOUR PHOTO

STORE

MOUNTAIN HOME, Idaho
Mini-lab Printer

BOISE CENTER

BOISE, Idaho
Researcher / Curator

IOWA HISTORICAL SOCIETY

DES MOINES, Iowa
Curatorial Intern

IDAHO SYMPHONY SOCIETY
BOISE, Idaho
Photo Researcher
THE RED RIVER
(Documentary of Cattle
Ranching)
NAPA, Idaho
Photo Researcher
Assistant Editor
Assistant to Producers
BEAR REALTY COMPANY
BOISE, Idaho
Secretary

CAREER OBJECTIVE
CUSTOMER SERVICE / Inside Sales position utilizing my extensive professional experience.

RELEVANT QUALIFICATIONS

Management / Customer Service
► Quickly attain responsible track record / diligently earn management status.
► Entrusted my senior executives to complete all administrative responsibilities.
► Assist client in accurate assessment of needs.
► Perform comprehensive interviewing, training and supervision of staff.
► Coordinate complex schedules for training programs.
► Regularly compile monthly corporate reports for international headquarters.
► Competently manage advertising, accounts, inventory / accounts, inventory, / purchasing, requirements.
► Handle product orders with attention to detail.

OTHER QUALIFICATIONS

Museum Research / Historical Film Production / Processing

► Expert photographic and textual researcher for museum exhibits, publications, films.
► Compile artifact collection / construct exhibit with regard to space requirements.
► Descriptively compose labels for artifacts on display.
► Practice safe storage and transport of exhibit items.
► Maintain precise edit logs for film-to-video transfer.
► Complete fund-raising proposals, and grant and film festival applications.
► Professionally operate color processor / printer for refined photographic development.

EDUCATION

BOISE COLLEGE
Bachelor of Arts Degree, Film Studies / History Minor
Graduated **Summa Cum Laud**

Awards and Scholarships
Merit Scholarship (Upper Class)
CAS Alumni Award (Outstanding Academic Achievement)
University Scholar (1991-1992 / Golden Key National Honor Society
Dean's list

Relevant Seminars
Dale Carnegle Course in Effective Speaking and Human Relations
Dale Carnegle Management Seminar

Personal Highlights
Creative / Team player / Quality Oriented / Strong Detail Emphasis

Note: This is a strong functional résumé that presents the applicant's qualifications in two up front ways. First as stated through both work experience and volunteer experience over several years. Note that the dates are omitted. This is can very important for older workers.

Mary Roseberry
2107 S. E. !4th Des Moines, Iowa
Telephone: (501) 343-9864
Mary.Mary.R@aol.com

Career Profile

Multi-faceted individual with many years of experience in varied areas of business ranging from business ownership and operation to academic and banking positions. Growth within banking industry started with responsibilities as a bank teller and loan closer, later promoted to loan officer. Additional interpersonal skills developed though working and volunteering in Singapore for five years.

Skills Summary

- Excellent Customer Service
- Business Management
- Typing / Data Entry / Word Processing
- Real Estate
- Telephone & Switchboard Handling

- Diversified Office Support & Secretarial
- Bookkeeping (Full-Charge) and Collections
- PC & Mainframe Operation
- Cash Handing & Balancing
- Banking Operations

Experience

Fundraiser (American Women's Association, Singapore) (Volunteer)   1995-2002
- Leveraged international military relationships, tapping network to raise funds for local charities.

Banking Position (Wells Fargo Bank, Des Moines, Iowa)   1989-1995
- Started as a bank teller part-time in operations, transferred to sales in 1991 as a loan officer. Opened checking, savings, and CD accounts, processed car loans and small consumer loans. Resolved problems with customer accounts and various reports.

Owner / Operator (My Flower Shop Des Moines, Iowa)   1887 – 1989
- Managed all areas of business (including all accounting functions)

Secretary / Registrar (Washington Elementary School, Des Moines, Iowa)   1985 – 1987
- Handled all student enrollment performed general secretarial and switchboard operational duties.

Bank loan Closer (Washington Mutual, Des Moines, Iowa)   1980 – 1985
- Processed documents for mortgage loans and worked with clients to ensure all were completed properly, entered necessary data on computer and distributed funds for loan.

Education

Associate Degree in Business	Riverside Community College, Riverside, CA
Bachelor of Arts in Accounting & Banking	University of California, Riverside, CA
Des Moines Technical School (Diploma)	Des Moines, Iowa

References Available upon Request

Note: As you can see here a lot of space was spent on detailing skills with just a brief description of each position (paid or volunteer). This approach is a concise profile of the applicant.

CLARA F. BOND

4534 6th Street ● **Salt Lake City, Utah 78909**
(515) 589-0974 Clara_Bond@aol.com

STATEMENT OF QUALIFICATIONS

Multi-dimensional and highly competent administrative and creative4 professional with 15 + years
Experience in all aspects of successful event/program and fundraising management.
Demonstrated Ability to recruit, motivate, and build cohesive teams that achieve results.
Sourced vendors, negotiated contracts, and managed budgets. Strong organizational,
interpersonal, and communication skills, Professionalism, poise, and diplomacy.

- **Special Event Management:** Conceptualization, coordination, and implementation of special events, providing strategic and tactical actions to meet objectives. Developed and administered budgets.

(**Fundraising and Public Relations**: Created, planned, and managed all aspects of several major fundraising campaigns resulting in significant contributions. Recruited volunteers and developed sponsorships. Generated media coverage through effective promotional and public relations strategies.

- **Administration:** Consistently effective in providing administrative leadership, enhancing work processes, and improving productivity. Experience in organizational, implementation, and team building/leadership.

RELATED EXPERIENCE

Utah Art Institute   1985 - 2000

- President (2 years), Board of Directors (8 years), Chair – Publicity Coordinator (2 years)
- Projects: Spring Feast Co-Chair/Founder (4 years)
    Summer Festival Chair – Prop/Costume Design Committee
    Christmas Pageant Chair

Ogden Medical Center Wives Group   1983 - 1998
- President (2 years)
- Annual Tea Party (5 years)
- Summer Fund Raiser Co-Chair (10 years)

Ogden Children Art Program
(Children's Art Committee   1990-1998

East High School   1990-1997
- PTA – Fundraising
- Football team booster Club – President (2 years); Chair Fundraising (4 years)

EMPLOYMENT HISTORY

Petco, Ogden, UT.   1997 - 1999
CUSTOMER SERVICE: Provided customer service and specializing in customized dog beds, pet foods, grooming and pet accessories. Presented community awareness programs. Sponsored an adoption program for pets without homes.

ABC School, Ogden, UT   1993 – 1997
SALES TECHNICIAN, School Coordinator: Recruited to coordinate magazine displays and sales in The Ogden School District. Recruited, trained, and supervised volunteers in operations, finance, and promotional incentives.

EDUCATION
BS, Vocational Home Economics, BYU University,   Provo, UT

NOTE: In this résumé you will discover more than ten years of volunteer work. These strong skills have been exploited to show the applicants abilities that can be transferred into the work place and paid position. This expansive summary takes up nearly a half of a page.

PROFESSIONAL PROFILE

High-energy individual offering the value of an advanced degree in Education with a solid background in counseling, therapeutic approaches, and training – combined with extensive experience in finance, database systems, and program management, offer a strong commitment to the delivery of high-quality educational programs with a personal and professional interest in the area of autism.

Hellen B. Fox

4201 Orange Grove
Orange, CA 92889

714-514-1991
HellenB.123@snet.com

Skilled lecturer, presenter, and writer. Published in *The Newport Journal and Spirit of Counseling Magazine*.

Successful in developing and presenting case studies, capturing, students' interest, and creating, an innovative, progressive learning environment that prompts critical though and class participation. Detail-oriented and perceptive: determined spirit and character. High professional ethics and personal integrity.

EDUCATION

M.Ed., --Cum Laude --**UNIVERSITY OF CALIFORNIA**, Fullerton, California

Coursework Highlights:

Principles of Guidance	Counsel & Guidance
Measurement & Group Tests	Theories of Counseling
Group Counseling	Counseling Practicum
Fundamentals of Research	Families in Crisis

BS, 1982 – Cum Laude – **FINANCE – UNIVERSITY OF CALIFORNIA** Riverside, California

TEACHING EXPERIENCE

Gained practical teaching experience through special assignments in fulfillment of the requirements of the graduated program in Education. Provided instruction to other graduate degree candidates in a formal classroom setting using teaching models, formats, and platforms pertinent to the topic. Developed lesson plans, defined learning objectives, developed materials and teaching tools, led classroom presentations, oversaw discussions, and assessed the effectiveness of the programs.

- **Case Studies** – Instructed students in client-centered and therapeutic approaches to resolve issues governing 'at risk' children, alcoholism, and divorce. Presented situation, knowledge, and foundation theories and outlined techniques of counseling.

- **Professional Development** – Led several presentations on contemporary counseling methodologies and techniques. Demonstrated and effectively communicated an understanding of the role/function of counseling, best professional practices (including legal and ethical considerations), and individual / group approaches to effective assessment and evaluation.

- **Internship, Orange Hills Middle School** – Counsel adolescents in the areas of substance abuse, attention deficit disorder, family relationship, depression, peers, and school Assisted trouble youths with building self-esteem, formulating realistic goals, and understanding the importance of positive peer models. Encouraged family members to take an active role in their children's development and progress. Demonstrated ability to incorporate effective counseling skills in a school setting.

Note: What we have here is a highly qualified applicant. In this case the applicant combines work experience and volunteer work to paint a strong picture. As you can see the applicant is showing teaching experience combined with diverse volunteer experience.

HELLEN B. FOX

Page Two   HellenB.123@snet.com

COMMUNITY / VOLUNTEER EXPERIENCE:

Volunteer/RI Representation – Autism Network for Dietary Intervention 1997 to Present
Assist parents with the implementation of Beat Autism Now! A biomedical protocol and gluten/casein-free dietary program for the disorder's underlying metabolic and immune dysfunction, concurrently, conduct ongoing research and serve as Utah Representative for the sponsoring national organization.

Union Steward – National Association of Government Employees, Ogden, Utah   1996 to 1997
Member of a community-base human-services organization specializing in employment related services for personnel with the Army Chemical Weapons Center. Provided one-on-one counseling to employees with varying backgrounds in grievances, employee rights, and other work issues.

- Served as a direct intermediary between union and management officials. Credited with facilitating negotiations, forging positive relationship, and promoting conflict resolution.

Volunteer Counselor – Child & Family Agency, Salt Lake City, Utah   1996 to 1997
Provided volunteer counseling services specializing in marriage, relationships, depression, stress, abuse, trauma, chronic illness, and grief. Designed individualized treatment plans and objectives, maintained/update client documentation, and built a strong working rapport with clients.

- Evaluated needs identified appropriate coping mechanisms, and designed/implemented individualized counseling programs.
- Effectively conducted counseling sessions with particular emphasis on promoting self-actualization and healthy integration of difficult life experiences. Resulted in a high number of successful completions.
- Documented benefits of treatment and discussed future interventions.

Mentor Program Coordinator -- Chemical Weapons Center, Ogden, Utah   1995 to 1997
Led the development and implementation of a mentor program between the Chemical Weapons Center and Orange Hills Middle School. Focused on partnering engineering professionals (service as volunteers) with student candidates. Charted the program's vision, established objectives, and coordinated schedules.

- Orchestrated training/orientation programs and served as liaison between volunteers and student. Successfully developed opportunities for participants.
- Contributed ongoing motivation and support and served as a mentor to several students.

BUSINESS EXPERIENCE:

Chemical Weapons Center, Ogden, Utah   1983 to 1997
Data Management Specialist (1990 to 1997)
Configuration Management Specialist (1985 to 1990)
Program Analyst (1983 to 1995)

Sally R. Campbell

592 California Ave
Riverside, California 92889

951-277-8382 Home
Sally1964@aol.com

MANAGEMENT / ADMINISTRATIVE PROFESSIONAL
Strengths in Project Coordination & Management

Highly motivated and hard-working professional with a track record of streamlining systems and systems and procedures to maximize productivity, minimize costs, and directly contribute to organizational goals. Resourceful in meeting challenges and solving problems. Work well under pressure to meet critical deadlines. Possess outstanding written and oral communication skills including correspondence, public speaking, and presentations

Work well independently as well as collaboratively in a team setting. Get along well with diverse clients and coworkers at all levels. Computer expertise on PC and Macintosh.

Strengths include:

Project Management / Office Administration / Client & Vendor Relations / Hiring, Training & Supervision
Oral & Written Communications / Consensus Building / Conflict Resolution / Analysis
Budget Management / Team Building & Leadership / Meeting & Event Coordination.

Program Director – 1996 to 2002
THE RIVERSIDE VALLEY COMMUNITY CHURCH, Riverside, CA   (1998 - 2002)
THE FIRST COMMUNITY CHURCH OF PERRIS, CA   (1996 – 1997, concurrent with full-time studies)
As a volunteer, coordinated and directed programs and business functions for small congregations.

- Instituted sound business and administrative practices, including introduction of computer technology, to ensure smooth functioning of operations with minimum staffing and budgets.
- Coordinated promotional efforts, including cable TV and radio spots, to increase public awareness of community events. Drew attendance of 2600 over six evenings for special events in small community.
- Established and nurtured partnerships with business community.
- Grew youth-group participation fivefold.
- Produced youth concert that drew record attendance.
- Completed community demographic studies and implemented computerized database to facilitate communication and community outreach efforts.

Partner / General Manager – 1984 to 1994
Packer Engineering, Riverside, CA

Oversaw day-to-day operation, marketing efforts, and project management for civil engineering firm specializing in 'overnight' corporate identity changes for major banking and franchise operations, Supervised cross-functional team of 25 project managers, engineers, and clerical staff.

- Represented company at trade shows throughout the U.S. to generate new business. Developed and delivered comprehensive slide and PowerPoint presentations.
- Generated and analyzed competitive bids from prospective vendors, awarded contracts.
- Surveyed facilities, developed specifications, and planned and managed field work. Multimillion-dollar Union 76 gasoline stations and 432 Big Boy restaurants. Other corporate accounts included Wells Fargo, Union Bank, and Carl's restaurants.
- Established internal administrative and operating procedures to streamline productivity minimize cost.
- Implemented cutting-edge computer application.
- Designed and delivered training classes.
- Coordinated meetings and travel arrangements.

Note: What we see here is an applicant that has been out of the workforce. Now that this individual is ready to return to the world, the work is focusing on her career goals, using recent volunteer experience which is valuable in achieving this goal.

Sally R. Campbell
Resune' Page Two

EDUCATION

Master's Degree – Baptist College of Riverside, CA
Bachelor of Science (*Civil Engineering*) – UNIVERSITY OF CALIFORNIA RIVERSIDE, Riverside, CA

Professional Development

Completed Management Course, Chapman University School of Management, Chapman University, Orange, CA
Delivered public presentations and published numerous articles

COMPUTER SKILLS

Proficient on PC Platforms and Macintosh

Hardware

PC, Scanner, Digitizer, Plotter, Digital Camera, PC Presentation, and Projection Equipment

Operation Systems
MS DOS, Windows x XP Professional / 2000

Software Applications

Microsoft Office (Word, Excel, PowerPoint, Corel Office Suite (WordPerfect, Presentations) AutoCAD,
QuickBooks, Lotus 1-2-3; timekeeping, group organization, mapping software.
Hebrew and Greek language software, Email, Internet

Other

BASIC Programming, Web Page Design

-- Excellent personal and professional referrals available on request --

Judy J. Jacoberger
456 Apple Valley Road, San Mateo, CA 93434
415-234-0233 Home ■ JJJ62@aol.com

Profile

- ☑ 15 years of administrative, volunteer and team experience in the coordination and implementation of educational, non-profit and community service projects.
- ☑ Quick and eager learner. Proven ability to adapt quickly to a challenge.
- ☑ Demonstrated ability to manage multiple projects simultaneously within deadlines.
- ☑ Outstanding team player with proven record of accomplishments.

Key Skills

Administrative Management
- Increased the visibility of a resale clothing shop, which benefits local charities, while serving as volunteer Store Manage. Raised $100K in 2001-2002, the best year in the history of the shop. On target to surpass sales records in 2002.

Project Management
- **Coordinated** and solicited 400 auction items (products and service) from northern California businesses and Wetlands Fund raising Auction. Managed the acquisition of and arrangements for guest speakers involved in a fundraising seven-part lecture series (1999 and 2000).

Leadership
- **Spearheaded** successful annual fund-solicitation programs as class agent for The San Mateo County School from 1997 to 2000, achieving 80% parent participation rate. Chaired fundraising events for the San Mateo Art Museum and the California Wetlands Association's 2000 Garden Tour.

Interpersonal Skills
- Proven persuasive communication skills. Adept at building and maintaining effective professional relationships. Easily able to win the trust and confidence of diverse individuals. Resolve a wide array of problems, applying diplomacy and assertiveness, while implementing organizational policies and procedures.

Writing & editing
- **For** the San Mateo County School; wrote successful fundraising solicitation letters that were instrumental in raising $42k to $53k. Wrote weekly community-action newsletters that provided information about zoning, water quality, traffic, and business-expansion issues to 400 community residents.

Work History

2000 - Present	Store Manager / Volunteer, Good Will Resale Shop, San Mateo, California
1998 – 2002	Volunteer, San Mateo Art Museum, San Mateo, California
1996 – 2000	Volunteer, California Wetlands Association, San Mateo, California
1998 – 1999	Chairperson, San Mateo Neighborhood Watch Association, San Mateo, California

Education

Bachelor o Arts — History, cum laude, University of California at San Mateo, California
Master's Degree Program – History (30 credits), University of California, San Jose, California
2001 Introduction to Computing, Santa Clara University, Santa Clara, California.

Note: Here we have an applicant re-entering the labor force. In this case functional style headings are being used to present Key Skills to prove diverse skills.

Norma W. Witbe

453 Littlehorn Lane Rock Springs, Wyoming 78931
(303) 732-3242
NomaW@aol.net

■ PROFILE

Conferences ● Fund – Raising ● Trade Shows ● Meeting Planning ● Cultural Programs

Creative professional with expertise in all aspects of successful event/program planning, development and management. Excel in managing multiple projects concurrently with strong detail, problem solving and follow-through. Demonstrated ability to recruit, motivate and build cohesive teams. Sourced vendors negotiated contracts and managed project budgets. Superb written communications, interpersonal and presentation skills.

■ SELECTED ACCOMPLISHMENTS

Special Events Management:

Planned and coordinated conferences, meetings and events for companies, professional associations, arts / cultural, other organizations, Developed program content and administered budgets. Arranged all on – site logistics, including transportation, accommodations, meals, guest speakers and entertainers, and audiovisual support. Coordinated participation and represented companies at industry trade shows. Recognized for creating and planning some of the most successful events held statewide.

- **Created cultural events for an arts organization that boosted membership enrollment.**
- **Organized 8 well-attended conferences for 2 national professional associations.**
- **Designed successful community educational campaigns promoting safety awareness.**

Fund-raising & Public Relations:

Created, planned and managed all aspects of several major fund-raising campaigns resulting in a significant increase in contributions raised for each function over prior years. Recruited volunteers and developed corporate sponsorships. Generated extensive media coverage through effective promotional and public relations strategies. Created newsletters distributed to employees, customers and others.

- **Co-chaired capital fund campaign raising $4.5 million for new facility.**
- **Coordinated 4 auctions raising over $175,000 for an educational institution.**
- **Initiated successful publication generating $45,000 to finance community programs.**

Sales & Marketing:

Selected by management to spearhead opening regional office, including all logistics, staff relocation and business development efforts. Designed and implemented creative sales and marketing strategies to capitalize on consumer trends and penetrate new market Coordinated and conducted sales training.

- **Developed and managed 20 key accounts generating $12 million annually.**
- **Recognized for managing top revenue-generating program company-wide**
- **Consistently exceeded sales forecast and led region to rank #1 out of 8 profitability nationwide.**

■ EXPERIENCE

Event / Program Coordinator (Volunteer**),** CHINESE ARTS AND GARDEN, Rock Springs, Wyoming (1998 – present).

Promoted from **Regional Manager, Account Executive and Financial Underwriter,**   HOUSEHOLD FINANCIAL SERVICES COMPANY, Rocksprings, Wyoming, (1988 – 2000)

■ EDUCATION

B.A. in Business Administration, University of Wyoming at Cheyenne, Wyoming

Note: This applicant was faced with layoffs, so as you can see the focus of experience is based on volunteer work to seek out her 'dream job'.

Jerry G. Lambert

SALES MANAGEMENT / RETAIL OPERATION

Manager with high integrity always eager to produce high-quality work.

PROFESSIONAL PROFILE

- Excellent leadership skills combined with an ability to motivate others while delivering projects on time.
- Highly effective communication and interpersonal skills; ability to work with diverse groups both internal and external
- Outstanding abilities in problem identification, resolution, and follow-through. Talent for troubleshooting and making maximum use of available resources.

QUALIFICATIONS

- Two years' management experience with focus in the entertainment industry.
- Managed and directed all phases of daily business operations including hiring, training, staff supervision, scheduling, payroll, and maintenance.
- Coordinated company events from fruition to completion.
- Skilled in all areas of personnel management.
- Extensive background in customer service.
- Proficient operation of basic computer programs.

KEY MANAGEMENT SKILLS

• Customer Service	• Office Management	• Budge Analysis
• Sales	• Document Management	• Project Management
• Merchandising	• Staff Development	• Presentations
• Bookkeeping	• Training	• Public Speaking

PROFESSIONAL EXPERIENCE

Twilight Zone Gaming, Inc. Riverside, California — 1996 – 1998
GENERAL MANAGER / PARTNER

The Castle Fun Zone, Inc. Ontario, California — 1995 – 1998
RIDE OPERATOR

AAA Insurance Company　(Bill Smith C.F.P.) — 1995 – 1996
PERSONAL ASSISTANT

OTHER EXPERIENCE

The First Methodist Church of Riverside California — 1998 – 2000

MISSIONARY, ASSISTANT TO THE MISSIONARY PRESIDENT
- Earned the Masters Teacher award

1492 California Street Riverside, California 92889 ● Cell phone 951-277-9073

Note: Here we have another functional format that highlights the applicant's qualifications that relate to his job objectives and recent experience.

Niki W. Le

IT TESTING / TECHNOLOGY MANAGEMENT / TECHNICAL SUPPORT

IT Management
SQL
Quality Control
Enterprise
Maintenance
MS Office
Troubleshooting
Fortran
End-User Support
Pascal
Sybase
Assembler
Oracle
Enterprise
Customer Service
Desktop Support
Installations
Conversions
MS Visual Basic
C C++
Fpreogm
Languages,
Chinese, French

PROFILE OF TRANSFERABLE SKILLS

- **Strong training and transferable skills**: returning to the workforce after missionary trip to China, Taiwan and Cambodia, during this time continued some self-study in technology and software.
- *Professional skills include strong educational training in mechanical maintenance with professional experience in the technology field.*
- *Able to conceive and develop new methods that expedite troubleshooting processes and reduce cost.*
- *Have demonstrated ability to accept diverse responsibility; understand the need to communicate and promote communications with those associated with competitive developmental technology / electronics environment.*
- *Able to troubleshoot electrical and complex mechanical systems in addition utilizing mechanical engineering training skills.*
- *Continuous working experiences with all levels of decision-makers, from the worker in the field to the functional department head to the upper-management level.*

PROFESSIONAL WORK HISTORY

UNIVERSITAL TELECOM, Huntington Beach, CA
IT & Database Support Technician (1991 to 1997)

- Provided extensive coaching and development of testing systems to support maintenance, sales and other administrative areas of the company. Experience base in this area totals nearly three years of dedicated network / software support management from 1994 to 1997.
- Provide environment for testing of new software and hardware installations as well as network troubleshooting and security testing.
- Help oversee design and implementation of enterprise-wide business workstation builds.
- Planned and deployed and build of various programs.
- Controlled inventory through critical data analysis, accurate data entry, procedural tracking, and development of enterprise-wide inventory system.
- Assisted in inventory management and tracking functions for the company.
- Consulted with customers on purchase and investment decisions regarding network choices and new systems.
- Resolved security problems during migrations and changes as well as unexpected shutdowns.

Systems X Inc., Santa Ana, CA
Computer Support Specialist II (1988 – 1990)
Computer Technician – Co-op (1986 – 1988)

- Assisted in inventory management and tracking functions.
- Consulted with customers regarding network choices and new systems from the ground up.
- Resolved security problems.

EDUCATION

BYU UNIVERSITY, Provo, Utah, **Masters of Science in Computers Engineering (January 1985)**

5453 Foxfire Road
Westminster, California 98733

Home: 714-674-1214
Cell: 714-674-1215

OGDEN COLLEGE, Ogden, Utah, **Bachelor of Science in Computer Technology (May 1982)**

Note: The applicant has been gone from the workforce for some time, but explains her absence with the missionary work. But the résumés overall focus is on her professional skills and experience to show qualifications for a 'high tech' job.

Ashley I. Young
921 Lincoln Ave
Riverside, CA 92889

Telephone: 951-278-2925

Email: AshleyIYoung@aol.Net

CAREER PROFILE

Exceptional Customer Service Representative with extensive experience in retail and real-estate, service, and related support functions. Skilled at managing multiple departments and staff. Experienced buyer having worked with extensive clothing lines and accessories for men, women, and children. Successful real-estate sales individual with the ability to follow through while applying a keen attention to detail. Willing to put to use transferable skills in most an interest and challenging position and business environment.

TRANSFERABLE SKILLS

- Proven skills in sales and customer service, strong attention to detail.
- Effective business manager and staff trainer/supervisor.
- Thorough knowledge of retail clothing buying, marketing, and sales.
- Earned credentials for real estate sales in the State of Maine.
- Knowledgeable in varied clerical functions and office procedures.

WORK ETHICS

- Dependable, loyal, and punctual.
- Ability to accept responsibility while consistently meeting deadlines.
- Experienced in handling and working with large amounts of cash.
- Previously screened, cleared, and employed by the Federal Government.

WORK EXPERIENCE

Realty Home Sales (Colton, California)   1987 – 1999
Licensed Sales Agent

Mervyn's (Corona, California)   1975 – 1986
    Hired as a Salesperson in the Children and Infants Department. After four months, was promoted to Buyer /Department Manager with a varied of responsibilities including personnel management, accurate record-keeping of merchandise ordered and received, and department display setup. Made frequent buying trips to New York and Boston markets. Demonstrated efficient merchandise management, inventory, control, and merchandise history-keep skills.

(Continued on Page 2)

Note: This applicant shows flexible skills that are transferable, also highlights personal attributes.

This résumé supports several job targets.

| Ashley I. Young | Resume' (Page 2 of 2) |

WORK EXPERIENCE (continued)

Penney's (Riverside, California)   1975 – 1986
Buyer/Department Manager

> Promoted to Buyer/Department Manager Sportswear and Accessory Departments
> (1977), then the management of the Women's Department was also added (1980)

> Functioned as Fashion Coordinator (simultaneously), with responsibility for the organization of fashion shows including
> selection of models and merchandise, writing commentary, preparing advertising, and coordinating all aspects of the show.

> Organized special events such as the annual Back to School Sale, 100 year Anniversary Sale and other special promotions
> as needed.

> Promoted to Floor Manager (1985) responsible for overseeing the entire store with regard to employee job performance
> and other general management issues and problems. Involved in management policy decisions.

Personal Services (Miramar, California)   1971 - 1973
Naval Air Station
Worked as a Personal Services Coordinator, Started out as a Volunteer beginning with a few hours per week; eventually became the
Personal Services Coordinator working forty hours per week. Position involved complex and varied duties including answering the
telephone, keeping cash records, operation and managing a rental service (household items), and making babysitting arrangements.
Also involved in varied crisis and emergency situations.

California Attorney Generals Office of Investigation   1971 – 1971
Identification Division
> Classified and researched fingerprints sent to the Attorney Generals Office.

EDUCATION

- Completed requirement of Real Estate Stale & Licensing – State of California.
  (Served as Chair for the Riverside, California Real Estate Board)
- Complete extensive training to Retail Sales, Service, and Management & Merchandising.
- Attended United Airlines Institute (Seattle, Washington) – Completed one Year.
- Ramona High School (Riverside, California) – Diploma, Cum Laude

References Available Upon Request

Randy R. Child

1278 Apple Valley Road
Stanton, CA 97233

714-514-8279
RRC@aol.net

QUALIFICATION

- Successful record working with children/adolescents with severe special needs.
- Strong behavioral management background.
- Positive and encouraging attitude, combined with consistent, patient manner
- Experience managing complex cases.
- Effective working independently and as a member of a team.
- Ability to coordinate services with multiple care providers and agencies.

RELEVANT EXPERIENCE

CHOC (Children's Hospital), Santa Ana, California 1983- 1988

Teacher II (1984-1988)
Teacher I (1983 – 1984)

- Provided case management for special-needs children ages 11-19, assigned two of the more complicated cases, requiring coordination with multiple agencies and professionals.
- Coached and instructed children and adolescents in activities of daily living, behavior management, and academic and vocational skills, according to needs of each child.
- Wrote individualized educational plans and student behavior plans that resulted in measurable behavioral improvements.
- Consulted with other professional to develop and implement effective strategies.
- Collaborated with speech/language specialist to develop communication books designed for non-communication children.
- Trained new staff in standard procedures for the care of autistic children.
- Communicated with parents on a regular basis to inform them of their children's progress, and instructed parents on effective techniques for working with their children.
- Offered management position but elected to continue in a case management and direct teaching role.

OTHER EXPERIENCE

Friday's Restaurant, Costa Mesa, CA, 1988 - 1997

Manager

- Trained, supervised, and scheduled employees, ensuring high employee morale.
- Greeted guests and maintained friendly atmosphere, which generated repeat business.

EDUCATION

University of California Fullerton, CA, 1988 – 1997

Note: As you can see in this résumé that it supports extensive caring and educated sick children with his prior professional teaching experience. Also as you see the most recent experience does not support the applicant's job target, therefore it is placed last.

Eugene B. Brown

2929 Blue Berry Road
Riverside, California 92873
(951) 277-9820

CUSTOMER SERVICE

Staff training / Employee Supervision / Support

Professional Profile

Mature worker with a solid work history that shows reliability, responsibility, and high-quality performance. Team member with an interest in learning and applying new skills. Strengths include customer support and staff training.

Core Skills:
Customer interface...Sale / Marketing... Communication ... Employee Relations ... Banking............

Summary
- Assisted individuals with accessing medical, insurance, and legal services, including Medicaid.
- Performed a wide range of human resource functions, including recruiting, interviewing, hiring, training, motivating, and evaluating employees.
- Supervised sales, customer service, cashier, maintenance, food service, stock, and office personnel.
- Handled purchasing, security, marketing, and merchandising, and secured licenses and permits.
- Conveyed a friendly, helpful, and positive attitude to customers and co-workers.
- Developed reliable and profitable relationships with vendors.
- Interacted effectively with people of all ages and backgrounds.

Experience

Family Caregiver   Riverside, California (1985 – 2002)

Manager   Cowboy Steak House, Corona, California, (1975 – 1985)

Insurance Adjuster   AAA, Riverside, California (1974)

Field Representative   KCE Corp. Corona, California (1970 – 1974)

Education
Los Angeles Employment and Training Center, Los Angeles, California
        Microsoft Office, 2002
Moreno Valley Continuing Education, Moreno Valley, California

References
Furnished upon request

Naomi J. Anderson, RN

745 Honey Bear Road Ontario, CA 92598
(909) 278-3234 Home (909) 278-3235 Cell
NJA32@aol.com

PROFILE

Registered Nurse ● Case Manager ● Medical Auditor with clinical / auditing experience, including medical treatment documentation review, DRGs, CPT coding, and ICD-9-CM ending. Knowledgeable of the disease process, findings, course of treatment, quality assurance, and risk management, Demonstrated track record in:

(Medical Records Auditing	(Practice Compliance Auditing	(Medical Bill Auditing
(Practice Site Reviews	(Managed Care Case Management	(HEDIS Assessment
(Medicaid Auditing	(Field Utilization Review	(Electronic Chart Review

Background in managed care protocol and case management for catastrophic trauma, soft tissue damage, and orthopedic injuries Recent case management professional development, Skilled M & R guidelines, as well as new hire orientations. Proven ability to interact effectively with healthcare and office staff professionally.

PROFESSIONAL EXPERIENCE

Montclair Healthcare mentoring, (healthcare accreditation firm), Santa Ana, California 1997-2000
Nurse Reviewer
Field position with multiple long- and short-term assignments. Audited, examined, and verified medical records and monitored practice sites to ensure documentation accuracy and compliance with standard medical practices and criteria. Conducted 15-20 on-site appointments weekly at medical clinics, hospitals, health plans and physicians' offices. Reviewed 50-70 charts daily. Completed 4-6 site reviews daily.

- **Monarch Health plan,** Performed HEDIS effectiveness of care audits, Medicaid audits, and Healthy Start Program and follow-up visit tracking. Practice compliance audits involved medical record reviews for specific disease conditions and/or routine care, including diabetes blood work, asthma management, immunizations, OB-GYN well visits, and OB care.

- **Blue Cross Health Plan,** Conducted medical record documentation reviews and practice site reviews for medical standards and credentialing purposes.

- **California Medical Accreditation Program (CMAP)** – California foundation for medical case information systems. Managed data collection for the Los Angeles Medical Society, Performed medical-record review and site assessment to determine clinical performance based on a set of standards and criteria.

EAGLE INSURANCE COMPANY, Brea, CA   1987-1997
Out-of-network utilization Review Specialist –Summer Healthcare, Santa Ana, CA (1996 – 1997)

- Identified and implemented appropriate level of care based on health insurance policy provisions and medical need. Scope of authority included pre-authorization, review, and discharge planning.

- Monitored or quality of care based on ethical and medical standard and criteria, as well timeliness and cost effectiveness. Ensured compliance with federal, state, and industry medical-management regulations. Utilized computer-based records-management procedures for documenting and retrieving clinical data.

Page 1 of 2

Note: Here we have an applicant leading with a strong profile of skills in Case Management. There is a two year gap in employment, but this is down played with mentioning of strong and recent professional experience. You can continue with a traditional chorological format.

Naomi J. Anderson, RN
(909) 278-3234 Home -- NJA32@aol.com

PROFESSIONAL EXPERIENCE

Field Concurrent Review Nurse – Western Healthcare, Los Angeles, CA (1993 – 1996)

- Performed on-site concurrent chart reviews for in-patient populations at area teaching medical centers, investigation medical status, appropriateness of stay, and quality of care.
- Monitored clinical outcomes and consulted with network physicians and medical director for case management review, ensuring timely delivery of optimum-level patient care.
- Proactive addressed network gaps by researching and recruiting specialty physicians and facilities to provide continuum of care within the network.
- Effectively balanced patients' medical needs with health plan benefits to appropriately implement discharge planning to home of alternate-level setting.

Rehabilitation Coordinator –United Property & Casualty Insurance Trust, Huntington Beach, CA (1987 – 1993)

- Designed and delivered field case management within the Personal Injury Protection (PIP) unit. Caseload consistently averaged 50-75 catastrophic and/or traumatic personal injury case. Coordinated client benefits between Western Healthcare and the State of California.
- Audited medical bills and hospital charts, evaluating coding and reviewing all reviewing all related medical treatment documentation Negotiated and resolved discrepancies.
- Monitored cases from initial medical assessment through ultimate disposition, coordinating healthcare at all levels in compliance with the State of California No-Fault statute.

- Received Western Healthcare's **Annual Customer Service** and **Leadership Award** in 1993

CUCAMONGA, REHABILITATION CONSULTANTS, INC., Ontario, CA   1983-1987

Insurance Rehabilitation Specialist. Consultant for California based insurance companies; Case managed traumatic injury cases from initial assessment through resolution, addressing all medical, legal, and financial issues.

EDUCATION

Diploma – Nursing, Los Angeles County School of Nursing, Los Angeles, CA
California State University – College of Nursing, Continuing Education Certificates:
The Nurse as Case Manager (65 contact hours), 2002; RN re-Entry into Practice (200 contact hours), 2001 Professional development (clinical experience and seminars) in healthcare delivery practices.

CERTIFICATIONS

Registered Nurse – State of California (License # 343232)
Certified Case Manager – 1993 (Certification # 456439)

Nancy C. Mason

655 Warmsprings Road , Riverside, CA 92889

(951) 278-3256 Home ■ (951) 278-8772 Cell

NancyCMason@aol.com

ADMINISTRATIVE PROFESSIONAL

Management / Training / Sales & Business Development

- Extensive background in training and education, working with adults, elementary education and developmentally disabled.
- Vibrant and expansive communication style with ability to build rapport with anyone, skilled in public relations, staff development and as a company rep.
- Comfortable with bottom-line responsibilities such as setting goals and directing teams to accomplish those goals. Extremely intuitive problem solver.
- Talented salesperson with awards for outstanding performance.

PROFESSIONAL EXPERIENCE

Home Care to Family Members, Riverside, CA, 1996 – Present
Director Recruitment, A-1 Employment Services, Colton, CA 1991 – 1995
Resident Assistant, Riverside County Academy for Women, Riverside, CA 1988 – 1990
Sales Manager, Best Marketing, City of Industry, CA 1986 – 1988
Third Grade / Special Ed. Teacher, East Side Elementary, Rialto, CA 1982 – 1985

Management & Business Development
- Hired and trained all recruiters at A-1, setting goals and encouraging high performance levels through team building and motivational techniques.
    o Developed recruitment programs, achieving quotas and winning company sales competitions.
  Performed business development for advertising sales through Best Marketing for a new California territory encompassing Northern California.
    o Handled recruitment, hiring and training of staff.
    o Performed administrative detail involving money collection, banking and record keeping.

Troubleshooting & Streamlining
- Troubleshot recruitment problems at A-1 locations throughout California, increasing enrollments in stagnating locations.
- Designed training manuals and implemented new policies and procedures at A-1 and Best.

Communications & Teaching

- Managed a multi-cultural dormitory of young ladies as Resident Assistant, monitoring behavior, accompanying on field trips, providing private counseling and resolving conflicts.
- Taught math, reading comprehension, language arts, writing and other core subjects to third-grade students at East Side Elementary.
- Worked closely to assist children with special-education needs in taking steps toward self-sufficiency and literacy at East Side Elementary.

EDUCATION & AFFILIATIONS

B.S. Adult Education. California State University at Riverside, CA, GPA. 3.8

Member, Adult Literacy Abroad Program

Note: Here we have an extensive functional résumé depicting strengths and Professional Experience. This applicant has a gap in employment, but this is explained in the résumé.

BUDDY MASON

323 BITTERN BOULEVARD
(408) 327-3462 HOME
(408) 327-3463 CELL

SUNNYVALE, CA 93223
BUDDY1@HOTMAIL.COM

COMPUTER PROFESSIONAL
Database Specialist / Web Site Developer / Designer

Professional Profile:

Creative database manager and website administrator with superior microcomputer training and hands-on Programming experience. Skilled in training users on new and enhanced technology. Able to interface with customers, identify their business needs, and develop computer systems and applications to fulfill those requirements.

Core Skills:

Advanced Access 2000	FrontPage 2000	Crystal Reports 6.
Publisher 2000	Visio 2000	Quicken 2000
PowerPoint 2000	Advanced Excel 2000	Internet Explorer

Programming with Access, FORTRAN and Ingres (Embedded SQL)

Education:

University of California at San Jose - School of Technology, San Jose California
Certificate in Access Database Specialist, 2001
Certificate in Advanced Word 2000, 2001
Certificate in Word Processing Specialist, 2001
Certificate in Microcomputer Applications Specialist, 2000

University of California at San Jose
Bachelor of Arts – Mathematics, 1981

Experience:

The Learning Center, Sunnyvale, CA   1998 - 2000
Part-time Tutor
Provided remedial tutoring to individuals and groups to reinforce academic skills.
  • Assisted students in improving classroom performance.

Bechtel Contracting, Inc. San Francisco, California   1992 – 1997
Associate Engineer
Assisted senior management and engineers with proposal development and packaging for local and international clients. Performed market research, estimated definitive costs, and prepared chemical process plant contracts. Worked with engineers in procuring and inspecting equipment and raw materials.
  • Made significant contributions to company's being awarded major contracts.
  • Negotiated rates and enabled company to benefit from price breaks and discounts.

Note: You can see in this résumé a strong flow of technical experience. The highlighting extensive computer knowledge and training, plus the employment work experience indicate business savvy and technical expertise. This résumé should be clear where this applicant wants to go.

BUDDY MASON   **PAGE TWO**

McDonald Aircraft, San Francisco, California   1984 – 1990
Software Engineer
Participated in software design, and testing of three major applications, Off-Line Date Reduction (OLDR), Track History (TH), and Radar Control Systems. Documented, coded, tested, and maintained various scientific software applications. Utilized FORTRAN and Ingres on DEC VAX/VMS network.

Northrop Aviation Company, Sunnyvale, California   1982 - 1984
Associate Engineer
Designed and documented a software application which performed data analysis from experimental laser weapon system.

References:
Furnished upon request.

Nancy W. Wayne

(415) 789-9822   231 Orangewood, Orange, CA, 93899   NancyW@aol.com

MANAGEMENT PROFESSIONAL

- 12 years of successful administration, supervision, and management experience.
- Caring, resourceful, flexible, practical, and self-motivated professional. Strive to improve upon processes and task.
- Strong interpersonal and communication skills.
- Consistent pattern of realizing profits and surpassing projections.
- Strengths in delegation, organization, long-range strategic planning, and project implementation.

EDUCATION

California State College at Fullerton, CA
POST GRADUATE STUDIES (3.7 GPA)
- Interdisciplinary Studies including Performing Arts.
- Received outstanding commendation for submitted work.
- Self-supporting while attending graduate school.

BACHELOR OF ARTS, BIOLOGY

WORK HISTORY

CONTRACTED TOURISM MANAGER   CALIFORNIA TOURISM INFORMATION CENTER, Orange, CA

- Contracted to update, upgrade, and operation the facility.
- Surveyed major tourism businesses to assess needs.
- Addressed Chamber of Commerce with goal of stimulating interest for meeting future tourists' needs.
- Assisted visitors with information regarding sites and accommodations in area. Hired staff.

ON-SITE PROJECT MANGER   ORANGE COUNTY FINANCIAL HOUSING CORPORATION, Orange, CA

- Rented, set policy, and managed new apartment complex for profit and non-profit ownership.
  Adhered to strict government guidelines.
- Hired and supervised staff of 5.
- Successfully negotiated terms that led the corporation out of harmful litigation.

WEEKEND MANAGER   LONG BEACH AQUARIUM, Long Beach, CA
- Manage 'The Aquarium Shop,' an educational learning center for children and adults
- Accompanied Field trips.

ASSOCIATED DEAN OF STUDENTS / HOUSING DIRECTOR ROCK SPRINGS JUNIOR COLLEGE, Rock Springs, WY.
- Assisted Dean with student affairs such as Foreign Student advisement, and sex and drug abuse workshops.
- Prepared $150,000 housing operation budget.
- Supervised staff of 20
- Made room assignments and determined rents.

WRITER/EDITOR   ORANGE COUNTY PROJECT AREA COMMITTEE, Orange, CA
- Produced and edited a newspaper or a large community.
- Ensured residents received all information regarding government guidelines and rights in this major housing rehabilitation project.
- Performed marketing survey.

GROUP SALES MANAGER   THE ORANGE COUNTY COMMUNITY THEATRE, Orange, CA
- Promoted to this position after one season in sales associate.

COMPUTER KNOWLEDGE

- Microsoft Word and WordPerfect for Macintosh and Windows.

Note: As you can see in this résumé this applicant has 10 years of unemployment, dates have been left off to down play this fact. This applicant has a sporadic work history which is also down played by leaving dates off.

Bob Gonzalsa, AIA
516 Dear Creek Road
Aguirlar, CO 81022
Phone: 712-612-3444
Cell: 712-612-3442

Home Designed by Bob Gonzalsa

ARCHITECT
Member of The American Institute of Architects
CUSTOM RESIDENTIAL DESIGN
NEW HOMES -- REMODELING -- SPACE PLANNING

"Committed to Architechural Design Excellence for More than 18 years"

Creative and accomplished Architect with 18 plus years experience with an excellent reputation, and a solid and verifiable record of achievement; gaining the trust and confidence of many of Dallas' top building contractors. Recognized for the ability to turn a dream into a reality. Not only involved with the design stage of a project, but hands-on involvement in actual construction through final completion.

Profile of Strengths

- **Unique, imaginative, and livable. Comfortable floor plans** tailored to the needs of each client. Designs provide for the maximum use of space, and create total environments that are functional and exciting places in which to live.
- **Strong management skills,** including strategic planning, project development and scheduling, problem solving, client relations, and quality control. Reduce building costs, improve energy efficiencies, and increase future value through good design.
- **Seasoned sales and marketing skills.** Demonstrated ability to gain trust and confidence of both builders and clients.
- **Expertise in managing major/minor project renovations.**
- **Solid design and construction experience in commercial projects** in addition to residential expertise.

PROFESSIONAL EXPERIENCE

Owner / Architect
Trilogy DESIGN GROUP, Denver, CO

Architectural designing company specializing in retirement residential homes ranging in price from $250K to $5 million with up to 8,500 sq. ft. establishing a **regional reputation** for excellence and developed a loyal following with several of the top builders in California, Arizona, and New Mexico.

- K B Homes
- Hancock Homes, Inc.
- Trilogy Homes International

EDUCATION

Bachelor of Environment Design in Architecture
School of Architecture & Design, University of Colorado, Denver, CO

Note: This applicant is looking for a position with a firm, not as an independent contractor. He has been away from the labor force therefore he is omitting dates. Since he is an architect the graphic is appropriate to bring attention to his résumé.

Dick T. Tracy
453 Shady Grass Lane
Riverside, CA 92884
(951) 277-29999 ● DickTT@comcast.net

> "Chief Tracy is a talented, tireless dynamo I count on for flawless
> assistance, advice, and products..... He's a first class all the way!"
>
> 1996 Peformance Evaluation

Management Profile

High-energy, results-driven professional offering illustrious military career reflecting continuous
Contribution and achievement backed by diverse leadership roles in the private sector, Dynamic problem-solver able to innovate
compelling, win-win solutions to complex situations. Exceptional relationship building skills, fostering unified teams and cohesion
across all levels of staff, management, and customers.

Core area of expertise encompass

(Vision & Mission Planning	(Business Administration	(Strategic Problem Solving
(Training & Development	(Change Management	(Human Resources
(Project Lifecycle Management	(High-Impact Presentations	(Team Building & Leadership
(Budget Control	(Sales & Marketing	(Team Building & Leadership

Value Offered

Strategic Administration / Operations Management: Top management authority for all aspects of marketing, sales, delivery, and administration, Oversaw inventory display and control, facility management, supplies and equipment, safety, database maintenance, work schedules, and customer service. Military budget, resources and quality management advisor.

Results-Focused Project/Program Management: Linchpin in base quality improvement programs. Managed U.S. Navy's complaint program at all levels on ten bases throughout the United States. Devised new program to ensure equitable tasking, successfully eliminating assignment complaints. Catalyst in success of intramural programs and numerous fundraising projects.

Bridging Gaps through Communication & Relationship Building: Interviewed custodial parents to gather data for child support cases and coordinated with diverse legal and government factions in support of payment orders. Cultivated relationships with prospective customers, served as point of contact for existing accounts. Negotiated contracts to close sales. Strengthened communication between commander and squadron members.

Proactive Human Resources: Supervised operations of 100-person personnel office providing office providing support to more than more than 10,000 military personnel assigned to 150 organizations in 30 locations, Interviewed, hired, and trained new employees. Oversaw morale, welfare, and discipline of the Navy population. Key participant in formulating policy and direct management of various training and personnel services.

Professional Overview

Dynamic 15 plus year career, demonstrating excellence in diverse areas of business, operations, relationships building, and personnel management with broad-based roles including:

Series of progressive leadership position in the U.S. Navy.

Assistant Operations Manager / Human Resource & Training Manager for Target.

Sales Consultant for Howards Home Alliance and New Wonder Homes & Development Corporation.

Business Manager for Fast Delivery Service.

Revenue Specialist II California State Department of Revenue / Child Support Enforcement.

Note: As you can quickly pick-up this is a serviceman with a number of good years of valuable experience. The elimination of dates helps him to get over his absence from the workforce. His recommendation is very supportive of his key qualifications.

Dick T. Tracy   Page 2

Highlights of Professional Achievements

- Superbly coordinated division's quarterly video teleconference training program.
- Authored 9-page complaint processing checklist to better assist field inspector commanders, resulted in new management tool to ensure 100% accountability from complaint intake to final response.
- Flawlessly managed office during 75% turnover in personnel with no service degradation.
- Pumped new life into weak in-house training programs; designed forms for work centers to serve as documentation and set up impressive continuity book in critical short-tour environment.
- Orchestrated administrative support of squadron by personally editing and finalizing all reports.
- Guided personnel programs through difficult period of rollbacks, early outs, and new evaluation programs with zero degradation in missions.
- Directly responsible for achieving 133% of the goal for drive project, collection 42% of entire amount from the Riverside County, California.
- Achieved success in managing personnel requirements for 30,000-man joint exercise associate with cleanup of largest oil spill in Los Angeles history.
- Selected to breathe new life into Naval Commander's Youth Relations Program, effecting immediate result in such programs as the Navy Sea Scouts of America, and Junior NOTC Program.
- Applied dynamic leadership to overcome tough budget and personnel shortfall issues.
- Took unsatisfactorily rated unit-retention program and turnover around to satisfactory status by resolving discrepancies within 90 days.
- Persuaded The United States Navy to cancel 15% reduction in command training quotas, accomplishing what no other command was able to do.

Character References

'**The best of the best! A hands-on self-motivated complaints specialist who provides blue-ribbon service...Always willing to pitch in and help get the job done...a team player extraordinaire...**'
--1995 Performance Evaluation

'**A superb leader and role model for all...Totally dedicated leadership is his strong suit.**'—1994

'**Dynamic senior Chief Petty Officer who comes through every time, on time.**'—1994 Performance Evaluation

'**An exceptional leader...He inspires achievement.**'—1992 Performance Evaluation

'**He is a standout performer with unlimited potential.**'—1991 Performance Evaluation

'**He's our Personnel Superintendent of Year because he's the best there is!**' –1989 Performance Evaluation

'**His ability to foresee potential problems and reach quickly to short-notice changes in schedules made the entire trips a complete success**' 1985 Performance Evaluation.

Home: 714-849-3432
Cell: 714-849-3433

8593 Garden Lane
Yorba Linda, CA 92714

Jim "Bo" Linsey
Email: JimBoLinsey@Comcast.net

SECURITY / LOSS PREVENTION

Professional security advisor with proven leadership skills and a comprehensive knowledge of security, whose effective management of people and resources minimizes criminal activity and maximizes the safety and protection of the public and employees. Provide optimal productivity and efficiency by training clients' personnel to effectively utilized crime and loss prevention techniques. Excellent communication skills with the ability to teach individually and make presentations to groups. Set the highest standards of excellence for myself and team members. Acquired substantial intuitive wisdom and completed extensive course related to law enforcement, safety, and security as an Officer during nine years with the Orange County Sheriff's Department.

AREAS OF EXPERTISE

Personal and Corporate Background Checks
Counter-Surveillance
Retail / Industrial Theft
Personal Injury
Highly Publicized Event Security
Labor-Related Investigations
Missing Persons

PERSONAL QUALITIES

Professional, Dedicated, and Ethical
Motivated, Energetic, and Enthusiastic
Resourceful, Diligent, Decisive, and Results Oriented
Work independently and as a Team Member
Quickly Identify, Assess, and Resolve Problems
Work Well under Pressure
Adaptable and Flexible

PROFESSIONAL EXPERIENCE

Law Enforcement Office, Orange County Sheriff's Department, Orange, CA   1991 - 2001
- Make arrests and restored order in a major riot during my first assignment.
- Subsequently assigned to the men's central jail in downtown Orange, CA. Duties included writing criminal reports and supervising and escorting high security inmates.
- Assigned to an emergency response team in 1994. Duties included responding to countywide emergencies, county jail riots, and major disturbances.
- Promoted to training office duties (1996 – 2000). Trained new deputies in laws of arrest, report writing, officer safety, and all necessary duties to be a qualified law enforcement officer.
- Sustained injuries that required a medical retirement in 2001.

EDUCATION / TRAINING

Suicide Prevention, Legal Update, Advanced Officer, First Aid/CPR Course   1995
- Costa Mesa Junior College, Costa Mesa, CA
Certificate of Completion, Orange County Sheriff's Department, Orange, CA   1992
- Finished in the Top Ten (of 200 Cadets) in Academics and Physical Fitness
Criminal Investigations Course, Orange College, Orange, CA   1991
Graduate, Fullerton High School, Fullerton, CA   1985

COMMENDATIONS

- **Personal courage and ethics** in subduing a volatile inmate that resulted in a colleague being cared for and deploying the absolute minimum amount of force necessary to resolve the situation. These actions personified the Orange Sheriff Department's core values and brought credit to the law enforcement profession (1996).
- **Willingness to step forward and help with a task;** put forth the effort and go the extra mile to recover lost property that belonged to an inmate. The teamwork attitude and concern displayed was an example of service-oriented policing (1995).
- **Quick response to a potentially violent situation** of racial tension in the Central Jail that was subdued with minimal altercations. Recognized for professionalism, tactics, cooperation, teamwork, and good solid police work (1995).
- **Involvement in helping to subdue a mini-riot** and reinstating order in the Central Jail. Acknowledged for self-discipline, clear thinking, professionalism and custody expertise (1994).

Note: It is very clear that this applicant is a law enforcement officer. He is trying to transition into the private-sector. He has strong skills and his 'Commendations' make a great impression. He shows both expertise and personal qualities that are very valuable.

Bill A. Handle

3421 Green Leaf Circle
Fullerton, CA 94232
(714) 342-5601
Thisismyhandle@aol.net

INTERNATIONAL CONSULTING / PROJECT MANAGEMENT

Proven ability to train, lead teams and manage advanced civil engineering projects with extensive experise in, but not limited to the design of reinforced concrete, composite and steel structures. Seeking R & D position based in the U.S. that will require some but not extensive trave.

QUALIFICATIONS

- *Familiar with engineering and team management principles that guide one-of-a-kind, advanced-technologies structural projects.*
- *Project leader, innovative project developer and communicator with outstanding technical development achievements.*
- *Developer of innovative structural solutions utilizing a variety of design, software and integrated material-structural engineering techniques. In all projects utilize strong foundation in mechanics, structural and materials engineering.*
- *Skills in research, writing, engineering and innovations with transferable consulting skills that will guide advanced-technologies structural projects.*
- *Able to act as liaison to clients to understand and define their specific, high-tech needs while delivering those solutions through the management of small, research-and-development focused engineering teams.*
- *Present complex engineering problems in clear technical-writing format to various audiences and customers without high-tech engineering skills or background.*
- *Outstanding overall balance of highly technical skills along with the ability to focus multiple internal entities and external customers on products requirements and products solutions.*
- *Technical reviewer for various engineering organization including National Science Foundation, American Concrete Institute, American Society of Civil Engineers, English Concrete Institute.*
- *Citizenship: United States.*
- *Fluency: Italian, Croatian, German, Japanese, Spanish, Portuguese, and English.*

SKILLS SUMMARY

- *Damage Assessment/Analysis*
- *Non-Destructive Testing*
- *Seismic/Non-Repair/Retrofit*
- *Procedure Design & Analysis*
- *Bridge/Building Deign & Analysis*
- *Structural System Analysis*
- *Solid Mechanic, Fracture Mechanics*
- *Micro-Mechanics of Cementitious Composites (Steel, glass, Kevlar, carbon, concrete, and etc.)*

- *New Technology Development/Implementation*
- *Product Development*
- *Technology Transfer*
- *Computer Programming/Modeling*
- *Auto-Adaptive Structures*
- *Project Management*
- *Technology Evaluation*
- *Procedure Development & optimization*

EDUCATION

1987	**UNIVERSITY OF IOWA, AMES,** IOWA
1986	**UNIVERSITY OF NEBRASKA,** OMAHA, Master of Civil Engineering (Specialization in steel Design)

Note: This applicant shows strong qualifications and key skills. He has been out of the work force with an employment gap of two years for a work related disability. You will notice a good chronology of his work on the second page of this résumé.

Bill A. Handle Page 2

1997-99	**Assistant Professor** of Civil Engineering, University of Colorado
1995-97	**Director of Scale Structural Testing** Laboratory (Constructed Facilities Laboratory – Engineering Graduate Research Center, University of Nebraska, Omaha
1992-95	**Assistant Professor** of Civil Engineering, Devonshire, London, England
1991-92	**Visiting Assistant Professor** of Civil and Environmental Engineering, University of Wyo., Cheyenne, Wyo.
1987-91	**Research Assistant,** Civil and Environmental Engr., Unv. CA, (European Campus, Belgrade, Yugoslavia)
Summer 1988	**Structural Engineer**, XYZ Consultants, Inc., Manchester, England
1986-87	**Research Assistant**, London Institute of Science and Technology, London, England

DESIGN HONORS, AWARDS AND RECOGNITIONS

- **The University of California Junior Faculty Enhancement Award** (1997)
- **Edward R. Muir Memorial Prize** for excellence in Concrete Structures and Technology (1987)
- **U.S. Concrete Production Design Award** – Industry Excellence (1986)
- *Featured on numerous national and international television and radio interviews and shows including CNNfn (financial) network, CNN Heading News, CNN Airport Network, CNN international Network, CNN Science and Technology Week, FOXTV, National Public Radio, Voice of America, Associated Press, CNNRadio, KNX Radio –Los Angeles.*
- Featured in popular press articles in ASCE *News*, Concrete Construction.

DEVELOPMENTAL AWARDS, TRAINING AND TEAM MANAGEMENT

- Recruited, developed, trained and managed R&D-focused engineering teams that included a total of 125 Research Engineers, 45 Research Associates, 25 Research Scientists and one Visiting Research Scientist from various academies across the U.S. and Europe. Developed and taught numerous undergraduate and graduate course on Reinforced Concrete Design, Concrete Design, Static's, Structural Mechanics, Construction Materials, Concrete Materials, and Statistics and Probability.
- Won and managed, as the main investigator, a total of $50 million in federal (International Science and Concrete Studies Institute), national and Industrial R & D projects on various aspects of assessment of non-seismically designed reinforced concrete frame buildings, development of improved seismic retrofit techniques and design guidelines for bridges and buildings, and development of multi-axial plasticity models for high-performance fiber composites.

COMMUNICATION SKILLS

Presented and published in numerous national and international journals, conferences and meetings on issue related to development of design guidelines for flexural and shear retrofit of reinforced concrete (R.C.) members, seismic retrofit R.C. buildings, punching shear failure of reinforced concrete slabs, reinforcing bar bond behavior, bridge-deck overlays, auto-adaptive and 'smart' structures, non-destructive testing of concrete structures, mechanisms of concrete cracking, and development and behavior of high-performance concrete and fiber composites.

- Published 22 **peer-reviewed papers** in national and international journals (*e.g. American Concrete Institute International Materials Journal, U.S. and European Structural Journal, and Journal of Cement and Concrete Composites) and three books chapters.* Presented 39 invited – lectures (presentations to select audiences by personal invitation only; *these don't include invitations to conference presentations*).
- Published 25 conference and workshop papers. Presented 80 conference and international meeting papers.

PROFESSIONAL AFFILIATIONS

- American Concrete Institute (ACI). Full member of ACI Committee 325 – Concrete Pavement, 348 – Structural Safety, 446 – Fracture Mechanics and 544 –Fiber Reinforced Concrete
- Associate Member of ACI Committee 440 –FRP Bar and Tendon Reinforcement
- American Society of Civil Engineers (ASCE)
- Earthquake Engineering Research Institute (EERI)
- International Association of Bridge and Structural Engineering (IABSE)
- Materials Research Society (MRS)
- Society for Experimental Mechanics (SEM)

References, reports, seminar and publication information available upon request.

Henry Anderson

901 Bell Ave Kanas City, Missouri 64225
816-667-4122 Home 816-667-4123
HA@comcast.net

AREAS OF RELEVANT SKILLS

Multi-dimensional individual with experience as heavy equipment operator, driver, or laborer with technical abilities in surveying, welding, and general maintenance. Excellent safety record and willingness to do more than what is expected. Communicate and interact effectively with diverse cultures.

- **Heavy Equipment Operations**: Forklift, Tractor, Loader, Backhoe, Motor Grader, Track Loader, Bulldozer, Bobcat Skid/Steer Loader, and Scraper
- **Driver** Dump Truck, Over-the-Road
- **Technical:** Surveying, Welding
- **Maintenance:** General, Preventive, Carpentry, and Painting

EDUCATIONAL BACKGROUND

Missouri State Technical College   Kansas City, MO
>   Heavy Equipment Operator Certificate Course
>   Welding; Blueprint interpretation, Surveying, Preventive Maintenance

U. S. National Truck Driving School   Corona, CA
>   Over-the-Road Truck Driving Certification Course

Western Wyoming Junior College   Rock Springs, WY
>   Introduction to Computer Information Systems, Basic Programming
>   Data Files, Structural Programming; Microcomputer Operating Systems

EMPLOYMENT HISTORY

TEMPORARY ASSIGNMENTS, Kansas MO   1992-2000

- Store Clerk/Stocker
- Library Clerk/Data Entry Clerk
- Computer Operation/Data Entry Clerk
- Chapel Head Clerk
- AM/PM Baker/Store Clerk

WESTERN WYOMING JUNIOR COLLEGE, ROCK SPRINGS, WY   1992
- Maintenance Technician – General maintenance, cleaning, carpentry, and lawn care

KANSAS CITY PARKS AND RECREATION DEPARTMENT, Kansas, City, MO   1991
- Laborer, Park Maintenance

SHAKEY'S PIZZA, Kansas, MO   1990-1991

DRIVEWAY PAVING, Toledo, OH   1988-1990

KESSEL VAN LINES, DES MOINES, IA   1987-1988

Note: What you need to know about this applicant is that is he is trying to emerge into the workforce from incarceration. He addresses this under Temporary Assignments. He is addressing his target employment with experience and certification which would relate to these jobs. If you are in a similar pickle this may be a good approach for you.

Mike F. Wade Jr.

908 Warm Springs Road ■ Rivereside, CA 92893
951-277-440-95 Home ■ 951-277-440-9541 Cell Phone

OBJECTIVES

To assist restaurant in attracting and retaining a strong customer base
by applying a *passion for the culinary arts and a strong work ethic.*

PERSONAL PROFILE

- Experience working in a kitchen environment, filling orders and developing menu items.
- Ability to get the job done by employing critical thinking and problem resolution skills.
- Work well as a *team player and independently with very little supervision.*
- Received commendations for being *dependable* and *hardworking.*
- Bilingual, Spanish and English.

COOKING SKILLS

- ☑ Prepared a selection of entrees, vegetables, desserts, and refreshments.
- ☑ Cleaned the grill, food preparation, surfaces, counters, and floors.
- ☑ Men high quality standards for food preparation, service, and safety.
- ☑ Maintained inventory logs and placed orders to replenish stocks of tableware, linens, paper, cleaning supplies, cooking utensils, food, and baked goods.
- ☑ Oversaw food preparation and cooking.

RESTAURANT EXPERIENCE

Kitchen Worker – State of California (Fontana Correctional Facility); Fontana, CA
Short Order Cook – Honey Bear Restaurant, Corona, CA
Prep Cook/Laborer – Normans Restaurant, Riverside, CA
Lunch and Dinner Cook – The Panda, Corona, CA

MILITARY SERVICE

U.S. Navy –Aircraft Hydraulic E-6 Honorable Discharge

GED obtained

Note: As you can see this is a functional –style résumé. In this situation the applicant used Restaurant Experince to down play that it was work done while in incarceration in hopes that it will be interpereted as paid employment. This style of résumé was used to emphasize work-related skills.

Ricky J. Hilton

456 La Serria Riverside, CA 93885 ● Phone 951-277-3412

Career Scope

Office Assistant position where acquired skills and experience gained during part-time employment while raising a family may now be applied on a full-time basis to a permanent career position in a professional environment.

Summary of Qualifications

□ Comprehensive knowledge of and experience in office procedures – reception, administrative support, and accounting – across multiple industries, including retail, distribution, manufacturing, and hospitality.

□ Demonstrated record of successfully executing day-to-day tasks in fast-pace, time-sensitive environments.

□ Proficient with Microsoft Office Suite products utilized to process correspondence, develop financial spreadsheets, and create presentations for executive-level personnel.

□ Background processing insurance contracts, purchase orders, and transportation vouchers and preparing reports.

□ Skill in assisting customers with product and service inquires and addressing and resolving problems.

□ Experience processing payroll, training employees, and scheduling appointments.

Experience   1992 – 2001

ABC Club Distributors, Inc.	Riverside, CA	Inventory Control
Holiday Inn	Orange, CA	Accounting Clerk
International House of Pancakes	Corona, CA	Office Assistant
7 – 11 Convenience Mart	Ontario, CA	Assistant Manager
Mayflower Transit Company	Ontario, CA	Reservation list
Green Lawn Associates	Riverside, CA	Customer Service
Texaco Distributors, Inc.	Colton, CA	Secretary

Training & Education

Riverside Community College, Riverside, CA
Business Communication and Administration Certification

Fullerton Community College, Fullerton, CA
Small Business Management Certification

KEYWORDS: Office Assistant, Administration, Customer Service, Accouinting, Training, Data Entry, Reception Scheduling, Problem Resolution, Quality Control, Inventory Control, Management

Note: As you may be able to see this applicant has a history of 'job hopping', but has attempted to cover this up by not giving details of each position. This employment history may have been because of an economic situation, or self generated, never-the-less it is down played in this résumé.

Juile Harris
1810 Borderline Road ● Colton, CA 94889
909-278-5691 Home   909-278-5692 Cell
JuileH@comcast.net

QUALIFICATIONS PROFILE

Extensive experience and practical knowledge of high-volume **Industrial Warehousing / Distribution and Manufacturing** environments. Hard-working, enthusiastic, dependable, and self-motivated: take responsibility to get the job done. Work cooperatively with a wide range of personalities. Excellent work history and attendance record. Computer skills. Take pride in achieving best possible results.

Special Achievement Award – Navy Test Center Norco, California
Certificate of Recognition for 10 Years Successful Government Service
Certificate of Appreciation – Defense Logistics Agency
Material Handling Equipment Operation Award (Forklift) – 2 years
Material Handling Equipment Safe Driver Award

EXPERIENCE

Norco Navy Test Center, Norco, California

Warehouse – WGG5 Step 5

Operated IMC warehouse forklift and sit-down crane. Experience in shipping and receiving, weekend shift supervisor.
- ☑ Skilled machine operator, good sense of balance, distance, and eye-hand coordination.
- ☑ Well -liked, effective shift supervisor
- ☑ Effectively executed shipping receiving procedures and regulations.
- ☑ Worked will independently and as part of a team.

EDUCATION

Orange Coast Community College, Costa Mesa, CA
Earned 40 credits / Liberal Arts

Complete 22 on-the-job training courses in safety and policy/procedures.

References Available on Request.

Note: In this résumé you will notice limited work experience as well as limited educational background, however the applicant exploits his personal attributes and awards to 'soft sell' his skills. An employer may see these personal characteristics as valuable and important attributes that can be utilized in his firm.

Ron R. Rogers
1345 Kirkwood Way -- Orange, CA 98233
714-514-6642 -- RRR@aol.com

HVAC TECHNICIAN

Provide primary and specialized hands-on support for HVAC. Furnish routine and miscellaneous inspections regarding new installations, repair, preventive maintenance, and procedures. Experienced with state-of-the-art equipment and technology. Learn quickly and follow directions. Work well with supervisors and peers.

EDUCATION
Salt Lake Technical College, Salt Lake, Utah
Industrial Building Maintenance –Diploma 1998
Basic-skills studies Carpentry, Electrical, and Plumbing with special training in Heating and Air Conditioning maintenance, Hands-on training at off-site locations.

Computer Experience: Word, Excel, Access

Polytechnic High School, Riverside, CA
Diploma, 1992

WORK EXPERIENCE
Heating and Air Conditioning Assistant
Executive Heating and Air Conditioning, Corona, CA
- ☑ Assisted owner with installation of new units, replacement of older units, and general troubleshooting on residential and commercial systems.
- ☑ Handled electrical work and made ducts form flat sheet of metal.

Park Maintenance Personnel
California State Park Huntington Beach, CA
- ☑ Gutted and remodeled entire work center building.
- ☑ Hand-crafted wood park signs and laid cement pads for picnic areas.
- ☑ Installed fencing for 3-and 4-wheelers on 3.5 acre for in 2 months.

Assistant Manager
3 day Carpet, Orange, CA
- ☑ Quickly learned all facets of carper business.
- ☑ Trained new employees in cleaning, repairs, patching, and tack stripping.
- ☑ Balanced cash drawer and receipts; opened and closed store.
- ☑ Promoted from general employee to Assistant Manager.

Other positions held: Gutter Installer, Gas Station Attendant, Building Supply Route man.

COMMUNITY INVOLVEMENT
Orange County AYSO Soccer League, Coach

Note: This is a sharply focused résumé. The applicant's goals are supported with clear relevant work experience and education. As you can see the dates have been omitted to reduce the possibility of pit falls.

Russ T. Thomason

2245 Rose Blvd. -- Orange, CA 94532
Phone: 714-514-6234 --Russ T. Thomason@aol.net

PROFILE

Experienced in machine operations, customer relations, and organizing materials. Willing worker, able to work independently or as part of a team. Bilingual English/Spanish.

EXPERIENCE

Packager, High Tech Packaging Company, Orange, CA   2000-2002
- Packaged items for Electronic firm using variety of packaging machines.

Machine Operator/Molding, Star Injection Molding, Orange, CA   1996-1999
- Molded plastic on injection and compression machines.
- Mixed ingredients for plastics.

Delivery Driver, Taylor Rentals, Orange, CA   1994-1996
- Delivered and picked up merchandise for customers.
- Assisted customers with concerns.
- Handled currency.
- Serviced damaged equipment.

Casual Mail Handler, DHL Parcel Service, Stanton, CA   1992-1994
- Sorted and distributed mail to various departments.
- Weighed airmail and dispatched to appropriate airlines.
- Operated and maintained postage machines.

Returned Goods Clerk, Best Electrical Wholesalers, Santa Fe Springs, CA.   1991-1992
- Received goods.
- Stocked shelves.
- Picked and checked orders.
- Coordinated with purchasing departments.
- Kept records and inventory.

EDUCATION

Center for Professional Advancement, Rancho Santiago Community College, Santa Ana, CA
Studied basic computers and job skills.

Note: This applicant used all relevant work experience. What you do not see is this individual was incarcerated but used packaging jobs to help show a flow of work qualifications and job stability.

Bruce T. Hoffman

2301 Clovis Ave
San Jose, CA 94963

408-343-4532
BriceH@comcast.net

Network Engineer /Technical Support

SUMMARY OF QUALIFICATIONS

- Solutions-driven network engineer providing technical support to improve performance, operational efficiencies, and expense reduction.
- Flexible and focused, with unique analytical problem solving ability.
- Solid theoretical knowledge of computer and network architecture and Microsoft Operating System.

Education

Foot Hill Community College, Mountain View, CA
Network Engineer: Windows NT, CompuVista Business Institute, Sacramento, California   2002

Information technology Certifications

MCSE	WORKSTATION	Windows 95
MCP+I	NT Server/Enterprise	Windows 3.x
A+ Certified	Networking Essentials	Windows NT
Microsoft NT	Windows NT Server 4.0	Internet Info-Server
MS DOS 6.22	TCP / IP Implementation	Internet Explorer 5.0

ACCOMPLISHMENTS

- Resolved security issuers on Windows NT involving group account policies and end users.
- Engineered effective Windows NT security structure and implementation in work networks.
- Installed software, provided peer-to-peer technical support, and consulted on LAN development.

WORK HISTORY

Computer Technician, San Jose School District, San Jose, CA	1999-2002
Press Operator, ABC Industries, Sunnyvale, CA	1998-1999
Painter, Easy Painting Company, Mountain View, CA	1997-1998

Note: As you can see this résumé focuses on computer skills, certifications, and achievements. What you may not see is the applicant gained this training during a rehabilitation period. What you see is a positive gain of skills focusing on employment goals.

Danny S. Williams

985 Hill Top Road --Placentia, CA 98343

714-514-7162--DannySW@hotmail.com

SALES REPRESENTATIVE

Self-confident and motivated with good track record in sales and construction with start-up companies. Communicate clearly and effectively with people of diverse backgrounds. Use tact and patience when dealing with difficult customers. Goal oriented and persuasive. Areas of expertise.

RELATED SALES EXPERIENCE

Sales Rep
Yager Construction, Orange, CA   1999-2001
Start-up to high-growth residential, commercial, and farm building company

Prospected new accounts utilizing a variety of effective sales techniques including cold-calling, direct mail, and telephone campaigns. Emphasized service, quality, and price. Handled bids and accurately estimating materials and labor costs for remodeling and new construction. Located hard-to-find materials and supplies; arranged for on-time delivery. Kept records of jobs to determine profitability. Supervised construction crews of up to 75 people; hands-on building experience.

- Grew business from 10 employees to 75
- Drove revenues from zero to more than $5,000,000

Manager/Owner
Williams Custom Golf Clubs, Placentia, CA   1990-1998

Assessed golfers' level of expertise, utilizing knowledge of the sport, to design and build custom golf clubs. Promoted the business through print advertising, networking, and customer service. Built and maintained client base and customer loyalty through quality product and service, resulting in high number of referrals.

- Slashed advertising budget 65% due to high referral business.

EDUCATION

Placentia High School, Placentia, CA

Computer Experience Windows, Microsoft Office, Construction specific software, and Internet.

Note: Here we have an applicant concentrating his résumé on relevant career goals, and prior experience that is relevant to his career goals. He avoids the short period of time that he was incarcerated. Your résumé should be as positive as it can.

Michael E. Sims
654 Pine Drive
Fantana, CA 94305
909-278-8114
MichaelE.42@aol.net

MANAGEMENT PROFESSIONAL

Leadership   Training   Communications   Quality   Control

Dynamic management professional with effective verbal and written communication skills, exemplary organizational skills, and attention to detail. Able to multi-task without sacrificing quality or timeliness of results. High level of discretion, familiar with risk management concepts and techniques, and proficient in variety of computer applications. Skilled in time and schedule of busy day, demanding senior executive, Identified as a 'key contributor' on evaluations each year. Received numerous performance awards. Full trilingual, English/Spanish/German.

'It is reassuring to know that you will bring in a project on time or ahead of time and done well.' Agnes Schiraldi, Supervisor, describing actions leading to performance award.

COMPUTER SKILLS

WordPerfect, Word, Excel, PowerPoint, Access, Publisher, Front Page, Adobe Photoshop, Internet, and Intranet Networking Systems. A+ Certification.

RELATED ACCOMPLISHMENTS

United Air Technical, San Francisco, CA   1990-1999
Senior Technical Assistant / Credit and Collections Analyst, 1996-1999
- Transferred hardcopy microfilm order form into Word document that, in turn, allowed company to send microfilm orders via email rather than via fax; this saved the company money for producing multi-copy form and telephone toll charges, as well a saving time. Worked with vendor to setup email procedure to ensure it was in place before actual orders were sent.
- Created variety of forms to expedite processing orders and record-keeping.
- Improved customer satisfaction by processing orders to a timelier manner.
- Filed and maintained historical records of price and cost. Completed financial projects to enable Technical Publication Department to implement new policy for non-paying customers.
- Reviewed and analyzed requests for new or additional technical publications materials from current and potential customers and company personnel. Determined eligibility, and applicable charges.

Note: This applicant has moved to the second page so that it does not detract from his strong experience and achievements earlier in his career.

Michael E. Sims   Page 2

Senior Technical Assistant / Credit and collections Analyst, Continued

- Generated and processed customer invoices, refunds, and collections, interfaced with internal and external personnel to provide, collect, clarify, and interpret information, explain or justify established prices, substantiate variations, and resolved discrepancies.
- Initiated authorization to fill approved orders and coordinated release of publications.
- Created charts to plot increase of revenues.
- Computerized maintenance of specialized records as directed, such as customer, exception to distribution policies, customer responses to special offers, and policy changes. Accumulated and prepared records and statistics for planning purposes.
- Originally hired for data entry work, but within weeks was given considerably more responsibility when supervisor realized my skills.

Supplier Publication Coordinator, 1990-1996

- Created standardized forms for recording and maintaining data. Reduced vendor publication backlog through increased follow-up and training.
- Improved coordination of supplier publications and saved management time by delegating clerical task.
- Implemented training course for new recruits, speeding profitability.
- Contracted, coordinated, and maintained status of worldwide vendor publications.

ADDITIONAL EXPERIENCE

State of California, Chino, CA
PC Service Technician   2000-2002
- Repaired and updated computers for state offices.
- Earned A+ certification.

EDUCATION

University of California, at San Jose, CA   **Computer Institute**, Santa Clara, CA
B.S., Business Management   Access I, II, III
Minors: Financial Management and MIS   PowerPoint I, II, III
3.89 GPA   Excel I, II, III

Harrit A. Zoolu

895 El Camino Park Way
Riverside, CA 93883

951-277-0987 Home   951-277-0986 Cell
HAZ@comcast.net

INTERNATIONAL MANUFACTURING CONSULTANT
Seeking Management-Focused Consulting Opportunities for U.S.-Based Companies Doing Business in Africa and Asia
International Food Processing --Chemical -- Pharmaceutical Industries

SUMMARY OF QUALIFICATIONS

- One of the only female executives on the continent of Africa to lead international manufacturing operations despite great, challenges and brief political imprisonment during a career.
- Proven, multi-year international management/leadership expertise with transferable skills form overseeing critical financial aspects in the manufacturing industry, including Controller-level Leadership (Multi-Projects), Plant Management, Debt Reduction Strategies, Safely Program Design and implementation, Manufacturing, Marketing, and Profit and Loss analysis.
- Regarded as an innovative, complete financial leader who successfully leads new strategic partnerships while managing teams on outsourced contracts with annual revenue in the millions of dollars.
- Strong production environment experience, operation management, and supervision of hourly employees. Able to review administrative and financial aspects of production plans as well as determine optimum business strategies in very difficult market, political, and economic conditions.
- Outstanding ability to establish strategic business plans that include evaluating and implementing leading-edge financial solutions while anticipating technology and personnel trends to meet a company's immediate and future needs.
- Able to direct financial-team activities that focus on design and implementation of new programs and strategies in financial areas that support leading-edge growth operations.
- Outstanding customer-driven financial solution management focus built through multi-year high-level partnering with international companies U.S and European primarily); track record of highly accurate forecasting, cost reductions/controls, and productivity enhancements across multiple corporate services and business areas.

- **Transferable skill set current positions includes:**

(**Strategic Planning/Initiatives**	(**Production Management**
(**Controller/Financial Leadership**	(**Political Experience/Sensitive Line Funding Issues**
(**United Nations Liaison (Corporate)**	(**Production/Process/Procedural Troubleshooting**
(**Union Negotiations/Labor Experience**	(**ISO 9002 Management**
(**Corporate Cost/Budget Management**	(**International Trade/Business Expertise**
(**Food/Chemical/Pharmaceutical Expertise**	(**Total P&L Responsibility/Engineering Projects**
(**Distribution Center Management**	(**Banking/Credit Relationship Development**
(**System Operational Evaluations**	(**Capital Program Management**
(**Safety Control/Design Issues**	(**New Market/Opportunity Development**
(**Cross-Functional Team Leader**	(**Business Strategy/Channel Profitability**

EDUCATION

THE UNIVERSITY OF IOWA, MS Political Science, May 2000
THE UNIVERSITY OF OKLAHOMA, BS, Chemical Engineering and Food Process Engineering, May 1996

PROFESSIONAL DEVELOPMENT

The University of California at Santa Cruz, CA three-month USAID-Funded course in Plant Management
The University of California at San Jose, CA three-month -USAID-course in Food Plant and Cost Management

Note: This applicant has a strong professional background. Even with the fact that she was a political prisoner her background and experience carry forward and should be of interest to a potential employer.

Harrit A. Zoolu   Page 2

PROFESSIONAL EXPERIENCE

WORLD SECURITIES, Pretoria, South Africa
Managing Director, 1996-1998

Led this manufacturing and holding company with turnover of $225 million annually (aggregate value of over $355 million): held complete management responsibility for the company's three distinct business units with 300 employees, including Petroleum and Petroleum Products Distribution through three channel: gas station/convenience stores (30); petroleum/fuel distribution; supply of cooking gas (butane) to institutions and retail outlets.
- Worked with contractors to produce goods to meet the company's order; this work included close knowledge of land contracts with governments, parasitical organizations, and international relief agencies (to procure goods on their behalf). Goods included commodities to scientific equipment.
- Relief Distribution focused on international relief efforts in Sudan and Vietnam; successes included distributing hundreds of thousands of pounds of food to these war-torn and economically/politically and socially distressed areas. Designed and implemented an aggressive safety-first program to reduce time lost due to injuries.
- Successfully completed bid-proposal preparation to secure business by assessing competition and industry trend despite still built-in traditional conflicts with South Africa and its citizens.
- Strengthened working relations with employees and built the company from small to large.

Directly controlled comprehensive multi-unit management functions. Led cross-functional teams on the company's major projects. Oversaw organizational recruiting, training, structure, and held P&L of technical department, which handled engineering projects. In this comprehensive management position, reviewed all employee performances and kept a hands-on, active role on all levels of personnel and financial management functions.

Held comprehensive controller/financial responsibilities for multimillion-dollar production and manufacturing division. Drove major imitative and management enhancement strategies across multiple departments through initiatives in these areas: Safety, Quality, Finance, and Production Management.

CHEVRON-CHEMICALS, Cape Town, South Africa
Production Assistant (1989-1991); **Production Liaison** (1992-1993); **Production Manager** (1993-1996);
International Relations Specialist (1992-1996)
- Help company develop liaison relationship with Fortune 500 companies in the United States to keep funding and financial support during political upheaval and racial-segregation challenges following termination of Apartheid.
- Successfully increased ethanol and citric acid recovery by 67% through efficient process design and control.
- Reduced employees from 500 to 300 while simultaneously increasing production out put through efficient use of new technology and overall cost reductions.
- Coordinated all operations and managed 300 employees for this facility, including ensuring ISO 9002 standards and EU-based food-safety procedures/standards.
- Directed both the Citric Acid and Ethanol (power alcohol) production divisions using molasses from sugar cane and the fermentation substrates. Successfully conducted pilot fermentations to determine optimal citric acid yields in line with different sources and different chemical clarification treatments of sugar juices (resulting in molasses of varying fermentation requirements).
- Improved production and operational reporting, which led to resolution of multiple manufacturing and operational delays. Neighboring sugar factories and U.S./European companies.
- Union work included solving workers' grievances and negotiation directly with unions to positive effect each time there was an issue; issues were resolved from management to floor workers—black and white/all cultures.

Led production improvements and initiatives that resulted in outstanding quality reputation and safety records. Drove Organizational changes that led to improved Best Practices SOP for the business across the board. Reviewed, standardized, and followed up to ensure these practices gained full support of all managers and other personnel. Held budgetary and P&L oversight. Change Agent Leadership leading culture shift toward customer-focused teams, better race relations, and team goals throughout the plants.

Leroy S. Snodgrass

4321 6th Street
Des Moines, Iowa 59892
512-916-3804   512-916-3805
LeroyS.Washere@aol.com

Objective Assistant Director, Center for Troubled Youth

PROFILE

Possess understanding of business protocol, a pleasant attitude and skills required to succeed in the position, willing to learn, work hard, and apply good work ethic.

Currently enrolled in business-management class; consciously trying to make a positive impact by tutoring young people. Ability and desire to effectively communication to kids' first-hand why they want to change their lives now before they waste their youth.

QUALIFICATIONS

- Excellent numbers and financial-management skill.
- History of developing and maintaining loyal repeat customers.
- Excellent memory for names and faces.
- Skilled in recognizing and creating business opportunities
- Demonstrated ability to successfully build upon limited resources.
- Demonstrated ability to successfully build upon limited resources
- Spanish fluency.

EXPERIENCE

Men's *Correctional Facility*, Des Moines, Iowa 1999-2002
Assigned position of **Kitchen Supervisor**

- Directed activities and performance of 30 men in the preparation, service, and clean-up of meals for inmates.
- Applied strong leadership, leadership, conflict-resolution, and mediation skill. Monitored and kept records of kitchen inventory. Commended for consistently excelling management and job performance.

Self-Employed, throughout Iowa State, 1995-1999
Pharmaceutical Sales

- Built and maintained loyal customer base.
- Created extensive contacts network.
- Managed cash flow.
- Kept accurate bookkeeping records.
- Polished communication and mediation skills

Construction Laborer, Part-time and seasonal work, various employers, 1987-1995
Developed finish carpentry skills and learned to operate heavy equipment such as bulldozer, caterpillar, dump truck, and cement mixer, worked with crews with diverse backgrounds and personalities.

PROFESSIONAL DEVELOPMENT / EDUCATION

Business Management, Iowa State University, Ames, IA, Currently attending
Tutor/Advisor, Youth Group, Baptist Church
Street-wise, on-the-job training -- illegal economy
Graduate, Lincoln High School, Des Moines, IA

Note: This is a straight forward résumé where the applicant present skills and personal experience and doesn't cover-up a problem period. This applicant makes a strong case for a life turnover as a way to move forward.

Helen C. Rosenberry, M.Sc.

2421 Draper Lane ▲ Salt Lake City, Utah 84020 ▲ HCrosenberry@aol.com

801-571-4556

OBJECTIVE: Committed to developing a career in translational research.

SUMMARY OF QUALIFICATIONS

- Strong academic qualifications at the post-graduate level.
- Lifelong interest in medical research-published thesis.
- Understanding of research techniques and technologies.
- Full range of laboratory research and laboratory management skills.
- Exposure to clinical analysis, assembling and organizing data.
- Supporting business experience with a strong management component.
- Able to plan and oversee projects form concept to conclusion—an efficient multi-tasker.

EDUCATION

BYU University, Department of Medical Science, Provo, Utah
M.Sc. Molecular Biology, 2002

Coursework: Human Anatomy, Physiology, and Pharmacology
Thesis: **Molecular Biology of Aging and Neurodegenerative Diseases**

University of Colorado, Colorado Springs, CO
B.Sc. Biology, 1992

PUBLICATIONS

'The Influence of Harvesting Technique on Measures of Dis-Hydration'. America Journal of Physiology, Volume 81, #10. 1998

RESEARCH EXPERIENCE
Thesis (2000-2002)
Coordinated and implemented all aspects of thesis research project.
- Developed these statements; created and implemented the protocol.
- Managed lab and academic course time effectively.
- Applied for and obtained funding.
- Operated and maintained a variety of lab equipment.
- Delivered progress reports to advisor and peers.
- Ethically treated and cared for lab animals.
- Performed statistical analysis on results, compiled research, and successfully defended thesis.

(Continued)

Note: In this résumé the applicant presents advanced education, while most recent skills and experience is presented on the first page.

Helen C. Rosenberry, M.S.c. -- Page 2

Additional Research Experience

Worked as a research assistant to professor and PhD Candidates (UCI Medical School) for four summers while completing undergraduate degree (1988-1992)

- **Virology**: Grew virus cultures.
- **Biochemistry**: Assisted in developing alternate kidney dialysis solutions to be used at the time of transplants.
- **Cardiovascular Pharmacology**: Studied the effects of anesthetic on vascular tissue of rats.

Other Professional Experience

Owner of Water Gardens Plus, a family business (1995-1998)

- Created a vision for the business and coordinated, with the assistance of the management team, day-to-day business operation.
- Grew the business from start-up to employing 20 personnel-doubled sales annually for 5 years.

Pharmaceutical Representative with Amgen Pharmaceuticals (1992-1995)
Organized and managed a territory in the State of Utah.

- Helped launch a new cardiovascular drug and supported physicians prescribing the product.
- Educated pharmacists and doctors on the company's cardiovascular product line.

COMPUTER SKILLS

Microsoft Office: Word, Excel, and PowerPoint
Windows: 95, 98, 2000
Managed large volumes of data using spreadsheets and databases in research settings.

INTERESTS

Medical Research – Reed medical periodicals and conduct Internet research on topics of interest.
Physical Fitness and Athletic – Participate in 10K and marathon races.
Volunteer Activities – Parent coordinator for the Junior Shooting Program, Salt Lake Shooting Club. Chairperson for the Salt Lake AYSO Soccer Club Executive.

Mary Ann Smith

1935 Compton Ave
Riverside, CA 92881
951-277-3713 H / 951-277-3714
MaryAS@comcast.net

DATABASE ADMINISTRATION / IMPEMENTATION CONSULTANT
-- Seeking Senior Technical Support Position --

Technology professinal with excellent business operations and IT consuling and suppor skills. Utilize cooperative leadership, a consultative project management approach, and proven skills in Information Resource Management.

TECHNICAL SKILLS SUMMARY

PATLAT	*Installation & Configuration*	**CERTIFIED TRAINING**	*Introduction to Visual Basic*
	Service Pack & Patch Application		*Perl Introduction*
	Issue Troubleshooting & Resolution		*Administration Microsoft SQL Server 6.5*
	Migration – Import Export (NT)		*Administration Windows NT 4.0*
	Master Scheduler & Poll Configuration		*Transact SQL Programming*
	Job Scheduler Job Setup & Scheduling		*Introduction to UNIX*
	Training & Security		*UNIX Administration*
	Batch Structure Processing		
SYBASE	*Configuration*	**REPORTING**	*Cognos Administration*
	Patches		*Cognos Report Development*
	Database Management		*Impromptu 5.0*
	Transact SQL Programming		*Powerplay 6.5 (Open Analyzer)*
	Backup & Restore		*All FastLine DSS Tools*
UNITS	*HP UNIX & Solaris*	**CODING**	*C++ Maintenance*
	Security		*Perl Scripting*
	Disk Partitioning		
	File System Setup		
DOCS	*Visio*	**IT**	*NT Security*
	PowerPoint		*NT User Account Setup*
	Microsoft Office Professional Suite		

General skills

- *(IT Systems Administration*
- *(Fluent in Russian*
- *(Client Relations/Client Communications*
- *(Technical/Reporting Consulting*
- *(Crisis Resolutions/Problem Solving*
- *(System Backup/Restoration Procedures*
- *(Disaster Recovery/Security Procedures*
- *(Senior Business Analysis*
- *(Requirements Definition Work*

- *(Programming/IT Project Management*
- *(Operations Analysis/Needs Analysis/Evaluations*
- *(Network System Administrative Management*
- *(Strategic Planning/Consulting*
- *(SOP Development/Implementations*
- *(User/IT Staff Training Initiatives*
- *(System Installations/Configurations*
- *(Senior Programmer Analyst*
- *(Database Performance/Tuning*

EDUCATION

UNIVERSITY OF California at Santa Barbara, CA
Master of Electrical Engineering and Technology Transfer, My 1991
Bachelor of Science in Information Technology with a Minor in Foreign Language Studies May 1987

(Continued)

Note: This résumé is one of a highly qualified applicant who has been on a sabbatical. The résumé is very powerful, depicting deep skills and powerful broad experience in the telecom industry. The applicant can be very flexible with her job skills.

Mary Ann Smith

Page 2

PROFESSIONAL EXPERIENCE

WORLD COMMUNICATIONS TECHNICIANS INTERNATIONAL, Riverside, CA
Technical Support Analyst, 1995-1999
Key Project Accomplishments include:
- *Successful implementation of FastLine Modules including: Financials, Procurement, and HR.*
- *Provided a unique key tie between separate application systems.*
- *Restructured test system's database and restoration from backup.*
- *Provided client technical support and training for Sybase, HP UNIX, and FastLine 6.0/0.2.*
- *Continued support of Fascine System and trained new IT Staff during multiple charges and growth.*
- *Updated system reports to contain divisions and train general ledger users how to make their own updates.*

(Served as key technical and reporting consultant, offering services for the implementation of Financial, Human Resources, and procurement Modules for U.S. and Russian business operations.
(Responsible for the installation and configuration of Sybase, FastLine File Servers, FastLine job servers, and FastLine clients. Applied Service Packs and Patches to FastLine system.
(Performed UNIX, Sybase, FastLine, and NT administrative duties.
(Set up and implemented backup and restoration procedures.
(Assisted with disaster recovery of the database system as well as updating security procedures.
(Troubleshot and resolved user requests, data, and system issues. Provided user and IT staff training as well as support for the FastLine environment. Documented FastLine system and developed new reports.
(Resolved payroll, HR, and custom reporting issues.

TELECOM SYSTEMS, Riverside, CA
Support Analyst, 1991-1995
(Provided support for FastLine decision Support module: Query, Reporter, Management reporter, Structures, and personnel, in addition to support staff.
☑ (Created and taught the first in-depth training class on Structures – started training developers and maintenance personnel, in addition to support staff.

PDQ SYSTEMS, Riverside, CA
Support Analyst, 1919-1993
- ☑ Provide support for FastLine decision Support module, Query, Reporter, Management reporter, Structures, and Analyzer.
- ☑ Created and taught the first in-depth training class on Structures – started training developers and maintenance personnel, in addition to support staff.

BACKGROUND SYNOPSIS/QUALIFICATIONS

■ Demonstrated ability interfacing with users and management to gather requirements for new application projects.

■ Prepare system environments such as applying UNIX patches, installing and configuring databases, NT file server space and patch level on NT systems at the required levels.

■ Strong experience dealing with Sybase and SQL Server databases; experience installing, configuring, setting up startup and backup scripts, monitoring locked processes, recycling the server, and performing database disaster recovery for the test databases.

■ Excellent verbal and written communication skills, including the ability to plan, write, and present arguments and recommendations on the abortion of technology, workflow changes, project-management plans, and new technology integrations. Explain products or solutions to administrators, executives, and end users.

■ Known for a very high level of customer service and satisfaction.

References Available Upon Request

Jay J. Flatt

880 Santa Fe Boulevard
Austin, TX 78746
e-mail: JJF@aol.net

home (512) 330-7578
cell (512) 892-3301

Senior Management / Executive Profile

Results-oriented operations executive with diverse experience and strond record of achievement spanning four independent franchises. Projected MBA in International Business and Finance, December 2003

- Manufacturing
- Warehousing
- Logistics
- Inventory Management

- Sales Management
- P& L Accountability
- Acquisition
- Team-Based Organization
- Community Leadership

- ISO 9000
- ERP, MRP, DRP, MPS, JIT
- Statistical Process Control (SPC)
- Theory of Constraints

Professional Experience

Education Sabbatical — 2001-2002

The Texas West Bottling Company, Dallas, TX — 1998-2000
Director of Operations

Accepted offer to lead The Texas West Bottling Company's flagship Dallas operation within six months after acquisition of 'All — State Bottling Company'. Led beverage production, syrup manufacturing, quality assurance, warehousing, inventory control, production planning, logistics, and transportation. Managed $155 Million annual operation budget and $6 million capital projects. Led organization over 500 employees, produced 45 million cases annually.

- ☑ Increased plant productivity 23%, resulting in 11.45 percent growth.
- ☑ Implemented a Total Quality System for process improvement.
- ☑ . Attained a 12 percent increase in quality index score after reviving a Statistical Process Control system that utilized automated data collection equipment and moving some of the test equipment of the QA lab and into the hands of the line operators.

All-State Bottling Company, Oklahoma City, Oklahoma — 1983-1998
Vise President of Operation, 1995-1998
Operations Manager, 1989-1995
Plant Manager, 1987-1989
Production Manager, 1983-1986

Successfully advanced career through three acquisitions; recognized with promotion after each. Also led beverage production, syrup manufacturing, quality assurance, warehousing, inventory control, production planning, logistics, transportation, and fleet maintenance. Managed $140 million annual operating budget and $3 million in capital projects. Led organization of 423 employees.

- ☑ Played leadership role during Texas West Bottling Company' acquisition of All-State Bottling Company.
- ☑ Developed a JIT system to service 30 distribution centers across the three-state area. Resulted in annual savings of $890,000 and the following reductions: material handling cost, 12%; accidents, 72 percent turnover, 89 percent inventory levels, 43%.

- ☑ Utilized the Theory of Constraints to avoid $4 million in capital cost and improve the output in syrup manufacturing by 17%.8

Note: You can clearly see that this applicant went on a sabbatical and he is right up front with this information. Also, he has detailed clearly his professional skills and experience. The second page of his résumé details Education and Community Service.

Jay J. Flatt,   Page 2

- ☑ Championed a project team, primarily hourly employee and front-line supervisors, charge with purchasing and installing a high-speed production line. Achieved full production in 62% projected time and with full product conversion cost 16% under budget.
- ☑ Developed an operator training and cortication program that resulted in an overall productivity increase of 7%, reduced accident cost by 64% and reduce turnover by 42%.
- ☑ Launched a contract packing business that contributed over $6 million annually to the bottom line.
- ☑ Successfully implemented Manufacturing Resources Planning (MRP) and Distribution Resource Planning (DRP) systems.
- ☑ Participated on the All-State Bottling Advisory Council, a prestigious, invitation-only group of senior-and executive-level managers and a think tank for coordination efforts across the bottling network.
- ☑ Facilitated teaching of Covey Leadership Center modules across the All-State Bottling organization.
- ☑ Recognized with All-State Bottling's highest quality recognition, the President's Award, which was presented to the plant in 1963.
- ☑ Played key leadership role during All-State Bottling Company's acquisition The Texas West Bottling Company in 1987, merged mine production plants into one over a period of a year and a half, which resulted in $17 million annual savings. Promoted to plant manager within six months of months of acquisition.
- ☑ Managed growth of Oklahoma City plant form 4 million cases to 27 million over a five-year period.

Education

University of Arizona, Phoenix, AZ
Matter of Business Administration, anticipated graduation December 2003 (Current GPA 40.

Bachelor of Arts in Business Studies, 2001 (GPA 4.0)

Continuing Professional Education

ERP, MRP, DRP, JIT, and Master Production Planning
Theory of Constraints, Oklahoma University

Covey Leadership Center –Facilitator Certification
The Seven Habits of Highly Effective People
Principle-Centered Leadership
Four Roles Leadership

Community Service

A strong advocate of Adult Education. Established a company-sponsored in-house program that guided people through obtaining GEDs, learning English as a second language, and gaining basic computer skills; provided tutoring for TASP and SAT testing Coordinated college-level classes taught onsite and at the local universities.
☐Organizational Leaderships: Texas Scholars Program, Adult Literacy Council, Oklahoma City Industrial Foundation.

Sandy E. Angle

6062 Flower Lane, Riverside, CA 92870

Home: 951-277-9235■Cell: 951-277-3138
E-Mail: SandyDanyEAngle@aol.com

■ **Summary**

BUSINESS & OPERATION MANAGER - MULTI-SITE, TURNKEY OPERATION
Facility, Operations, and Administrative Procedures for a highly visiable retail store

Intricately seasoned manager and 'business connoisseur' with a polished history of utilizing word-of-mouth advertising for longevity, while incorporating diverse Medias, unique marketing strategies, and a no-questions-asked service department. Pillar in the community and recipient of several awards from area businesses and non-profit groups throughout the state of California in recognition of the development and implementation of 'Community and Safety'.

Planning / Program Development --
(Incentive / Sales Programs
(Customer Satisfaction Policies
(Special Events / Safety Training

Networking --
(Multimedia Advertising
(Press Releases / Affairs
(Public Promotion / Affairs

Administrations --
(Front- and Back-Stone Logistics
(Infrastructure & Processes

Personnel --
(Labor Relations / Staffing
(Workflow Optimization

■ **Career Highlights**

Created and implemented a 'Head Smart' Program; sought area sponsors, volunteers, and media coverage designed to expose the relines of head injuries. Integrated a reward program for children wearing helmet protection although no helmet law exists in the state of Wyoming.

Rallied and spearheaded the start of a Salt Lake City Police Department Bike Program. Visited various departments, taught how to start the program, the equipment needed, soliciting startup funds, and citizen / community support.

Participated in the beginning stages of Injury Prevention Center (IPC) designed to bring attention to accident rates and fatalities caused by lack of or improper use of equipment.

Involved in all facets of the business, from demography selections, bank financing, and groundbreaking to store schematics and product lines –oversaw the purchasing and buying of each line based on store location and season.

Founding father of the North Salt Lake BMX Association, enabling Big 5 Sporting Gooding stores to form the area's first team that won national recognition for three consecutive years.

Focused on 100% quality customer care and vendor/supplier relations designed to increase productivity to augment long-term, strong business relations.

■ **Professional Experience**

GENERAL MANAGER, 1984-2000
Big 5 Sporting Goods store, North Salt Lake, Utah
Operated corporate franchise of bike, sports, and fitness business that grew from $75,000 in revenues to $4.5 million per year, including the addition of 5 store locations (60 employees), a mail order program, and warehouse facility. Oversaw all business logistics from simplistic processes to complex administrative logistics, including on-site staff training, point-of-sale processed, advertising, marketing, new facility design, and cost management.

- Modified the product line to provide consumers with products pertaining to their lifestyles and needs (i.e., provided Mopeds in the '80s, bike products in the '90's and subsequently fitness products).

■ **Training & Continued Education**

Attended several classes covering software, sales motivation, operations, management, and time-management topics.

Note: As you can see in this résumé, it shows deep and clear experience. This applicant is ready to transition in to a new job.

Mellissa S. Goodfellow

35 Greenleaf Dr. Boise, Idaho 78992 – 802 -788 -2310 – MSG@Yahoo.com

Marketing Management Professional

Event Prodction & Marketing – Trade Show Coordination -- Sales Management

Professional Training

University of Utah at Salt Lake
- Began studying for Master of Business Administration degree in 8/ 00.

Univeristy of Iowa at Ames, Iowa
- Bachelor of Science degree received 8/98 with major in Marketing/Merchandising Management.

Relevant Courses

(Statistics

(Accounting

(Fashion Buying/Merchandising

(Marketing Research

(Marketing Strategies/Decisions

(Contemporay Retail Management

(Expository Writing

Professional Highlights

Macy's – Boise, Idaho, and Salt Lake City, Utah – *Assistant Store Manager*

(Managed up to 25 sales associates in a retail classic clothing and department store for business and professional women.

(Achieved sales goals daily and annually by maintaining customer service levels.

(Handled marketing events including direct mailing, in-store fashion shows, and events.

(Trained new associates, covering all aspects of the company manual and exposing associates to all areas of the operation.

(Designed and merchandised all windo displays and sales floor daily.

(Conducted inventory bi-annually, prepared daily schedules, processed payroll data, and handled office duties including copying, faxing, and data entry.

Henry Jones Enterprises – Salt Lake City, Utah – *Showroom Assistant*

(Assisted buyers inselecting merchandise at major trade show events in showrooms and convention center.

(Conducted inventories and compared inventory data with customer needs.

(Prepared orders and assentieed displays.

(Prepared flyers for diredct mail and performed offfice duties including copying, faxing, and data entry.

Internship

Fashion Institute of Technology – Long Beach, California

(Mentored by the Vice President of Public Relations in a goal-proemted. Evaluated position

(Conducted market research through direct mailing, target marketing, creation and implementation of trade show specials, promotions, and window display development.

(Maintained exemplary client/tenant and home furnishing industry retations.

Skills

- Computer -- Windows 98, Microsoft Office 2000, Word 8.0, Asscess 8.0 PowerPoint 8.0
- Language – Conversational Spanish

Note: This applicant developed her résumé to re-enter the fashion world. What you do not see is a military transfer. In this case a functional style résumé is used to highlight relevant skills and down play the sporadic employment history.

Evy A. Craft

225 Blair Road
Riverside, CA 92883

951-284-5558
EvyA@aol.com

Career Objective: A Sales or Customer Care position employing my abilities to create a positive experience for the client while generating profits for the company.

Professional Strengths Summary

- **Able to direct others and clearly relate key concepts / goals.**
- **Build confidence in colleagues to gamer results.**
- **Understand value of attention to detail combined with excellent time-management skills.**
- **Practice patience when dealing with difficult situations.**
- **Expertly adapt to the behavioral styles of others to maintain diplomacy and understanding.**

Customer Service / Qualifications

Track records for utilizing expert communication abilities to promote professionalism in customer care.

- ☑ Award-winning telemarketer with outstanding capability to lead successful campaigns.
- ☑ Communicate regularly with potential customers to assess needs / recommend appropriate services.
- ☑ Accurately quote current rates and prices.
- ☑ Develop superior product knowledge to increase strength of services.
- ☑ Accurately report sales statistics.
- ☑ Experienced with data-entry record-keeping routines.

Employment History

ABC	**Vern's Carpet /Upholstery**	**Riverside**
Communication	**Cleaning & Auto Detailing**	**School District**
Riverside, CA	Norco, CA	Riverside, CA
Telemarketer	*Assistant*	*Teacher's Aide*

Personal Development / Education

High Potential, Inc
Communication Styles Course

Poly-High School, Riverside, CA
Diploma

Note: This is a functional style résumé, as you can see it can be used to highlight relevant skills.

In this case the sporadic employment is down played.

Myra A. Cheyenne

142207 Running Springs
Orange, CA 91442
714-637-4283
MACheyenne@alo.com

Career Summary

Fifteen years of progressive sales, supervisory, and training experience.
Demonstrated and documented track record of exceeding sales goals.
Training, interviewing, hiring, and management experience.
Probing, negotiation, and organizational skills.
Business-to-business self-generated sales ability.
Effective territory-management skills.

Articulate and creative, offering innovative and practical solutions.
Assertive, self-motivated, goal-oriented, and efficient
Adept at both oral and written communications.
Energetic and results oriented.

Professional Experience

East Coast Scientific Products (major distributor of lab chemicals, supplies, and equipment)   Los Angeles, CA
Telesales Representative   *March 1997 - 2002*

(Top performer, January 1999

Responsible for the development of new and existing accounts within the Los Angeles metropolitan area. Communicated with scientists, engineers, lab managers, quality-control managers, purchasing agents, and microbiologists for lab supplies, equipment, and furniture consultations and purchase. Coordinated technical assistance and support between the manufacturer and end-user. Negotiated a national contract for over $500k in new business revenue. Won an exclusive contract, locking out the competition. Managed territory by telephone, with occasional on-site visits. Increased stability of a difficult-to-manage territory within one year of assignment.

World Search Consultants (contingency recruiting firm)   Orange, CA
Sales Manager / Owner   1994-1997

Contingency recruiter for senior-management, middle-management, and various other positions in sales, marketing, finance, and human resources within the restaurant and manufacturing industries. Initiated new business throughout the United States utilizing telephone and in-person presentations and increased revenue to over $90K within the firs two years of business. Responsible for accounting, purchasing, profit-and loss statements, new business development, advertising, and public relations.

Note: The approach taken here was to highlight relevant experience and notable achievements in the Professional Experience section. The Career Summary shows both professional qualifications and personal attributes.

Myra A. Cheyenne

Page 2

714-637-4283
MACheyenne@alo.com

Professional Experience

WestMed Products (*medical supplies and equipment company*)
Medical Sales Representative

(Top performer June 1992, August 1992, October 1992
Expedited sales of disposables, educational materials, and topical medication and topical medications through detailing. Target market was OB/GYN and other medical specialties. Coached OB/GYN residents in the OR and outpatient clinical environments on the medical indications and insertion / removal of OB/GYN prosthetics. Utilized detailing, short lectures, journal reports, and demonstrations to generate new revenue. Territory responsibilities included time management, budgeting, sales projections, and forecasting. Turned a low-revenue territory around within 12 months.

Polaroid Corporation (*office equipment and supply manufacturer*)

Marketing Representative
(Top performer May 1988, March 1989, August 1989
Entry-level sales position with demanding quotas, Developed a customer based from 0 to over 200 companies, which generated revenues of over $500k annually. Increased sales solely from cold-calling activity. Actively conducted product demonstrations and formal slide presentations and prepared proposals for prospective customers. Coached and trained new hires, utilizing formal internal training methods and practical on-the-job sessions

Education

University of California at Fullerton
BS – Mass Media Broadcasting / Journalism

Fullerton, CA
1987

Joan A. McCormick

6166 Cayon Road
Ontario, CA 93512

JoanAMcCormick@comcast.net

Cell Phone 909-715-8693
Home: 909-715-8639

MORTGAGE LOAN OFFICE

A goal-oriented professional whose proven record of achieving productivity and service objectives has produced valuable results. Recognized as a contributing team member with outstanding analytical skills and high standards of quality customer service. Capable of expanding business in a highly competitive marketplace.

Highlights of Qualifications

(Prepare analyze, verify, and approve loan applications
(Knowledgeable of loan products and loan approval processes
(Oral; and written communication skills
(Problem contact and interface
(Customer service abilities
(Bilingual - English / Spanish
(Skilled with accounting and financial procedures
(Ability to inspire trust, respect, and confidence
(Work independently and as a team member
(Develop effective working relationships with management and clients

PROFESSIONAL EXPERIENCE

<u>Green Light Mortgage Company</u>, San Bernardino, CA
Senior Loan Office, 1994-1998

Originated conventional real-estate loans and specialized in FHA loans, developing business and providing service primarily to the Hispanic community.

(Fulfilled corporate objectives and closed several loans per month.
(Accessed loan documentation and programs for placement with appropriate lender.
(Processed loans from conception to completion and followed through to timely closure.
(Reviewed loan application, interviewed applicants, verified accuracy of documents.
(Assisted borrowers to understand the loan process and complete application.
(Helped consumers qualify to purchase a home or to refinance an existing mortgage.
(Kept abreast of new mortgage products to meet customers' needs including reverse-equity mortgage products to meet customers' needs, including reverse equity mortgage, shared-equity mortgage, and adjustable-rate mortgages.
(Met with customers, gathered data, answered questions, and processed required forms.
(Reviewed completed financial forms for accuracy and requested additional data if necessary.
(Requested credit reports from manor credit-reporting agencies and ensured that the consumer met the lending institution's requirement.

Note: This is a straight chronological résumé and it works well. What you do not know is that this applicant is following a career husband. The applicant has displayed current experience which is a good approach and works well here.

Joan A. McCormick   Resume' - Page 2

PROFESSIONAL EXPERIENCE (Continued)

Internal Revenue Service, **Riverside, CA**
~~**Internal Revenue Agent,** 1988-1994~~

Conducted intensive investigations of numerous individuals and corporations to resolve problems involving tax-law compliance.

(Interviewed individual taxpayers and corporate executives to determine to validity of financial statements and performed detailed analysis of statements for accuracy.
(Upon completion of investigation, wrote reports recommending appropriate action.
(Attended ongoing training seminars to stay informed of federal taxation laws.
(Received Public Service Award for volunteering time to VITA, a program to assist underprivileged adults and senior citizens with tax preparation.
(Served as bilingual interpreter, assisting other IRS agents in telephone communications and correspondence with Hispanic taxpayers.

University of Riverside, Riverside, CA
Accountant, 1983-1988

Handled all accounting activity associated with university donations, including accounts receivable, bank reconciliations, general ledger, and year-end closing.

(Received commendation letter from Vice President for outstanding performance.
(Gained a broad knowledge of accounting as an assistant for the first three years.

EDUCATION and TRAINING

LICENSES

Enrolled Agent License, 7/94 – Present

Real Estate License, 9/00
State of California

Notary Certification, 10/00

Jackie P. Oliver

1551 Sandstone Road - Riverside, California - 951- 277-2924 - JPOliver@aol.net

CAREER TARGET PHARMACEUTICAL SALES

Dynamic professional with a strong medical background and experience in sales. Energetic and outgoing with great communication skills. Outstanding organization and time management abilities.

STRENGTHS AND SKILLS

▶ **Highly** creative, self-motivated professional with excellent interpersonal skills.
▶ Strong medical background obtained through education and work experience – familiar with medical terminology and diagnostics.
▶ Ability to conceptualize and generate new ideas, analyze problems and develop effectiveness.
▶ Dependable team player who relates well and works cooperatively with diverse personalities.
▶ Fast learner with demonstrated initiative and dedication to the achievement of organizations.
▶ Focus on providing exceptional service resulting in customer satisfaction and repeat business.
▶ Computer capabilities include: MS word, the internet, and Outlook.

EDUCATION

BS, Physiology, University of Nevada, Reno, Nevada
Courses included: Biochemistry, Organic Chemistry, Physics, Anatomy, and Biology

EXPERIENCE

ROSS, Corona, CA
Sales Associate

- ☑ Designed creative window displays for this children's clothing boutique.
- ☑ Sold merchandise to 72% of the customers browsing during assigned shift, including many add-one.
- ☑ Assisted owner with selecting merchandise for the shop.

RIVERSIDE HOSPITAL – EMERGENCY DEPARTMENT, RIVERSIDE, CA
EMERGENCY MEDICAL TECHNICIAN

- ☑ Assisted nursing staff and physicians with invasive and non-invasive procedures. Averaged 43% new admissions over any eight-hour period.
- ☑ Took basic vitals, and provided patient care and comfort measures.
- ☑ Charted procedures and maintained medical supplies for trauma 1 center. Know CPR.

Unit Clerk

- ☑ Organized charting, and provided follow-up with patients attending physician regarding various information
- ☑ Utilized available resources and systems to efficiently facilitate procedures.

Note: What we see here is an applicant that wants to focus her career objective in the area of pharmaceutical sales. Her extensive summary brings together her experience and education. What you do not know is that her motivation to seek out this new career area is because of relocating.

Sandy Maxwell
Legal Assistant / Paralegal

Highly motivated legal assistant dedicated to professionalism and quality.
A proven record for providing dependable assistance as a team member in a law environment.

- ☑ Aptitude for effectively interfacing with supervisors, professional staff, and clientele.
- ☑ Strong communication, grammar, and interpersonal skills.
- ☑ Knowledge of Corel WordPerfect, Microsoft Word, TimeSlips, and various software and office equipment.

PARALEGAL CERTIFICATION (1910)
Focus: Litigation
University of Santa Barbara, CA

GENERAL COURSEWORK
Focus: Business / Social Sciences
University of Nevada, Reno, NV

LEGAL ASSISTANT (1999 – 2002)
Jones and Jones, Santa Ana, CA
- ☑ Aided litigation partner in coordination real estate transactions and corporate documents.
- ☑ Expedited preparation and editing of correspondence, discovery, and pleading.
- ☑ Assisted counsel in preparing foe court hearings, depositions, and trials.
- ☑ Responsible for maintaining court calendar, attorney's personal calendar, billing documents, and files.

PARALEGAL (196-1996)
Riverside Management Company, Riverside, CA
- ☑ Responsible for daily review and organization of litigation files and calendar.
- ☑ Prepared corporate minutes and assisted with administrative support.
- ☑ Appointed to correspond with outside counsel regarding ongoing litigation.
- ☑ Reviewed and supervised monthly billing statements of outside counsel.

LEGAL ASSISTANT / PARALEGAL (1991-1993)
Baker, Smith, and Wilson at Law, Orange, CA
- ☑ Drafted discovery motions and correspondence, prepared court forms for filing and service, and maintained court calendar.
- ☑ Prepared deposition summaries and maintained files.

PARALEGAL (1911 – 1993)
West Coast Management Company, Stanton, CA
- ☑ Assisted with the preparation, filing, and service of litigation documents.
- ☑ Prepared unlawful detainer pleadings, court forms, and motions for Bankruptcy Court.
- ☑ Monitored court calendar and prepared miscellaneous office correspondence.

California Association of independent Paralegals
California Real Estate License

Note: What we have here is a résumé of a relocating applicant; it shows relevant education, and certification. The recent experience makes for a strong résumé along with an eye-catching format. What you do not see is that this is a relocation spouse.

396

CINDY JO WASHINGTON

714-514-9823   12334 California Street, Orange , CA 92838   CindyJoWashington@aol.com

PROFESSIONAL OBJECTIVE

Sales/Management

PROFESSIONAL PROFILE

- ☑ Profit-minded, bottom-line driven professional focused on results, quality, and teamwork.
- ☑ Highly motivated, goal-directed team member/mentor with strong leadership abilities and trails.
- ☑ Valued by employed for extraordinary contributions to building peak annual revenues.
- ☑ Number one ranked Team Manager/Leader in the nation for four consecutive years.
- ☑ Respected by others for knowledge, consistent performance, and witty, caring personality.

EXPERIENCE

CORPORATE FRANCHISE MANAGEMENT,   **1996-2002**

Team Manager/Leader, 10/97-9/02
- ✓ Reporting to franchise owner, entrusted to manage all facts of the day-to-day operations with accountability for and compensation based on annual profit performance. Mentored and motivated employees to perform at highest levels to ensure customer satisfaction and retention.

Key Results:

- ✓ Provided sound leadership in establishing vision and direction to achieve desired goals.
- ✓ Fostered cooperation among team members, contributing to a productive work environment.
- ✓ Exceeded annual growth goals, with averages at 20% to 25%.
- ✓ Retained key accounts in a highly competitive and cyclical market — accomplished through networking, sales prospecting, and outstanding customer focus.
- ✓ Collaborated with clients, identifying budget parameters and vision to deliver superior-quality end product: successfully maintained 75% of total sales orders per month.
- ✓ Recipient of *National Excellence in Leadership Awards: 2002* – Gold; 2001—Gold; 1999 –Gold; 1998 – Silver; 1997 – Bronze.
- ✓ Active member of Business Council; completed various seminars on Leadership/Management.

Customer Service Representative, 6/96 – 10/97
- ✓ Hired by owner to perform entry-level duties: assisted walk-in customers; phone quotations; prospecting; data entry. Performed daily account reconciliation of sales and sash register; followed through on a myriad of details, ensuring customer satisfaction; make thank-you calls and wrote personal notes of appreciation; managed project deadlines and quality assurance.

EDUCATION

Bachelor of Arts – Art and Design – Baker College, Long Beach, CA May 1996
- ✓ Emphasis: Drawing, Art History, and Sociology
- ✓ Dean's List – Five Semesters
- ✓ Personally paid for over 82% college education

'CINDY is one of those rare individuals you discover (and hire) once in a lifetime. I would not be where I am today – for certain – without her vast contributions and commitment to our company'.
Henry Wilson, Owner/General Manager, **CORPORATE FRANCHISE MANAGEMENT, Irvine, California**

Note: This is a straight chronological format résumé. What enhances this résumé for the applicant is the quote and profile from the former employer.

SHA KATOBI

773-348-9400   250 Arlington, Reno, NV 89501   SKatobi@aol.com

MARKETING -- PROJECT MANAGEMENT -- MIS MANAGEMENT

Self-mtivated professional with unique combination of skills in marketing, project management, and technology. Proven results: Increasing company revenue, developing cost-saving programs, developing new markets, and building product awareness.

SUMMARY OF QUALIFICATIONS

- Attuned to ever-changing needs of business; service oriented with strong intuitive and analytical abilities.
- Astute, identifying areas in need of improvement, with the vision to develop and implement successful action plans.
- Excellent program/project and general business management skills.
- Creative in problem-solving and cost-cutting issues.
- Work cooperatively on team, as well as independently, toward excellence and quality in corporate objectives and goals.
- Strong management and organizational skills.
- Able to set goals, prioritize tasks. Structure operation, and handle multiple projects simultaneously.
- Computer skills: MS Office, Oracle, Visual Basic, and Web Development.

EXPERIENCE

MARKETING STRATEGIST (VOLUNTEER) AMERICAN RED CROSS, Reno, NV   1995-Present
Work on blood drive, The Great American Blood Drive, consulting with prospective advertisers and developing a strategic advertising concept to promote the campaign.

SENIOR EXECUTIVE, CLIENT SERVICES PRESSMAN ADVERTISING AND MARKETING Bombay, India 1990-1991
A leading financial advertising firm in India.
Analyzed the competitiveness of existing products, developing new technologies and redefining market niche.
Restructured PR strategies and crested new sales collaterals, and advertising and trade-show materials to support market expansion,
Handled financial advertising for stocks and mutual funds.
- Directed successful media campaigns, including ad layouts, media buying, and cost analysis.
- Completed major projects within budget through proper planning and coordination of resources.
- Monitored the status of various projects, tracking cost and manpower utilization and keeping management informed of project status at all times.

EXECUTIVE OF CLIENT SERVICES   ABC ADVERTISING & MARKETING CO., Calcutta, India   1986-1990
A major advertising company in India.
Prepared strategies for media campaigns and materials for local, regional, national, and global advertising. Handled sales-promotional materials such as POP displays, trade-show exhibits, circulars, catalogs, booklets, and direct-mail advertising. Handled many major clients in India.

MARKETING EXECUTIVE   INDIA BREWERIES & BOTTLING, LTD, Calcutta, India   1986-1989
Supplier of beer to exclusive clients in India and abroad

Handled marketing, sales, advertising, and PR; coordinated with distributors to supply major hotels and nightclubs in Calcutta.
Managed PR Programs, launching materials to increase awareness, recognition, and market share. Outperformed competition by sponsoring sporting events and holiday parties.

EDUCATION

Master of Arts, *International History*, UNIVERSITY OF CALCUTTA, Calcutta, India
Master of Arts Candidate (52% complete), *Advertising & PR* HAWAII STATE UNIVERSITY, Honolulu., Hawaii
Post-Graduate Degree, *Management*, UNIVERSITY OF CALCUTTA, Calcutta, India
Bachelor of Arts, *Clinical & Industrial Psychology*, MITHIBA COLLEGE OF ARTS & SCIENCE, Bombay, India
Seminar, *Import/Export Management*, Calcutta, India
Computer Skills, COMPULEARN, Orange Coast College, CA
Workshop, Public Speaking for Executives

Note: What you can pick up very quickly is that this applicant has strong professional experience and impressive educational credentials. You will note that in this example the applicant is an immigrant that is trailing a spouse, but shows relevant volunteer work that is supported by her career.

JOHNY C. HARAJ
CIVIL ENGINNERING PROFESSIONAL
8091 Rose Road -- Riverside, CA 92883 --Residence: 714-514-8296 -- Office: 714-514-8295

Strong leader with extensive experience in lifecycle project management - from design, development and testing to completion. International and updated BSCE credential; recipient of mutiple awards for engineering excellence.

EXPERIENCE

Project Experience

Land Reclamation & Bridges
(Paved road construction & infrastructure
(Vehicle bridge construction
(Concrete lining for canals
(Open and covered drains
(Land leveling

Dams & Lakes
(Excavation
(Filling & compacting
(Intake, escapes, weirs, regulators and culverts
(Pumping stations
(Drains

Buildings & Steel Structures
(Foundation design and soil investigation
(Concrete piles
(Brick & reinforced concrete construction (homes, schools)
(Steel structures (garages, factories, warehouses)

Project: Reconstruction of Concrete Riverbeds Surrounding Ancient City
Role: **Executive Engineer**
 Challenge: High ground water level throughout site plan.
 Actions: Open side drains along canal and incorporated pumping stations.
- Excavated the river in cross sections.
- Converted open drains to cover drains.
- Began lining while operating pumping stations to reduce the risk of collapse.

Results: Time saved = 42%

Project: Issyk Riverbed Land Reclamation
Role: **Executive Engineer**
 Challenge **1:** Collapse of cover field drain sides due to high water level and collector drains not working sufficiently.
 Action; Integrated pumping station; drained water from collector to main drain.
- Decrease ground level on field drain alignment to reduce risk of collapse.
Results: Time saved = 21%

Challenge 2: High temperatures and evaporation of soil moisture led to hairline cracks in canal concrete lining.
Actions: Wet concrete section before lining.
- Reduced time cap between trimming and lining
- Decided to lay concrete at night instead of daytime.
Results: Time saved = 17%

Project: Hadded Hiram Development
Role: **Resident Engineer**

Challenge: Develop irrigation structure (head regulators, intakes, siphons culverts)
Actions: Wet canal section before lining.
- Redesigned structures as pre-cast units.
- Developed pre-cast plants at site locations.
Results: Time saved=39%

Note: In this résumé we have an Engineering Professional that has all of his relevant experience out of country, which is presented in a project format. Plus the applicant has since obtained additional education after coming to the United States.

PROFESSIONAL HISTORY

Greater Central Asia Reclamation Company – OSH, KYRGYZSTAN (1989 to 2001)

Led the development of project plans throughout Asia and Middle East, as well as site investigation, structure irrigation, materials testing, dams and intake structure, and lake, drain and canal excavation. Also provided quantity estimation.

RESIDENT ENGINEER

Issyk Kul Project – ISSYK KUL, KYRGYZSTAN (1989 to 1989)

Planned design and edited original drafts for concrete structures and filling and compacting projects. Provided design and cost negotiation consultation for Pellicar Company (Greece) and Sribona Company (Russia).

SUPERVISING ENGINEER

ARGA AGRICULTURAL DESIGN & CONSTRUCTION COMPANY – (1977 to 1980)

Supervised building site of steel and concrete structures: provided soil testing expertise.

ESTIMATION ENGINEER

PRINCIPAL CONSTRUCTION COMPANY – BISHKER, KYRGYZSTAN (1975 to 1977)

Responsible for cost analysis and quantity estimation.

EDUCATION

B.S. – Civil Engineering (2002)
California State University at Berkley, CA
B.S. Civil Engineering (1977)
University of Bishkek
Bishkek, Kyrgyzstan

Other courses:
Scientific and technical training in integral reclamation, project planning, and business administration.

Awards detailed upon request.

Johny C. Haraj
8091 Rose Road – Riverside, CA 92883
Residence: 714-514-8296 – Office 714-514-8295

1492 Sunset Blvd. Los Angeles, CA 90453
213-456-2234

Captain Kangaroo

Uniquely qualified for

on-air talent -- radio imaging -- commercial voiceover -- documentaries -- music production -- acting

- ☑ personable, articulate, and professional with elements of uniqueness
- ☑ proven ability to adapt to challenges and changing environments
- ☑ poised in public speaking and widely experienced in communications
- ☑ comfortable with powerful personalities and celebrities
- ☑ great communicator, 'in-the-trenches' experience

Voiceover/radio imaging talent

Prestige communications, Hollywood, Hollywood, California   1993-2001
- ☑ **radio imaging** – Radio KNBC Children program

Western communications, Hollywood, Hollywood, California   1993-1997
- ☑ **Voiceover** – Disneyland Cruise Line
- ☑ **Voice** – International Balloon Festival, Temecula, California

On-air talent

ABC radio group, Hollywood, California   1985-1993

Radio Play
'hot nights' (late night romance) 10:00 pm-2:00 am
- ☑ #1 adult 25-54 program, 1995

Radio Play
'hot nights' (late night romance 9:00 pm-12:00 midnight
- ☑ #1 adult 25-54 program (from 7th), capturing 39% of viewing audience, 1993
- ☑ 'People's Choice Award,' 1995
- ☑ 'Citation of Excellence,' Category: Local Radio, 1994

'Saturday night oldies'
- ☑ #1 adult contemporary, Saturday night

metro – Hollywood
'sweet facts'
- ☑ News, traffic, guest interviews, live broadcast, music programming...the whole thing!
- ☑ Weekly radio documentaries.

acting (actors equity # 13245)
Movies 'Paper Chase' Hollywood, California
Television "Fast Times' and 'Look Who is here' Hollywood, California

Personal data

Military (12) years US Army Airborne Forces, Special Forces
Active Duty: Malaysia, Indonesia, Kenya, Oman, Jordan, and Falkland Islands
Well-traveled: Far East, Middle East, Europe, Eastern Bloc, Scandinavia, North Africa, Canada, Caribbean

Note: In this résumé it shows strong qualifications in broadcasting. Notice that the applicant has an interesting name and graphics that add to the résumé as an attention getting addition.

Maggie L. Hamilton
8978 Haven Av Rancho Cucamonga, California 91737
909-941-3245   MaggieLHamilton@aol.com

OBJECTIVE

An administrative assistant position in the SEE Program

HIGHLIGHTS

- ☑ 34 years of government experience at various administrative levels.
- ☑ Extensive college level business courses.
- ☑ Outstanding follow-up skills; goal-driven, always seek to bring projects to completion.
- ☑ Self-starter who sees what has to be done then does it.
- ☑ Recipient of many Outstanding Service Awards.

RELEVANT SKILLS AND EXPERIENCE

OFFICE TECHNOLOGY
- ☑ Keyboarding skill of 52 wpm.
- ☑ Mastery of MS Office Suite (Word, Excel, Access) and Windows 95 environment.
- ☑ Expertise in various other software packages including SAS, WordPerfect, CODAP, SPSS, PROPS, Harvard Graphics, and Lotus 1-2-3/

ADMINISTRATION
- ☑ Developed organization and command budgets.
- ☑ Recommended distribution of bulk software purchase.
- ☑ Scheduled training classes and served as an instructor.
- ☑ Coordinated and conducted monthly Information Management Office meetings.
- ☑ Organized CODAP conferences.
- ☑ Processed travel orders.

LEADERSHIP
- ☑ Supervised 7 to 9 employees as Team Leader for the Configuration Management and Requirements Team.
- ☑ Served as lead officer in the development, implementation, and operation of CAPRMIS (Capability Request Management Information System) for the Personnel Information System Command.

WRITING
- ☑ Wrote policy statements, procedures manuals, and programs of instruction.
- ☑ Wrote the user manual for the PERSINSCOM (Personnel Information Systems Command)
- ☑ Wrote Comprehensive Analysis Reports for the Army, Navy, Air force, and Marines.

WORK HISTORY

1982 - 1984	**Program Analyst**	Department of Army, Washington, DC
1980 – 1982	**Management Analyst**	Department of Navy, Washington, DC
1976 – 1980	**Administrative Assistant**	Department of Army Washington, DC

EDUCATION

Chaffey Community College, Rancho Cucamonga, CA
 Associate Degree in Business Management/Personnel Administration
 Addition coursework in Business Management and Personnel Administration
Riverside Community College, Riverside, CA
 Courses in Business Administration

Note: This résumé presents strong relevant skills and experience. This applicant wants to return to the work force after being retired, and as you can see the résumé keys in on skills.

Jeanne H. Kasier

383 Redwood Road
Riverside, CA 92884
951-277-7717, 951-277-7716 Cell
JeanneH.Kasier@comcast.net

SUMMARY OF QUALIFICATIONS

In-depth experience in the following areas:

- **Billing and Invoicing** – Managed accounts payable and accounts receivable invoices at the Hudson Generating Station of Public Service Electric and Gas. Evaluated invoices for accuracy and checked material orders. Worked with statistical documentation.

- **Computers** – Familiar with Lotus 1-2-3, WordPerfect, and Word for Windows; knowledge of customized mainframe payroll systems (APPO Operating System)

- **Clerical Administration** – Performed payroll functions, word processing, data entry, and various secretarial duties. Reported to regional business manager and site manager. Implemented special financial projects needed. Distributed petty cash funds.

- **Customer Relations** – Interfaced with distribution employees and procurement analysts. Communicated with managers regarding payment and approval of bills. Worked as part of a clerical team encompassing generating-station personnel and field personnel. Served as a Member of the Corporate Committee for APPO Users. Analyzed current systems for defaults and made recommendations for the future. Served as the generating station Notary.

- **Person Strengths** – Developed excellent communication skills. Enjoyed helping employees and working with people in all areas. Known as a cooperation team player and a diligent, responsible employee. Career encompassed 14 years of increasing responsibilities and promotions in the administrative areas of a major utility company.

PROFESSIONAL EXPERIENCE

1980-2001   **RIVERSIDE UTILITIES**
Magnolia Generating Stations
Administrative Clerk 'A' – Senior Level/Staff Support
Offered an early-retirement package after 20 years of service.

Promoted three times to the highest administrative step. Worked closely with APPO Project Team. Demonstrated expert knowledge of DWAC and PACE Accounting Systems. Responsible for vendor relations and various financial duties. Maintained contact with station supervisors, ordered all supplies for the station, and performed related secretarial duties.

EDUCATION

THE UNIVERSITY OF CALIFORNIA, Riverside, CA
AS in Liberal Arts
Continuing Education: Customer Service, Effective Speech and Writing

Note: This is a functional format résumé that highlights this applicant's skills. As you can see this individual was employed by one employer. As you review this sample you note that this person took early-retirement, but now wants to re-enter the workforce.

Mike Van Riper

3421 Pine View Drive
Orange, CA 91602 -- 714-514-6543, 714-514-6541
MikeVR@comcast.net

QUALIFICATIONS

- ☑ 30 years of Management, Sales and Customer Service experience.
- ☑ Stable employment history with more than 25 years at same local company.
- ☑ Background in production and printing.
- ☑ Possess mechanical aptitude with experience in basic repairs/maintenance.
- ☑ Keyboarding/data entry skills.
- ☑ Known for loyalty, honesty, enthusiasm, willingness to learn, interpersonal/communication skills, and sense of humor.
- ☑ Use creativity in approaching new situations and solving problems.

HIGHLIGHTS OF EXPERIENCE

Production Management

- ☑ More than 20 years' experience overseeing planning, scheduling, and tracking the use of human and physical resources in a production environment.
- ☑ Supervised departmental activities as well as all factory operations (four departments), directing the activities of a small staff, and later four production managers and their staffs totaling 120 employees, operating in a 24x5 environment with monthly sales of $690K.
- ☑ Monitored expenses to remain within budget guidelines and effectively utilized time and equipment to achieve sales goals.
- ☑ Applied solid organizational abilities to meet the demands of these positions.

Personnel Management

- ☑ As a manger, performed diverse human-resources functions, including Interviewing, hiring, disciplining, terminating, training, motivating, scheduling, and performance assessment.
- ☑ Used interpersonal, analytical, and decision-making skills effectively on a daily basis.
- ☑ Developed a pre-employment screening tool that tests basic language, math, and reasoning skills, which is still in use by the company today.

Customer Service & Sales

- ☑ For the last 10 years of my career, assisted customers with questions, problems, and orders via telephone.
- ☑ Handled assigned accounts (including one of the company's largest accounts, $5 million in annual sales) as well as inquires from potential new customers.
- ☑ Contacted forms dealers and brokers to market the company's services and expertise.
- ☑ Designed business form solutions to meet diverse customer needs, specializing in complex numbering and mailer forms.
- ☑ Entered orders, following through production to completion and keeping customers informed of status.
- ☑ Maintained excellent customer relationships, resolved problems effectively, and served as a resource to other customer-service and sales team members.

Note: Here we have another sample of a functional style résumé. The applicant does have a lot of experience and qualifications, but does not want to overwhelm the reader. All dates are moved to the second page.

404

Mike Van Riper -- Page 2

EMPLOYMENT

WEST COAST FORMS INC. -- City of Industry, CA   1968 to 1997
Senior Customer Service & Sales Representative
Press, Collator & Bindery Liaison
Factory Superintendent
Foreman, Collator Department
Forman, Bindery & Hand Assembly Department
Equipment Operator/Shipping Clerk

CALIFORNIA BINDERY --City of Industry, CA   1979 to 1992
Owner/Operator
- Home-based company servicing forms for manufacturers who required hand or piecework, such as labeling and stringing.

U.S AIR FORCE   1964 to 1968
Airman Firs Class/Personnel Specialist
- Honorable discharge

AFFILIATIONS

Member, Circle of Support for DDSO Client involved in ORANGE, CA OMRDD Self-Determination Pilot Program
Member, Orange County Traumatic Brain Injury Support Group & Volunteer Drive, DDSO

EDUCATION

Graduate St. Joseph Military Academy --Riverside, CA

James P. White

P.O. Box 143, Ball Road Colton, CA 93220 -- Tel. 909-234-4213, Cell 909-234-4214 -- 909-234-9999 (F.D. HQ)
Email: JamesPWhite@aol.net

MANAGEMENT PROFILE

PUBLIC SAFETY /CODE ENFORCEMENT / FIRE SUPPRESSION & PREVENTION / EMERGENCY MEDICAL SERVICES

Accomplished Senior Manager combining strong management skills with expert capacity to build and nurture cohesive, productive teams to achieve optimal levels of performance.

QUALIFICATIONS SUMMARY

- □ Extensive background and training in all facets of emergency operations including fire, emergency medical, and hazardous-handling.
- □ Recognized for consistent ability to identify opportunities to employ innovative processes and procedures to revitalize operations and affect bottom-line results. Strong ability to identify, analyze and solve problems.
- □ Flexible leader and expert strategist delivering unique change management initiatives. Explore innovative paths and procedures to achieve outstanding results. Initiate good conceptual ideas with practical applications.
- □ Demonstrated ability to effectively influence key decision makers. Take decisive action based on well-documented facts. Excellent ability to cope with stressful situations and multiple priorities.
- □ Strong leadership skills with a genuine interest in growth and development of staff, inspiring team members to achieve success through developing individual strengths.
- □ Excellent interpersonal skills and capacity to optimally utilize all channels of communications. Innate ability to effectively communicate goals and interplay of ideas and concepts to convey clear understanding of the corporate mission and philosophy.

CORE COMPETENCES INCLUDE:

Project Management	Strategic Planning	Operations Management
Team Leadership	Staff Training / Development	Problem Analysis / Resolution
Process Reengineering	Inspection / Enforcement	Purchasing
Budget / Finance	Grant Writing / Administration	Liaison Skills

MASTER OF DEVELOPING AND IMPLEMNTING STRATEGIC PLANS AND OPERATIONS INTIATIVES THAT ACHIEVE RESULTS

PROFESSIONAL CAREER PLAN

SAN BERNARDINO COUNTY FIRE DEPARTMENT, San Bernardino, CA   1980 – 2002
Fast-track promotion through increasingly responsible positions commencing as Firefighter and ultimately leading to Battalion Chief.

DIRECTOR OF EMERGENCY MEDICAL SERVICES –BATTALION CHIEF
SHIFT COMMANDER—CAPTAIN
ENGINE COMPANY OFFICER –LIEUTENANT
EMERGENCY MEDICAL TECHNICIAN – ENGINEER
FIRE FIGHTER

Supervised Emergency Medical Services comprising 50 EMTs and paramedics at three fire stations. Participated in the direction of all aspects of personnel relations including hiring, disciplinary actions, and structure fires. Coordinated all phases of emergency medical service (EMTS) and served as chairman of EMS Operations Committee. Wrote and implemented EMS protocols.

Continued.......

Note: It is clear here that we have a fire chief who is looking for a second career. And this résumé make it clear that he has management experience.

406

James P. White

Page 2 of 2

- Planned, organized, and executed EMS training, testing, and recertification for 75 EMTs. Served as Emergency Medical Services Training Officer.
- Catalyst in the conceptualization of paramedic program for San Bernardino County Fire Department. Aspects of state licensure became model for other fire departments.
- Instrumental in developing a medical-director contract that became model for other EMS agencies.
- Orchestrated groundbreaking legal inter-local agreement with neighboring fire department to share personnel, which enhanced public relations and augmented learning opportunities for firefighters.
- Established and launched Fire Cadet Program (paid internship) to allow 17 to 21-years-olds to participate in fire service through a comprehensive training and mentoring opportunity.
- Appointed as Special Commander during Los Angeles Olympics.
- Streamlined process to provide medical oxygen to EMS through small cylinders, eliminating rental **fees and saving 53% on oxygen cost.**

EDUCATION

Associate of Applied Science in Fire Science
San Bernardino Junior College, San Bernardino, CA

Associate of Science Degree
Riverside Community College, Riverside, CA

CERTIFICATIONS

Fire Science Officer II
Apparatus Driver / Operator
EMT and CPR Instruction
EMT -- Basic National Standard Curriculum

Fire Fighter I, II, III
Fire Inspector I -- Fire instructor
Hazardous Materials
EMS Training Officer

PROFESSIONAL DEVELOPMENT COURSEWORK

Managing Emergency Medical Services
Leadership and Decision Making
Pesticide Fire and Spill Control
Preparing for Incident Command
Handling Hazardous Materials Incidents
Life Safety Code
Leading People Effectively
Aerial and Quint Operations & Tactics
Weapons of Mass Destruction
Public Information Officer
Fire Service Communications
Executive Analysis of Multiple-Venue Operations

Advanced incident Command
Hazardous Materials Incident Analysis
Incident Command
Commanding the Initial Response
Servicing Fire Extinguishers
Conducting Basic Fire Training
Stewart Rose Fire Training
EMS Leadership Course
Supervising Today's Workforce
Advanced Leadership issues in EMS
Fire Service Organizational Theory
Emergency Medical Services Special Operations

AFFILIATIONS

New York State Fireman's Association
National Five Academy Alumni Association

New York State EMT Association
District 3 B inter Hospital Committee

New York State Fire Chief's Association
New York State Department of Public Safety Division of Community Emergency Management

Richard E. Siegel

922 Chapman Road
Orange, CA 92503
714-514-9833, Cell 714-514-9834
E-Mail: RESiegel@Comcast.net

> "....You are the most highly organized engineer I have met....the thoroughness your work and youf dependability are excellent... your assumption of responsibility for assignments scheduling and accomplishment outstanding...." -- John Smith, Former Dept. Chief, Rocket Sciences Corportion

EXECUTIVE PROFILE

High-energy, results-driven professional, blending formal education in Civil Engineering with in-depth experience in Mechanical Engineering focusing on project engineering. Exceptional leadership, management, and relationship-building skills; foster team unity and project cohesion across all levels of staff, management, and customers. Technically fluent, rapidly assimilating cutting-edge technologies, ideas, and processes. Reputation for unsurpassed loyalty, dedication, professional ethics, and integrity.

AREAS OF EXPERTISE

-- Project lifecycle Management	-- Product Development	-- Team Building & Leadership
-- System Testing & Qualification	-- Component Design	-- Operations Improvements
-- Change Management	-- Production Processes	-- Strategic Problem Solving
-- Budgeting / Cost Control	-- International Sales	-- Contract Administration

SELECTED ENGINEERING CONTRIBUTIONS

- ☑ Directed four Integrated Product Development (IPD) design teams to develop ECS components for Japanese Experimental Module (JEM) program of International Space Station project.
- ☑ Full authority for engineering budgets ranging from $150,000 to $5 million.
- ☑ Leader of 'Tiger Team' to resolve high rejection rate on new vendor castings, saving loss of 632 castings, avoiding recall of 221 delivered units, and restoring customer confidence.
- ☑ Reduced design costs by transferring schematic preparation from design department to project engineering. Verified feasibility of transfer, established departmental and design procedures, and conducted training of personnel.
- ☑ Represented division in two-year technical definition and sales campaign with three major Japanese contractors for the Japanese Experimental Module (JEM) Resulted in first-phase contracts of more than $4 million and potential for final qualified hardware contracts exceeding $65 million.
- ☑ Led division in five-week in two-year renegotiation of $234 million corporate contract with Space Station contractor.
- ☑ Created and filled unique position of Engineering Business Manager for International Space Station, monitoring all business, financial, and technical program activity.
- ☑ Recipient of engineering excellence awards for impact on manufacturing production and delivery: 'F-18 Outstanding Customer Relations Award,' Lockheed Corporation, and 'Valued Ethics and Trust Award,' Japanese consulting firm.
- ☑ **'Your ability to relate to the various personalities with whom you come in contact, your positive attitude and your written communication skills are valuable assets for your future development...' --Bill Franklin Group Manager, Orbital Science Corporation.**

Note: As you see in this résumé the dates are left out to assist this retired engineer to re-enter the workforce. The focus is on the applicant's background and specific achievements. Plus quotes make strong recommendations about his engineering skills.

Richard E. Siegel

Page 2

Professional Highlights

PROJECT ENGINEER / PRODUCT DEVELOPMENT – Orbital Sciences Corp., Tempe, AZ (16 years)
Key contributor in six separate aerospace programs culminating with assignment as engineering program manager for sale of control components to Japan, a joint partner in International Space Station with Lockheed. Excelled in four additional special assignments achieving success through versatility of strategic planning, organization, and implementation. Program engineer for component development on major subsystems and development engineer for individual value systems.

Built track record of consistent program success to contribute to company's long-term success. Managed all phases of integrated Product Development (IPD) for control system components manufactured for multiple environments in both aviation and space-related applications. Oversaw all phases of proposals, design, development, testing, qualification, and initial production.

SENIOR ENGINEER – Lockheed Missile and Space, Hawthorne, CA (3 years)

Fast-track promotion from product-support analyst to senior engineer, designing and manufacturing environmental control and fuel subsystems for F-18 tactical aircraft program. Gained expertise in project management from OEM viewpoint, coordinating engineering actions with component suppliers. Functioned in additional roles of engineering project coordination for subsystem design, engineering change-board coordinator, and logistics-support analyst for ECS system design.

Additional Experience

Computer Consultant – MM Enterprises, Los Angeles, CA
Customer Service Representative – American Airlines, Salt Lake City, UT
Transportation Specialist – Systems Enterprises, Denver, CO
Officer / Instructor Pilot – United States Air Force

Education & Training

Bachelor of Science in Civil Engineering
United States Air Force academy at Colorado Springs, CO

Master in Business Administration Degree Program in Computer Information Systems
University of California at San Jose, San Jose, CA

Management Training

Total Quality Leadership (TQL), Integrated Product Development (IPD) team procedures, and ISO 9000/9001 Conversion Requirements for international markets.

AutoCAD R14 Professional Level Training – Orange Cost College

Technical Expertise

Capable of rebuilding personal computers, upgrading existing equipment to include latest technologies.

Microsoft Office Suite, Technical Management Programs, AutoCAD Design Products, and various support and educational software.

Certifications

Licensed Commercial Pilot with Flight Engineer Certification

S
F
C

Susan F. Clifford

1410 Birdbath Lane, Riverside, CA 92877 ● Home:951-277-2327 ● Cell: 951-277-2328 ● SFClifford@aol.net

Manufacturing/Production/Office
Management

Results-driven professional with 20 years' management experience in manufacturing with consistent achievement in productivity and quality, personnel management, and team building. Aggressive with exceptional ability to motivate team workers.

Accomplishments
- Developed 'World Class Manufacturing Training Program' for the Kinston plant.
- Managed the transfer of the Quality Assurance Lab form Kinston to Cove City.
- Participated in the implementation of Demand Flow Technology into the Cove City Plant.
- Received Silver and Gold Cup Awards for $123,000 and $252,000 company savings, respectively.

Career Highlights

Classic Faucets, Incorporated, City of Industry, CA
1976-2002

Warehouse Supervisor (Walnut and City of Industry, CA) (2001-2002)
> On special assignment supervise on-and off-site warehouses including activities of team leaders, shipping and receiving attendants, and salaried shipping/receiving clerks, managed the Kanban System providing inventory to the appropriate locations.

New Products Materials Planner, City of Industry, CA (1995-2001)
> On special assignment with the Materials Department to assist in getting components approved and manufactured for a significant number of new products according to scheduled lead-time requirements.

Senor Quality Assurance Supervisor, City of Industry, CA (1995-2000)
- Transferred the Quality Assurance Systems Laboratory to City of Industry and assumed supervisory responsibility for the dimensional, functional, fit, cosmetics, and bill-of-material audits to ensure good product for the customer.
- Trained technicians, clerks, and auditors at the new location in the use of all instruments and processes.
- Maintained compliance with all standards agencies such as the international Association of Manufactured Plumbers Organization, Canadian Standards Association, American National Standards Institute, and the International Standards Organization.
- Produced all necessary reliability reports.
- Developed all job descriptions and method sheets for this department.
- Managed quality holds for the corporation, new product approvals, and releases.

Note: This is a standard chronological format résumé which the applicant has put together to cover early retirement from her company. The format is effective in showing experience and progress that was made during her career.

Production Supervisor, Johnson (1980 – 1995)
- Supervised final assembly, cartridge subassembly, brass buffing, brass polishing and tipping, subassembly of components, ring and seat buff, spout buffing, CNC Buffing, brass, and black nickel plating.
- Managed 72 to 200 operators, machinists, buff house operations, and material handlers.
- Coordinated the schedule and job assignments of all operators with production and materials management.
- Identified and managed out sourced tooling suppliers.
- Developed budget and ensured compliance.
- Supported activities of self-directed work teams.
- Coordinated machine run-offs on a timely basis.

TACHNICAL SKILLS

Quality Equipment: Calipers, Comparators, micrometers, flow meters

Processes: Nickel, brass, and zinc plating; injection molding; screw machines; PVD (Physical Vapor Deposition); buffing; silver-solder brazing; sonic welding; air-decay testing; water functional testing; vibratory finishing processes; and die casting.

Machinery: Bodine, Kingsbury, Astro, Fusion, Vibramatic, Cincinnati Milicron, packaging/bagging machines

EDUCATION/TRAINING

Industry Training-Variety of courses in Management/Supervision, Process Training, Materials Management; Quality Management; Demand Flow Technology & Business Strategy Workshop and Advanced Mixed-Model workshop: and Systems, Applications; and Products (SAP-integrated business systems solutions-7 modules)

Computer Training-Microsoft Word, Excel, Access, PowerPoint, WordPerfect, Cullinet, Lotus Norton Commander

Riverside Community College, Riverside, CA Industrial Management Curriculum 1983-1988

AFFILLATIONS

American Society of Quality – Member from 1995 to 2000

Mike J. Hamilton
Cellular Phone (951)-354-0437

May through December
4532 La Sierra Ave
Riverside, California 92505
Residence Phone (951)- 354-7426

January through April
5803 East 14th Street
Riverside, California 92506
Residence Phone (951) - 354-9301

Business & Investment Consultant
Long term Growth .... Profit Building.... Business Development
COMMODITIES/STOCKS... LAND DEVELOPMENT...PROPERTY MANAGEMENT... FRANCHISING

A visionary, innovative, goal-oriented, and business-development professional with 30+ years of cross-functional expertise in sales, marketing, administration, and management. Excellent interpersonal communication, presentation, and training skills. A strong mentor with the ability to teach 'out of the box' thinking. Demonstrated competency in the following areas.

(Executive Leadership
(Startups & New Ventures
(Market timing & Market Positioning

(Market Research & Analysis
(Executive Road Shows
(Stockholder Relations

PROFESSIONAL EXPERIENCE

QUICK MUFFLER SHOPS – California and Arizona   1975 to 2000

OWNER/FRANCHISEE
Owned 10 franchises in 2 states, oversaw general management team, and developed new business opportunities.
GOLDEN CAPITAL LIFE INSURANCE – Riverside, California   1966 to 1975
GENERAL AGENT
Monitored agent sales activity and assisted with training and regulatory compliance issues.
Developed prospect lists, identified sales opportunities, and presented/sold insurance and investment plans to individuals within the Southern California territory.

INVESTMENT EXPERIENCE

☑ Seat Holder and Active Floor Trader on Los Angeles Board of Trade, Mercantile Exchange, Los Angeles Board of Options Exchange and the New York Cotton Exchange, 1971 to 1999.
☑ Speaker at the international investment conventions discussing hard currency, gold, silver, and oil. Quoted in the *Wall Street Journal*.
☑ Property Owner/Manager of residential and commercial properties in Los Angeles, Arizona, and Costa Rica.
☑ Land Developer of residential and commercial property in Los Angeles, California.

EDUCATION

Bachelor of Business Administration: The University of California at Fullerton, CA
Continuing Education: Numerous Investment Conferences worldwide from 1971 to present

COMMUNITY ACTIVITIES

Riverside City Development – Led redevelopment efforts of Market Street commercial area in conjunction with William Smith of Riverside School of Architecture. Riverside Country Club Member

Note: What we have here is a highly qualified retired professional who is presenting his expertise without overwhelming the reader with details.

Richard S. Knight

17176 White Tail Road, Apt. 3 B
Riverside, CA 92506
Phone: 951-335-9338 -- E-mail: RSKnight@aol.com

Professional Overview

Active, broadly talented professional, offering enthusiasm for challenges, aptitude for new ideas and situations, and uniquely diverse life and career experiences. Expert in all aspects of business administration through more than 25 years of successful business ownership. Strong leader in community and professional organizations. Keen motivated by diversity and complexity of activities.

Value Offered

Experienced Business Manager & Administrator
- Managed all aspects of a successful practice including hiring and supervising staff, directing sales and marketing, purchasing, record keeping, and financial control.
- Delivered top-notch customer service as an optometrist, building strong report patient and referral-based business.

Organizational Leader
- Long-standing officer and director, 2 years as president of Optometric Council of California.
- Championed causes for organization, liaising with California State legislators to influence pending legislation.

Creative Mastermind & Wordsmith
- Wrote and edited monthly column for industry newsletter, giving due attention to current standards in grammar, punctuation, and common usage of the English language.
- Conceived and encoded more than 500 cryptograms to date, surpassing common crypto quotes in complexity and devising impediment at code-breaking of cryptograms with computer programs.
- Self-published two pocket-book-sized, 59-pages volumes of 'Original Cryptograms,' each containing 250 cryptograms. Market and sell first volume through website.

Multi-talented. Hands-on Expert
- Fully familiar with Medicare, Medicaid, and other third-party insurance programs from both sides-provider and beneficiary. Experience gained through own optometry practice and assisting close family member through two complicated surgeries.
- General contractor for extensive office renovations, hiring laborers, designing layout, drawing floor plans, calculating room areas, purchasing furniture, and selecting accessories.

Active Community Contributor
- Member of Riverside County Democratic Committee for 2 years.
- Current Advisory Board member of the Riverside Jewish Center.
- Chairman of the United Jewish Appeal -- Federation of the Jewish Philanthropies Appeal, Riverside Division, for 4 years.

Career & Academic Experience
Optometrist -- Western Vision Services, Riverside, CA (1997 – 1999)
Business Manager / Optometrist – Dr. Richard S. Knight, Optometrist, Riverside, CA (1975-1996)

B.S., Optometry — University of California, Davis, CA
B.A., Iowa State University, Ames, Iowa

California State Optometry License.

Note: As you can see in this résumé is a very flexible applicant offering expertise in key areas which should be interesting to an employer. What you do not see is that this is an 80-year-old retiree looking to return to the world of work.

Kenneth E. Thomas
505 Rose Drive
Orange, CA 91623
Home (714) 635-0441 E-mail: KET@aol.com

FOCUS

To obtain a responsible and challenging administrative support position

HIGHLIGHTS

Software

(Word, Excel
(Access, PowerPoint
(SAP, Cullinet

Office Machine

(Copier
(Fax
(Computer
(Printer

Strengths

(Organized
(Customer-Service Oriented
(Fair

CAREER EXPERIENCE

West Coast Production   1980-2001
Stanton, CA

Shipping Coordinator (began as Production Operator, then promoted to Quality Control Technician, Inventory Control Clerk, Shipping Clerk, and shipping Coordinator)

✓ Supervised shipping personnel including loaders, administrative processors, and finished-goods transport personnel
✓ Trained, cross-trained, and ensured compliance with shipping procedures.
✓ Ensured smooth material flow from manufacturing to shipping and from one shift to another.
✓ Maintained manifest shipping accuracy of 99%.
✓ Processed over/shorts on a daily basis and reconciled the shipping bin daily.
✓ Maintained adequate supplies of oil, fuel, stretch film, and pallets.
✓ Maintained a safe work environment, including the battery charging area.
✓ Followed budget guidelines and developed cost reductions.
✓ Communicated with accounting, distribution centers, and supervisors.
✓ Served as Fist Aid Attendant and Fire Brigade Member, 1983-1999.

Note: This applicant is trying to refocus his career toward an administrative role. In this case the applicant was downsized which opened up the opportunity to redirect his career.

Kenneth E. Thomas -Page 2
Home (714) 635-0441 E-mail: KET@aol.com

EDUCATION

Orange Coast Community College, Coast Mesa, CA

Received the following certificates during 1985-1987: Orientation & Study Skills, Introduction to Personal Computers, Lotus 1-2-3, Harvard Graphics, Bookkeeping, Math Concepts, Business Mathematics, Quality Assurance Concepts, Shop Math, Industrial Blueprint Reading, Precision Measurement Concepts, Instrument, and Statistical Process Control.

Coast Mesa Community College, Coast Mesa, CA

Introduction to Computers Data Processing, 1985

CERTIFICATES

SAP Training (Systems, Application, and Products-integrated business systems solution) –2001

Team Leader Training – 2001

Ambulance Attendant –1990-1994

CPR Training – 1990-1994

First Aid Attendant –1991

Emergency Medical Services Seminar – 1991

Aeromedical Safety for Emergency Response Teams (East Care) –1989

RECOGNITION

Operation Filter Team promoting anew kitchen faucet (water filter) at various Lowe's location in Santa Ana, CA Represented Team in Irvine, CA –2000

President's Achievement Award –1992

Perfect Attendance Awards –1986, 1987, and 1989

CIVIC / COMMUNITY INVOLVEMENT

Rotary Club, Orange, CA –Treasurer 2000-2001

Rotary Club, Santa Ana, CA – President 1985-1986

Raised funds for crippled children in Orange and Santa Ana for more than 20 years.

Lee L. Benson

456 Waiwai Drive ■ Honolulu, Hawaii 95822
(808) 555-8978 ■ LLB@aol.net

GENERAL MAINTENANCE MECHANIC

Air Conditioning • Refrigeration • Electrical • Plumbing

19 years of broad-based maintenance experience. Promoted through increasingly responsible decision-making positions. Place priority on safe working environment.

CERTIFICATIONS AND TRAINING

ESCO Institute

UNIVERSAL TYPE I, TYPE II: Certificate No. 455590002256, Section 608
MOTOR VEHICLE: Certificate No. 4533346, Section 609

Sears Extension Institute
Basic Refrigeration, Advanced Refrigeration, Central Air Conditioning,
Understanding and Using Test Instruments

Hawaii Hotel and Restaurant Industry
Basic Refrigeration, Blueprint Reading, Plumbing

RELEVANT EXPERIENCE

WAIKIKI INTERNATIONAL RESORT   Honolulu, Hawaii
(formerly Hawaiian Hotel at Waikiki Beach)

General Maintenance 1st Class	1996-2001
Maintenance 2nd Class	1988-1996
Maintenance Trainee	1982-1988

Accountability and Accomplishment Highlights

- Performed comprehensive property-equipment checks, service, and repair to ensure normal guest service and building operations.
- Collaborated with foreman to handle recurring challenge of air in chilled-water air-conditioning system. Conceived innovative solution to bleed air from system, resulting in reliable and efficient operation.
- Given authority to select new fan-coil units for major room-renovation project, Met with competing vendors and made suitable product recommendations to hotel management.

Note: As you can see clearly that this applicants résumé is applying for a specific position which is backed up by experience and knowledge in the air-conditioning maintenance area.

Lee L. Benson
Page 2

Sears, Hardware department   **Honolulu, Hawaii**

Sales Associate

Sold hardware products; educating customers on tool operation and uses. Performed minor tool repairs.

EDUCATION

Associate in Science Program
Refrigeration and Air Conditioning
Honolulu Community College – Honolulu, Hawaii

Associate in Science Degree
Merchandising Mid-management and Hotel Operations Mid-Management
Kapiolani Community College – Honolulu, Hawaii

RECOGNITION

' Your alertness and quick response to the smoke exiting from the compactor aided in averting a possible fir from occurring...I would like to add my persona thanks for being such a conscientious and valued employee.'

> Letter of Commendation - April 1994
> General Manager John Jeffrey

'Your quick response and bravery beyond the call of duty were instrumental in the proficient handling of the fire emergency. We are truly proud of your performance and feel privileged to have you at the Hawaiian Hotel.'

> Letter of Commendation – September 1992
> Executive Assistant Manager Henry Samson

'...in recognition of outstanding and valuable service to the Hawaiian Hotel.'

> Certificate of Recognition –September 1982
> General Manager Bill Baker

-- References Furnished on Request --

Marvin M. Cash
342 Ford Street, Orange, CA 92985 (714) 514-9933

Machinist

Career Highlights

Machinist — 1996-2001   California Machining, Inc, Orange

- ☑ Determined the sequence of operation from blueprints and drawings to manufacture products for the pharmaceutical industry.
- ☑ Machined parts to specifications using metal-working machine tools.
- ☑ Designed fixtures and tooling.
- ☑ Assembled parts into units with tools.
- ☑ Laid out and verified dimension of parts using precision measuring instruments and mathematics.
- ☑ Calculated and set machine controls.
- ☑ Selected, aligned, and secured fixtures.
- ☑ Measured, examined, and tested completed parts.
- ☑ Cleaned and lubricated tools and equipment.
- ☑ Conferred with engineering and manufacturing.
- ☑ Restored out-of operation equipment.

Sales / Stock Associate –1994 — 1995   Orange Hardware, Orange, CA

- ☑ Assisted customers in finding desired items.
- ☑ Processed sales transactions-cash and credit card
- ☑ Priced coded stock.
- ☑ Stocked merchandise for sale and display and maintained cleanliness.

Machine Skills

Metal and Wood Working Machines

(Manual Milling Machine	(Manual Lathe	(CNC Hurco 40/20 M
(Flex/Arm Tapping Machine	(Wood Lathe	(EDM Machine
(Grinder	(Band Saw	(Table Saw
(Jointer	(Radial Arm Saw	

Education and Certifications

Journeyman Certification, Southern, California Apprenticeship Council, Southern California Department of Labor – November 2001

Coast Mesa Community College, Coast Mesa, CA – Advanced Machinist Degree, 1996
Degree, 1996

Fullerton Community College, Fullerton, CA — Graduated 1991

Note: This résumé is one of a laid off job applicant. He has strong competitive skills to compete for a similar job with companies in the same area.

Herman H. Fredericksen

71716 Ocean Side Drive
San Diego, CA 93882

HHF@yahhoo.com

714-571-7878 Home
714-514-7877 Cell

PROFESSIONAL OBJECTIVE

Outside Sales /Account Executive

PROFFESSIONAL QUALIFICATIONS

(Successful sales/customer relations experience with a Chicago-based Fortune 500 company.
(Effective relationship-builder who is personable and caring; aggressive in pursuit of new accounts.
(Goal-oriented team player who is ethical, versatile, and has what it takes to do a job well.
(Well-liked by others and known as a fast learner who works hard, has drive and ambition, is efficient, and believes in providing extraordinary customer service, competitive by nature.

EXPERIENCE

JD Accounting, San Diego,   **12/00 to 5/02**

(Senior Corporate Account Manager
Managed over 400 accounts for this financial service firm. Accountable all facets of cold-call prospecting, account profiling, and meeting demanding sales and call goals. Position downsized.

Key Results

(Exceeded sales goals for 14 consecutive months.
(Increased profit margin by at least 9 percent each month
(Provide timely responses and business solutions to customers' inquiries to ensure business.
(Performed duties with efficiency and productivity: named 'Employee of the Month' five times.
(Increased sales 129% in a 12-month period while improving overall profits by 35% during time of organizational transition.

Petco Pet Clinic, San Diego, CA   **9/00 to 12/00**
(Veterinary Assistant – During college

Dennis Restaurant, San Diego, CA   **5/00 to 9/00**
(Server/Bartender – during college

EDUCATION

B.S. University of California at San Diego, CA December 2000
(Major: Business Marketing – Minor Corporate Communication
(Captain, Football Team; Team All-American

Professional Sales Training: Three months of extensive sales training sponsored by UCLA
Computer Knowledge: Network 2 Certified, Word, PowerPoint, Excel, Access, and Outlook.

Note: What we have here is an applicant that has been laid-off, had a short tenure with his most recent employer, but was able to come up with several strong achievements that helped focus on an effective résumé.

Gary G. Grass

9454 Magnola Way ■ Riversive, CA 92884
Home: 951-737-7855 ■ Cellular: 951-737-7854 ■ E-mail: ggg@aol.com

NETWORK MANAGER / ENGINEER
Expertise Includers: WANs ■ LAN ■ WLANs ■ VPNs ■ Servers ■ Firewalls
Cisco Certified ■ Thorough Knowledge of OSO Model and TCP/IP

Seasoned Network Administrator with 14 + years of broad-based IT experience; skilled at planning, implementation, and oversight of network infrastructure upgrades and maintenance. Background includes demonstrated ability to solve problems quickly and completely without risking system reliability. Adaptable to organizational and industry change. Driven professional with high level of personal integrity.

TECHNICAL PROFICIENCIES

Cisco: Catalyst 5500 / 5000 / 6500 / 3500 switches – 3600 / 2600 7513 / 4000 routers – Aironet 340 / 350 wireless bridges – Cisco Works 2000 – VPN Concentrator 3005

SERVERS: Win2K – WINS – Windows NT (dual and multiple domain models) – PDC – BDC – DNS – DHCP – RAS – SQL – SNA – Novell – Microsoft Exchange –MS Proxy Server

PROFESSIONAL CHRONOLOGY

Network Analyst   Santa Ana, CA
UCI Hospital   1998 to 2002

(Handled all network improvements including 2001 upgrade from flat model to hierarchical routed system that resulted in increased security and additional broadcast control.
(Managed 14-clinic wide area networks. Configured, planned capacity for, and maintained WAN, incorporating facilities throughout the state. Converted all outpatient clinics from DSL to frame relay.
(Oversaw network infrastructure and horizontal cabling project, collaborating Cisco Systems to design and implement new LAN GB backbone. Integrated wireless network utilizing state-of the-art-bridges and NICs.
(Accomplished cutting-edge upgrade replacing Fast Ethernet with progressive Gigabit Ethernet, positioning backbone to handle new standard.
(Installed, and maintain hospital's VPN connection.
(Configured and oversaw Windows 2000 Active Directory domain.
(Managed and administered user migration from Novell to Windows 2000 domain.

Network / Facilities Manager   Anaheim, CA
West Coast Link Networks, Inc.   1997

(Planned and constructed firm's internal and external networks. Configured and maintained Internet and VPN routers.

Note: As you can see here this applicant is clearly a techie with a great deal of solid systems and network administration background. His résumé showcases his problem solving capability and expertise.

Gary G. Grass

Page 2

- ☑ Configured and installed Microsoft SQL Server in Microsoft Clustered environment, Including Active/Passive and Active/Active Failover SQL Cluster designs.
- ☑ Managed Windows NT dual domain, Microsoft Exchange Server, and Proxy server.

Decision Support Systems Analyst   Santa Ana, CA
West Coast Medical Services

(Provided all levels of PC support as Team Lead for User Support Center
(Managed and maintained Cisco routers and switches.
(Administered organization's RAS, Windows NT, Novell, Microsoft Exchange, and SNA servers.

PC / Programmer Analyst   Costa Mesa, CA
ABC, Inc.

Performed network management, installing and administering Novell Netware, Handled claims system database program support, Carried out hardware and software maintenance. Performed JCL and COBOL batch programming.

TECHNICAL TRAINING AND CERTIFICATION

Cisco CCNA 2.0 Certification, June 2001

Data Communication Systems: Implementation, and Management, December 1997
Orange High Tech Park – Orange, CA

NetWare 3.11 Systems Manager / NetWare 3.1x Advanced Systems Manager, July 1996
Riverside Community College - Corona, CA

EDUCATION

Associate of Science, Data Processing, 1991
Riverside Community College – Corona, CA

(References Furnished On Request)

Jerrold J. Street.

2521 Camel Trail Road ● San Diego, California 92901
Home: (858) 555-3204 ● Cellular: (858) 555-3205 ● E-Mail: JJStreet@aol.com

Seeking Position in...

URBAN FORESTRY / TREE CARE

Tree ID and Selection   Plant Health Care   Tree Haazared Assessment   Three Appreaisal

ISA Certified Arborist with demonstrated ability to plan and implement ecosystems that include trees. Extensive knowledge of San Diego area trees, geography, and climate. Absolute dedication to professionalism and ongoing education. Outstanding communication skills. Computer proficiencies include Word, Excel, and Access. Speak Japanese and some Spanish, Ethical, observant, and thorough.

CERTIFICATIONS, TRAINING, AND RESEARCH

ISA CERTIFIED ARBORIST: License No. WC-23212 (2001)
CALIFORNIA CERTIFIED NURSERY PROFESSIONAL: License NO. 34331 (1983)

American Society of Consulting Arborists (ASCA) Consulting Academy:
Report Writing and Professional Practice Workshop (Feb. 2002)

Arbor Learn: Online Tree Appraisal Course (Jan. 2002)

Utah community Forest Council: Tree Hazard/Appraisal Workshop (Dec. 2001)

Self-Directed Research in Japan: Performed Private study on significance of trees and flora as well as their influence in Japanese culture, politics, commercial, and religious life.
For future publication, (1993-1995 and 1997-1999)

RELEVANT EXPERIENCE

Landscaper / Gardener   2000 to 2002
Private State of Mr. John Moneybags   Rancho California, CA
Ten-acre, multimillion-dollar property

> ➢ Oversaw 142 plus trees (21 to 25 species), single-handedly performing ongoing ecosystem and landscape management. Also included 7,800-square-foot lawn and rose garden.
> ➢ Planned and implemented 6-month mission to prepare landscape for private wedding. Project was total success.
> ➢ Implement organic-gardening procedures. Recycle majority of green waste.
> ➢ Successfully performed comprehensive redesign of rose garden.

Southern California Sales Associate   1992 to 1993
Southern Gardens   Rancho Santa Fe, CA

(Performed sales and customer service functions while educating public on basic planting decisions and offering troubleshooting tips.

Note: What we have here is an applicant that at the headline has showed cased his Qualifications, Competencies, and knowledge; also, his essential certifications and training.

422

Jerold J. Street
Page 2 of 2

- Maintained nursery and stock. Oversaw seasonal sales promotions of roses and bulbs.
- Gave widely attended gardening seminars.

Nursery Sale Associates   1980 to 1986
San Diego Home Nurseries, Inc.   Santa Ana, CA

- Planted trees, shrubs, bedding plants, and grass in residential gardens and commercial lots.
- Handled wholesale purchasing and customer deliveries.
- Led rose-pruning workshops.

PROFESSIONAL AFFILIATIONS

American Society of Consulting Arborists (new)   San Diego Horticultural Society (since 2000)
International Society of Arboriculture (since 2000)   American Horticultural Society (since 1996)
California Urban Forestry Council (since 2000)

EDUCATION

Business Management Certificate Program
University of California at San Diego Extension, anticipated completion 2004

Master of Science, Education, 3. 5 GPA
California State University at Long Beach, 1997

Bachelor of Arts, English, 3.3 BA
California State University at Fullerton, 1989

Associate of Arts, Ornamental Horticulture
Riverside Community College, CA, 1984

OTHER EXPERIENCE

English Teacher, New Day School – Sendel, Japan   1997 to 1999
Japanese Language Teacher, Park Villa High School – Park Villa, California   1996 to 1997
ESL instructor, Rancho Diego Community Collage District – Orange, California 1996 to 19997
English Teacher, AEON Intercultural Corporation – Toyohashi, Japan   1990 to 1995

Tomas B. Bush

213 Sweet Road ● Atlanta, GA 30043
770-555-2121
TomB.Bush@aol.com

Qualifications Summary

Strong Leadership (Full Lifecycle Management (Technical Management
Sales & Presentation Skills (Risk Analysis (Web Development
Negotiation (Problem Solving (Team Motivation (Results Orientation (Interpersonal Skills

A dynamic leader with excellent qualifications in driving new business development initiatives and managing divers multimillion-dollar projects that position commercial enterprises for prosperity and Technological advancement. Known and respected for having outstanding presentation, negotiation, Mediation, and closing skills, and for applying the practices of the Project Management Institute's 'Project Management Body of Knowledge.' Innovative solutions provider offering client-centric solutions. IT trendsetter and mentor producing a large network of accomplished team member.

Telecommunications Expertise

Metropolitan & Long-Haul Networks (Managed Wavelength Services
Long-Distance Networks (Data Networks (Voice & Data Protocols

Internet Expertise

Internet & Intranet Design (Content Development
E-Commerce (Affiliate Marketing (Ad-Hoc Reports

Auditing & Security Experience

User Authentication (Access Management Security Policies (Disaster Recovery
Contingency Planning (Security Policies & Procedures (Information Assurance
Controls Auditing (Risk Assessment & Management

Professional Experience

SOUTHERN COMMUNICATIONS, Alpharetta, GA   **2000 to 2002**
Senior Systems Engineer
Managed multimillion-dollar optical system deployments by leading cross-functional teams on several concurrent customer engagements across the U.S. and Canada.
- Closed a $1.5M contract in equipment and engineering services by carefully reassessing customer requirements and internal software release issues, and by developing a workaround solution that kept the customer's delivery timeline intact.
- Led and trained a team of engineers in flaw in a flawless European network implementation resulting a cost savings for our European counterparts of $120K.

Note: As you see this applicant is a highly qualified senior-level manager with diverse experience in communication, software, and professional skills who have been affected by a downturn in the telecommunications industry.

Tomas B. Bush ● Page 2   77-555-2121   TomBBush@aol.com

——————————————— Professional Experience Continued ———————————————

HIGHTOWER AFFILIATES, ATLANTA, GA   **1999 to 2000**
SENIOR Project Manager
- Secured a multimillion-dollar contract with a major retail grocer by establishing and documenting an effective project-management process that included procedures for managing software development release.
- Facilitated project-status meetings for issue determination/resolution.
- Identified and mitigated project risks.
- Implemented MS Project web interface for more efficient tracking of project status.
- Advised Chief Technology Officer on business planning and strategies.

ABC CORPORATION, Atlanta, GA   **1998 to 1999**
Supervisor/Analyst, Network Operations (1998)
Project Manager/Lead Negotiator (1897 – 1998)
Access Network Manager (1996 – 1997)
- Led a team of 30 members and successfully negotiated an agreement that enabled the entry into the local service provider market.
- Successfully negotiated reform to access network-payment agreements that accounted for an increase of over $2M annually to company's bottom line.
- Participated in company's leadership-development program, for which less than 1 percent of 150,000 employees are selected.

————————————————————————— Education —————————————————————————

Iowa State University of Science and Technology, B. S. in Industrial Technology

Professional Training
Situational Leadership / Stephen R. Covey Effective Leadership
Interpersonal Effectiveness and Listening Skills / Project Management
Network Architecture / Nodal Service / ASB High-Speed Data Networking Curriculum
Internet Development and Architecture / Networks Optical Products Training

2001 recipient of the Outstanding Team Member Award for Leadership
Selected for prestigious Leadership Development Accelerated Executive Program

Alfred A. Cleveland
International and New Business Development / Relationship Management
Market and Competitive Analysis / Multilingual

7878 El Camino Real Drive
San Diego, California 99120

855-543-1991
Alfred39ACleveland@aol.com

NEW BUSINESS SPECIALIST

Sales and marketing professional with effective combination of analytical and interpersonal skills. Proven international trade expertise, especially in Europe and Asia, with emphasis in strategic planning and market development and client relationships. Advanced skills in solving key account challenges through designing country-specific sales / marketing strategy and recruiting in-country sales professionals.

Strengths include: (1) client relationship management / communication with client-company top officers; (2) strategic business planning, sales planning, market planning, and product development and management; (3) advertising, marketing, media relations, and corporate image development. Fluent in English, French, German, Dutch.

- ☑ Impressive ability to create business opportunities.
- ☑ Consistent history of accomplishments in new business / new market development.
- ☑ Top performer; ready and eager for new challenges.

Company Affiliations:

The Gap	The Limited Group	Blockbuster	Adidas
Wal-Mart	Food Lion	Home Depot	Nike

PROFESSIONAL ACHIEVEMENTS

VP MARKETING SALES   BBC, INC., SAN DIEGO / TOKYO / LONDON / PARIS / Beijing, 1995 to 20002

Directed domestic and international sales for $300 million world leader in high-technology motion and presence sensors. Prepared all objectives, budgets, and forecast. Coordinated marketing and sales for Europe and Asia, advertising and promotion activities, distribution channels, product positioning, market-management, market surveys, and competition monitoring. Served as liaison with strategic partners. Developed corporate image.

(**Led sales team to # 1 position in the world.**
- ☑ **Increased sales from $19 to $63.5 million in three years.**

MARKETING MANAGER   WILLIAMS TEXTILES, RICHMOND, VA,   1993 to 1995

Managed all marketing-consulting assignments for Fortune 1000 companies. Specialized in diagnostic analysis, strategic business plans, and establishing key relationships.

- ☑ **Contributed to repositioning that resulted in #2 position to the United States.**
- ☑ **Increased sales by $19 million in 12 months.**

MANAGEMENT CONSULTANT   DME, BRUSSELS, BELGIUM, 1992 to 1993

Completed management consulting assignment for Fortune 1000 companies, Specialized in diagnostic analysis, strategic business plans, and establishing key relationships.

EDUCATION

MBA with an emphasis in Marketing
BS Economics and Management

University of California at San Jose, CA
Vrije University, Brussels, Belgium

Note: Here we have a résumé of a senior executive; this one page résumé profiles this applicant's key company affiliations and achievements. The boldfaced print brings attention to the candidate's strengths.

PROJECT / DESIGN ENGINEER

HIGHLIGHTS OF QUALIFICATIONS

PROFESSIONAL EXPERIENCE

--Project Management
--Research and Development
--Total Quality Management
--Product Development
--Integration Techniques
--Budget / Schedule Compliance
--Production / Manufacturing
--Military Programs

--Resources Management
--Military Compliance
--Quality Assurance
--Technical Liaison
--Product Improvement
--Systems / Component
--Communication Skills
--Problem Resolution

<u>The Boeing Company</u>, Long Beach, CA
Senior Engineer, 1989-2002
- ☑ Planned, scheduled, conducted, and coordinated detailed phases of C-17 Aircraft fuel system technical projects.
- ■ Superior project skills in orchestrating, organizing, and managing.
- ■ Strong background in aircraft fuel systems and components.
- ■ Expertise in aircraft component design and specification.
- ■ Aircraft systems design and development knowledge.
- ■ Extensive laboratory testing experience.
- ■ Troubleshooting and isolation techniques on aircraft.
- ☑ Provided technical and field support to staff in production, manufacturing, technical, and engineering environments.
- ☑ Designed and coordinated parts for a new center-wing fuel system, including preparation of specifications, scheduling, and qualification of new parts. Achieved desired goals by working closely with staff at Parker Hannifin.
- ☑ Recognized for superior performance, quality, effort, and teamwork.

<u>Naval Weapons Station</u>, Seal Beach, CA
<u>Mechanical Engineer,</u> 1982-1988
- ☑ Project engineer for quality assurance, reliability, and environmental testing of complex missile systems and subcomponents.
- ■ systems and subcomponents.

<u>Naval Civil Engineering,</u> Port Hueneme, CA
Mechanical Engineer, 1980-1982
(Conducted research and development of alternative-energy for incorporation at Naval facilities.

EDUCATION

Bachelor Science Degree, Mechanical Engineering, 1979
California State University, Fullerton, CA

Note: What you can clearly see is a highly qualified applicant with 10 years of solid experience with Boeing. The highlight of his qualifications details these key areas of his ability.

Patrice P. Johnson

65432 Warm Springs, Corona 92883　　　PatP1492@aol.com　　　951-277-9451

CAREER PROFILE

A 20-year progressively responsible, professional career, in management, marketing, and HR. Consistently met or exceeded company goals, significantly impacting profits. Advanced rapidly based upon demonstrated results in: customer service / satisfaction, selection and training of personnel, merchandising, sales growth, organization, and leadership. Professional qualifications include:

- Management / Organization
- Team Building / Leadership
- Public Relations / Promotions
- Strategic Planning / Implementation
- Administrative Policies / Procedure

- Public Speaking
- Sales / Marketing
- Customer Service
- Community Outreach
- Human Resources Affairs

Experienced in MS Excel, Word, and PowerPoint; Quicken and Windows 98

PROFESSIONAL EXPERIENCE

ADMINISTRATION /MANAGEMENT: Program management, planning, development, budgeting, and supervision

- Organized, detail-oriented, and skilled in managing multiple tasks, as evidenced by supervising three department managers and 60 employees, ensured that all aspects of the departments ran effectively – merchandising, personnel, and sales plan / budget.
- Controlled shortages and inventory, exceeding company standards.
- Passed all shore audits at satisfactory above ratings.
- Earned **Team Leader of the Month** for the District.
- As interim store manager during a change in leadership, created a positive yet hard-driving environment.

'Patrice, you have added back to Odessa stores an atmosphere that is congenial and positive again.... A great turnaround from the previous level of morale...you accept challenges head on, as when you stepped into the acting Team Leader position'

--Bill Smith, Mervyn's District Manager

SALES / MARKETING: Customer relations, presentation, advertising, and marketing

- Degreed in Marketing: completed comprehensive training in advertising and marketing.
- Awarded Merchandiser of the Year from District Manager.
- Developed innovative 'survivor game' that boosted credit solicitations so that goals were met at 110%--recognized as a store leader in driving profits.
- Applied marketing concepts to achieve departmental sales success that met or exceeded company goals.

'Patrice led her teams effectively to drive sales. She has very high standards and holds her teams accountable for results.'

--Helen Geihs, District Team Leader

HUMAN RESOURCES: Personnel selection, hiring, training, and development

- Hired, trained, and developed over 2200 employees.
- Scheduled weekly over 72 personnel and reviewed time sheets for submission to payroll.
- Managed employee performance.

'...worked to performance-manage the Support Team Coordinator to help improve our in-stock numbers and get better results from that team.'

--Carman Johnson

Note: In this situation we have a highly qualified retail manager transitioning in to a new field. This applicant has 'testimonials' to verify her abilities. She is also a laid-off individual that has highlighted transferable skills in a functional format.

Patrice P. Johnson

951-277-9451 Page 2 PatP1492@aol.com

PROFESSIONAL EXPERIENCE (continued)

- ➤ Administered medical benefits.
- ➤ Maintained and documented personnel files.
- ➤ Conducted safety meetings and managed workers' comp claims.
- ➤ Assisted with college recruiting program, interviewing and hiring college graduates, four of the **Recruits became successful district team leaders.**

'Patrice took on college recruiting with the STL and helped select new management trainees for our district. She learned to asses the candidates and knows if the match was right for our stores.'

--Emil Arguello, Store Manager

COMMUNITY: Event planning and coordination

Spearheaded numerous community and company outreach events:

- ➤ Directed the Community Closet assisting 26 women from Women's Protective Services over a two-day period with personal improvement and interview training.
- ➤ Organized March of Dimes Walk-a-Thon for employees, increased participation over a 10-year period by 145%.
- ➤ Organized and implemented 'Child Spree,' a one-day event bringing 25 to 40 children to the store and soliciting donations for school attire from other businesses to help with the effort, helped 900+ children over a 16 year period. Project showed a 221% increase in donations and numbers of children served within 6 years.

EMPLOYMENT HISTORY

Experience includes retail team leader, operations manager, interim store manager, area manager, department manager, buyer, and sales and visual merchandising, Excellent record with former employers, Mervyn's in Odessa, Midland, and Lubbock (1985-2001); Cross & Cross, Alpine (1983-1985); and C. R. Anthony's , Alpine (1976-1983).

EDUCATION

B.B.A., Marketing, Sul Ross University, Alpine, TX, 1984

Received scholarships and worked throughout university studies.

Completed 16 additional graduate hours after completing degree.

Graduated with hundreds of hours of professional training, workshops, and seminars on topics such as ADA, EEO, interviewing, leveraging diversity, DISC Dimensions of Behavior, decision-making, management, marketing, sales, and others.

Excellent Professional References Provided Upon Request

Alfred F. Murphy

785 Pine Drive Corona, CA 92883
AlFMur@aol.com

Home: 951-277-8878
Cell: 951-277-8879

Health Service s Administrator

General Primary Care / HIV-AIDS / HEALTH Promotion Programs
Substance-Abuse Treatment / Diverse Patient Population

- ➤ Successful track record of delivering quality care while championing operational efficiencies.
- ➤ Expertise in management information systems and data analysis.
- ➤ Experience with budgeting, fiscal policy, third-party reimbursement, purchasing, training, research studies, OASAS funding/program regulations, and Joint Commission on the Accreditation of Healthcare Organization (JCAHO) standards.
- ➤ Effective supervisor with solid decision-making, interpersonal, and communication skills.
- ➤ Master's degree in Public Health from The University of California at Irvine, CA

Relevant Experience

UCI MEDICAL CENTER, Anaheim, CA   20+ years

Administrative Director, Substance-Abuse Treatment Program
Oversaw business operation of $6 million substance-abuse treatment program with on-site continuity and general primary care. Accountable for resource acquisition & allocation, quality-control initiatives, capital projects, and MIS. Participated in research studies of health services costs and utilization.

Administrative Director, Methadone Treatment Program
Supervised funding and operation of $3.1 million Methadone Maintenance Treatment Program, providing care to 900 patients in 3 clinics with a staff of 60. Served as on-call administrator for both drug-treatment program, and entire medical center.

Unit Supervisor, Methadone Program
Accountable for administration of clinic treating 150 patients. Involved budget administration, personnel, management, quality assurance, and regulatory compliance.

Counselor / Assistant Supervisor
Treated 75 heroin addicts maintained on methadone or in varying stages of detoxification. Confirmed eligibility and assessed needs of applicants, prepared and maintained patient charts. Assumed management responsibilities during supervisor's absence.

SELECT ACHIEVEMENTS:

- ✓ Improved consistency of clinical care and streamlined business operations by consolidating three methadone treatment clinics, with different standards and operations, into a unified treatment program, Developed policy and procedure manuals, job descriptions, and forms.

- ✓ Instrumental in creating a model program for substance abuse clinics to address AIDS-related issues early in the emergence of this epidemic. Secured funding for health educators who trained staff and patients on HIV transmission and risk reduction.

- ✓ Substantially improved the physical environment of the clinics, minimizing health risks (due to inadequate ventilation and asbestos) and increasing privacy, security, and space utilization. Obtained capital funding from governmental and private sources.

- ✓ Pioneering the successful 'one stop shopping' model of substance-abuse treatment and general and HIV-related primary care services. Provided 10,000 primary-care encounters annually without losing money, planned and implemented all aspects of linking these services from obtaining a license to establishing computer systems.

- ✓ Created a quality-assurance program that eliminated charting deficiencies and resulted in excellent reports form federal, state, and hospital review teams.

Note: What we have here is a highly qualified health-services administrator who had been laid off. In this case while presenting his specific and general skills, he also at the same time had to downplay his age. In this résumé achievements are broke into functional areas to improve readability.

Alfred F. Murphy

SELECT ACHIEVEMENTS: MANAGEMENT INFORMATION SYSTEM

(Introduced and maintained systems for collecting data from multiple locations, validating it, and importing into a database used to support business and academic projects.
(Automated the weekly process of patient Medicaid coverage verification, reducing man-hours from 24 to 2.
✓ Initiated billing commercial insurance carrier for methadone maintenance treatment and collected $50,000 in the first year.
✓ Streamlined the Medicaid accounts-receivable management system and brought in $75,000 to $100,000 per year in non-routine billing for methadone treatment.
✓ Created a system to produce data reports that has practical application in day-to-day clinic operation (such as a monthly alpha listing of all patients by caseworker) and support adherence to federal and state documentation requirements.
✓ Collected $30,000 to $50,000 annually through generating NYS OASAS-approved sliding-scale invoices for self-insured patients.

Teaching/Training Experience

PC/MIS Consultant, Data Com, Orange, CA	1989-Present
Lecturer, University of California, Fullerton, CA	1987
Lecturer / Field Instructor, Orange Coast College, Orange, CA	1982-1986

Education

Master of Public Health, University of California at Irvine, School of Public Health, Irvine, CA
Bachelor of Arts, University of California at Fullerton, CA

Memberships

American Public Health Association
American Society of Law, Medicine, and Ethics
☐New York Academy of Science

Judith Hackwood, MBA

Suite 234 - 219 South Shore Drive, San Francisco, CA 90480
Phone: 444-667-8383   E-mail: Jhackwood@aol.com

SENIOR SALES EXECUTIVE

Results-driven professional with an exemplary record of developing strategic initiatives to enhance sales. Initiate action and thrive on challenge. Entrepreneurial in business approach; able to seize opportunities: demonstrate excellent networking skills. Build profitable rapport with peers, management, consultants, clients, other stakeholders. Capable of critically evaluating and responding to diverse sales patterns and trends. Recognized as an inspirational, motivational manager who celebrates diversity and proactively leads and challenges a sales team. Tactful and diplomatic communicator able to disseminate ideas and generate action across all levels of an organization. Exude energy and enthusiasm. Consistently meet or exceed sales targets. Critically analyze the marketplace with respect to feasibility and profitability.

PROFESSIONAL EXPERIENCE

Southwestern Giftware, Inc.. Dallas, Texas
Held the following 5 progressively responsible positions prior to downsizing:
DIVISION SALES MANAGER, BAY AREA, San Francisco, CA   1998-2001
- Directly accountable for generating the following unprecedented revenue growth in Premier Giftware's second largest sales base in the United States.

	2001	2000	1999
Revenue Increase	$453,787	$945,718	$2,023,620
Order Count Increase	2,584	3,326	3,332
Average Order Increase	$4.74	$1.73	$8.09
Area % Increase vs. National	2.6% to 1.2%	4% to 2.7%	9.4% to 7.1%
Renewal Rate %	70.2 to 100+%	72.3% to 100+%	83.2% to 100+%
Rep. Count Growth	2.9%	3.1%	3.5%
Fundraising	54.2% vs. 2000	47.7% vs. 1999	199.7% vs. forecast

- Won the following prestigious award for impressive sales strategies, team leadership. And overall revenue growth.
- Directed 21 geographically dispersed Sales Managers dispersed Sales Managers within the Northern California Territory.
- Oversaw recruitment, training and development, human-resource issues.
- Selected by corporate head office to initiate, administer, and test Premier Giftware's MLM project.
- Devised implemented, and monitored the territory's $7 million operation budget.
- Created unique and aggressive marketing strategies, coupled with motivational incentive programs, designed to elevate, sales.
- Initiated partnerships with community groups to facilitate fundraising and escalate Premier Giftware's profile and market share.
- Acknowledge by staff for instilling confidence, enthusiasm, and encouragement to deliver and optimum performance.
- Pinpointed community and trade events, using sale booths to promote the 'Great Buy, Great Sale' plan and achieving phenomenal sales activity and growth.

2000	1999
National Leader - "Best Decile" (Coverage & productivity)	National Leader - "Staff Gain"
3rd Place - "World Sales Leader"	3rd - "World Sales Leader"

- Planned, organized, and facilitated staff-appreciation banquets for the presentation of awards.

Note: In this résumé the applicant uses tables to bring attention to sales results. This is a striking approach to stress ability and success.

JUDITH Hachwood, MBA   Page 2

MANAGEMENT ASSOCIATE

- **Acknowledged by senior sales management for producing outstanding result in the 1998 fourth quarter in the following areas:**

DIVISION SALES TRAINER   1992-1998

- Seconded to New York for four months after selection by Vice President-Sales, West Coast, to develop comprehensive manuals and training course for the U.S marketplace.
- Developed and delivered the 'Premier Giftware National Recruiting' seminar and trained Premier Giftware personnel to implement program across the country.
- Taught Sales Managers in a classroom or field environment: Prospect Marketing, Presentation Skills, Planning and Organizing, and Understanding Business Opportunities for Growth.
- Selected to test the new Representative Development Program; provided training to National Sales Managers; played the key role in the national launch of the 'Train the Trainer' program.

NATIONAL SALES TRAINER

- Conceived and designed the 'District Manager Guide to Premier Giftware,' an informative manual still utilized by Premier Giftware 12 years later.
- Recognized as the youngest National Sales Trainer in the U.S.
- Devised and conducted the wee-long Premier Giftware Training Modules I and II, provided to District Sales Managers semiannually.

DISTRICT SALES MANAGER

- Named 'Sales Manager of the Year' in 1988 for 19% revenue increase, in territory, one of only 3 in the Western U.S.
- Achieved 'The Circle of Excellence' in 1989 for 32% revenue increase, the top 10% in the U.S.
- Employed, trained, motivated, and managed 450 independent Sales Consultants.
- Surpassed sales and profit objectives established by senior management in 1988 by 2.9% and 1989 by 33.1%.

EDUCATION

California State University, Fullerton, CA   1996
MASTER OF BUSINESS ADMINISTRATION

California State University, Fullerton, CA   1990
BACHELOR OF ARTS – Mass Communications

Fashion Institute of Hollywood, CA   1985
DIPLOMA – Mass Merchandising

Selected courses, workshops, and seminars have included the following subjects:

Leadership	Instructional Tehniques	Six Thinking Hats
Train the Trainer	Instructor raining	Motivation for Impact
Action Writing	Managing People, Process & Preformance	Dealing with Difficult People
The :eadersjo[Grid	Behavioral Interviewing	Instructional Design

Peter P. Sellers

2346 Clearview Road
Fontana, CA 92564
909-790-0766
PeterP.@yahoo.com

Summary of Qualifications

Project Management
Planning
  Organization
  Work Plans
  Subcontractors
Control
  Budget/Schedule
  Documentation
Execution
  Communications
  Quality Control
  Technical Quality
  Health & Safety

Supervision & Team
Leadership

Motivational "We Can
Do It" Attitude

Training & Career
Development for Field
Operations Personnel

Working Superfund
Knowledge
  RCRA, TSCA,
  CERCLA,
  SARA, UST, CWA

Emergency Response/
Crisis Management
  Site Assessments
  System Design &
    Installation
Solidification &
  Stabilzation
Cleanup & Shutdown
Electrical & Plumbing
  Maintenance

Contaminants Experience
  Hydrocabons
  Pesticides
  Toxic Metals
  Explosives
  Radioactive Materials
  PCBs

Hand-charging **OPERATIONS MANAGER** with 20+ years of sound environmental project experience in all aspectsof planning and implementing site remediation and closure while reducing cost and achieving regulatory compliance. Strong leadership skills demonstrated by an instinctive ability to guide and motivate a diverse workforce to work at optimum levels in a fast-paced environment.

Professional Experience

XYZ Corporation (formerly ABC CORPORATION), Fontana, CA
A member company of the Fortune 1000 XYZ Group, XYZ CORPORATION is a leading environmental – and facilities-management from with 8,000+ employees at 83 nationwide locations.

Operations Resource Manager of Craft Labor

- Directed a craft labor pool of 1500+ with 14 staff coordinators' assistance.
- Deployed key field workers to numerous ongoing projects, maintaining a 98% billable rate at XYZ, and ABC during the merger.

ABC REMEDIATION SERVICES CORPORATION, Riverside, CA

Regional Operations Manager
- Established objectives and directed 300+field personnel in a 13-state Madwest region, maintaining a 93% billable rate as Regional Operations Manager.
- Organized interview and training process for multiple candidates for local projects as well resources offices.

Site Superintendent
Investigated, analyzed, and identified objectives for remedial action/cleanups, monitored project teams; managed outside liaison affairs with contractors and regulatory-agency personnel to successfully complete disposal actions.

- USACE IT Industries/Bakercorp Superfund Site, Chino, CA
  Coordinated remediation of 50,000 tons of lead-contaminated soil from 150 residential sites two weeks ahead of schedule and $500,000 under budget, leading to additional remedial activity of $1M per month for XYZ. Awarded USACE North Central Division "Best Safety Program for Large Construction Contractor," 1995.
- Other Cleanup Sites USACE: Colton, CA; Rialto, CA
                          USEPA, Ontario, CA

Senior Electrician
- Installed electrical, plumbing, and gas systems in decontamination, office, lab, and propect site
- Maintained electrical and plumbing systems: equipment, controls, and pumps.

EDUCATION/SPECIALIZED TRAINING

UNIVERSITY of CALIFORNIA, Riverside, CA
        B.S., Environmental Safety and Occupational Health Management

Certified Hazardous Materials Management Training, University of California OSHA: 40-hours Sepervisors' Training, 40-hour HAZWOPER Training Approved USEPA Response Manger for EPA Regionsl, II, III, & V Nuclear-Reaction, Chemically Contaminated First Aid for Self & Victims, and Related Decontamination Procedures

Note: In this resume the applicant used the column on the left to summarize key-word qualifications. This resume is packed with relevant experiences and achievements.

Sally M. Kight

1812 Centry Road
Riverside, CA 92884

SMKight@hotmail.com

Home: 951-277-0437

Profile

Dynamic, creeative designer offering extensive experience in a wide variety of venues: special events, theatre / stage, and retail. Scope of knowledge includes set design, lighting, and sound effects. Resourceful, felxble individual, with an ability to effectively solve problems quickly, and consistent, sharp eye on 'the big picture.'

Education

University of California at Riverside, CA
B.A. Candidate, Technical Theatre

January 2001 to Present

Relevant Course: Scene Design, Scene Building, Costume Construction

John Moore University, Liverpool, England
Fashion & Texile Studies

1980 to 1982

Relevant Courses: Fashion Design, Textile Design, Color, Life Drawing, Fine Art, Art History, Communication Art, Fashion Drawing, Apparel Fabric, Fashion Show Production, Silk Screen, Painting, Etching, Woven Design, and Print Design

ST. HELENS COLLEGE OF ART & DESIGN, ST. Helens, England
Art & Design Studies

1978 to 1979

EMPLOYMENT

EVENT COORDINATOR Orange, CA
Center Stage Events

1999 TO 2001

Planned and executed all logistics for exclusive, large-scale corporate, ploitical, and social events.

- Carried out the opiening welcome party at the Music & Arts Academy for the 200 Republican National Convention's California delegates, an event featuring a cocktail gathering, entertainment, and dessert, coffee, and cordials on the stage.
- Coordinated a bruch for 1,000 guest at Radance Square, featuring former First Lady Nacy Reagan as leynote speaker.

EXECUTIVE DIRECTOR
The Main Events, Orange, CA

Directed sales, managed a sales team, and personally conducted presentation, using design and space-planning expertise expertise to successfully communicate themes and concepts to clients.

- Organized the opening of the Hawaii National Convention Center. Supervised set construction, Coordinated the vive-day series of event, most notably the opening black-tie gala with 2,000 guests and an outdoor lei-tying coremony with local government figures. Led a team in coordination log-distance equipment transport as well as local rentals.
- Conceived and facilitated the stage and ambient lighting design for the opening of Orange County Convention Center, transforming the convention hall into an elegant event space, Subsequently carried out numerous logistical duties, including aneging communications with rival unions.
- Directed a major events for Young & Watson, LLP, the 25th anniversary of thier Entrepreneur of Year. Incorporated lighting and special sound effects to keep interest high. Designed lighting, sound, and a set intermingling the Orange County skyline and the Entrepreneur award itself. Finally, constructed a laser tunnel as a quest passageway from dinner to dessert and dancing.

Note: As you can see this applicants résumé brings together current goals and recent education to maximize the impact of this résumé.

435

7001 Resumes-Plus Second Edition

Now that you have had a chance to review a variety of résumés, you can adopt or modify any one of them to meet your needs or use a combination to present your background and experience; or you can develop one of your own from scratch.

Let me point out my philosophy and the philosophy of many others on résumé style; the best résumé style is the one that gets you the job. However, many will argue in favor of the Chronological résumé while others might say the Combination résumé is better. I believe that in this book I have suggested that you present data in your résumé in the best light that makes you look like the best candidate for the job you are applying for.

However, I would like to say a few words about presentation and your résumé as an art form. I myself would be impressed with a résumé or applicant that took the time to design a résumé that showed creativity and that was prepared to impress the reader, but that is me. You will find that this may or may not be the case with many others, and it certainly is not the case if you are presenting your résumé over the Internet. What I am going to suggest here is that you keep your résumé simple, concise, and to the point; and try to incorporate what you have accomplished in relationship with what the company is asking or looking for. I am going to suggest that you use their words, phrases, and statements, but do not lie or make stuff up. You may get the job, but if they find out you lied, this is grounds for dismissal.

The reason I am suggesting you use their statements, phrases, and wording is simple; many companies that do job search on the Internet employ programs that are specifically looking in these areas and will dismiss, reject, or disqualify those applicants that do not have them. Personally I am not impressed with job search on the internet, but I am from the old school and still believe in face to face, and that there is more to people or individuals than paper, but you are not going to work for me and this seems to be the trend at this time. But I am a guy that likes to talk to a person when you call a company and not an answering machine, shame on me huh!

My choice is the Tailor-made résumé; you will design it to match the ad or job announcement that you see in the Newspaper, Magazine, or on the Internet. I know this is a

436

The Job Search Tool to Get You That Job

lot of work to create or prepare a new résumé every time, but you can save the basic design on a disk if you do not have a computer; I save mine on both just in case. Sometimes I look for a lecture position, or I use my résumé to 'test' some of the job search engines that I find. Also, remember you are looking for a job and you need to do whatever it takes to put yourself in the best light you can. Plus, I think you forget sometimes that we are competing, in most cases, against hundreds of other applicants or even more. I remember several years ago I was applying for a Sales Manager position at 'Staples' and was told that there were over 80 applicants. If you are applying in good times on the Internet I would suggest that the number could be in the hundreds if not more. So if you're going to take the time to apply for the position; do it right!

Now you will want this 'one' clean and crisp résumé, and even your cover letter, on a disk or USB flash drive that is easy to get to, also backed up on your hard drive because you will be asked to down load it. You have saved them so they can be easily accessed.

MARKET STUDY PACKAGE:

Use this page to plan and lay-out your job search program

CHAPTER TWENTY-NINE

TOP 100 COMPANIES IN THE COUNTY

In this chapter, we are going to explore the top companies in America that would be worthwhile in taking your time to apply. Along with getting prepared to do job search one thing I am going to suggest is a number of places that you might want to consider for long-term employment. The following information is not just going to be an opinion, but the companies that you find in this chapter will be based upon researched data, and information that I have compiled.

I will try to give you as many facts as I can and avoid hear say information. However, I cannot guarantee that with this information in hand you are going to get your first choice. There may be many facts that contribute to your being able to get the job of your choice or the number one company in the industry. You may not have all the qualifications necessary, or, it may not be the right time, or it may be necessary that you would have to relocate, and the list goes on.

Some years ago, I went to work for one of the top companies on this list: Proctor-Gamble. You will find that it is <u>68</u> on this list. My experience was I found that the division I worked for was some what run Military like, in my view, I hadn't been out of the military very long, I was not comfortable with this type of management style and sales organization, and I did not like selling in the Soap Division; so I left. I wanted something different. However, you

439

7001 Resumes-Plus Second Edition

can set your sites and work towards your objective and needs. I want to say this, that during my career, I have worked for at least two if not more top companies in Business and Industry. Nevertheless, as my needs changed I had to find something that met those needs and you may too. I think what I am trying to say is do not feel disappointed if you have to settle for number two or three, at least during the beginning of your career. That's not bad and you can always work your way up to where you want to be, as well as make the moves that put you in the right place to reach that dream job and top company.

WHAT MAKES A GREAT PLACE TO WORK

Any company can be a great place to work.

The trust between managers and employees is the primary defining characteristic of the very best workplaces. At the heart of this definition of the great place to work is a place where employees: *trust the people they work for, have pride in what they are doing, and enjoy the people they work for for having pride in what a great workplace is measured by, the quality of the three interconnected relationships that exist there:*

(The relationship between employees and management.

(The relationship between employees and their job / company.

(The relationship between employees and others.

1. Google
2. Genentech
3. Wegmans Food Markets
4. Container Store
5. Whole Foods Market
6. Network Appliance
7. S. C. Johnson & Son
8. Boston Consulting Group
9. Methodist Hospital System
10. W.L. Gore & Associates

The Job Search Tool to Get You That Job

11. Cisco Systems
12. David Weekley Homes
13. Nugget Market
14. Qualcomm
15. American Century Investments
16. Starbucks
17. Quicken Loans
18. Station Casinos
19. Alston & Bird
20. QuikTrip
21. Griffin Hospital
22. Valero Energy
23. Vision Service Plan
24. Nordstrom
25. Ernst & Young
26. Arnold & Porter
27. Recreational Equipment, Inc. (RET)
28. Kimley-Horn and Associates
29. Edward James
30. Russell Investment Group
31. Adobe Systems
32. Plante & Moran
33. Intuit
34. Umpqua Bank
35. Children's healthcare of Atlanta
36. Goldman Sachs
37. Northwest Community Healthcare
38. Robert W. Baird
39. J.M. Smucker Company
40. Amgen
41. JM Family Enterprises
42. PCL Construction
43. Genzyme

7001 Resumes-Plus Second Edition

44. Yahoo!

45. Bain & Company

46. First Horizon National

47. American Fidelity Assurance

48. SAS Institute

49. Nixon Peabody

50. Microsoft

51. Stew Leonard's

52. Ohio Health

53. four Seasons Hotels

54. Baptist Health Care

55. Dow Corning

56. Granite Construction

57. Publix Super Markets

58. PricewaterhouseCoopers

59. Pella

60. MITRE

61. SRA International

62. Mayo Clinic

63. Booz Allen Hamilton

64. Perkins Cole

65. Alcon Laboratories

66. Jones Lang LaSalle

67. HomeBanc Mortgage

68. Procter & Gamble

69. Nike

70. Paychex

71. AstraZeneca

72. Medtronic

73. Aflac

74. American Express

75. Quad/Graphics

76. Deloitte & Touche USA

77. Principal Financial Group

78. Timberland

79. TDIndustries

80. Lehigh valley Hospital and Health Network

81. Baptist Health South Florida

82. CDW

83. EOG Resources

84. Capital One Financial

85. Standard Pacific

86. National Instruments

87. Texas Instruments

88. CarMax

89. Marriott International

90. Men's Wearhouse

91. Memorial Health

92. Bright Horizons Family Solutions

93. Milliken

94. Bingham McCutchen

95. Vanguard

96. IKEA North America

97. KPMG

98. Synovus

99. A.G. Edwards

100. Stanley

<u>WHAT MAKES THESE COMPANIES SO GREAT</u>

I am going to provide you compiled information about a number of companies that suggest why individuals and employees believe these companies are the best to work for. These firms are considered the <u>top</u> companies in America. Take the time to read and evaluate the information given to see if these companies fit what you are looking for in an employer. You may find one or more of these firms meet your need for long-term employment. However, you

7001 Resumes-Plus Second Edition

will also discover that you may have to re-locate to go to work for one of these firms if you are selected to be one of their employees. It may be very necessary when advancing your career to be very flexible as to where you are willing to live. What I want to point out is that the following firms have been identified as the top companies to work for, but are not necessarily in order of preference.

Valero Energy

This is a San Antonio headquartered company with revenue of $54,691 million a year. What makes this company great is when disaster hit this team seemed to pull together. It supplied goods and temporary housing for its employees and donated $1 million to the Red Cross. The company had 701 new jobs in one year and boasted a 26% turn-over. The average annual income in this company is Store Manager – Retail at $38,227. The most common job is hourly customer service.

Griffin Hospital

The Griffin Hospital is headquartered in Derby, Connecticut with revenues of 87 million dollars. The hospital employs 1,049 with 10% being minorities, 78% of the employees are women. You will find that the hospital boasts an 8% voluntary turnover. What is interesting about this hospital is that even with a pay scale 5% to 7% lower than other hospitals in the area they receive 5,100 applications for a range of 160 open positions in 2005. This is largely due to its top-notch reputation for patient care. The most common job (hourly) is registered Nurse with an average pay of $64,454.

Wegmans Food Markets

Wegmans is a large company in the Food and Drug business. You will find their headquarters in Rochester, New York. The company is privately held; it's a real family business. Before it opened two new stores last year, Wegmans chartered a jet to fly all new full-time employees to Rochester to be welcomed by the CEO, Danny Wegman. The company has 31,890 employees with 15% being minorities and 54% women.

The most common job (salaried) is Store Department Manager with an average income of $46,741 and the most common job (hourly) Customer Service with an average pay of $26,047.

The company is quoting an 8 percent voluntary turnover rate. At Wegmans you will find a job growth in one year of 7 percent. The company provides 40 hours of professional training a year. Going to work for this firm you will find challenging with a 127,588 applicants to contend with.

W.L. Gore & Associates

The headquarters of W.L. Gore & Associates is in Newark, Delaware. The company is a High-Tech Manufacturer, and ranked as a midsized company. What is interesting in this firm is the fact that you will find no bosses, job titles or organization charts, just sponsors, team members, and leaders. The company has 4,537 employees with 2,247 employees working outside the country. The company boasts 15% of their workforce being minorities with 40 percent women. New job development was 261 for one year, and the job growth is 6 percent.

You will also find that the company has a low level of turnover, with a 5% voluntary ratio. During the year the company offers 18 hours of professional training.

The most common job (salaried) is Field Sales Associate, and the most common job (hourly) is Medical Device Assembler. What you might find interesting is that 37,936 people apply to work for this firm.

7001 Resumes-Plus Second Edition

Container Store

This midsized 375 million dollar firm is headquartered in Coppel, Texas. You will find that this company is in the Specialty Retailer business. The firm has 36 sites in the United States and boasts 2,857 employees with 400 working outside the country. You will find that 29 percent of the workforce are minorities with 62% being women. At this storage retailer, even part-timers can receive bonuses, and drivers are rewarded for long service and safety driving records. In 2004 one driver took home $5,000 for ten years of perfect driving.

The company indicates new job development for one year at 117, with 18 percent of voluntary turnover. The company also offers a whopping 108 hours of professional training. The most common job (salaried) is Store Sales with an average annual pay of $40,394 and the most common job (hourly) is Distribution Center with an income of $29,227.

I would suggest the only down side here is the fact that this company receives 31,794 applications a year so you have your job cut out for you to beat out the competition if you are interested in employment at this firm.

Vision Service Plan

If you are interested in the Health Care industry, you may want to consider this Rancho Cordova, California Company. This small firm employs 1,915 people in the United States of which 30 percent of them are minority, and 68% of them are women.

Unfortunately the company's new jobs are down and the growth is down. However if you have gotten a job with this firm you will find that they provide 40 hours of professional training. The most common job (salaried) is Application Developer $91,699, and the most common job (hourly) is Customer Service Representative II at $33,993. The company receives about 8,653 applicants a year.

J.M. Smucker

I have worked with this small food company and found it an interesting firm to be involved with. This 109-year old jam and food company has family feelings that are still sweet. Tim and Richard Smucker, two brothers, are still at the wheel. What is interesting is that employees interview job applicants to make sure future colleagues will fit in to the company culture.

The company employs 2,930 employees in the United States with about 1,047 who are employed outside the country. You will find 24 percent of the employees are minorities or which 44 percent are women. Job growth is down this year. But the upside the company can boast of a voluntary turnover of only 5%. However, if you do find a position with this firm you can plan on 90 hours of professional training.

The most common job (salaried) is Production Supervisor with an average income of $51,165 and the most common job (hourly) is Customer Service Representative at $32,527. Getting employed at this firm is competitive with the 9,500 applicants they get a year.

Note: Information herein on U.S. employees include part-timers as the time of the survey, job growth, new jobs, and voluntary turnover are full-time only. Average annual pay: yearly pay rate plus additional cash compensation for the largest classification of salaried and hourly employees. Revenues are for 2004 or latest fiscal year. All data based on U.S. employee

Relocation

One of the things that I have to point out and stress is if you are interested in a great many of these companies, it is important that you stay flexible and be willing to relocate. The more flexible you are the better able you will be to take advantage of these job opportunities. It is very simple; you must go where the jobs are.

7001 Resumes-Plus Second Edition

Some of you may be in an area that you can take full advantage of job opportunities and some of you may not. This will be a decision each one of you will have to make to further your career. I will share this with you, and your conscious will have to be your guide.

Easily, in my career, I wanted to teach at the Junior College level and I could have, however, I was unwilling to make the move to a small community where the opportunities were. As a result I was never ever able to get a full-time position, the best I could do was teach as an Adjunct professor at several Junior Colleges because of the competition and timing in the large communities where I have lived.

Point being, I was not willing to relocate to take advantage of the opportunity at the time. I have had many other interesting and stimulating opportunities, but I had to give up this one dream for other career choices.

Genentech

Here we have a midsized Biotechnology firm ranked number one. This company is headquartered in South Francisco, California. What makes this company better? First the firm is a cancer-fighting organization and being a valued member can be a good thing. Employees find working for this company motivating, and 95% of the workers are shareholders so they benefit handsomely from soaring stock value.

The company employs 8,121 in the United States, with two outside the county. Of the total employees 42 percent are minorities, with 50% being woman. The company can boast 1,364 new jobs in one year, and has reported only a 5% voluntary turnover.

The percent of job growth for one year was 20%.

You will find if you are employed by this firm you get 51 hours of professional training. The most common job (salaried) is Research Associate with an average annual pay of $69,425, the most common job (hourly) you will find is Mfg. Technician with an average annual income

448

The Job Search Tool to Get You That Job

of $47,817. If you are interested in going to work for this firm it is important that you be aware of the fact that this company receives 246,000 applicants a year.

Recreational Equipment

This Specially Retailer was ranked 45th in 2005, but has moved to number 5. You will find this midsized company headquartered in Kent, Washington. The company has 7,443 employees in the United States and you will find that the common ground that unites the company employees with its customers is the passion for roughing it. The company regularly hosts environmental-service projects.

Here at Recreational Equipment you will find 12 percent of the employees are minorities, with 40% being woman. The company has created 192 new jobs in one year with a job growth of 9 percent. The firm offers 30 hours a year of Professional training.

The most common job (salaried) is Retail Store Manager at an average annual pay of $80,144, and the most common job (hourly) Retail Sales Specialist with an average annual income of $21,835. The company quotes a 12 percent voluntary turnover. This organization sees 23,166 applicants a year.

S.C. Johnson

For those interested in living in the mid-west you should take a look at S.C. Johnson whose headquarters is in Racine, Wisconsin. This is a family-owned consumer-products manufacture that has a devoted workforce. Witness to this company loyalty is a low 2 percent voluntary turnover, which is nearly unheard of. The company has 3,404 employees here in the United States with 6,596 employees outside of our county. You will find 15% minorities, with 36 percent women. The company only reported an 8 percent new job rate, with a zero percent of job growth. However, the company does provide 40 hours of Professional training a year.

7001 Resumes-Plus Second Edition

The most common job (salaried) is Sr. Research Scientist at an average annual pay of $102,161 and the most common job (hourly) is Assoc- Production with a salary of $58,300. The company has 6,131 applicants a year.

Plante & Moran

What we will find here is a consulting service firm that is ranked number 4 for a small company. This firm is headquartered in Southfield, MI. You will find this is a 196 million dollar company. What is interesting about this firm is that they work hard to have a 'jerk-free' workforce. The employees are encouraged to live by the Golden Rule and abide by the credo 'Speak up! If it is not right, we'll change it.'

The company has 1,356 employees in the United States, with no employees outside the country. Five percent of the employees are minorities with 56% being women. The company boasts 102 new jobs with a job growth (one year) of 9 percent. This firm has 60 hours of professional training a year.

The most common job (salaried) is Auditor at $65,000 annual average and the most common job (hourly) is Secretary at $32, 600 annual average. If this is the kind of firm you like to work for you will be facing around 6,000 applicants of competition.

Intuit

Here at Intuit, who are financial software developers (Quicken, Turbo Tax); the employees get to make suggestions to the CEO, Steve Bennell, at a quarterly Web cast which leads to more vacation time for longtime employees. The company is headquartered in Mountain View, California and has locations also in San Diego, and Tucson. They are ranked 17th.

Sunnyvale is a nice place to live and the brainiacs at Intuit know how to party. The inventors of Quicken, TurboTax, and other financial tools, are legendary for their Friday afternoon socials, summer cookouts, and beach parties at the end of tax season. My kind of company!

You will find that the firm employs 6, 889 employees in the United States and 466 out of country. The company boasts of 387 new jobs with a job growth of 6 percent. You will find that there is about a 12% voluntary turnover. I might suggest that going to work for this firm is very competitive with the company receiving 112,906 applications a year. The percentage of minorities working for this firm is 25 percent with 45% of the employees being women.

The most common job (salaried) is Software Engineering; average annual pay is not available. The most common jobs (hourly) is Technical Support; no information on pay available.

Umpqua Bank

This community bank, which we find headquartered in Portland, Oregon and with 131 offices on the West Coast, allows employees 40 hours a year of volunteer work. You will also find lobbies of some 'stores' offering free internet access and complimentary coffee (Umpqua's own blended roast).

The company employs 1,435 employees in the United States with no employees outside the country. The company has 95 new jobs with an 8 percent job growth, and a voluntary turnover of 20 percent which is a little high, but I have data on the reason way. You will find that this firm receives about 1,818 applicants a year. An area of interest, unlike many companies, this firm offers a job sharing program.

The most common job (salaried) is Store Manager at an average annual salary of $50,078 and the most common job (hourly) is Universal Associate at $26,162 average annually. The company offers 42 hours professional training, but does not offer a paid sabbatical, however they do have a 100% paid health care coverage. You will discover that 11 percent of the employees are minority with 77% of the workforce being women. This firm also has a nondiscrimination policy that includes sexual orientation.

In addition, you will find that this firm offers 24-hour ATM banking, and features extended business hours: Monday through Thursday 9 a.m. to 5 p.m. and Friday until 6 p.m. and Saturday from 10 a. m. to 2 p.m. The company is designing new neighborhood stores that feature distinctive merchandise form local businesses.

Children's Healthcare of Atlanta

This pediatric hospital system is regarded as one of the country's top hospitals of its kind. By adding a 'manager of work-life balance', his job is to keep adding amenities like backup care for children and the elderly, and such. You will find that this firm had 294 new jobs with a one year job growth of 7 percent. The hospital reports a 9 % voluntary turnover. It is reported that the hospital gets 43,039 applicants a year.

The most common job (salaried) is Business operations Coordinator at $42,354 average annual pay and the most common job (hourly) is staff Nurse Colleague at $63, 228 annual average income. The hospital does offer a job sharing program, and has 20 hours of professional training a year. You will find that the hospital does not offer any type of sabbatical or 100% health care.

Forty-one percent of the employees are minorities and 82% of the employees are woman. It is estimated that there will be 120,000 additional children in metro Atlanta by 2009. They will have a need for talented employees and dedicated volunteers. Children's Healthcare has been recognized as a premier employer by Fortune magazine.

Goldman Sachs

What we have here is a Wall Street firm that offers great salaries, plus for the company made up to $6,000 in contributions to eligible 401(k) accounts. The company employs 12,542 in the United States and 8,924 employees outside of the county. The company had in one year

THE JOB SEARCH TOOL TO GET YOU THAT JOB

655 new jobs with a job growth of 6 percent. The voluntary turnover at this firm is 10%. You will find amazingly 70,220 applicants applying to this firm.

The most common job (salaried) is Analyst, Program Analyst, and Associate at an average annual pay of $129,000. The company does offer job sharing programs and also 33 hours of professional training. You will find that the company offers a sabbatical program but doesn't off 100% health care coverage. 31 percent of the employees are minorities and 35% are women.

Northwest Community Hospital

I think that you will find it interesting that this is the second hospital that has scored extremely high on the best company list. Northwest Community has revenues of 942 million, is headquartered in Arlington, Ill, and is also located in Buffalo Grove, and Schaumburg.

What makes this company/hospital so great is employees enjoy benefits not commonly found in hospitals. There is a $3,500 tuition reimbursement, enhanced loans for nursing or radiology school, concierge service, and a $5,000 forgivable loan to buy a new home. There are 3,299 U.S. employees. The hospital reports 95 new jobs with a job growth of 7 percent; and a very low 4 % voluntary turnover. With some very unique 'Perks' the hospital had 8,800 job applicants.

The most common job (salaried) is Clinical Coordinator with an average annual pay of $81,224 and the most common job (hourly) is Acute Care Staff Nurse with an average annual pay of $67,245. The hospital does offer a job share program and offers 52 hours of professional training. Twenty-six percent of the employees are minorities and 83 percent are women.

Robert W. Baird

You will find that this is one of the top three out of 74 investment advisor firms. The company is employee-owned and they believe in a personal touch. New hires often are greeted with flowers and meet with the CEO at an event for new associates. The company employs

7001 Resumes-Plus Second Edition

2,080 in the United States and 75 outside the county. The company reports a -2 percent of job growth for the year, with a voluntary turnover of 10 percent.

The most common job (salaried) is Financial Analyst with an average annual pay of $116,000 and the most common job (hourly) is Client Relationship Assistant with an annual pay of $37,900. You will find that the company offers job sharing, and 186 hours of Professional training a year. Forty-four percent of the employees are woman, with 6% of the employees being minorities. This firm reports that they have 13,029 applicants a year.

Milliken

This family founded textile company Headquartered in Spartanburg, SC is ranked 38th in best companies. There seems to be great employee affection for the companies CEO, Roger Milliken. 'They feel thankful that someone in this country cares about the American worker and what he stands for'.

The company was founded in 1865 and employs 9,300 in the United States and has 1,700 people outside the country. The company is made up of 38 percent minorities and 38% are women. Unfortunately the jobs are down by 300 positions, or a job growth of a -3 percent. The company does offer 57 hours a year of professional training, and shows a voluntary turnover of 13 percent. The company is reporting no applicants.

The most common job (salaried) is Product/Process Improvement with an average annual pay of $60,000, and the most common job (hourly) is Machine Operator with an average annual pay of $30,000.

Amgen

We will find this top Pharmaceutical Headquartered in Thousand Oaks, California. This biotech leader keeps their employees onboard by giving generous benefits. One important benefit is the fact that the company offers a generous 90 percent contribution toward health-insurance premiums, and an automatic 5% 401(k) company contribution with a 5% match, plus 16 paid holidays.

They employ 11, 374 persons in the United States with 3,461 outside of the county. Of these employees 28 percent are minorities with 49 percent being woman. The company has added 649 jobs or a job growth of 6 percent. They offer 80 hours of professional training a year. We see a voluntary turnover of 8 percent, and some 63,114 job applicants; so if you are interested in this firm get your résumé and application in early and make sure it is correct.

JM Family Enterprises

You will find this largest distributor of Toyota offering perks. This Automotive Retailer Services offers a free good grooming with their hair and nail salon on site. Located in Deerfield Beach, Florida it has been socking away 15% of pay for their employees via profit sharing every year since 1969.

The company employs 4,114 people in the United States with no employees out of country. The company has developed 333 new jobs with a job growth of 9 percent. You find a slightly high voluntary turnover of 15 percent. With this firm you will experience 35 hours of professional training a year.

The most common job (salaried) is District Manager, JM&A Group (a subsidiary) with an average annual pay of $118,950.00 and the most common job (hourly) Customer Account Representative with an average annual pay of $31,180.00. Don't be surprised when you discover that there are 11,227 applicants.

Timberland

If you are interested in working for a small top company, Timberland just might be your company. You will find the firm headquartered in Stratham, NH. This company is a boot and outdoor gear label. The attitude in this firm is to help save the world. To do this, employees who buy a hybrid car get $3,000 credit, and the company pays for up to 40 hours of volunteer work in the community.

You will find 1,975 employees in the U.S. with 3,307 working outside the country. Thirty-one percent of the employees are minorities, with 51% being women. New jobs are down by a -26 or a job growth of -2 percent. You will find the company reporting a 15 percent voluntary turnover. The company offers 38 hours of professional training.

The most common job (salaried) is Manager Store Sales with an average annual pay of $53,509 and the most common job (hourly) is Assistant Manager Sales with an average annual pay of $26,167. This company reports 48,300 applicants a year.

Boston Consulting Group

You will find that Boston Consulting is ranked 3rd as small companies. They are headquartered in Boston, MA. The overall attitude in this firm is knowledge really is power. When you arrive at this management consulting firm with a B.A., the firm will send you to a top institution for a MBA, pick up the tuition bill, and double your salary if you agree to stay on.

The company employs 1,261 individuals in the United States with 3,868 outside the county. Twenty percent of the workers are minorities, with 44% being women. It is reported that new jobs are 167, or a job growth of 17 percent. In spite of the education and income benefits the company reports a voluntary turnover of 12 percent.

While employed at this firm you will find a whopping 106 hours of professional training a year. The most common job (salaried) is Consultant with an average annual pay of $120,776 and Most common job (hourly) Executive Assistant at an average annual income of $56,477. You will find applying to this firm somewhat competitive with 20,186 applicants.

Quicken loans

This midsized commercial bank ranking 7th is headquartered in Livonia, MI. A supercharged mantra culture rules at this mortgage bank. Saying such things as: 'Every client, Every Time', and 'No exceptions, No excuses' are plastered on posters, t-shirts, travel mugs, notepads, and portfolios.

The company employs 2,951 individuals in the United States with no out of county employees. Of these, 19 percent are minorities and 52% are women. The company has developed 1,093 jobs showing a new job growth of a whopping 60 percent. But I am sad to report that this firm has a depressing 23 percent voluntary turnover rate. If you go to work for this firm you will experience a 250 hours of professional training a year.

The most common job (salaried) is Web Mortgage Banker with an average annual income $76,400, and the most common job (hourly) is Loan Analyst with an average annual income of $38,250. The company gets 40,258 applicants a year.

HomeBanc Mortgage

Do you want to work for a spiritual mortgage bank? If so here you go, this company frequently opens meetings with Prayers. This firm is headquartered in Atlanta, GA. In 2004/05 they reported revenues of 57 million dollars. The company has 1,342 employees in the United States with no people overseas. 24 percent of the company's work force is minorities with 53 percent women. This company has 105 new jobs or a 9 percent job growth rate with a voluntary turnover of 10 percent and offers 131 hours of professional training.

The most common job (salaried) is Underwriter with an average annual income of $57,942. The most common job (hourly) is Customer Service Specialist with an average annual income of $38, 671. HomeBanc reports an annual applicant rate of 24,000.

7001 Resumes-Plus Second Edition

Whole Foods Market

Want to work for a Food and Drug Store chain? Why not this one? With its headquarters in Austin, Texas, Whole Foods Market is one of the top ranking large companies in this category. You will find employees up and down this food chain benefiting from the rapid growth of this natural foods company. The stock has tripled in the past three years and even part timers are eligible for stock options.

The company employs 33,246 individuals in the United States with 1,120 employees out of country. 45 percent of these employees are minorities with 43 percent being women. The company is reporting an astonishing 4,579 new jobs with a job growth of 18 percent. As an employee you will see 112 hours of professional training per year. But I would suggest somewhat of a down side when you see a voluntary turnover of 25 percent.

The most common job (salaried) is Associated Store Team Leader with an average annual income of $75,061, with the most common job (hourly) of Prepared Foods Team Member with an average annual pay of $25,451. Applicant information was not available.

Edward Jones

Let's take a look at Financial Services Company. We find this large firm ranked 4th and headquartered in St. Louis, Missouri. At Edward Jones, education here ends with spending 2.5% of payoff on training. We also find a mentoring program at the firm where new brokers are paired with veterans for a year, and lots of workers take subsidized business school classes.

The company employs 29,197 employees in the United States and 2,048 outside the country. The company only employs six percent minorities with 55 percent of their workers being woman. You will find a voluntary turnover rate of 15%, and if employed with the firm you will experience 105 hours per year of professional training.

The most common job (salaried) is Sr. Programmer Analyst with an average annual pay of $74,323, and a most common job (hourly) is Branch Office Administrator at an average annual income of $27,396. You can count on facing around 539,523 applicants if you are interested in applying to work for this company.

Republic Bancorp

Is a Commercial Bank your desire as an employer? Take a look at this small company headquartered in Owosso, Michigan. The have revenues of 67 million and are ranked 6th in small companies. The company is a 20-year-old firm with a rah-rah atmosphere. They have offices in the Midwest, and anyone can submit questions to the CEO's monthly TeleRap conferences, or nominate a co-worker as a 'local hero.'

The company employs 1,190 employees in the United States with no one employed out of county. They employ 10 percent minorities while 75% of their company employees are women. The company is experiencing a little down turn with a -104 new jobs or a job growth of a minus 9 percent. The company does offer 50 professional training hours a year. You will find a voluntary turnover of 15%.

The most common job (salaried) is Mortgage Loan Turnover with an average annual income of $165,000 and the most common job (hourly) is Customer Service Representative with an average annual income of $35,500. You will find that this firm is reporting an application rate of 22,000.

Baptist Health Care

What makes this Health Care Company so great? New employees at this Southern hospital group wear an ID badge sticker for the first 90 days so that co-workers can offer a helping hand. To brush up on company culture, after five months they're invited to a day of skills, contests, and speakers. This midsize firm is ranked 8th in the country. They have 4,303 employees, of which 25 percent our minorities, and 79 percent of the employees are women. At this point the Health Care Company only shows 6 new jobs, or a job growth of zero. There is a voluntary turnover 13 percent at this firm. If employed you would experience professional training of 60 hours per year.

The most common job (salaried) is Manager with an average annual income of $43,000 and the most common job (hourly) is Registered Nurse at an average annual income of $52.727. If you were to apply you would be one of the 19,308 applicants.

Alston & Bird

This legal service company is headquartered in Atlanta, Georgia. This is considered a small company but ranked 7th with revenues in the $402 million range. The company keeps open discussions and communication, which is vital at this national law firm, by a monthly open loop of firm meetings, fireside chats, 'town hall' meetings, and a daily online newsletter.

The company has 1,509 employees in the United States, with no one working out of country. Twenty-four percent of the employees are minorities with 56% of the workers being women. The firm is suggesting 48 new jobs or a job growth of 3 percent. As an employee of Alston & Bird you would have 50 hours of professional training a year. The company shows a voluntary turnover of 12 percent.

The most common job (salaried) is Associate Attorney with an average income of $131,239 and the most common is Legal Secretary (hourly) with an average income of $59,088. It has been reported that over 16,096 apply to work for this firm.

Pella

Do want to live in the Midwest and work for a manufacture. Well take a look at Pella. They are headquartered in, where else, but Pella, Iowa. I always think of my youth because I grew up in Iowa. Anyway, Elders aren't taken for granted at this maker of windows and doors. For

THE JOB SEARCH TOOL TO GET YOU THAT JOB

employees with 25 years' service, the company places a brick bearing their name and hometown in Pella Plaza at the Iowa State Fairground.

The company employs 8,758 employees in America with 51 out of county. They report that they employ 7 percent minorities with 35 percent of their workers being women. The company is showing some 579 new jobs with a job growth rate of 7%. As an employee you would see 48 hours of professional training and a voluntary turnover of 13 percent.

It is suggested that the most common job (salaried) is Department Manager and Engineer with an average annual pay of $52,569, and the most common jobs' (hourly) average annual income here is $36,940. You need to be aware that the company gets approximately 39,092 applicants a year.

Microsoft

Let us take a look at one of the most recognizable companies around. Microsoft is headquartered in Redmond, Washington. This computer software company offers what may be the most generous health-insurance plans in the United States. The premiums are zero, with no deductible. And it's the first U.S. Corporation to pay for therapy for dependents that are autistic.

This large company is ranked 11. The firm employs 39,011 people in the United States with 23,460 outside the country. Of these employees 28 percent are minorities, with 25% being women. The company has generated 1,509 new jobs or a job growth of 4 percent. While with the firm you will experience 45 hours per year of professional training.

The most common job (salaried) is Software Design Engineer at an average annual income of $107,300; and the most common job (hourly), you will find is Administrative Assistant at $47,000 average annual income. If you decide that this is the firm for you, you will be competing with over 166,184 other applicants.

7001 Resumes-Plus Second Edition

SRA International

SRA International is a Consulting Service company located in Fairfax, Virginia. This midsized company is ranked 19th. This IT firm and government contractor is helping employees develop healthier habits. So far it has enrolled more than 500 workers and significant others in GET FIT, an 18 week program to exercise more and eat healthier foods. The company employs 3,986 people in the United States with only 3 people working out of country. You will find that 30 percent of the employees are minorities with 36% being women. The company is reporting 717 new jobs with a job growth rate of 23 percent.

The most common job (salaried) is Software Engineer with an average annual income of $87,592. The most common job (hourly) you will find is Administrative Assistant which pays an average annual income of $40,500. The company reports a voluntary turnover rate of 14 percent. The firm has about 4,748 applicants per year.

Nordstrom

For those of you who are interested in general merchandising you may want to set your sights toward this large retail firm. Ranked 12th, Nordstrom is headquartered in Seattle, Washington. At this upscale specialty store the salespeople have the power to make decisions about refunds or exchanges, and top sellers can earn over $100,000 a year in commissions.

The company employs 45,112 people in United States with 8 working out of country. You will find that 41 percent of the company's employees are minorities with 72 percent of these employees being women. The organization is reporting 783 new jobs or a job growth of 3 percent. As an employee with the firm you will experience 60 hours of professional training per year.

The most common job (salaried) is Sales Department Manager with an average annual pay of $46,200 and the most common job (hourly) is Salesperson with an average annual pay $34,500. There is no information available on the number of applicants per year.

AFLAC

This company I believe has come a long way to develop their identity. Headquartered in Columbus, Georgia this firm is a midsized life and health insurance company, with a rank of 20th. What makes this company great is some of the PERKS, and the way management treats employees. For Employee-appreciation week at this health insurer, which is a seven-day party featuring food, concerts, movies, plays, and a minor-league baseball game, prizes, and amusement park outings, family members are invited.

The company employs 4,034 employees in the United States and 3,204 out of country. Forty-two percent of the employees are minorities while 69 percent are women. The company is indicating 179 new jobs or a job growth of 5 percent. You will find that the company is quoting a voluntary turnover of 10 percent. If you work for this insurance firm you will experience a whopping 90 hours of professional training.

The most common job (salaried) is Supervisor with an average annual pay of $53,919, and the most common job (hourly) is Customer Service Specialist II with an average annual income of $25.598. If you apply for a position with this firm you will be competing with over 20,940 other applicants.

Perkins Cole

A small legal service firm, but Perkins Cole is doing things to make it stand out. Located in Seattle, Washington you will find this company offering incentives galore to its staff. They are offering a 5% bonus at the end of the year in addition to a 7.3 Percent contribution to retirement

7001 Resumes-Plus Second Edition

accounts. The company is also offering recognition awards including roundtrip airline tickets and gifts.

The company has 1,553 employees working in the United States and only 2 working out of country. It is indicated that the company has 15 percent of their employees being minority with 58 percent being women. On the downside the company is reporting a -59 job reduction or a -4 percent job growth rate. Also the voluntary turnover is a little on the high side with 13 percent. But you will find the company offering 50 hours of professional training.

The most common job (salaried) is Associate with an average annual pay of $139,112, and the most common job (hourly) is Legal Secretary at an average annual income of $55,993. You will find that this company is reporting a job applicant level of 4,590.

Nixon Peabody

You may ask 'who is Nixon Peabody', well they are a small company that is ranked 17th. They are a legal Services firm based in Boston Massachusetts and because of four mergers between 1999 and 2003 were catapulted into a national law firm with 630 lawyers. Employees give the company high marks for diversity. 15% of the employees are minorities and 16 percent are women. The company now employs 1,563 people. The company can boast that they have developed 56 new jobs or a job growth of 4%. If you get a chance to work for this firm you will be involved in 40 hours of professional training. What I believe the company can also boast about is their low voluntary turnover of only 4 percent.

The most common job (salaried) is Associate Attorney with an average annual pay of $154,719.00, and the most common job (hourly) is Legal Secretary with an average annual pay of $62,450. Over 8,500 applicants apply to this firm.

464

Genzyme

This midsize firm is ranked 22nd, is in the Pharmaceutical Industry, and is based in Cambridge, Massachusetts. An interesting point about this firm is that they recently moved to a new 'green' building that uses less water and electricity and has a top-floor cafeteria with a sweeping view of Boston.

The company employs 5,399 in the United States and 2,250 outside the country. Of these employees 24 percent are minorities and 55 percent are women. The firm has 415 new jobs or a job growth of 9 percent. The company is reporting a surprisingly low voluntary turnover, 7 percent. You will find that the company offers 50 hours of professional training.

The most common job (salaried) is Researcher at an average annual pay of $85,499, and the most common job (hourly) is Cytogenesis Technicians/Technologists at an average annual pay of $56,740. However if you apply to work for this firm you will have to contend with the other 61,902 applicants.

Eli Lilly

Here is another top Pharmaceutical company headquartered this time in Indianapolis, Indiana. The company is ranked 13th. One of the neat things that this drug maker does is help their employees stay healthy with free Pap smears, mammograms, and colonoscopies. The company has an on site clinic with physicians, psychologists, and nurses. They have 50,000 visits a year to their clinic.

The company employs 21,898 people in the United States and 21,463 outside the country. Of these employees 15 percent are minorities and 45 percent are women. The company is reporting a down turn in jobs of -1,711 or a job growth of a -7 percent. However the company does have, I feel these days, an impressive low voluntary turnover of 7 percent. If you were

7001 Resumes-Plus Second Edition

employed by this firm you would more than likely participate in 90 hours of professional training a year.

The most common job (salaried) is Sales Representative with $88,314 average annual income, and the most common job (hourly) is Technician at an average annual pay of $64,001. You will find a whopping 44,282 applicants applying to this firm.

Hot Topic

At first glance, you might ask 'who is Hot Topic'; well they are a Specialty Retailer located in City of Industry, California. They rank 23rd out of 656 million midsized companies. This is somewhat of a unique company where the employees express themselves with tattoos, nose piercings, and saying what they want. This is a music-inspired clothing retailer that employs nearly 80% of their workforce under the age of 25.

The company has 8,314 employees in the United States and 75 outside the country. In this firm only 17 percent of their people are minorities with 63 percent being women. The company indicates 401 new jobs or a job growth of 22 percent. The turnover is somewhat high in this firm at 24 percent. If you were employed with this firm you will find yourself involved in 35 hours of professional training.

The most common job (salaried) with this firm is District Manager with an average annual income of $71,096 and the most common job with this firm (hourly) is Full Time Assistant Manager at an average annual income of $23,876.

I have to report that if you apply to this firm for employment you will be in competition with a whopping 200,000 other applicants.

Arnold & Porter

You will find this small legal service ranked 18th and headquartered in Washington, DC. Revenue for this company is in the 410 million dollar range. You will find that the lawyers at this firm are socially responsible. They contributed 8,714 hours of attorney work pro bono. This is equivalent of 39 people on a full-time basis. You will find associates volunteering for six months at the legal Aid Society.

The company employs 1,283 here in the States with 68 working out of country. Within the firm there are 32 percent minorities with 57 percent being women. The company shows a slight down turn with a -49 percent new jobs or a job growth of -1 percent. Professional job training varies within this firm.

The most common job (salaried) is Associate with an average annual pay of $133,593. And the most common job (hourly) is Legal Secretary with an average annual pay of $51.345. The firm is quoting an application level of 16,020 per year.

Station Casinos

Here is a first to our list of top companies and one that I was surprised to see. Station Casinos, located where else, but in Las Vegas, Nevada. The company is running a Hotel, Casino, and Resort. In seeking the interest of their 1,200 employees they discovered that of these, some indicated that they wanted to be American citizens. So the company offers free English courses, a 24-hour bilingual hotline, and citizenship clinics.

The company has 10,957 employees in the United States with none working outside the country. They also suggest that they employ 48 percent minorities with 49% being women. The company is boasting 544 new jobs or a job growth rate of 6 percent. The company does have a little high voluntary turnover of 19 percent, but you will see a little higher turnover in this type of business than you would in other industries.

7001 Resumes-Plus Second Edition

The most common job (salaried) in this firm is Blackjack Floor person with an average annual income of $42,220 and the most common job (hourly) is Table Games Dealer with an average annual pay of $50,972. The company is stating that they have 89,180 applicants so you have got your job cut out for you as you apply to this firm. I would suggest that you have a very well done résumé to submit.

Publix Super Markets

Here we have a large 100% employee-owned Southeastern supermarket chain. The company is headquartered in Lakeland, Florida and ranked 15th. To celebrate the company's 75th birthday in 2005, 850 stores hosted parties with balloons, banners, costumes, and musical performances. The company employs 129,412 employees in the United States and of these, 38 percent of them are minorities and 49 percent are women. The firm has created 1,987 new jobs or a job growth of 3 percent. Voluntary turnover in this firm is 12 percent. If you were working for the company you would receive 50 hours of professional training.

The most common job (salaried) is Store Manager with an average annual income of $101,800, and the most common job (hourly) is Deli Clerk at an average annual income of $23,623. You should be aware that this company has 482,799 applicants a year.

Synovus

What is Synovus? Well, they are a large Commercial bank. We do not know them in the West, but this bank is headquartered in Columbus, Georgia and ranked 16th. At this firm, feedback matters. This processor and bank holding company solicit employee opinion via an intranet that can now be accessed from home, and workers are surveyed online every month.

The bank employs 11,860 employees in the United States with 418 out of country. Of these employees 26 percent are minorities and a whopping 64 percent are women. The organization has developed 38 new jobs or a job growth of 0. You will find that the bank

The Job Search Tool to Get You That Job

registers a 13 percent voluntary turnover and if you are employed by them you would participate in 52 hours of professional training a year.

The most common job (salaried) would be Project Analyst Lead at an average annual income of $63,333 and the most common job (hourly) is Machine Operator 1 at an average annual income of $20,867. You will find that this processor and bank holding firm identifying 4,191 applicants.

Stew Leonard's

Let us take a look at this Wholesalers, Food and Grocery firm headquartered in Norwalk, Connecticut, and ranked 19th as a small company with 293 million dollars in revenue. What seems to be unique about this firm is that they try to promote 'Moms hours'. These are hours that mothers can work while their children are in school, and take the summer off to tend to them. The three giant supermarkets in New York City suburbs are soon to be joined by a fourth.

The firm employs 1,819 people in the United States of which 55% of them are minorities and with 45 percent being women. The company is showing -26 new jobs, or a job growth of -2 percent. The company can boast about a low voluntary turnover of 8 percent which I believe is quite good these days. So there is something that is holding these employees. If you go to work for the firm you will be involved in 38 hours of professional training a year.

The most common job (salaried) is Store Manager with an average annual income of $62,374, and the most common job (hourly) is Production Assistant with an average annual pay of $29,915. This company reports that they have 5,275 applicants a year.

Baptist Health South Florida

This large Health Care Company is Ranked 59th, but 17th as a large company headquartered in Coral Gables, Florida. What makes this company so good? Well for one thing these hospitals encourage employees to go the extra mile with lots of incentive bonus programs. Employees donate to a fund to assist co-workers which are then matched. To help workers meet weight targets, they'll even pay for Weight Watchers.

The Hospital system employs 10,706 people of which 70% of them are minorities with 75 percent being women. The organization is reporting 245 new jobs or a job growth of 3 percent. What is interesting is the hospital shows only a 7 percent voluntary turnover. At this point as an employee of the hospital you would receive 8 hours of professional training a year.

The most common job (salaried) is Assistant Manager, Patient Care which pays an average annual income of $83,125 and the most common job (hourly) is Clinical Nurse which has an annual average income of $56,842. As an applicant you will be facing another 16,203 applying for employment at this Health Care system.

Vanguard Group

Ranking 60th this Financial Service firm is headquartered in Malvern, Pennsylvania. This large company also ranks 18th of the top lager companies. One of the ways that makes this mutual fund operator to standout is that they recognize exemplary service with $250 spot-bonus awards. To show appreciation during an especially busy period, CEO Jack Brennan, gave everyone a double bonus.

The company employs 11,070 in the United States and just one out of country. The job has reported 800 new jobs or a job growth of 8 percent. The company also is reporting a low voluntary turnover of 7 percent. As an employee you would be involved in professional training of 64 hours a year.

The most common job (salaried) is Superior Information on Income. The most common job (hourly) is Client Relationship Associate; no income information available. The firm reports 4,000 applicants.

THE JOB SEARCH TOOL TO GET YOU THAT JOB

<u>Sherwin-Williams</u>

How would you like working for a top Chemical company. This firm is reported 61st overall and 19th as a large company. One thing this firm is so great at is 90 percent of placements in managerial and professional positions come from within at this paint seller. About 600 college recruits are hired every year and receive training in different divisions and functions.

The firm employs 27,938 employees with 4,215 who are employed out of country; of these, 20 percent are minorities and 20% are women. The company is reporting 2,536 new jobs with a job growth of 14 percent. The company has a low voluntary turnover of 9 percent.

The most common job at this firm (salaried) is Store Manager with an average annual pay of $57,487 and the most common job (hourly) is Operating Technician with an average pay of $34,307. You will find that this firm gets 29,795 applicants so make sure if you apply you have an outstanding résumé.

<u>Memorial Health</u>

Headquartered in Savannah, Georgia, this Health Care firm is ranked 62nd as an organization, and 24th as a midsized company. This firm offers an above and beyond benefit for their employees which includes a 3 percent-of-pay contribution to their 401(k) plans, a $4,200 tuition reimbursement, relatively inexpensive onsite child care ($440 a month), and $5,000 in adoption aid.

The Health Care firm employs 4,301 employees in the United States with 38 percent minorities and a whopping 81 percent of their employees being women. The organization is reporting 88 new jobs with a job growth of 2 percent. The company reports a 9 percent voluntary turnover.

The most common job in this company (Salaried) is Senior Staff Registered Nurse with an average annual pay of $63,098 and the most common job (hourly) is Staff Registered Nurse at an average annual income of $48,222. This firm reports that they receive 9,204 applicants a year.

Russell Investment Group

You will find this small company Ranked 63rd as a top company headquartered in Tacoma, Washington. The firm has revenues of around 925 million dollars and they are ranked 20th as a small company. What is interesting about this investment service firm is its HQ was designed to showcase views of Mount Rainier.

The company wants to help their employees stay fit so they have installed a state-of-the-art fitness center. The company has 1,092 employees in the United States with 812 people out of country. Of these employees 12 percent are minorities and 53% are women. Russell Investment Group is reporting 198 new jobs or a job growth of 22 percent. They also indicate a voluntary turnover of 16 percent. As an employee of the firm you will find yourself involved in 16 hours or professional training.

The most common job (salaried) Sales (Regional Directors) with an average annual pay of a whopping $574,373, and the most common job (hourly) Office/Clerical Administrative Assistant (Project Coordinators) with an average annual income of $44,130 a year. If you apply to this company you need to be aware that there are about 11,500 other applicants a year.

FedEx

There are as you know several Mail, Package, and Freight Delivery organizations. However, here we find FedEx headquartered in Memphis, Tennessee ranking 64th in the top companies and ranks 20th as a large company. One of the things that makes this company shine is the fact that they promote from within: Ninety-two percent of managers came up from the ranks. This makes going in a little rough, but once you are in the firm you have a good opportunity for

THE JOB SEARCH TOOL TO GET YOU THAT JOB

upward mobility. And the fact that the company has doubled in size since it debuted in 1998, and the founder Fred Smith is still is at the helm shows stability and promise.

The company employs 212,241 employees in America and 29,639 outside the country. You will find that the firm employs 41 percent minorities with 29% of them women. The company is boasting 8,246 new employees or a job growth of 7 percent. As an employee you would participate in 34 hours of professional training a year. You will find a 7 percent voluntary turnover.

The most common job (salaried) is Operations Manager at an average annual income of $74,070. And the most common job (hourly) is Courier with an average annual pay of $37,351. This company has 460,742 applicants, so if you are interested in this firm make sure you submit an outstanding résumé.

PCL Construction

Here we have a midsized company ranked 25th as an organization and ranked 65th of the top 100. This General Contractor was in charge of the Staples Center, and Denver Airport. The firm is headquartered in Denver, Colorado. This company is employee owned, breeding a strong camaraderie. And to maintain a position of no single control, no one owns more than 8 percent of the company stock.

Another area of interest is that 70 percent of the employees volunteer regularly. The company has 2,543 employees working for the firm in the United States and another 3,650 working out of country. You will find that 38% of the firm's employees are minorities with 9 percent being women. The company has developed 523 new jobs or a job growth of 26 percent. In this firm they have a voluntary turnover of 21 percent which is a little high.

The most common job (salaried) in this company is Superintendent at an annual average pay $83,078 and the most common job (hourly) is Carpenter with an average annual income of $52,215. As an employee of this firm you will be involved in 34 hours of professional training.

473

7001 Resumes-Plus Second Edition

If you decide to apply to this firm for employment be aware that this company sees 6,500 applicants.

Mitre

This is a little different type of organization. Mitre does research for the government. They are headquartered in McLean, Virginia. The firm is ranked 66th and 26th as a midsized company. They are classified as a diversified outsourcing firm. What makes this firm standout is the fact that they have an outstanding retirement for those in the golden years. Their program allows employees to replace up to 75% or more of full pay when they stop working.

The company has 5,575 employees in the United States with 65 out of country. Of these, 13 percent of the employees are minorities and 31 percent are women. The company is reporting the development of 191 new jobs or a job growth of 4 percent. You will find their voluntary turnover is a low, low 5 percent. As an employee you will be involved in 45 hours of professional training a year.

The most common job (salaried) is Information System Engineer Lead at an average annual income of $109,849 and the most common job (hourly) is Technical Project Support III at an average annual income of $47,840. This firm has 24,753 applicants a year.

Ernst & Young

This large Financial Services firm is ranked 67th, but 21st as a large firm. You will find the company headquartered in New York City, New York. What sets this company apart is the fact that they put 'people first'. This Big Four accounting firm emphasizes diversity. Today minorities make up 24% of its workforce, up from 16% in 1996. The firm's nondiscrimination policy now includes gender identity.

The company has 23,657 employees working in the United States with another 76,343 working out of country. Of these employees 40 percent of them are women. Over the year the company has developed 1,059 jobs or a job growth rate of 5 percent. Even with this 'people first' policy the company is reporting a 23 percent voluntary turnover. As an employee with the firm you will be involved in 97 hours a year of professional development.

The most common job (salaried) is Senior – a client serving position at an average annual pay of $61,905, and the most common job (hourly) is Administrative Assistant. If you are inclined to apply to this firm be aware there are 298,870 other applicants.

Bronson Healthcare Group

Here we go with another health care operation. Looks like this industry is doing a good job to develop and keep employees. This company is ranked 68th overall, and 27th as a midsized firm. It's based in Kalamazoo, Michigan. The Health care system has gross revenues of 526 million dollars.

As we all know Nurses are the heart of most hospitals and this is more than true here. In this firm you will find a chief nursing office on the senior management team. Employees who buy houses in certain areas are eligible for an up to $10,000 no-interest loan. The Hospital system employs 3,395 employees in the United States. You will find that of these employees 16 percent our minorities with a whopping 88 percent being females. The company has developed 160 new jobs or a job growth of 6 percent. And looking at the voluntary turnover I believe says something about the firm, Bronson Healthcare Group is quoting only 6 percent. If you are employed by the Hospital system you will experience 95 hours of professional training each year.

The most common job (salaried) is Leaders at an average annual income of $79,991 and the most common job (hourly) is Registered Nurse with an average annual pay of $60,935. If you apply to this firm I would suggest that you have your credentials in order as well as try to use the information this book offers; having a Champion. You're going to be facing 7,902 other applicants.

7001 Resumes-Plus Second Edition

Valassis

Here is an interesting company. Valassis is a small firm, but has an overall ranking of 69th, with a small company ranking of 21st. The organization is headquartered in Livonia, Michigan. The firm is in the Advertising and Marketing industry. They print a Sunday newspaper insert. The firm has been credited of having more award programs than anyone else; they have at least 50. The new 'Global Thinker Honor' awarded airfare for two to any place in the world, along with $3,000 for expenses.

The firm has 1,803 employees in the United States with 2,626 outside the country. Of these you will find 16 percent minorities and 52 percent women. The firm is reporting 40 new jobs or a job growth of 0. I am happy to say that this firm also has a very low voluntary turnover of 6 percent, so they are doing something right. As an employee of the firm you will experience some 48 hours of professional training a year.

The most common job here (salaried) is Account Coordinator with an average annual pay of $50,082. The most common job (hourly) is Press Operator with an average annual income of $59,672. I need you to look closely at the number of applicants here which is about 3 to 1 or 15,179. Here again, you do need a super résumé, but the real secret is to have a Champion working for you. Be it from inside the firm or from the outside.

A.G. Edwards

I am surprised to see a number of Securities companies placing in the top 100. Here we have the 70th ranked overall, and 22nd as a large company. This brokerage firm is 118 years old, so I believe you can be assured that the firm is going to be around. The company is headquartered in St. Louis, Missouri.

The company sees themselves as a classroom. It hired 650 financial consultants not to long ago and spent $75, 000 to train each one. Employees can also earn college credits onsite via in-house classes at A.G. Edwards University.

You will find that the company has 15, 708 employees in the United States with only 8 out of country. Of these, 8 percent are minority which I find surprisingly low based on the trend of the company in this evaluation and survey. Of all the employees however, 46 percent are women.

On the downside, depending on how you look at it, the company has reduced the jobs at the firm by a -71, with a job growth of 0. But this means that there is a good chance as the economy comes back there could be some openings to fill within this firm. The voluntary turnover of 10 percent isn't real high. If you happen to be working for the company you can expect 73 hours of professional training a year.

The most common job (salaried) is HDQ Managers & Professional Support with an average annual pay of $68,825 and the most common job (hourly) you will find is Branch Support Employees with an average annual income of $34,379. This firm gets 22,387 applicants.

PricewaterhouseCoopers

I am very surprised to see so many Financial Services firms doing so much to benefit their employees. Here we have this New York City, New York headquartered firm rated 71st over all and 23rd as a large company. The company is piloting a program designed to reduce work hours. It also invented a new position for career employees who are not on a partner track, thereby getting rid of the old 'up and out' culture.

The firm has 26,309 employees in the United States with about 250 employees who work outside of the country; with 24 percent minorities and forty-eight percent who are women. Also the company is reporting 2,583 new jobs or a job growth of 11 percent. As an employee you will be involved in a whopping 150 hours of professional training. You will also find that the company is reporting a voluntary turnover of 13 percent.

The most common job (salaried) is Manager/Supervisor with an average annual income of $83,334 and the most common job (hourly) is Executive Assistant with an average annual income of $51,021. But be prepared, this firm receives 283,374 applicants a year.

Booz Allen Hamilton

Yes that is right, a little different name, but this firm is ranked 72nd overall and 24th as a large company. You will find this company headquartered in McLean, Virginia. This Consulting Services provides an in-house university that offers hundreds of courses. A partnership with John Hopkins has helped 100 employees earn an MBA degree.

The company has 15,582 employees in the United States and 1,523 people working outside the country. Of these employees 26 percent are minority with 38 percent being women. The company is reporting 1,237 new jobs or a job growth of 9%. The voluntary turnover rate is 13 percent at this firm. However if you are employed with this consulting service firm you will experience 60 hours of professional training a year.

The most common job with this firm (salaried) is Associate at an average annual pay of $99,000 per year. And the most common job (hourly) is Executive Assistant at an average annual pay of $56,700. When applying to work for this firm, beware, there are over 10,071 other applicants.

Standard Pacific

Here we have a Homebuilder that is ranked 74th overall and 22nd for a small company. Standard Pacific is headquartered in Irvine, California. What is interesting, and making this company standout, is the fact that they give discounts on home purchases: 1% after one year of service, and 2% after two years, and 3 percent after three or more. Top employees also get coupons to use at the company store.

The company has 2,317 employees here in the United States. Of these, 16 percent are minorities with 43 percent being women. You will find that this firm is reporting 403 new jobs or a job growth of 22 percent. They are reporting a voluntary turnover of 14 percent. If you work for the firm you will experience 40 hours of professional training.

The most common job (salaried) is Construction Superintendent at an average annual income of $76,000, and the most common job with the firm (hourly) is Sales Assistant with an average annual pay of $29,040. You will be very surprised to discover that this firm receives over 3,060 applicants a year, which is about one and a half times the number of employees in the company. This only goes to show you that in job search it is important to have a plan as well as a back up plan if your first one doesn't workout.

Quad/Graphics

You will find that this firm is ranked 75th overall and 25th as a large Company. Quad/Graphics is a publishing and printing firm headquartered in Sussex, Wisconsin. So what makes this company so great? Well you will find that half of the employees at this catalog and magazine printer are related by blood or marriage. So for best results you may want to start dating someone that works for the firm, just joking.

Anyway, the close-knit workers can take advantage of four onsite medical clinics, there onsite child-care centers, and a 325-acre recreational park. The company employs 10,399 individuals here in the United States with 112 outside of the country. Of these, 13 percent are minorities with 24% women. The company is reporting 133 new jobs with a job growth of one percent. In addition, you will find that the firm has a voluntary turnover of 11 percent. As an employee you'll be involved in 23 hours of professional training.

7001 Resumes-Plus Second Edition

The most common job (salaried) N.A. at an average income of $68,490 and the most common job (hourly) N.A. at an average of $28,029. This firm is also reporting an amazing 25,214 applicants a year. I'll be very clear to you here that a champion in this firm will be very helpful in getting a position here. I would strongly recommend that you review the section on getting a champion in this book.

Children's Healthcare of Atlanta

If you have been reviewing company overviews, you will recognize that there are a great many health care organizations in this report, such as this one. Here we have another Children's Hospital, located in Atlanta, Georgia. They are ranked 76th overall and 29th as a midsized company. You can be assured that working at a children's hospital can be stressful, so employees here are offered onsite child care, a 'Club Med.' wellness program, baby showers for expectant mothers, and a concierge service for things like meals and trip reservations.

The hospital has 4,910 employees in the United States, of these, 41 percent are minorities with 81% being women. The healthcare organization is reporting 151 new jobs or a job growth of 4 percent. What is interesting is you will find that the hospital has an 8 percent voluntary turnover. As an employee you will be involved in 20 hours a year of professional training.

You will find that the most common job with this hospital (salaried) is Business Operations Coordinator with an average annual pay of $36,421 per year, and the most common job (hourly) is Staff Nurse II at an average annual income of $57,633. Let me give you a heads up at this point, if you are looking for a career path and are so inclined, I am going to strongly recommend that you take a look at Nursing, based upon not only personal background, there are very strong trends that suggest you could do worse. Be aware that this organization gets 26,076 applicants a year.

480

National Instruments

Here is a Computer Peripherals company located in Austin, Texas that is rated 77th overall and 23rd as a Small company. What is 'neat' here at this firm is the company suggests that employees never face a layoff. I am sure everyone is hoping this is true. In addition, when employees are not working, they play football, socialize with co-workers at onsite deck parties, and participate in annual talent shows.

The firm employs 2,148 individuals in the United States and 1,455 out of country. Of this number, 25 percent of these are minorities with 28% women. The company is reporting 89 new jobs or a job growth rate of 4 percent. In addition, the voluntary turnover is a low 8 percent. If you happen to be employed with this firm you will participate in 50 hours of professional training per year.

The most common job in this firm (salaried) is Entry-Level Engineer at an annual average pay of $57,991, and the most common job (hourly) you will find is Material Handler with an average annual income of $26,090. No information on applicants applying to this firm.

Methodist Hospital System

Here we go; another hospital system. As you can see if you have gotten this far we have had a number of medical operations to review and evaluate. This one is ranked 78th overall and 30th as a midsized company. The system is headquartered in Houston, Texas. So what sets this system apart from any other company, well this is one of the nation's largest nonprofit hospitals.

The system has a very high patient-satisfaction score to an I CARE mission launched in 1998. The hospital has 6,714 employees here in the United States. Of these 64 percent are minorities and 77% are women. New jobs are up with 475, and a job growth of 6 percent. The voluntary turnover rate is what I would suggest seems to be in the average range of 10 percent. I

7001 Resumes-Plus Second Edition

was surprised to see a low professional training per year of only 11 hours. I would have expected much more.

The most common job (salaried) here at this hospital is Manager, Nursing with an average annual pay of $86,551, and the most common job (hourly) Registered Nurse-Clinical Colleague at an average annual income of $67,733. What I see is somewhat astronomical; this hospital system gets 45,000 applicants per year.

East Penn Manufacturing

What we have here is a battery manufacturer headquartered in Lyon Station, Pennsylvania. The firm is ranked 79th overall and 31st as a midsized company. What is interesting is the heart of the firm is made up of lifers. This maker of the Deka battery still has the founder, Delight Breidegam, at the wheel. And top senior employees have 418 years of combined service.

The staff includes 246 married couples. You will find that the firm employees 4,082 in the United States and 100 out of country. The company is quoting 87 new jobs or a job growth of 2 percent. Voluntary turnover at this firm is a low 6 percent. As an employee you will be involved in 100 hours of professional training a year.

The most common job (salaried) here at East Penn Manufacturing is Engineer with an average annual pay of $57,236 and the most common job (hourly) you will find is Finish Line Production and the average annual pay is $40, 251. Last but not least here at this firm you will discover that the company has 7,704 applicants.

CH2M Hill

An interesting named Engineering Construction firm headquartered in Denver, Colorado. The company is rated 80th overall and 26th as a large company. What we see here in this firm is that ownership breeds loyalty. This is an employee owned firm. Some of the jobs tackled by this firm are 'demolition of nuclear plants'. Nearly two thirds of the employees have been with the company 10 years; and 10% more than 20 years.

You'd be interested to know that the company employs 17,770 people in the United States with 2,478 out of country. The company is boasting about 5,533 new jobs or a job growth of 48 percent. With all the expansion I was surprised to see only 6 hours of professional training a year. The voluntary turnover at this firm is 8 percent.

The most common job at this firm (salaried) is Associate Engineer at an average annual income of $65,502 and the most common job (hourly) is Administrative Assistant 3 at an average pay $41,616. You will be taken back somewhat at the 48,474 applicants that apply to this firm. As I have suggested, if you're interested in really working for this firm you will need to do much more than just send in your 'paper'. For best results, as in most job search situations, you will need to work from the inside; it would be to your advantage to have a 'Champion' in your court.

Autodesk

For those of you who don't know, Autodesk is a Computer Software firm headquartered in San Rafael, California. They show an overall ranking at 81st and a small company rank of 24th.

This firm is known for their design software and there counterculture roots. Wear what you want to work and bring your dog too. I kind of like that, since these days I take my dog with me nearly every place I go. Want to take a six-week paid sabbatical every four years, will here you go. And the CEO, Carol Bartz, hosts 'coffee with carol' chats.

You will discover that the company has 2,098 employees in the United States with another 1,690 outside the country. Of these, 22 percent are minorities with 30 percent being women. The company can boast and be proud about their 5% voluntary turnover. You will find that the company is reporting 97 new jobs or a job growth 5 percent. As an employee of this firm you can expect to spend 42 hours of professional training a year.

7001 Resumes-Plus Second Edition

The most common job with this firm (salaried) is Programmer Software Engineer 1 with an average annual income of $125,527 and the most common job (hourly) is Customer Service Rep with an average annual income of $43,850. Are you sitting down, as I stated, this firm employs around 3,600 or so employees but they have over 26,263 applicants; as you can see this is around 9 to 1. So, make sure that you have something more to offer than just paper.

Bingham McCutchen

I was also surprised to see the number of legal services that was on our list. Here we have another one. Bingham McCutchen is ranked 82nd overall and 25th as a small company. As an employee you will not go unnoticed at this national law firm. The company fetes the non-lawyer population with staff-appreciation week and gives gift baskets for new babies and weddings.

The firm has 1,542 employees in the United States and 47 out of county. They have 0 new jobs or a job growth of zero. The voluntary turnover is 16 percent at this company. The company offers 100 hours a years of professional training.

The most common job at this firm (salaried) is Associate at an average annual pay of $173,391 and the most common job (hourly) is Legal Secretary with an average annual income of $63,821. Bare in mind that if you apply to this company you will find that you are facing nearly 7,000 other applicants.

Texas Instruments

Here is a company name that many of you may know, Texas Instruments. You will find that they are ranked overall at 83rd and as a larger company at 27th. They are headquartered in Dallas, Texas. This high-tech pioneer supports diversity through 30 employee-groups. Among them: 'Lesbian and Gay employee network', 'Christian Values Initiative', and 'Muslim Initiative,' as well as other affinity groups.

The company has 15,102 employees in the United States and 18,710 out of country. Thirty-four percent of their employees are minorities with 25% being women. The company is reporting a reduction of jobs at this time of -1070 suggesting a job growth of -6 percent. You will find what I believe is an impressive voluntary turnover of only 5 percent. As an employee of this firm you will experience professional training of 43 hours.

The most common job with this firm (salaried) is Electrical Design Engineer with an average annual pay of $111,752 and the most common job (hourly) is Water Fab Specialist with an average annual pay of $38,115. If you are going to apply to this firm for employment bare in mind two things, one, the reduction of employment as indicated, and the fact that there are 41,481 other applicants.

Worthington Industries

This is a midsized company with an overall ranking of 84th, and 32nd as a midsized firm headquartered in Columbus, Ohio. The steel processor's culture is based on trust and great benefits. Factory workers get a piece of monthly profit sharing, which augments monthly salaries 40% to 100%. Join the wellness program and you health premiums are covered.

The company has 6,233 employees in the United States with 1,146 working out of country. The company reports a down turn of a - 217 jobs or a -4 percent of job growth. As an employee you will find 60 hours a year of professional training, with a voluntary turnover of 9 percent.

The most common job at this firm (salaried) is Senior Inside Sales Rep at an average annual income of $64,492 and the most common job with this firm (hourly) is Helper with an annual average income of $38,137.

If you decided to send this firm an application because you feel that you would like to work for the company, just be aware that this firm has 10,000 applicants a year. So not only should your cover letter and résumé be pristine, I would recommend that you get someone

7001 Resumes-Plus Second Edition

to become your champion to help you get your job. I recall doing this some time ago when I wanted to work for Lockheed Missile and Space Company, and I assure you it works.

First Horizon National

As we have been going through this list of companies we have seen a few financial institutions. This one, First Horizon National, is ranked 85th overall and 28th as a large company. You will find this commercial bank headquartered in Memphis, Tennessee. Culture puts bank employees ahead of customers and shareholders. The bank has added vision care and enhanced dental coverage, and this year the bank is boosting the lifetime maximum benefit in health insurance coverage. What you may find interesting is some firms are cutting back on these benefits so this is a real plus for the new employee.

The firm has 13,228 employees in the United States of which 23 percent are minority with 63 percent being female. In addition the company is reporting an impressive number of new jobs 1,274 or a job growth of 11%. However, I am surprised to see such a large voluntary turnover rate of 21 percent. As an employee of this firm you will experience up to 68 hours of professional training.

The most common job (salaried) with this firm is Enterprise Technician with an average annual income of $69,023 and the most common job (hourly) in the company is Teller with an average annual pay of $23,035. The company is reporting that they are involved with 51,571 new applicants. With the high voluntary turnover rate even with this high applicant rate they are going to be looking for new employees constantly. So polish up your résumé and send it in if you are interested in working for this Commercial Bank.

Principal Financial Group

Headquartered in my old home town, Des Moines, Iowa, I have not been there for a very long time but I can remember some of the great places to eat. Principal Financial Group has

The Job Search Tool to Get You That Job

an over all ranking of 86th and is ranked 29th as a large company. What is interesting about this firm is that the employees love the flexibility at this retirement and insurance services Company. What we see is 69% use flexible hours, another twenty percent use compressed weeks, and 17 percent spend at least 20% of there time working from home. I am sure some of them are down to the Des Moines River fishing.

The company employees 12,723 people in the United States with 1,672 working outside the country. Eight percent of the employees are minorities, with 70 being women. In addition, the firm is claiming 251 new jobs or a job growth of 2 percent. As an employee you will experience 38 hours a year of professional growth training. The company suggests that they have around a 9 percent voluntary turnover rate.

The most common job (salaried) is Sr. IT Application Analyst with an estimated Annual pay of $86,951 and the most common job (hourly) is Client Transaction Tech with an average annual income of $22,790.

If you are interested in working for this firm more than likely you are going to have to relocate to a new environment. I can tell you one thing about Des Moines, the summer nights can be hot and sticky. I all cases with every one of these jobs, unless you live in the area, your decision on applying should also be based on your willingness to relocate. This is a decision like many you must make before you submit your résumé. I believe I deal with a few of these reasons and why. Plus in your job interview this very well might be a question you are going to be asked and you will need to have a prepared answer. In this case you are also facing 25,347 other applicants.

Washington Mutual

Here is a name we all recognize I think. Headquartered in Seattle, Washington, this savings institution is ranked 87th overall and 30th among large companies. It is suggested that the CEO, Kerry Killinger, is a fun guy and this 'fun' is the underlying theme of this nation's largest thrift; you often find this CEO being an enthusiastic emcee.

7001 Resumes-Plus Second Edition

The institution employs 54,396 people with 42 percent being minority and 65 percent are women. The company is quoting some what of a down turn at a -3,399 or a job growth of a -7 percent.

The most common job (salaried) in the firm is Assistant Financial Center Manager with an average annual income of $50,024 and the most common job in the company (hourly) is Financial Center Teller with an average annual pay of $24, 948. The turn over rate is not available, but if you decided to apply to this firm you are going to be in the army of 350,165 other applicants. Let's look at that. You will find that at this rate it is nearly 6 applicants for every employee in the company; and with the down turn, maybe this firm is not one that should be high on your list to work for.

<u>Morrison & Foerster</u>

Sounds like a good firm to work for. You will find this small legal services company headquartered in San Francisco. A very cool city and I mean it can get cool there, but it can be a fun place too. This legal services firm has an overall ranking of 88th with a Small company ranking of 26th. What we have here is one of the nation's most premier law firms. The company pays well, $172,000 is an average base for lawyers, and $60,334 for legal secretaries. Each year it funds every employee's 401(k) with 5% of their total compensation. Sure makes me want to have a law degree if I were younger.

The company employs 2,145 people in the United States with 298 out of country. You will find 32 percent of the employees are minorities with 59 percent being female. The company has a 40 hour a year professional training program that you would be involved in. You will find that the company has 58 new jobs or a job growth of 3 percent.

The most common job with this firm (salaried) is Associate Attorney with an average annual income of $182,905 and the most common job (hourly) is Legal Secretary with an average annual salary of $67,800.

Let me tell you a little a bit about San Francisco. You may know this but it is hilly, it is hard to get into, many people live outside the city and commute in by driving, or by BART (Bay Area Rapid Transit). There are great restaurants with outstanding food and great sight seeing. However, is gets cold, and it is very expensive to live anywhere around the city as well as in the suburbs. This firm gets 10,544 applicants a year. I lived in the area for a number of years and I liked it, but will you?

Mayo Clinic

Here we have one of the top Health Care organizations in the country headquartered in Rochester, New Mexico. This firm ranked 89th overall and ranked 31st as a large company. What makes this company so great? What we first see is, Eighty-nine percent of employee's say they are proud to tell others they work at this hospital, known for both its cutting-edge research and unique collaborative style, in which doctors and other providers work on teams for each patient.

This health care organization has 38,085 employees in the United States with only 3 working out of country. You will find that 11 percent are minorities and 71 percent are women. At the Mayo Clinic they have developed 1,160 new jobs or a job growth of 4 percent, and you will find a very low voluntary turnover of 5 percent. As an employee of the Clinic you will find that you will be involved in 45 hours of professional training.

The most common job (salaried) is Staff Physician/PhD, salaries not available, and the most common job (hourly) is Registered Nurse, again salaries not available. If you have an interest in applying and working for this Health Care hospital be prepared to compete with 161,765 other applicants.

John Wiley & Sons

John Wiley & Son is a small Publishing and Printing Company which is ranked 90th overall and 27th as a small firm. You will find the company headquartered in Hoboken, New

Jersey. What you will find out about this book and journal publisher is it has that old fashioned feeling. This is a company that is being run by sixth and seventh generation family members; a 198-year-old firm. Bucking the national trend, the firm is enhancing the company's pension plan.

The firm has 2,090 employees in the United States with 1,415 working out of country. Of these, 23 percent are minorities and 58 percent are women. The company is reporting 25 new jobs or a job growth of one percent. As an employee you will find that you will be involved in 96 hours of professional training. This company reports a voluntary turnover of 10 percent.

The most common job in this firm (salaried) is Publisher Representative with an average annual pay of $56,015 and the most common job (hourly) is Editorial Assistant with an average annual income of $30,314. As an applicant you will find yourself with another 1,368, so make sure you have a good tailor made résumé that highlights skills and experiences that would be valuable to a publishing and printing company.

Granite Construction

Here we have an Engineering and Construction company headquartered in Watsonville, California. The company has an overall ranking of 91st and holds a rank of 33rd as a midsized company. What is neat about this highway builder is that they allocate up to 2 percent of their profit to charitable contributions and allows employees to select the recipients. In 2004, $1.1 million was donated to causes like Boys and Girls clubs and Habitat for Humanity.

The company has 4,300 employees working the United States. Of these you will find that 29 percent are minorities and of that total 13 percent our women. The company is reporting 92 new jobs or a job growth of 6 percent. The company has a voluntary turnover rate that seems to be in the normal range of 10 percent. As an employee you would experience 38 hours of professional training a year.

The most common job in this firm (salaried) is Engineering with an average annual income rate of $68,803, and the most common job in this firm (hourly) is Journeyman with an average annual income of $35,310.

If you have your sights set on working for this firm, here is a piece of advice. First, have a good solid résumé with support experience; next, before sending in your résumé try to find yourself a champion as I discussed in chapter ten on having a champion work for you. This could be someone who is knowledgeable about your work and who can contact with ease someone within this organization that could open the door for you. Going the extra mile at this end my save you a great deal of time in you job search. Let me point out that this firm has 14,750 applicants a year.

Men's Wearhouse

I think this is the next place I want to go when I buy my next suit; I might also say that one of my first part-time full-time jobs was working in a clothing store in Mountain View, California called Normans'. I worked for a great guy whose name was Norm Tobias. Anyway, let's look at this organization.

You see this company on TV all the time now and the President is always saying, 'You Will Love the Way You Look'. So what make this company standout? First you will find this company headquartered in Houston, Texas and Fremont, California. They are a Specialty retailer with an over all ranking of 92nd and a large business ranking of 32nd.

What is interesting is that the employees dress for success at this clothing chain. This makes me feel good to see dressing up coming back; there was a time not to long ago where capsule was in. Anyway, 98% of the regional and district managers started in the store position; good news if you are trying to work your way up. And more than 100 kids of employees are receiving college scholarships for $5,000 a year.

7001 Resumes-Plus Second Edition

I was surprised myself to discover that the company had 10,757 employees here in the United States and 52 percent are minorities, with 46 percent being women. The company is boasting about 668 new jobs or a job growth of 9 percent, I would say that is a healthy rate. However, I was surprised to see a voluntary turnover rate of 26 percent. I believe that this is a little high.

If you are working for this firm you can expect 85 hours per year of professional training which I would suggest is very valuable. The most common job (salaried) in this firm is Professional (Information & Technology) with an average annual pay of $77,280, and the most common job with this firm (hourly) is Full-time Tailor at an average annual income of $31,692. This firm provides no information on the number of applicants, but with the voluntary turnover so high I would believe if you are interested in retail sales and have some reasonable experience, a good résumé, and know how to interview, you should not have any problems getting hired.

CarMax

When you think of a place to buy a car do you think of a good place to work? That's the 64 thousand dollar question. Well This Automotive Retailing Service outfit is ranked overall at 93rd and 33rd as a large company. Headquartered in Virginia, it was a surprise to me that this 'ho haggle' car superstore lets employees buy any car left on the lot longer than 14 days for $200 over cost. I am still trying to understand 'no haggle'. Also, when an employee volunteers for a nonprofit, CarMax pays the organization $10 for each hour worked.

The company has 11,400 employees in the United States, of which 42 percent are minorities and 23 percent are women. The company is boasting the creation of 950 new jobs or a job growth of 12 percent, not bad by the way. The company suggests that their average voluntary turnover is 17 percent. As an employee you will be involved in 82 hours of professional growth training.

The most common job (salaried) is Buyer with an annual average pay of $55,000, and the most common job (hourly) is Sales Consultant that pays an annual income on the average of $44,000 a year.

CarMax reports that they have about 35,240 applicants a year; with this number I would suggest that they will be looking for people with prior car sales, or at least sales experience. I am only guessing but I would think that the company will lean away from people from the 'old' school of selling cars. In your best interest it would advisable to talk to someone who works or has worked for the company to see what they are really looking for in an applicant and design your résumé in that direction.

Bright Horizons

Here is something a little different. These folks are a Diversified Outsourcing firm headquartered in Watertown, Maryland. More commonly known as a child care provider, you will find that over 90 of the Fortune 500 companies use there care. Workers here get 50% discounts on their child care, and 20 times a year they can use backup child care for $10 a day.

The company employs 13,551 people here in the States and another 1,658 outside the country. Thirty-two percent of these employees are minorities and as you might expect 96% are women.

The company has created 836 new jobs or a job growth of 8 percent. The voluntary turnover is a little high at 20 percent. This is interesting, as an employee of the firm you will receive 100 hours of professional training a year.

The most common job (salaried) is Director with an annual average income of $50,900 a year, and the most common job (hourly) you will find to be a Teacher at $23,460 average annually.

With a somewhat low income, there was a whopping 10,202 applicants for these jobs. However, with the somewhat high turnover the qualified individual would still have a good chance.

Wm. Wrigley Jr.

Here is a name that has been around for a while Wm. Wrigley Jr. headquartered in Chicago, Illinois is ranked 95th overall and 34th as a midsized company. Traditions endure under CEO Bill Wrigley, who is the great-grandson of the founder. Every month the Gum Lady distributes free gum at company HQ. One-third of their employees have been with the company for more than 15 years.

In 1891 William Wrigley Jr. came to Chicago from Philadelphia when the was 29 years old with $32.00 in his pocket and with enthusiasm, energy, and a talented salesman, created the Wrigley chewing gum empire.

Today the company employs 3,372 employees in the United States and 11,978 out of country. Of these 30 percent are minorities with 38 percent being women.

The company reports that they have a slight down turn and they have lost 85 jobs or a job growth of – 2 percent. I was surprised to see a low voluntary turnover of 4%. The most common job (salaried) of Territory Manager with an average annual income of $56,936 and the most common job (hourly) is Wrapping Machine Operator with an average annual pay of $47,110.

If you want to be apart of a company that is steadfast in applying this basic principal: 'Even in a little thing like a stick of gum, quality is important.' But you will be among the 22,898 applicants that apply every year.

The Job Search Tool to Get You That Job

<u>Ikea (U.S.)</u>

I have to say we haven't too many Specialty Retailers like this one in our survey. Here we have this Swedish midsized company ranked 96th overall and 35th as a midsized firm. What makes this company stand out is that they have been expanding in the United States. The company is looking to add three to five stores a year in this country. Eighty percent of employees agree that 'people are given a lot of responsibility here.'

The company has 9,499 employees in the United States with no employees working out of country. Of these 58 percent are minorities and of that a whopping 91 percent are women.

You will find 940 new employees or 18 percent job growth. The voluntary turnover rate at this firm is high at 34 percent. However, if you are an employee of this Specialty Retailer you will be involved in 40 hours of professional training a year.

The most common job (salaried) is Sales Manager at an average annual income of $57,268, and the most common job (hourly) you will find is Sales Co-worker with an average annual income of $18,300.

If your interest is in retailing and you select this firm as a place you would like to set your sights on, be prepared to be one of the 31,000 applicants that this firm gets each year.

<u>Intel</u>

By now I would believe that everyone knows that Intel is one of the big names in computer components. You will find this firm headquartered in Santa Clara, California. This company has an overall ranking of 97th with a large company rank of 35th. Intel is known for its tough, confrontational culture in which employees are encouraged to speak up. CEO Paul Otellini has his own blog. 'How cool is that?' says one employee. Workers get an eight-week paid sabbatical every seven years.

7001 Resumes-Plus Second Edition

The company employs 48,655 people in the United States with 35,974 outside the country. Of these, 33 percent are minorities with 24 percent being women.

The company has developed 488 new jobs with a job growth of 1 percent. This Semiconductor firm can boast about its low 4 percent voluntary turnover. I would suggest that this is impressive for the electronic industry.

The most common job (salaried) with this firm is Component Design Engineer with an annual average income of $101,816, and the most common job (hourly) Manufacturing Technician with an average annual pay of $55,690.

If you think that moving to Santa Clara, California and working for Intel would be your ideal job, make sure you have an outstanding résumé, and I would suggest that you try to do some networking because Intel receives 222,611 applicants a year.

General Mills

This Consumer Food Producer is headquartered in Minneapolis, Michigan. They hold an overall ranking at 98th with a large company ranking of 36th. What makes this company stand out? Well, you can bring your laundry to work and get your car serviced, your packages wrapped, and nails done at the headquarters of this food giant. Also available is an infant-care center for children ages 6 weeks to 16 months.

The company employs 17,993 in the United States with 9,868 working outside the country. Of this 23 percent are minorities with 40 percent being women.

Unfortunately the company has lost 992 jobs or a job growth rate of a minus 5 percent. The firm is quoting a 5 percent voluntary job turnover rate. If you find yourself an employee of the company you would be involved in 61 hours of professional training a year.

The most common job (salaried) is Retail Representative with an average annual income of $40,977 and the most common job (hourly) is Operator (semi-skilled) with an average annual pay of $48,975.

If you are looking toward General Mills as an employer you must consider the fact that they have reduced the number of jobs within the firm plus the fact that this firm has 58,155 applicants per year. I am not suggesting that you do not apply, but be aware of the low job growth at this time with this firm.

Marriott international

There are a lot of companies in the Hotel, Casino, and Resort industry; here we find this one holding an overall rank of 99th of top companies and ranked 37th of large companies. It's headquartered in Washington, District of Columbia.

This firm has a committed bunch at this hotel chain, where J. W. Marriott jr., the 73 year old son of the founder, visits the companies 200 sites a year. Nearly a quarter of employees have more than ten years of services; 5,000 more have 20-plus years.

This hotel chain employs 126,704 employees here in the United States with 6,600 out of country. Of this, 59 percent are minorities with 54 percent being women.

The company has developed 2,941 new jobs, or a job growth of 3 percent. This is a good number of jobs but with the overall size of the employment staff it does not seem so impressive. The firm does have a high level of voluntary turnover of 18 percent but you would expect a high level turn over in this industry. As an employee here you can expect 87 hours of professional training per year.

The most common job with this firm (salaried) is Sales Manager with an average annual income of $60,333 and the most common job (hourly) average annual pay is $22,075.

7001 Resumes-Plus Second Edition

There is no information available about the number of applicants, but you can be assured that it is a good number. However, with the high level of voluntary turnover and the company creating a large number of new jobs there is going to be jobs at this firm. You will just have to decide if you are interested in working in the hotel industry.

Nike

We all know what this firm does, the name says it all. Headquartered in Beaverton, Oregon, Nike holds the overall rank of 100th and is ranked 38th as a large company. Responding to criticism from activists, this sports giant now has 90 full-time employees monitoring overseas factories. The Perks in the U.S include a 50% discount on Nike gear and a campus with a pool, climbing walls, and trails.

The company employs 12,562 employees in the United States and 11,029 outside of the country. Of these 40 percent are minorities with 49 percent being women.

The company has developed 452 new jobs with a job growth rate of 5 percent. And I believe that the company can boast of its 7 percent voluntary job turnover.

The most common job (salaried) is Professional/Specialist General with an annual average pay of $52,086, and the most common job (hourly) is Material Handler Assistant with an average annual income of $34,648.

If you think you want to work for Nike you will have to get in line, they get 299,925 applicants a year. So here again, you will want to make sure you have done your work and prepared the best résumé you can. And if you do some networking this wouldn't hurt you either.

In conclusion

What we have done here is explored the top 100 companies in America. Though there are many more good firms that you might be interested in working for in your area and outside your community. There are a number of things you need to do before you apply to a company you would be interested in working for. One thing which is very important is to decide if the area is one in which you would be conformable living in. This may not be at the forefront of your consideration; however, it may become very important down the road and could cause you some grief or disappointment.

For example, if you are one of those individuals that could become depressed at that fact it is raining a lot, although this may give you a very 'green' community, you may not want to live in the state of Washington. A great state, but it can get very wet. Or you would like a more rural life; you may be unhappy in Santa Clara, California.

Once you have decided where you want to live, you need to make sure you take the time to prepare your résumé using the samples that have been outlined in this workbook. Tailor your résumé and cover letter to fit the company you are applying to. Also, when you can, try to find yourself a 'Champion' to assist you in obtaining the job of your choice. As you may recall we have discussed the value of a Champion in this book, take the time to review this section. And before you interview, take the time to review the interviewing techniques. Remember, the bottom line in getting the job of your choice is up to you.

CHAPTER THIRTY

HOW MUCH ARE YOU REALLY WORTH?

As you go through the process of job search it is important that you have some idea of what the positions you apply for are worth, and what you are worth based upon your education and experience. This information is going to help you to negotiate and secure the job you are going for. The following information is courtesy of the U. S. Department of Labor, and other research.

How much money does a Chef earn?

The salaries for chefs vary a great deal, depending on the size and location of the establishment, volume of business, and chef's reputation. According to the U.S. department of labor the average income is $32,650 for a head chef and up to $100,000 depending on training and talent. Chefs trained at the CIA (Culinary Institute of America) or Europe, especially France, earns the most, as do talented chefs at five-star restaurants. For someone with a two-year degree from a local community colleges culinary arts program, they will start at less than $35,000.

How much money does an Accountant earn?

Typical experience Entry Level income for an accountant is $33,000 to $34,000 the first year. Junior Staff accountants earn $36,000 to $63,000 the 1st year, second year and Senior Staff Accountants from $40,000 to $85,000. Managers can earn from $50,000 to $110,000. After 7 plus years Partners can earn $260,000 or more.

First you must consider the fact that you are going to be earning a Masters degree and work toward earning a CPA. The CPA goes beyond the duties of accountant which you will have to research, but to become a CPA you must study and take a test that evaluates your technical competences. You will take a test that licenses you to be a CPA in all 50 states and other U.S. territories. There are four parts to the test, and you must pass each part by 75%. The rate on passing the CPS test is 33 percent. But like a Doctor to practice as a CPA you must have a license.

In the Federal Government, the starting annual salary of junior accountants and auditors was $23,442 in 2003. Candidates who had a superior academic record might start at $29,037, while applicants with a master's degree or 2 years of professional experience usually began at $35,519. Supervisory and managerial positions averaged $69,370 a year in 2003; while auditors averaged $73,247.

How much does an Air Traffic Controller earn?

First what do they do? The Air Traffic Controller directs the flow of aircraft in and out of airports. There are specializations, such as ground controller, departure controllers, and route controllers. You will find that Air Traffic Controllers work at Airport control towers, radar rooms, and en route control centers.

To become an Air Traffic Controller you much have a Federal certification. Unless you come to the job with extensive military training and experience in air traffic controlling, prospective air traffic controllers must be trained by the Federal Aviation Administration (FAA). The minimum requirement to enter the academy is a high school diploma and some general work experience. The FAA does not hire entry-level air traffic control specialists older than 31. The age restriction does not apply to air traffic controllers coming from the military. To get into the FAA Air Traffic Control Academy, students must pass the FAA Traffic Selection and Training exam.

Earning: Usually in the $90-$146,000 range. And the job outlook is very good; in fact it is a good time to get into this competitive field because many new controllers are needed to replace those likely to retire soon.

What does a Carpenter earn?

The income of a Carpenter can very quite a bit, based on seasonal demands, regional factors, your qualifications, whether you're in a union (United Brotherhood of Carpenters and Joiners of America), and more. Earnings can be reduced on occasion, because Carpenters lose work time in bad weather and during recessions when jobs are unavailable.

In 2002, median hourly earnings of carpenters were $16.44. The middle 50 percent earned between $12.59 and $21.91. The lowest 10 percent earned less than $9.95, and the highest 10 percent earned more than $27.97. Median hourly earnings in the industries employing the largest number of carpenters in 2002 are shown below.

o Nonresidential building construction $18.31

o Building finishing contractors $17.30

o Residential building construction $16.02

o Foundation, structure, and building exterior contractors $16.01

o Employment services $12.58

The national average for an apprentice carpenter is $12.50 per hour plus benefits, after finishing the apprenticeship the average becomes $21-$25 per hour plus benefits.

7001 Resumes-Plus Second Edition

You can't really give an average income for a carpenter because there are some that build custom cabinets and other interior pieces and some exterior things that make good money. A good carpenter can expect to earn $800 to $1,000 per week, but on very good jobs it is possible to earn $400.00 in a single day.

How much money does a Dental Assistant earn?

First let us explore what the Dental Assistant does. As a Dental Assistant you would help the dental operator (Dentist or other treating Dental auxiliary) provide more efficient dental treatment. Your tasks include but are not limited to the following:

o   Holding and passing instruments

o   Retracting tissues and suctioning to assist better vision of the operating field.

o   Sterilizing dental instruments and equipment.

o   Developing dental radiographs

o   Charting

o   There are many other traditional and extended duties.

The pay for a dental assistant really depends on the area you live in, and what you consider 'good'. In large cities you would earn more than in small towns, and you could probably earn more if you received formal training (although there is some value in 'hands-on' experience. The work can be tedious and the hours can also be long, but many dental assistants love their job. Pay can start at $7.00 an hour and you can earn as much as $14.00 an hour or more. There are also pension benefits and medical plans available depending on the dental firm. You can also find vacation plans and other benefits.

It may be a good idea to get formal training to make yourself more salable. Dental Assistant training last about 39 weeks during the day or if you want to go to school at night

The Job Search Tool to Get You That Job

to get the training, it may be as long as 45 weeks. Schools will provide training in realistic laboratory environments, and many provide hands-on working experience called externships. This experience can be up to 160 hours or more of training.

A majority of Dental Assistants are employed by General Dentists. Some are employed by Specialists (orthodontists, oral surgeons, etc.), some assistants work part-time, and sometimes in more than one office. Assistants may have some freedom to choose their own hours.

How much does an Actor earn?

We all have a favorite actor or actress and may often say to ourselves, 'I could do that'. But just what kind of a career is acting and how much does it pay?

As we know, actors perform in stage, radio, television, video, or motion pictures. Most actors work hard to find steady work, but only a few become famous 'stars'. Some well known, skilled actors may be in supporting roles while others work as 'extras,' with no lines, or only one or two lines. They also teach in high schools or college drama departments, acting conservatories, or public programs.

Most acting jobs only last a short period of time, from 1 day to a few months, which means that they can have a long time between jobs. So, most actors must have extra jobs in order to make enough money.

Actors work long hours. They may do one show at night and another during the day. They also might travel with a show. Evening and weekend work is a regular part of an actor's life. As an actor you need to be in good physical condition. They must endure heat from bright lights. They get water breaks so they will not get tired or sick from heat or thirst.

To get ready to be an actor you may follow many paths. First, it is very important that you love to entertain others. Most new actors play a part in high school or college plays, work in college radio stations, or act with local groups. Some have local experience and work in summer plays, on cruise lines, or in theme parks. Some actors may start by doing commercials. This helps many young actors sharpen their skills and earn needed credits for membership in one of the actors' unions. Union membership and work experience in smaller communities may lead to work in larger cities, mainly New York or Los Angeles. Actors usually work their way up to larger parts and productions.

Actors usually train at an acting school or in a college programs. However, some people enter the field without it. Those who want a bachelor's take classes in radio and television broadcasting, communications, film, theater, drama, or dramatic literature. Many continue their college training and get a master's degree in fine arts. Training may have classes in stage speech and movement, directing, playwriting, and design, as well as acting workshops.

Actors often work with a drama coach. They research their roles so they can understand the story's setting and background. Sometimes they learn a foreign language or train with a coach to develop a certain accent to make their characters realistic.

You will find that actors need a lot of talent in order to play different parts. Skills such as singing, dancing, skating, or juggling may be important. Actors must have self control and be able to follow directions. Modeling experience also may be helpful. Physical appearance, such as the right size, weight, or facial look, often determines who gets selected for certain roles.

Most actors have agents or managers who find work, deal with contracts, and plan their careers. Agents earn a part of the pay in an actor's contract. Other actors try out for parts on their own. Many years ago my daughter was a model; she had an agent which received 10 percent of everything my daughter earned.

To become a movie extra, an actor usually must be with a casting agency. Actors only get small parts when more people are needed to perform in a particular movie. Very few actors actually get parts this way.

The middle half of all actors made between $15,320 and $53,320 in 2002. The lowest-paid 10 percent earned less than $13,330, and the highest-paid 10 percent earned more than $105,350, though the most famous actors earn much more. We all have heard of the $10,000,000 that Tom Cruise earned per movie, or the fact that Arnold Schwarzenegger is worth over $800,000,000 from his moving making. These are the exceptions to the rule.

The future for employment as an actor is expected to grow about as fast as the average for all occupations through 2012. Competition for jobs will be tough because many highly trained and talented people are trying to become actors. Many actors leave this job because the hours are long and they can't earn enough money. Only a few actors become a star.

There are other jobs like this:

- o Choreographers
- o Dancers
- o Designers
- o Disc Jockeys
- o Editors
- o Makeup artists
- o Musicians
- o Singers
- o Writers

How much does a Bank Teller earn?

If you are organized, efficient, and are good at interacting with others, you might want to consider a job in banking; most of the time you will start out as a Bank Teller. Today this entails long weeks or so (depending on the bank). The Bank Teller position can also serve as a 'gateway' to increasingly responsible positions in the banking/financial services industry. You will need a combination of work experience, on-the-job training, and the right education. With this it

7001 Resumes-Plus Second Edition

is possible to become a teller supervisor, vault teller, new accounts representative, loan officer, credit examiner, supervisor, branch manager, or mortgage loan processor.

A Financial services/teller position is available throughout the United States. Salaries range from $7.50 to $13.50 an hour, depending on hours worked and the position, financial institution, and the average wage in a community. Over the next years the expected need for financial service and tellers is expected to increase as banks and credit unions expand their services. In addition to traditional urban and suburban settings, banks, credit unions and other financial service businesses can now be found in shopping centers, grocery stores, even on college campuses.

How much does a Construction Equipment Operator earn?

Are you good with your hands? Do you have strong depth perception and good communication skills? Can you work in high places? If so, then Crane and Hoisting Equipment Operator may be the job for you!

You will need to choose a career path. There is the servicing and operating the hoist and swing equipment that is used to move machinery and other large objects at construction sites and industrial yards. Then there are other types of construction equipment jobs.

The out look for construction is terrific with 6.7 million wage and salary jobs and 1.6 million self-employed and unpaid family nongovernmental jobs in 2002; it was one of the Nation's largest industries. Jobs opportunities for construction equipment operators are expected to be good through 2013 – due to the shortage of adequate training programs. In addition, many potential workers may choose not to enter training programs because they prefer work that is less strenuous and has more comfortable working conditions. Construction equipment operators held about 416,000 jobs in 2002. Jobs were found in every sector of the country and were distributed among various types of operators.

About three out of five construction equipment operators worked in the construction industry. Many equipment operators worked in heavy construction, building, highways,

The Job Search Tool to Get You That Job

bridges, or railroads. About one out of five of all construction equipment operators worked in State and local government. Others, mostly grader, bulldozer, and scraper operators, worked in mining. Some also worked in manufacturing and for utility companies; less than one in twenty construction equipment operators were self-employed.

With the completion of a training certificate course you should be afforded opportunities from contractors to 'show your stuff.' The industry needs operators to replace the ones leaving and to fill the jobs required by the overwhelming increase in construction projects across the nation. With your formal training, heart, and integrity, no experience is required for employment.

As was indicated you will have to choose a career path, but an apprentice of a Tower Crane Operator for example, you could earn at least 70% of the journeyman wage rate in your place of employment in the first year, and 80% in the second year of your apprenticeship. As an apprentice Mobile Crane Operator (except for Hydraulic and Conventional which do not specify), you earn at least 70% of the journeyman wage rate in your place of employment in the first year, 80% in the second, and 90% in the third year of your apprenticeship. Since I referred to other types of construction equipment, you will find that the pay varies.

In this example the journeyman rate of pay is \$12 to \$28 an hour plus benefits. In addition to the basic hourly rate, employers provide statutory holiday and vacation pay. Employers may also provide other benefits such as group insurance for health, dental and vision care, retirement packages, and training benefits. In total, benefits can be worth 20 percent to over 30% over and above the basic hourly pay rate. You will find that this represents a 40-hour, five-day workweek which is normal. You may also have to work occasional overtime to meet construction deadlines.

To advance you can do so with experience and additional training, again advancement may vary with the type of equipment and work you are doing, but in this example you may advance to supervisory positions. If you want to relocate, you can take your skills with you. Like most careers in the construction industry, your skills in this occupation are portable.

7001 Resumes-Plus Second Edition

To become a Crane and Hoist Equipment Operator you will need training, and you must earn a certificate or registered apprentice of the trade. To register in an apprenticeship program, you will need to complete an application, have a 10th grade education, and pass an entrance exam. You are going to have to find an appropriate employer who is willing to hire and train you as an apprentice. Again, requirements for other construction training may vary. If you choose the Heavy Boom Truck path, your apprenticeship lasts 2 years (two 12 month periods). This includes a minimum of 1000 hours of on-the-job training and 4 weeks of technical training each year. The Medium Boom Truck apprenticeship will last 1 year (one 12- month period). This includes a minimum of 1000 hours of on-the-job training and 4 weeks of technical training. Again I want to point out that training for other constriction equipment will vary.

If you are still in high school, you can Jump-start your career in construction by checking out Career and Technology Study (CTS) courses. These hands-on courses can help you build the basic skills you will need for work in the construction industry. You can also begin an apprenticeship program and earn high school credits at the same time through the Registered Apprenticeship Program (RAP). After high school graduation, many RAP apprentices complete apprenticeship programs while working full-time.

How much does Computer Operators earn?

Under this heading I am going to talk about a few of the different jobs in the computer technology area. Therefore you will only get an overview; if you find one or more of these areas interesting it may require addition research. However, if you are trying to decide on a career but want to be sure you are choosing one that is in demand and that has potential for growth, your best choice may be Computer Software Engineering, or Computer Support Specialist. According to the bureau of labor statistics these careers are the fastest growing as well as the best paying fields in the local area.

The Job Search Tool to Get You That Job

If you like searching for facts and figuring out problems mentally rather than leading or persuading people, enjoy math and science classes, have an inquisitive nature and prefer work that involves ideas and thinking more than with physical activity, you may want to consider a career in the computer field. Typically, a person who does well in this field is an out-going, take charge type who likes change and sees obstacles as challenges. They tend to stay focused on resolving problems and reaching conclusions while mobilizing resources to achieve their long range goals. If you believe that describes you, a computer career could be ideal for you.

Let us look at the Computer Software Engineer. This job creates and modifies general computer applications software or specialized utility programs. Their job is to analyze user needs and develop software solutions that are customized for a particular business, with the goal of optimizing operational efficiency for the company. Examples of computer specialties under this category include Computer Engineering Technologist, Computer Software Engineering, Information Technology, and Medical Illustration.

Now the Computer Support Specialist provides technical assistance to computer system users by telephone or from a remote location. Many provide assistance concerning the use of computer hardware and software, including printing, installation, and word processing. Computer Support Specialist includes: Computer Customer Service Representatives, Network Control Operations, User Support Analysts, and Technical Support Specialists. Companies such as AOL and Dell Computers, have computer call centers where they employ a variety of computer specialties.

You will find that the Bureau of Labor Statistics suggest that the Computer Software Applications field is expected to grow by 100 percent throughout the United States with an average of 28,000 annual job openings. The growth rate countrywide for Computer Support Specialists is predicted to be 97% with 40,000 annual openings.

You can expect to receive an entry level wage of $18,660 as a Computer Support Specialist and earn a high of $33,000 with a high school diploma and experience. A Computer Software

7001 Resumes-Plus Second Edition

Engineer with a Bachelors Degree can expect to start at $61,511 and earn up to $99,530 with experience.

You can expect to work 40 hours a week, 8 a.m. to 5 p.m. Monday through Friday. Most employers offer benefits packages that include health, dental, vision, holidays and vacations, and retirement plans.

To enter this field can be simple; many companies are not looking for people with degrees to hang on a wall, but if you are a High School graduate with a strong interest in computers, have experience, and possess computer knowledge, this is the first prerequisite to success in the field. In my opinion if you train in High School and take this experience with you and develop additional computer education, plus have a strong desire, you will move up the career ladder. Persons without a college degree, and college graduates unfamiliar with data processing, will face stiff competition from the large number of experienced workers seeking jobs.

So if you are in High School go to your Career Center and check out the variety of assessments, labor market information, and career resources to guide you in making an informal decision. You can also get advice on school programs and sources of financial aid to help you to reach your goals. Also consult your guidance counselor.

In large data processing departments, persons who begin as junior systems analysts may be promoted to senior or lead analysts after several years of experience. If you show leadership ability you may also be advanced to jobs as managers of departments. Some computer experienced people may start their own computer consulting firms.

Finding employment should be simple; you can find positions advertised in your local and national newspapers. Information about no-advertised job opportunities can frequently be obtained from friends working in the industry or through contacts made at professional meetings and conferences. Those interested in civil service jobs should contact the federal, State,

The Job Search Tool to Get You That Job

county, and city personnel offices. Further information on employment may be obtained from your nearest Employment Development Department Job Service office.

How much does a Fire Fighter earn?

Fire-fighters are modern heroes. They have an undoubtedly dangerous job, yet it's one that many people are keen to find out more about, and to do. Whatever your reason for being interested in the fire service, whether it's the uniform, the chance to demonstrate extreme bravery, or just the chance to drive a fire-engine, you will find this the favorite career of children. No doubt the kids are fascinated by the bright red vehicles clanging down the road, and the dare devilry in rescuing victims trapped in infernos among the other things. But a fire fighter's work is no child's play. Fire is one of the most dangerous enemies of life – plant, animal, and human. Greatly so to urban existence, where the threat to human lives is multiplied manifold.

A firefighter's job is for those with plenty of guts and physical strength. It's the firefighters' job to respond to fire alarms and other emergency calls in the city. It is also their job to drive and operate firefighting vehicles and equipment.

On any given day a fire department may be called upon for the following:

- Airplane crashes
- Animal rescues
- Bomb threats
- Brush fires
- Car fires
- Childbirth
- Elevator rescues
- Floods
- Gas leaks
- Hazardous material spills
- And more!

Firefighters also play an important role in education and pubic awareness of fire safety. All this in addition to putting out house fires!

7001 Resumes-Plus Second Edition

First understand that salary for Firefighters' will vary from state to state and city to city. However in Seattle, Washington for example, they make about $42,000. The median hourly earning of fire fighters' was around $18.43 in May 2004. The middle 50 percent earned between $13.65 and $24.14. The lowest 10 percent can earn less than $9.71, and the highest 10 percent earned more than $29.21. Median hourly earnings were $18.78 in local government, $17.34 in the Federal Government, and $14.94 in State government.

In May 2005 the median annual earnings of first-line supervisors/managers of fire and prevention workers was $58,920. The middle 50% earned between $46,880 in May 2004 and $72,600. The lowest 10 percent earned less than $36,800, and the highest 10 percent earned more than $90,860. First-line supervisors/managers of fire fighting and prevention workers employed in local government earned about $60,800 a year.

In May 2004 the median annual earnings of fire inspectors and investigators was $46,340. The middle 50 percent earned between $36,030 and $58,260 a year. The lowest 10 percent earned less than $28,420 and the lightest 10 percent earned more than $71,490. Fire inspectors and investigators employed in local government earned about $48,020.

Understand there are different types of firefighter's jobs (Municipal, forest, industrial, and more).

In nearly all cases to be a fireman you will need to get some training. In most states you will have to pass a State or City physical test. You will also have to pass an academic performances test.

To meet these requirements you may want to go to a Junior College or approved Fire Training Academy. Academies are located in various parts of your state, and class schedules are usually stated in conjunction with the start of the college semester. Typically two classes are started each year. The minimum standard is about $450 for training. For additional information consult you local Junior College, or Association.

Getting hired

Although the hiring process is often seen by would-be firefighters as tricky and confusing there is information available. There are guides available where you can get advice from successful firefighters and people who hire firefighters. You may need to go on the Internet to get said guide. However, it will discuss the best places to be a firefighter, when and what departments to contact, details about the entrance exams, what fire chiefs are looking for, how to dress, taking physical, medical and psychological exams, and more. If you are interested go to www.fabjob.com/Firefighter.asp. You will find a Guild and also a CD available for a small price.

How much does a Nurse earn?

Like most occupations, the income will vary from state to state and job to job. Though in California on average a CNA (certified nursing assistant) makes $9.14 per hour, more being made on night shifts, and with experience. An LVN (Licensed Vocational Nurse) gets paid approximately $20 to $30 per hour, though many earn $22-25 dollars per hour. An RN (registered nurse) makes $30 plus per hour and some times more. This is in a real hospital, doing 'hour' health; there are places where you can make less, but at the same time more. You will find a great need for nurses with new and interesting positions depending on where and what type of nursing. A staff nurse starts off in a hospital at about $18.00, as a traveler you will make about $30. I am aware of persons in nursing making over $100,000 but I would suggest an average of $50.000 or more. This sounds like a good income, but consider that this is overall a very difficult, unappreciated and sometimes dangerous job. You have a heavy burden of responsibility and the lives of others are in your hands. One screw up can ruin you for life. Imagine if you made an honest mistake, like medicated a person (say a child or a baby) with the wrong med or gave the wrong dose by accident. The patient dies. You get sued, reprimanded, raked over the coals, all while experiencing the guilt and remorse for what you have done. You live with something like that the rest of your life. However though, you will find many opportunities for a career in Nursing out the United States.

7001 Resumes-Plus Second Edition

To understand the role of a nurse, take the time to chat with someone in nursing prior to starting a nursing course. No one will be able to provide a better insight into the life of a nurse than a nurse; it's best coming form the horse's mouth, so to speak.

If you do not know anyone that works as a nurse, you may be able to get in touch with your local health care trust and ask if they can arrange a meeting with a nurse so you can discuss it with them because you're interested in becoming one. I am sure if you contacted any of your local hospitals or University training hospitals you could also get answers to your many questions. Since I have been married to a Managing nurse for several years I can assure you that there are many new opportunities that were not around a few years ago, so I would suggest that you explore these career paths within the nursing industry.

There are some hospitals that are offering experienced nurses bonuses up to $14,000 at signing apart from their salaries. Statistics show that 400,000 nursing positions will be available coming 2012, and if nursing isn't the forte, there are plenty of health care programs that focus on lab tech training and lead to lucrative health care careers.

To become a nurse in most cases you will need a degree, this is the most obvious and popular route to becoming a certified nurse. Universities provide accredited nursing degrees. These courses, running at universities across the country, are to provide a combination of theoretical work and practical training by assigning students to attend healthcare practices such as nursing homes and such.

What you need to know is that courses should be accredited, so if you select a private school, and they are out there, such as: University of Phoenix, Keiser University, or American Intercontinental University, getting a nursing license requires the nursing education/training is attained from a school that is accredited by the National League for Nursing Accrediting Commission.

The Job Search Tool to Get You That Job

For more information about becoming a Nurse I would suggest that you go on line and do additional research, consult your career counselor, or contact your local University.

How much does a Police Officer earn?

You can very well take for granted that most Police Departments in the United States have the same philosophy as the New York City Police Department that their mission is to 'enforce the laws, and preserve the peace, reduce fear, and provide for a safe environment'.

The pay for new officers will vary across the country; in New York new hires earn $25,100 a year. Upon the completion of the Police Academy, in this case their training is six months (again this will vary from department to department), the annual salary increases to $32,700. Top pay for an officer in the New York Department is $59,588, not including overtime and other forms of compensation. Some Department pay is considerably more, up to $50,000 for new hires and over $100,000 for experienced cops. You will have to contact each department you have an interest in. I am sure you will find an established pay scale you can review.

Some departments have to take a test and run a background check. In the City of Mesa, Arizona, the Police Department suggests that the process could take up to 3 to 5 months with a target time of 3 month.

The age may vary some, but you must be 21 years of age at the time you graduate from the Mesa, Arizona Police Department Academy. Their department has no age limit but this may not hold true with others.

You will have to take a written test in some departments; Mesa's testing for example has 169 questions, multiple-choice, and timed. The questions are related to: common sense, reading comprehension, sentence structure, and observation skills. In the Mesa Department test you will have to score 70% or better to pass. I remember many, many years ago, being young and fresh out of the Navy, I was bumping around and decided to take the police officer exam for the Sunnyvale, California department. I was surprised to find police investigation questions. So,

517

each department designs the test their way, therefore you will need to ask a few questions to determine the direction each test might take.

A great many departments have a challenging physical agility test that you must pass; the Mesa Police Department is no acceptation. You must realize that the police academy and departments have high expectations. If you are not in good shape, you will not have the stamina or strength to complete the physical agility exam successfully. It is reported that 30% of the applicants fail this test the first time.

In many departments the academy allows recruits to attend at no charge and they are a paid employee, though the lengths may differ with each department. I have heard of some individuals going through the school at their own expense in hopes of finding employment. The schools provide training in such things as: night field problems, night shooting, criminal codes, domestic violence, multiculturalism, interpersonal communication, driving, and more. Typically classes start three times per year and usually run in February, June, and October. Once the applicant completes the process they can usually be placed in an employment position within a department.

Over the years criminal justice education has progressed, and some departments are looking for more and more policeman with college training. You will find this training being provided at the college level.

I am sure you will find Community Colleges in your area that are providing two-year associate degree programs. In most cases these will be purely academic courses; however some schools are incorporating basic law enforcement certification into their 2-year curricula. Many states have integrated their mandated-based police training into their two-year programs or a pre-service basis. Students who complete criminal justice programs in those settings often earn both an associate degree and certification necessary for employment.

An increasing number of police agencies now require the 4-year bachelor's degree as a hiring credential. Generally regarded as part of the social sciences, four-year criminal justice programs focus more on research than on skills training, in accordance with long dictates of disciplines.

Many police department are divided into several major bureaus, each sub-divided into sections, divisions, and units. This in turn will offer various types of positions and activities.

- Aviation Unit

    The aviation Unit responds to various emergencies and tasks, supporting Patrol as well as other units.

- Emergency Service Unit

    The Emergency Service Unit provides specialized support and advanced equipment to other units.

- Harbor Unit and Scuba Team

    It should be clear that this unit only exist in those communities where there are miles of waterways to cover. This unit of course is to provide protection of life and property.

- Special Victims Squad

    Here again the name, size, and existence of this unit will vary with each department, but this unit is involved in the investigations of sex crimes and attempted sex crimes of children less than 13 years of age. They are also involved in the investigation of aggravated sexual abuse (all degrees) and more.

- Major Case Squad

    This squad handles Kidnappings, burglary, larceny, extortion, robbery, and more.

- Movie and Television Unit

7001 Resumes-Plus Second Edition

You may not find this unit in every police department, but the NYPD does have such a unit. In fact, the NYPD was the first department in the county to have one. This unit has the greatest knowledge on how to assist production, particularly with complex shooting situations in a city that is dense with vehicular and pedestrian traffic. The also provide their services free to productions filming in their city.

- School Safety Division / Training Unit

Provided with entry-level basic training in the areas of Behavioral Science, Police Science, Law, and Physical Training Tactics (including CPR/First Aid Training), you may or may not find this Division in every department. You have to remember this type of Division is more prevalent in larger departments.

- Real Time Crime Center

This again is a unit normally found in larger departments. This department essentially collects and warehouses data. You will find search engine operations by a staff of detectives that assist and provide relevant and timely information to officers' conducting investigations.

- Auxiliary Police

Again more likely found in larger departments.

- Crime Scene Units

Because of Television we are all aware of CSI activities and forensic work.

- Housing Bureau

More generally found in larger departments.

- Detective work

The Job Search Tool to Get You That Job

Normally an officer enters patrol work and if you become interested in becoming a detective, as in the case of Mesa City Police, you must have a minimum of three years on the force, though there are some exceptions to the rule.

- SWAT

Officers work four 10-hour shifts per week, but this work day depends on each department. Individuals with active duty military can apply for the position of police officer, but need to apply six months before their discharge.

For more information about being a policeman you will need to contact the department in which you are interested in or you can contact your local college to get information on getting information on Criminal Justice Classes.

How much does an Insulation Worker earn?

Today with the entire hullabaloo about energy conservation, the Insulation Worker is going to be a busy occupation. Properly insulated buildings reduce energy consumption by keeping heat in during the winter, and out in the summer. Refrigerated storage rooms, vats, tanks, vessels, boilers, and steam and hot water pipes are also insulated to prevent the wasteful loss of heat. Insulation workers install the materials used to insulate buildings and equipment.

Insulation workers cement, staple, wire, tape, or spray insulation. When covering a steam pipe, for example, insulation workers measure and cut sections of insulation to the proper length, stretch it open along a cut that runs the length of the material, and slip it over the pipe. They fasten the insulation with adhesive, staples, tape, or wire bands. Sometimes, they wrap a cover of aluminum, plastic, or canvas over the insulation and cement or band the cover in place. Insulation workers may screw on sheet metal around insulated pipes to protect the insulation from weather conditions of physical abuse.

7001 Resumes-Plus Second Edition

As an insulation worker you could work in attics or on exterior walls of un-insulated buildings where you blow in loose-fill insulation. A helper feeds a machine with fiberglass, cellulose, or rock-wool insulation, while another worker blows the insulation with a compressor hose into the space being filled.

As an installer you could work on new construction and/or major renovations, insulation workers staple fiberglass or rock-wool batts to exterior walls and ceilings before drywall, paneling, or plaster walls are put in place.

Because of the danger, U.S. Environmental Protection Agency regulations require the asbestos be removed before a building undergoes major renovations or is demolished.

Insulation workers use common hand tools such as: trowels, brushes, knives, scissors, saws, pliers, and stapling guns. The may use power saws to cut insulation materials, welding machines to join sheet metal or secure clamps, and compressors to blow or spray.

If you select this occupation you should be aware that you would generally work indoors in residential and industrial settings, and more than likely spend most of your workday on your feet either standing, bending, or kneeling. As an insulation worker you may be working from ladders or in confined spaces; you could also work around vessels with temperatures that may cause burns. Minute particles may be blown around causing irritation to the eyes, skin, and respiratory system. Because of these problems there are strict safely guidelines to protect yourself.

Most insulation workers learn their trade informally on the job, although some complete formal apprenticeship programs for entry level jobs, insulation contractors prefer high school graduates who are in good physical condition and licensed to drive. High school courses in blueprint reading, shop mathematics, science, sheet metal layout, woodworking, and general construction provide a helpful background. If you are considering dropping out of high school or do not have a high school diploma, please be aware that applicants seeking apprenticeship positions should have completed high school or have its equivalent (GED) and be at least 18 years old.

As a trainee you will receive instruction and supervision from experienced insulation workers. You will start off with simple tasks such as carrying insulation or holding material while it is fastened in place. Your training may take up to 2 years depending on the nature of the work. A Certification program has been developed by insulation contactor organizations to help all workers prove their skill and knowledge.

The overall forecast is excellent for the insulation worker. There should be a lot of openings for limited skill workers and replacement workers who retire or leave the labor force for other reasons. Insulation workers held about 61, 000 jobs in 2004. The construction industry employed 4 out of 5 workers.

The medium hourly earnings of floor, ceiling, and wall insulation workers based on the most available information from 2004 is $14.57 an hour. The middle 50% earned between $10.63 and $20.20. The lowest 10 percent earned less than $8.53 and the highest 10 percent earned more than $27.35. Median hourly earnings of mechanical insulation workers were $16.03 an hour. The middle 50 percent earned between $12.16 and $21.15. The lowest 10 percent earned less than $9.82, and the highest 10 percent earned more than $28.85.

- Insulation workers, mechanical building equipment contractors

  Building equipment contractors $15.66

- Building finishing contractors $15.55

- Insulation workers, floor, ceiling, and wall

  Building finishing contractors $12.95

Note: Union workers tend to earn more than nonunion works.

7001 Resumes-Plus Second Edition

Related Occupations:

(Carpenters

(Carpet

(Floor and tile installers, and finishers

(Drywall installers

(Ceiling tile installers

(Tapers

(Roofers

(Sheet metal worker

For additional information about training programs of other work opportunities in the trade, contact a local insulation contractor, the nearest office of State employment service apprenticeship agencies, or one of the following organizations:

- National Insulation Association www.insulation.org

- Insulation Contractors Association of America www.insulate.org

*Source: Bureau of Labor Statistics, U.S. Department of Labor.

What does a School Teacher earn?

First, you must understand that there are hundreds, if not thousands of school districts across the country which have developed salary schedules. Plus, the salaries vary with region, and of course level of education, years of experience, and in some cases if there is a shortage for a specific area of education or specialty such as Special Education. However, we will try to take a look at some general information.

The median annual earnings for Kindergarten, elementary, middle, and secondary teacher ranged from $39,810.00 in 2002, the lowest 10 percent $24,960 to $29,850, the top 10 percent earned $62,890 to $68,530. Median earnings for preschool teachers were $19,270.

THE JOB SEARCH TOOL TO GET YOU THAT JOB

According to the American Federation of Teachers, beginning teachers with a bachelor's earned an average of $30,719 in the 2001-02 school year. The estimated average salary of all public elementary and secondary school teachers in 2001-02 school year was $44,397. Private school teachers generally earn less than public school teachers.

As a teacher you can boost your pay in a number of ways; in most school districts you receive more pay with years of experience on the pay scale. This is generally automatic; however, periodically Teacher Associations negotiate and generally improve the salary schedule. When I went into teaching many years ago, you could not go into the classroom until you had what was called '5 years'. One up side to this is the next way to boost your pay is by taking more classes.

Since the advent of 'No Student Left Behind' many districts have asked, and in some cases demanded, that teachers take special additional classes, but at the same time this has improved and moved teachers across the pay scale. Getting additional degrees, coaching sports, working with students in extracurricular activities, gets extra money. I myself was involved in an ROP (Regional Occupations Program) where I not only taught vocation class, which became a demonstration class for the state, I became a Consultant for the State, which got me 'special' money, and all I was involved with was student state competition. You can teach after school, and I, like a lot of teachers, earn extra income during the summer by teaching summer school. Also, there is what is known in some districts as a 'Six Period Assignment' which is to teach 6 periods a day and not the standard of 5 periods with a 'Prep'. They also perform other jobs in the system. In the later years, also available to many teachers, I became a department chair which provided me with a little more responsibility, and more pay.

What is interesting is that the average public school teacher was paid 36% more per hour than the average non-sales white-collar worker and 11 percent more than the average professional specialty and technical worker.

Preparing to become a teacher is not an easy task. First you need a plan. These plans start with doing well while you are attending High School. The paths to certification as a teacher

7001 Resumes-Plus Second Edition

are different depending upon your educational background and experience. After High School attend a Junior college to establish the first two years of college then move on to a four year school to get your bachelor's degree and become certified. Or on the other hand you could go directly to a credited four year school such as Sam Houston State University, California State University at San Jose, Iowa State University, or any of the hundreds of schools across the country.

How does the teaching job market compare to others? The job market for teacher varies widely by geographic area and by subject specialty. Many inner cities often characterized by overcrowded conditions and higher than average crime and poverty rates, and rural areas characterized by their remote location and relatively low salaries, have difficulty attracting enough teachers, so job prospects should continue to be better in these areas than in suburban districts. Currently many school districts have difficulty hiring qualified teachers in some subjects, such as: mathematics, science (especially chemistry and physics), bilingual education, physical education, and social studies. Teachers who are geographically mobile and who obtain licensure in more than one subject should have a distinct advantage in finding a job. With enrollments of minorities increasing, coupled with a shortage of minority teachers, efforts to recruit minority teachers should intensify. Also, the number of non-English speaking students has grown dramatically, especially in California and Florida, which have large Spanish-speaking student populations, creating a demand for bilingual teachers and those who teach English as a second language.

Overall employment of kindergarten, elementary, and secondary school teachers is expected to increase about as fast as the average for all occupations through the year 2009. The expected retirement of a large number of teachers currently in their 40s and 50s should open up many additional jobs. However, projected employment growth varies among individual teaching occupations.

Employment of secondary school teachers is expected to grow faster than the average for all occupations through the year 2009, while average employment growth is projected for kindergarten and elementary school teachers. Assuming relatively little change in average class size, employment growth of teachers depends on population growth rates and corresponding student enrollments. Enrollments of secondary school students are expected to grow throughout most of the projection periods.

The number of teachers employed is also dependent on state and local expenditures for education. Pressures from taxpayers to limit spending could result in fewer teachers than projected; however pressure to spend more to improve the quality of education could increase the teacher workforce.

For more information on licensure or certification requirements and approved teacher training institutions you can contact the State Department of Education in your state, or teacher unions. For example, you can contact the American Federation of Teachers, 555 New Jersey Ave NW, Washington, DC 20001 or The National Education Association, 1201 16th NW, Washington, DC 20036. National Council for Accreditation of Teacher Education, 2010 Massachusetts Ave. NW., Suite 500, Washington, DC 20036, The National Board for Professional Teaching Standards, 26555 Evergreen Road, Suite 400 Southfield, MI 48076.

What I have done for you is to give you an overview of a number of different jobs. At last count there were over 7,000, perhaps more, different jobs. So if you have an interest in one of the above jobs, or any of the following, you can find information similar to what I have presented here by going to various sites on the Internet. You can go to www.Google.com and/or www. Yahoo.com. Information is available at your local Department of Employment, or take a trip to your local Library and ask the Reference Librarian; she/he can help you search out information that will help with your quest. If you are a College or High school student I would suggest you visit your campus career center.

7001 Resumes-Plus Second Edition

Here are some additional Jobs and related salaries

Job Categories	Salary Range		
	Lower	Upper	Average
Administration	$6,185	$31,000	$16,172
Advertising, Marketing & PR	$10.000	$26,350	$18,794
Art, design & Crafts	$14,000	$15,000	$14,500
Construction & Property Mgr.	$10,135	$22,000	$14,798
Counseling, Social & Guid. Ser.	$10,000	$27,720	$18,468
Economists, Statisticians, etc	$16,000	$26,500	$22,657
Engineering	$12, 300	$119,900	$75,330
Auto Body Repair	$26,000	$26,000	$44.000+
Cashiers	$12,000	$18,000	$18,500+
Cost Estimator	$40,590	$41,000	$79,400
Dentists	$ n/a	$ n/a	$110,160+
Dietitians and Nutritionists	$35,020	$ n/a	$51,320
Funeral Directors & Morticians	$35,040	$ n/a	$ n/a
Financial Managers	$55,070	$ N/A	$ N/A
Glaziers	$12/hr	$ N/A	$21/hr
Guards	$16,240	$ N/A	$ more
Insurance Sales Agents	$34,370	$ N/A	$ more
Janitors, Clnrs & Instit. Cl. Super.	$15,340	$ N/A	$25,060
Jewelers & Prec. Stn. & Met. Wk	$23.820	$ N/A	$ more
Lawyers & Judicial Workers	$78,170	$ N/A	$1,000,000+
Librarians	$38,470	$ N/A	$ more
Mathematicians	$49,120	$ N/A	$ N/A
Occupational Therapists	$ 48,230	$ N/A	$86,540+
Painter & Paperhanger	$ 24,000	$ N/A	$ more
Psychologists	$48,050	$ N/A	$88,280+
Real Estate Agent & Broker	$28,020	$ N/A	$83,330+
Retail Salesperson	$7.00/hr.	$ N/A	$14/hr
Sheet Metal Worker & Duct inst.	$13/hr	$ N/A	$24/hr
Social Worker	$30,590	$ N/A	$49,080
Taxi Driver	$7/hr	$ N/A	$12/ht
Truck Driver	$11/hr	$ N/A	$19/hr
Veterinarian	$50,950	$ N/A	$106,370+
Water and wastewater Treat Pl.	$29,660	$ N/A	$44,710
Welders, Cutter, and welding op.	$25,810	$ N/A	$ More

As you see here I have given you a cross section of various salaries for a number of different jobs. In no way have I salaries for all the jobs there are; this is just a small cross section to give you a basic idea. For more information and to cover the job that you might be interested in you will need to take some time to do some research. If you have a computer you can start this research by going to www.studentsreview.com/salary.shtml or other websites on the Internet. As a suggestion you can use www.Google.com or www.Yahoo.com to start your search. Of course do not neglect your local Library or your Department of Employment for assistances.

CHAPTER THIRTY-ONE

DIGITAL RÉSUMÉS

Now on the horizon is a new fad, or an extra benefit, but definitely a milestone. In any event, this job search tool can be another option for you; it is the production of the Digital Résumé. This does however give you another job search strategy that can be sent to a potential employer. This approach is at the forefront in the job search techniques. Video résumé services are only starting to emerge on the Internet. If you have the right visuals this could be one way of getting a leg-up in your job search.

The job search has come a long way since the days of printing résumés on high-quality, linen paper and stuffing them in matching envelops. Today, employers typically accept electronic versions of traditional résumés, in fact, may require them while incorporating their own search of applicants' social-networking and personal profiles. You will find that you lose some of your formality and individualism that you might have had from a résumé that looked good and matched well.

So, to stand out, some job seekers are now turning to online services such as Workblast. com and ResumeBook.tv, or posting their clips on video-sharing sites like Google inc.'s YouTube. No longer limited to mailing video on tape or CD, they are e-mailing links to employers directly or adding them to traditional résumés.

7001 Resumes-Plus Second Edition

There are several basic approaches; one is to show the candidate speaking directly to a camera while the other is sitting in a mock interview. Some are a blend in visuals of related work or extracurricular activities, such as playing the piano, or some other activity outside of work.

Surprisingly many employers are welcoming the chance to see a candidate before committing to an interview. What the employers are discovering is that many job searchers know the right things to say because they know what the employers are looking for in their résumés. But the video presentation allows the employer to observer the candidate's presentation skills in real time. Employers are finding that this can cut interview time if they can view the applicant's video clips first. Some employers are concerned about the time it might take to review all the videos and the potential for discrimination based on race, age, and other factors that wouldn't be apparent from a traditional résumé. I can see how the Digital Résumé can be a major advantage for those who might be photogenic, or the so-called beautiful people, however, at the same time you are going to have to be somewhat of a performer.

What I want to point out here, and it's a point I suggested earlier, is whether or not you are going to use this Digital Résumé approach in your arsenal of job search tools, you need to practice job interviewing skills in front of a video camera. Clearly the employer is looking for not only the answers you give to the questions asked, but they are going to be evaluating your presentation. The more you practice, like Basketball, the better the player you will be come, and in this case you are playing the biggest game in your life, the career game. You want to be the best player you can.

As a job seeker you can make yourself look stupid, not by just having a weird or inappropriate e-mail address, but by being too casual, when in fact, you should be tops in professionalism. If you are not careful you can come across as the 'American idol.' Since the concept is new the Job Seeker has few, if any, good role models to copy; the only thing they have is trial and error, and what they see on television for inspiration. What I am advocating is developing good interview skills, practice answering the question I have given you, know

532

yourself, your goals, and where you want to go, and if you select this as one of your job search strategies, you will be prepared.

What do I really think, well I have not used this approach, but my feeling and suggestion is to use whatever job search technique that gets you a job. Use whatever approach you feel comfortable with, and that works. The best job search technique is the one that gets you the job, no more, no less. Is this Digital Résumé approach a 'flash in the pan', I think not, is it the only way to get a job, no, but it is one approach; one tool that you can have in your arsenal. I have to ask myself if I would use this approach, and I have to say that in the past when I was doing job search I used a variety of strategies, some worked, some didn't, but I tried them. I have to say yes, I would use any job search weapon/tool that would get me a job and I would hope that you would do the same.

Some advocates believe that video résumés may make sense in certain fields like broadcasting, marketing, and theater - the ones where job seekers are already asked to send in portfolios of past work. Unlike a portfolio though, a video résumé merely shows how one performs in front of a camera and it really shows a great deal of 'make believe'; it is not a true measure of your real ability. And like the résumé, it is a marketing piece 'high lighting' and 'show casing' what you can do, or what you have done for another employer, but does not necessarily show the real scope of your work.

REFERENCE:

Mags, Inc.

How to Sell Yourself, Jo Girard
Simon & Schuster, Inc, A. Warner Book

What Color is Your Parachute? Richard Nelson Bolles
Ten Speed Press

Who's Hiring Who, Richard Lathrop
Progressive Publications

Finding you ideal Job, Richard N. Diggs
Progressive Publications

Jobs'95, Kathryn and Ross Petras
Simon & Schuster, a Fireside Book

7001 RÉSUMÉS, Dr. Ferris E. Merhish
Authorhouse

RÉSUMÉS that KNOCK 'Em DEAD, Martin John Yate
Bob Adams, Inc.

Expert Résumés for People Returning to Work
JIST Works Publishing, Inc.

BUSINESS TODAY Fifth Edition, Rachman Mescon
Random House

The Management OF HUMAN RESOURCES, David j. Cheriton
Ally & Bacon, a Division of Simon & Schuster, Inc.

Sales Management, Dan H. Robertson & Danny N. Dellenger
Macmillan Publishing Co., Inc.

What you're not supposed to know, Boardroom, Inc.

15 New Rules For Job Hunting Success, Bob Gerberg
Mckenzie Scott Press

American Express Property Casualty Companies

Great Place to Work® Inc. Institute

The Press-Enterprise
Riverside, CA

JUMPSTART YOUR CAREER, Dr. Ferris E. Merhish
Authorhouse Publishing

SAMPLES OF APPLICATIONS

CONSOLIDATED STORES CORPORATION
EMPLOYMENT APPLICATION
This application is considered active for ninety (90) days.

DRUG FREE WORKPLACE
All employees are subject to the
drug and alcohol testing procedures

WOTC Registration # _____

PERSONAL DATA

Name (Last, First, Middle)

Street Address

Social Security Number

City | State | Zip | Home Phone Number

Position(s) Interested In?

Are You Under the Age of 14? ☐ Yes ☐ No
If Yes, state your age. _____

Salary Requirements

_____ Hour / Week (Circle One)

How were you referred? ☐ Newspaper
☐ Friend ☐ Other _____

Have You Ever Worked For Any Odd Lots, Big Lots, Mac Frugal's, Pic 'N' Save, All For One, ITZADEAL, Toy Liquidators, Toys Unlimited, Amazing Toy Stores, K•B Toys, K•B Toy Outlet,K•B Toy Works or other Consolidated Locations Before? ☐ Yes ☐ No

If Yes, When & Where

If Hired, Can You Supply Proof That You Are Legally Entitled To Work In The United States? ☐ Yes ☐ No

Do You Have Friends or Relatives Working For Us? ☐ Yes ☐ No

If So, Whom? _____

Can You Work: ☐ Anytime ☐ Days ☐ Evenings ☐ Weekends

Are There Any Times Or Days You Cannot Work? _____

If In Hawaii Do Not Answer

Have You Ever Been Convicted Of A Felony Or Retail Related Crime (i.e., shoplifting, credit card fraud, robbery)?
Note: A "Yes" response will not automatically disqualify you from employment. ☐ Yes ☐ No

If Yes, Please Describe: _____

MILITARY SERVICE

Have You Served In The U.S. Armed Forces? ☐ Yes ☐ No

If Yes, Please Complete The Following:
What Principal Duties Did You Perform While In The Service?

Branch Of Service

Are You Enrolled In The Military Reserves? ☐ Yes ☐ No

Expiration Date Of Reserve Status

If Yes, Check One: ☐ Active Status ☐ Army ☐ Air Force ☐ Coast Guard
☐ Inactive Status ☐ Navy ☐ Marine ☐ National Guard

EDUCATION

Have you ever attended school under a different name? _____

Type Of School	Name Of School	Location Of School	Area Of Study	Last Year Completed	Did You Earn A Degree or Diploma? Describe
High School				1 2 3 4	☐ Yes ☐ No
College				1 2 3 4	☐ Yes ☐ No
Graduate				1 2 3 4	☐ Yes ☐ No
Other				1 2 3 4	☐ Yes ☐ No

AN EQUAL OPPORTUNITY EMPLOYER
Consolidated Stores Corporation is an Equal Opportunity Employer and does not discriminate in making employment decisions based upon race, color, sex, religion, national origin, age, disability, marital status or sexual orientation.

K•B SKU 5518

OL/BL SKU 86860004S • 12/98

BEGINNING WITH MOST RECENT EMPLOYER, LIST ALL EMPLOYMENT INCLUDING MILITARY SERVICE AND SELF-EMPLOYMENT (Account for all periods of unemployment)

If presently employed may we contact your employer for references? ☐ Yes ☐ No

May we contact you at your place of employment? ☐ Yes ☐ No

Name of Present or Last Employer	Job Title / Responsibilities	From (Mo. & Yr.)	To (Mo. & Yr.)
Address		Supr. Name	
City, State, ZIP	Reason for leaving ☐ Resigned ☐ Discharged ☐ Laid Off	Starting Salary $	
Phone Number ( )	Explain	Last Salary $	
Name of Present or Last Employer	Job Title / Responsibilities	From (Mo. & Yr.)	To (Mo. & Yr.)
Address		Supr. Name	
City, State, ZIP	Reason for leaving ☐ Resigned ☐ Discharged ☐ Laid Off	Starting Salary $	
Phone Number ( )	Explain	Last Salary $	
Name of Present or Last Employer	Job Title / Responsibilities	From (Mo. & Yr.)	To (Mo. & Yr.)
Address		Supr. Name	
City, State, ZIP	Reason for leaving ☐ Resigned ☐ Discharged ☐ Laid Off	Starting Salary $	
Phone Number ( )	Explain	Last Salary $	
Name of Present or Last Employer	Job Title / Responsibilities	From (Mo. & Yr.)	To (Mo. & Yr.)
Address		Supr. Name	
City, State, ZIP	Reason for leaving ☐ Resigned ☐ Discharged ☐ Laid Off	Starting Salary $	
Phone Number ( )	Explain	Last Salary $	

REFERENCES

List names of three persons (other than relatives) we may contact who have knowledge of your job related abilities.

	Name	Telephone Contact	Address/City/State	Occupation
I				
II				
III				

AUTHORIZATION: I hereby voluntarily authorize Consolidated Stores Corporation to obtain consumer reports about me from a consumer reporting agency and to consider the consumer reports when making decisions regarding my employment at Consolidated.

Applicant's Signature _____ Date _____

I understand that Consolidated Stores Corporation (CSC) may contact the past employers and/or personal references I have provided in order to verify my past employment and work record. I authorize all past employers, educational institutions, government agencies and/or personal references to release any and all information concerning my past employment work history, performance and personal character. I hereby release all such past employers, personal references and CSC from any and all liability resulting from damages I may incur in the reference verification process.

I also understand that if employed by CSC my employment is "at will" and can be terminated at any time for any reason either by myself or the Company. This agreement cannot be modified by any representative of the Company either in writing or verbally.

Finally, I understand it is unlawful for CSC to employ anyone who is neither a citizen of the U.S. nor an authorized resident alien. I certify that the U.S. citizenship information I have provided the Company is authentic. Further I certify that all information I have provided on this application is accurate.

False information or omission of facts on the application may result in the termination of my employment with CSC.

Date _____ Applicant's Signature _____

Thank You For Your Interest And The Time You Have Taken To Prepare This Application

Pre-Screening Notice and Certification Request for the Work Opportunity and Welfare-to-Work Credits

▶ Use only for individuals who begin work after September 30, 1997.
▶ See separate instructions.

OMB No. 1545-1500

Job applicant: Fill in the lines below and check any boxes that apply. Complete only this side.

Your name _____ Social security number ▶ _____

Street address where you live _____

City or town, state, and ZIP code _____

Telephone no. (___) ___ - ___

If you are under age 25, enter your date of birth (month, day, year) ___ / ___ / ___

Work Opportunity Credit (For individuals who begin work after September 30, 1997)

1 ☐ Check here if you received a conditional certification from the state employment security agency (SESA) or a participating local agency for the work opportunity credit.

2 ☐ Check here if **any** of the following statements apply to you.

- I am a member of a family that has received assistance from Aid to Families with Dependent Children (AFDC) or a successor program for any 9 months during the last 18 months.

- I am a veteran and a member of a family that received food stamps for at least a 3-month period within the last 15 months.

- I was referred here by a rehabilitation agency approved by the state or the Department of Veterans Affairs.

- I am at least age 18 but **not** over age 24 and I am a member of a family that:
  a Received food stamps for the last 6 months, OR
  b Received food stamps for at least 3 of the last 5 months, BUT is no longer eligible to receive them.

- Within the past year, I was convicted of a felony or released from prison for a felony AND during the last 6 months I was a member of a low-income family.

- I received supplemental security income (SSI) benefits for any month ending within the last 60 days.

Welfare-to-Work Credit (For individuals who begin work after December 31, 1997)

3 ☐ Check here if you received a conditional certification from the SESA or a participating local agency for the welfare-to-work credit.

4 ☐ Check here if you are a member of a family that:
- Received AFDC or successor program payments for at least the last 18 months, OR
- Received AFDC or successor program payments for any 18 months beginning after August 5, 1997, OR
- Stopped being eligible for AFDC or successor program payments after August 5, 1997, OR limited the maximum time those payments could be made.

All Applicants

Under penalties of perjury, I declare that I gave the above information to the employer on or before the day I was offered a job, and it is, to the best of my knowledge, true, correct, and complete.

Job applicant's signature ▶

For Privacy Act and Paperwork Reduction Act Notice, see page 2.

Cat. No. 22851L

Date ___ / ___ / ___

Form **8850** (Rev. 9-97)

Form 8850 (Rev. 9-97) Page 2

For Employer's Use Only

Employer's name _____ Telephone no. ( ) _____ EIN ▶ _____

Street address _____

City or town, state, and ZIP code _____

Person to contact, if different from above __Mary Horton__ Telephone no. (800) 669-6000

Street address c/o CIC Enterprises, P.O. Box 40974

City or town, state, and ZIP code Indianapolis, Indiana 46240-0974

If, based on the individual's age and home address, he or she is a member of group 4 or 6 (as described under **Members of Targeted Groups** in the separate instructions), enter that group number (4 or 6) . . . . ▶ ___

DATE APPLICANT: Gave information / /   Was offered job / /   Was hired / /   Started job / /

Under penalties of perjury, I declare that I completed this form on or before the day a job was offered to the applicant and that the information I have furnished is, to the best of my knowledge, true, correct, and complete. Based on the information the job applicant furnished on page 1, I believe the individual is a member of a targeted group or a long-term family assistance recipient. I hereby request a certification that the individual is a member of a targeted group or a long-term family assistance recipient.

Employer's signature ▶ _____ Title _____ Date / /

Privacy Act and Paperwork Reduction Act Notice

Section references are to the Internal Revenue Code.

Section 51(d)(12) permits a prospective employer to request the applicant to complete this form and give it to the prospective employer. The information will be used by the employer to complete the employer's federal tax return. Completion of this form is voluntary and may assist members of targeted groups and long-term family assistance recipients in securing employment. Routine uses of this form include giving it to the state employment security agency (SESA), which will contact appropriate sources to confirm that the applicant is a member of a targeted group or a long-term family assistance recipient. This form may also be given to the Internal Revenue Service for administration of the Internal Revenue laws, to the Department of Justice for civil and criminal litigation, to the Department of Labor for oversight of the certifications performed by the SESA, and to cities, states, and the District of Columbia for use in administering their tax laws.

You are not required to provide the information requested on a form that is subject to the Paperwork Reduction Act unless the form displays a valid OMB control number. Books or records relating to a form or its instructions must be retained as long as their contents may become material in the administration of any Internal Revenue law. Generally, tax returns and return information are confidential, as required by section 6103.

The time needed to complete and file this form will vary depending on individual circumstances. The estimated average time is:

Recordkeeping . . . . 2 hr., 47 min.
Learning about the law or the form . . . . 37 min.
Preparing and sending this form to the SESA . . . . 36 min.

If you have comments concerning the accuracy of these time estimates or suggestions for making this form simpler, we would be happy to hear from you. You can write to the Tax Forms Committee, Western Area Distribution Center, Rancho Cordova, CA 95743-0001.

DO NOT send this form to this address. Instead, see **When and Where To File** in the separate instructions.

EMPLOYMENT APPLICATION

Coldwater Creek is an equal opportunity employer and all applicants will be
considered without regard to race, color, creed, gender, marital status, sexual
orientation, pregnancy, childbirth or pregnancy-related conditions, age, religion, national
origin, disability, handicap or any other basis protected by local, state or federal law.

PERSONAL

Name: *(please print)* _____ LAST _____ FIRST _____ MIDDLE   SS# _____

Current address: _____ NUMBER   STREET _____ CITY _____ COUNTY _____ STATE _____ ZIP CODE

Telephone number: (____) _____ HOME   (____) _____ WORK   (____) _____ CELL   _____ E-MAIL

POSITION

Position applied for: _____   Location: _____   ☐ Full-time   ☐ Part-time   ☐ Temporary

If you are not available to work Coldwater Creek's hours of operation, please list any exceptions: _____

Referral source: ☐ CWC employee / Name: _____   ☐ Employment agency   ☐ Job Fair   ☐ Newspaper   ☐ Radio   Other: _____

Have you ever filed an application with Coldwater Creek before?   ☐ Yes   ☐ No   If yes, please give date: /   /

Have you ever been employed by Coldwater Creek before?   ☐ Yes   ☐ No   If yes, please give date: /   /

Do you have any relatives currently working for Coldwater Creek?   ☐ Yes   ☐ No
If so, name of relative and employment location: _____

On what date would you be available to start work?   /   /   What are your salary requirements? $ _____   ☐ Hr   ☐ Mo   ☐ Yr

Are you over 18 years of age?   ☐ Yes   ☐ No

Have you ever been convicted of a felony crime or have you been convicted of a misdemeanor in the last seven years?   ☐ Yes   ☐ No
If yes, please list details, including date(s) of conviction(s) and jurisdiction(s) of crime(s).
(Convictions will not necessarily disqualify applicant. Each case is considered individually.)

WORK EXPERIENCE

May we contact your current employer?   ☐ Yes   ☐ No   If yes, please initial here

Employer:	Dates employed From: To:
Address:	Hourly rate/salary:
Telephone number: ( )	Supervisor:
Job title:	Reason for leaving:
Duties:	

Employer:	Dates employed From: To:
Address:	Hourly rate/salary:
Telephone number: ( )	Supervisor:
Job title:	Reason for leaving:
Duties:	

Employer:	Dates employed From: To:
Address:	Hourly rate/salary:
Telephone number: ( )	Supervisor:
Job title:	Reason for leaving:
Duties:	

Have you ever been fired or forced to resign from any employment?

☐ Yes   ☐ No   If yes, please explain: _____

Office of Human Resources
114 South Del Rosa Drive
San Bernardino, CA 92408
Phone (909) 382-4040 Website: http://www.sbccd.cc.ca.us

Application for Administrative/Managerial Position

Name: _____
         Last   First   MI

Address: _____
              Street Address
         _____
         City   State   Zip

Home: ( ) _____
Office: ( ) _____
Cell/Msg: ( ) _____
E-Mail: _____

Position Applying For: _____

Education and Training: Professional Preparation Beyond High School

Name of Institution	City & State	Major or Course of Study	Type of Degree Awarded	Date Degree Awarded

Professional Certifications or Licenses

Type of License/Certificate	Date of Issuance	Issuing Agency	License/Certificate Number

Professional References:
List persons who have first-hand knowledge of your administrative ability, technical skills, job performance and character. Former supervisors or managers are preferred.

Name	Title	Organization	Relationship	Telephone Number

Professional Experience:
List most recent experience first. Use additional sheets if necessary.
Do Not Complete This Section by Stating "See Resume"

Employer Information	Description of Duties and Responsibilities	May we contact this employer? Yes No
Company		Title:
Address		Salary:
City, State, Zip		Start Date:
Phone		End Date:
Supervisor	Reason for Leaving:	Hours per Week:

Employer Information	Description of Duties and Responsibilities	May we contact this employer? Yes No
Company		Title:
Address		Salary:
City, State, Zip		Start Date:
Phone		End Date:
Supervisor	Reason for Leaving:	Hours per Week:

Professional Experience (continued)

Employer Information	Description of Duties and Responsibilities	May we contact this employer? Yes No
Company		Title:
Address		Salary:
City, State, Zip		Start Date:
Phone		End Date:
Supervisor	Reason for Leaving:	Hours per Week:

Employer Information	Description of Duties and Responsibilities	May we contact this employer? Yes No
Company		Title:
Address		Salary:
City, State, Zip		Start Date:
Phone		End Date:
Supervisor	Reason for Leaving:	Hours per Week:

Teaching Experience (if applicable):
List most recent experience first. Use additional sheets if necessary.

Do Not Complete This Section by Stating "See Resume"

Inclusive Dates of Employment		Name of Institution or District	City & State	Subject and/or Grades Taught or Assignment	Reason for Leaving
To	From				

Special Qualifications: Indicate special studies, honors, experience, professional organizations to which you belong, offices held, special abilities, or any other information that would be helpful in considering your application as it relates to this position. (Attach additional page if necessary.)

General Information

Have you ever been convicted of any felony or of a misdemeanor that resulted in imprisonment?	Yes	No	If yes, please attach a written explanation
Have you been dismissed or asked to resign from a position?	Yes	No	If yes, please attach a written explanation
After employment, will you be able to provide verification of your legal right to work in the U.S.?	Yes	No	If no, please attach a written explanation
Do you have any relatives currently working for the San Bernardino Community College District?	Yes	No	If yes, please list:

Applicant Certification and Waiver

I hereby certify that the statements on this application are true and complete to the best of my knowledge and belief. I understand that any false statements or omission of pertinent information shall be cause for dismissal.

I authorize the San Bernardino Community College District to investigate my employment and educational background and all of the statements contained in my employment application and materials submitted in conjunction with my application for employment. I further authorize my previous and current employers, as well as all educational institutions that I attended, personal and professional references and public or private agencies that have issued me either a professional or vocational license to release any and all records and other information maintained in their custody and control and which pertain to my employment relationship, history and educational background. I understand and acknowledge that this authorization will permit positive as well negative information to be released. I hereby release from any liability all persons and organizations furnishing such information and hold the San Bernardino Community College District harmless for its investigation of my employability. Employees of the San Bernardino Community College District are required to submit to fingerprinting that will be checked by law enforcement agencies.

X Not valid unless signature appears here _____

Applicant's Signature   _____ Date

Pursuant to Section 504 of the Rehabilitation Act of 1973 as amended and Section I of the Americans with Disabilities Act, disabled persons who believe they need reasonable accommodations or help in order to apply or perform the necessary duties of a position may contact the Office of Human Resources at San Bernardino Community College District. San Bernardino Community College District is an Equal Employment Opportunity, Title IX, Section 504 Employer.

10/02

COMMUNITY COLLEGE DISTRICT

This information is only for statistical purposes with regard to affirmative action. Your cooperation in providing the requested information is appreciated. This information will be kept separate and confidential and will not be used in any way to make employment decisions.

Name_____ **Position Applied For**_____

Age: Under age 18_____ Age 18 to 39_____ Age 40 & over_____

Male_____ **Female**_____ **Disabled:** Yes_____ No_____

_____ White

_____ Black, African American

_____ Hispanic: Latino, Chicano, Mexican American, Puerto Rican, Latin American

_____ Asian or Pacific Islander (original people of the Far East, Southeast Asia or Pacific Islands)

      _____ Filipino   _____ Hawaiian   _____ Laotian   _____ Chinese

      _____ Japanese   _____ Samoan   _____ Cambodian   _____ Korean

      _____ Guamanian   _____ Vietnamese   _____ Asian Indian

_____ American Indian or Alaskan Native

_____ Decline to State

Ethnic Definitions

White (not of Hispanic origin): All persons having origins in any of the original people of Europe and North Africa, the Middle East.

Black (not of Hispanic origin): All persons having origins in any of the black racial groups of Africa.

Hispanic: All persons of Chicano, Mexican, Puerto Rican, Cuban, Central or South American or other Spanish culture of origin, regardless of race.

Asian or Pacific Islanders: All persons having origins in any of the original peoples of the Far East, Southeast Asia or the Pacific Islands. This area includes, for example, China, Japan, Korea, the Philippine Islands or the Indian sub-continent.

American Indian or Alaskan Native: All persons having origins in any of the original peoples of North America.

WHERE DID YOU LEARN ABOUT THIS OPPORTUNITY? _____Community Agency

_____Job Announcement _____Jobline Recording _____Job Fair _____Friend

_____Newspaper_____ (Name of Newspaper/publication)

_____State Chancellor's Registry _____Other_____

Statistical Information Sheet.Doc

GLOSSARY OF TERMS

A

Absenteeism: not showing up continuously for work. This negative practice is detrimental in acquiring a job as well as keeping one.

Agent: in this case and agent is typically a non profit organization such as a school district, Police Department, and county office.

Age discrimination: an employment act 1967: federal legislation requiring employers to treat applicants and employees equally, regardless of age.

Application: application (job) this is a document supplied by the employer in which you will supply your employment history and vital personal data as described by law.

Articles of partnership: a document that states clearly the rights and duties of a partner.

Assets: in this case intangible scales that economic value has in helping achieve your new employment

B

Battle plan: in this case the plan designed by you where you determine what kind of job you're going to go after so the employer has confidence in the fact that you know what you're doing and have goals.

Blacklist: a list developed by management of undesired workers or employees that will hinder them in finding new employment. This information or list may be passed around to other employers.

Body: (of a letter) this is the main part of your cover letter.

Body Language: an observable statement made by your body that may be different than ones verbal statement.

Business plan: a structural plan that is designed to help the businessman or employer consider alternatives that best meet the needs in the developing of the business or organization.

Bonus: cash payment in addition to the regular wage or salary, received by an employee Hans Sears has a reward for achievement.

Business cycle: the fluctuation in the rate of growth that an economy expenses over a period of several years.

Budget: a defined economic plan for saving and spending income.

C

Canned: a prepared and/or rehearsed presentation normally associated with telephone sales. You may want to develop this kind of job search technique if you are doing the job search cold calling.

Capitalist: businessperson, entrepreneur, or investor.

Champion: an individual that you can enlist their help and will be willing to assist you in the job search by enhancing your image and promoting your cause.

Combination résumé: has an element from other forms of résumés. Generally it does not have an occupational statement.

Collective bargaining: going together as a group, such as a union to negotiate with an employer for salaries, benefits, and other perks.

COBRA: this is a federal legislated health benefit that you can subscribe to while you are unemployed.

Commodity: a valuable product. You must recognize that you have something to offer. But realize you always will be in competition with others. You want to sell yourself to the highest bidder, but the employer is looking for people with the best overall skills and who can best state their organization.

Competition: people you will be going up against doing job search, research and interviewing.

Compensation: payment for your work.

Cooperative: working together and being supportive.

Contract: exchange of promises by individuals documented and enforced by law.

Continuousness: non stopping.

Creativity: you have the ability to do something unique, see problems as opportunities.

Cross - training: expanding your knowledge or experience that would make you more viable to a company or organization through training. For example, we worked in more than one task or job and/or have the skills to work in another department.

Coordinator: one who manages, directs, arranges, or plans.

Corporation: a legally chartered enterprise with most of the legal rights of a person, including the right to conduct business, own said property, to borrow money, and to sue or be sued.

D

Daydreaming: thinking about other things during the day and not your work or what you are currently doing.

Dependability: one who can be counted on. Being reliable.

Downsized: laid off due to no fault of your own, usually associated with companies trying to reduce employees or staff to become more efficient because of sales or profit downturns, however, this may not necessarily be true, the company may have another agenda.

Digital Résumé: new on the horizon, it is a fad, a benefit, or a milestone. In any event a job search tool that can be another option. This gives you another job search strategy that can be sent to a potential employer. This approach is at the forefront in the job search techniques.

Video résumé services are only starting to emerge on the Internet. If you have the right visuals this could be one way of getting a leg-up in your job search. You can make a video, CD, or DVD. You can do your own thing, or have it professionally made. Specially developed using digital video camera to produce an on line video résumé to use for job search. This video résumé can be sent to potential employers for evaluation. This visual allows the employer to see the applicant speaking directly to them, or in a mock interview, or a blend.

Direct mail: advertising (résumé & employment) sent directly to employment prospects through the U. S. Postal Service or by private carriers; also sent to prospective customers to sell products.

Detrimental: not good, or damaging.

Defensively: approaching in a defensive posture.

Divulge: giving up information or facts.

Division of labor: specialization by workers in performing certain portions of a total job.

E

Effectiveness: doing the right things in your job search campaign.

Efficiency: exceeding the minimum amount of work for the least amount of pay.

Expense item: all costs associated with job search may be deducted from your income tax. Remember to keep receipts and/or documents associated with job search in case you need to provide them to the IRS.

Entrepreneurs: individuals who organize, develop, and create a business, and people who sell such products or services and are willing to take the risk of failing.

Enthusiasm: full of zeal, eagerness. Employers look for this in an applicant.

Electronic Mail (E-Mail): text messages transmitted from one computer to another.

F

Family business: ownership or involvement of two or more family members in the life and functioning of a business.

Feedback: getting information back with regard to effectiveness of your résumé, or cover letter. Also getting information back from a customer on ideas or products; perhaps getting information/feedback from a customer on a sales presentation.

FDIC: news, statutes, regulations, banking data, publications, consumer and asset sales info from US bank regulators & insurers of American bank savings. *www.fdic.gov*

Follow-up Letter: a letter sent to a prospective employer after an interview.

Franchisee: person or group to who a corporation grants an exclusive rights to use its name/products in a certain territory; usually in exchange for an initial fee plus monthly royalty payments.

Fringe benefits: compensations other that wages, salaries, and incentive programs. It could be health benefits, vacation, and key to the executive washroom.

Functional Résumé: concentrates on your job skills, abilities, qualifications and what you have done under individual headings.

Fraud: the act of deceiving or misrepresenting yourself. As you fill out your résumé or job application, remember you can be dismissed from employment for misrepresenting information.

G

Gatekeeper: the gatekeeper is a person such as a secretary or receptionist who is placed between the general public as a buffer to control who is allowed to see busy executives.

General expenses: operating expenses, such as office and administrative expenses. Not directly associated with creating or marketing goods and services.

Goals: targets or aims, could be by the individual or a company.

Goal setting: the successful entrepreneur strives to make it happen after the goal is set.

H

Headhunter: individual or agent working for a job search company. The company or individual receives fees from the employer or you for finding and placing you into a job.

Human Relation Department: organization within in a company involved in screening and hiring of new employees; also involved in outplacement.

Human Skills: skills required in order to understand other people and to interact effectively with them.

I

Incentives: could be a cash payment to workers who produce at a desired level or whose unit produces at a desired level. Normally given for exceeding a quota; also could be other benefits such as a vacation, or special gift.

Interest: fees that you would have to pay for the privilege of using a credit card. Also monies paid to you for leaving funds in an institution (savings account).

J

Job analysis: a process by which jobs are studied to determine the task and dynamics involved in performing them.

Job hopper: one who gets labeled for changing jobs often, or for working only a short duration or time on their jobs.

Job instruction training: a system designed to make on-the-job training more effective.

K

Key: the most important element in accomplishing an idea or process. In this case most efficient way of finding a job is through 'Networking.'

Keynote: the number one most important element.

L

LIFO: last in first out. Method of pricing inventory under which the cost of the last in goods acquired is the first cost to be charged to cost of goods sold. Sometimes employees will be laid off because they were the last employee to be hired.

Long-range plans: plans geared to a two-to-five year span and in some cases longer.

M

Marketing Plan: this is an important document that presents steps in helping the businessman or organization seek the best alternative to promote the company or firm. On some occasions you may be asked to present a mini-marketing letter to show your planning 'savvy.'

Management: process of coordinating resources to meet an objective; also supervising people, time, and material.

Messenger – one who brings information.

Moonlighting: an employee working more than one job, usually the second job is the moonlighting position.

N

Networking: talking to friends, neighbors, business contacts, church members, and club members and asking them for help in finding a new position or a job. 64% to 85% of jobs are gotten through networking. In networking you are looking for referrals from one contact to another contact.

Newsletter: a job search tool used to present someone your assets and abilities in a special presentation such as information and achievements that may not show up on your résumé or cover letter.

Needs: things humans must have to survive.

O

Outplacement: a 'free' service offered by some employers to transition laid off employees in developing job search skills or to a new job. Outplacement assists with résumés, phones, job search training, and supplies.

Oxymoron: a figure of speech in which opposite or contradictory ideas or terms are combined.

Output per man-hour: the amount of goods that one worker on average can produce in one hour.

Offensively: being rude or unfriendly on approach.

P

Payoff: is finally getting an interview and/or getting hired by a potential employer after being consistent in promoting yourself through self-advertising.

Perks: a special class of fringe benefits made available to an employee by a company for being valuable.

Pigeon-holed: being recognized as only being able to working in one industry, field, or job.

Pruning: a new 'buzz' word for being laid off, or 'downsized.'

Partnership: an association or relationship between two or more persons operating a business as co-owners and sharing profits or losses.

Personality: the qualities of a person that make an impression upon other people.

Punctuality: always being on time. This is a very good trait you will want to cultivate and maintain. Employers will be always impressed.

Q

Qualified: verified as having the means, skill, and authority to make a purchase or do a job.

Quotas: fixed limits on the quantity as to who is going to get hired, or a standard that is set for salesmen to meet and exceed.

R

Relocation: being willing to move to a new area, city, state, or country as part of an employment offer or package.

Reputation: the image that is projected by you as seen or perceived by others; your character.

Résumé: a job search tool that summarizes ones education, working experience, interest, and other personal information presented to an employer.

Risk: the chance you take in any given situation.

Rule of thumb: this is a standard that is used to measure from; for example, a guide.

Roadmap: a path you have set up for yourself to follow on the way to developing your career.

S

Savvy: having the knowledge about an operation or skill, i.e. being computer savvy; your understanding of a subject.

Salaried worker: an employee who earns a stated amount for a given period of time regardless of the number of hours worked.

Severance packages: a compensation package or arrangement given to an employee by the employer for being downsized or laid-off; may also be given to an employee to avoid bitterness or a lawsuit. There is no guarantee that every employer will offer a severance or termination package.

Self-confidence: feel no threat to your authority.

Short range plan: all individuals should have a short term plan; it governs your actions for a specific period of time.

Script: this is a planned presentation that you develop to practice and sound professional up to the point when calling an executive of a potential employer.

SIC: is a code that manufactures, marketing companies, businesses, and the government use to identify products, materials, and types of companies. This code places organizations and companies into groups by what they do, manufacture, or market.

Stopgap: referring to a job or business opportunity which can provide a living until one finds that career position.

'S' corporation: corporation with no more than 35 shareholders that may be taxed as partners or investors. This company must have 3 or more officers.

Sole Proprietorship: a business owned and operated my one person.

T

Tabloid: a newspaper normally published by various industries which has information about new products, organizations, as well as sometimes jobs within its industry.

Target Market: a target which has been labeled and identified, such as certain industries, companies, individuals, or customers, by a business that they plan to go after to sell or market the companies' products or services to.

Technical skills: ability to perform the mechanics of a particular job.

Tough-mindedness: the entrepreneur must be able to make and stick to decisions.

Traits: those things that set you apart from others; your behavior or persona.

Tracking: being recognized as only able to do one type of skill, industry, or job; same as being 'pigeon-holed.'

Tailor-made: designed just for one party or person.

Two-tiered wage system: A pay system that discriminates between the same skilled employees based upon higher pay and benefits for newly hired employees over seasoned and other employees.

U

Under-value: believing that something is of less value then it really is.

Unemployment insurance: government sponsored program for assisting workers who are laid off, and to a lesser extent, those who quit their jobs.

V

Value: making yourself qualified by getting more education, training, or skills.

Venture capitalist: investment specialists who provides money to finance new businesses in exchange for a portion of ownership, with the objective of making a profit.

Voice mail: a computerized system for storing telephone messages.

W

Wages: cash payment based on a calculation of the number of hours an employee has worked or the number of units he or she has produced; can be paid by check.

Wants: those things that are not necessary to survival but make life much more enjoyable, such as a nice car, new clothes, etc.

Web page: a location on the internet placed there by a company, organization, or individual to promote a product, company, jobs, and/or services.

Work rules: policies during collective bargaining that govern what type of work union members will do and the conditions under which they will work.

Willing to take risks: you must be able to take chances based upon intelligent limits.

Window of opportunity: a job or business opportunity that suddenly develops almost overnight that you must decide to take action on quickly.

X

Y

Yellow-dog contract: agreement forcing workers to promise, as a condition of employment, not to join or remain in a union.

Z